# ENERGY AND EMISSIONS MARKETS

## COLLISION OR CONVERGENCE?

# ENERGY AND EMISSIONS MARKETS

## COLLISION OR CONVERGENCE?

Tom James
Peter Fusaro

**WILEY**

John Wiley & Sons (Asia) Pte Ltd

**Other Wiley Editorial Offices**
John Wiley & Sons, Inc., 111 River Street, Hoboken, NJ 07030, USA
John Wiley & Sons Ltd, The Atrium, Southern Gate, Chichester PO19 BSQ, England
John Wiley & Sons (Canada) Ltd, 5353 Dundas Street West, Suite 400, Toronto, Ontario M9B 6HB, Canada
John Wiley & Sons Australia Ltd, 42 McDongall Street, Milton, Queensland 4064, Australia
Wiley-VCH, Boschstrasse 12, D-69469 Weinheim, Germany

**Library of Congress Cataloging-in-Publication Data:**

ISBN-10 047-0-82158-2
ISBN-13 978-0-470-82158-9

Typeset in 11/13 point, Palatino by Superskill Graphics Pte Ltd
Printed in Asia
10 9 8 7 6 5 4 3 2 1

# Contents

# Foreword

Economic and environmental objectives are all too often considered to be mutually exclusive. However, with increasing concern over global climate change, regulators across the world are introducing market-based mechanisms that set out to demonstrate how economic objectives can go hand in hand with environmental objectives.

This is no easy task. In a world of increasing energy prices and concerns over the security of energy supply, long-term environmental goals almost always lose out to short-term economic objectives.

But this is only half the story. Increasing energy prices and the introduction of new market-based mechanisms such as emissions trading and renewable energy obligations are making alternative-energy sources more cost competitive. In addition, resolving concerns over security of supply potentially requires more, not less, diversity of sources, thus justifying the development of an appropriately weighted energy mix of coal, gas, nuclear and renewables.

This books looks to provide answers to those wanting to understand what these new environmental markets are all about. It is an invaluable resource for all people wishing to enhance their understanding of the new world paradigm, where traditional energy markets and new environmental markets are intrinsically linked. The authors have managed to provide both historical context and critical analysis of the key issues facing market entrants in what is, at present, a very complex and fragmented market.

I congratulate the authors for their well-informed, insightful and valuable contribution to the debate. I also encourage you to get involved. These markets require imagination, creativity and capital to make the convergence of economic and environment objectives a reality.

In years to come I would expect every student of economics and environmental issues to have a copy of this book. It demonstrates how market-based mechanisms can protect our environment and ensure economic prosperity which, ultimately, will help to safeguard the future for our children and generations to come.

**Robert Casamento**
*Head of Climate Change Services, Deloitte Touche LLP*
*Member of the Advisory Board, GLOBE Legislators & Business Leaders*
*G8 + 5 Climate Change Dialogue*
*Special Advisor G8 CEO Roundtable on Climate Change*

# Deloitte.

Deloitte offers its clients a broad range of fully integrated services in areas that include audit, tax, consulting and corporate finance. With over 120,00 people, operating in 150 countries, Deloitte has the global coverage and technical expertise to meet our clients' needs.

The Energy, Infrastructure and Utilities group (EIU) at Deloitte provides comprehensive and integrated solutions designed to meet the requirements and unique needs of this rapidly changing and dynamic sector.

These solutions address a broad range of challenges facing companies as they adapt to a changing regulatory environment, to political, economic and market pressures and to technological developments. In the United Kingdom, our team extends to 50 partners and over 450 staff in 23 locations, and globally we have over 4,000 staff dedicated to energy and resources.

Our Energy, Infrastructure and Utilities (EIU) industry teams serve clients in all links of the value chain — covering exploration, production, oilfield services, transport & pipelines, energy trading, emissions, refining, marketing, power generation, gas supply, emissions, water supply and waste disposal and decommissioning activities.

The Energy Markets practice, which Tom James is part of, is a specialist group within EIU made up of experts dedicated to the global oil, gas, power and emissions markets. The team has specific experience in helping clients across the world develop and enhance their risk management, trading and investment strategies and capabilities.

For further information visit our website or contact:

Don Kinnersley
Head of Business Development
Tel: +44 (0) 20 7007 0693
Email: dmkinnersley@deloitte.co.uk

www.deloitte.co.uk

# Glossary

**Additionality:** In projects taking place under the *joint implementation* and *clean-development mechanisms* outlined in the *Kyoto Protocol*, this is where there is a positive difference between the emissions set out in the baseline scenario and the actual emissions in a proposed project.

**Aggregation:** The policy under which all futures positions owned or controlled by a trader or group of traders are combined to determine reportable positions and speculative limits.

**ARA:** Amsterdam–Rotterdam–Antwerp area — a European port and refining area.

**Arbitrage:** The simultaneous purchase and sale of similar commodities in different markets to take advantage of price discrepancies.

**Arbitration:** The procedure of settling disputes between members, or between members and customers.

**Backwardation:** When the price of nearer (typically prompt or spot) crude, product or another underlying commodity, or instrument trades at a premium to the same commodity or instrument traded further forward. Also known as "an inverse".

**Barrel:** A unit of volume equal to 42 U.S. gallons.

**Baselines:** These are estimates of population, GDP, energy use and resulting *greenhouse gas* emissions, without policies and measures that address climate changes, as well as the impacts of climate change without remedial policy.

**Baseload:** The minimum amount of electric power delivered or required over a given period of time at a steady rate.

**Base year:** Targets for reducing GHG emissions are defined in relation to a base year. In the Kyoto Protocol, 1990 is the base year for the major GHGs for most countries.

**Basis:** The difference between spot (cash) prices and the futures contract price. Unless otherwise specified, the price of the nearby futures contract month is generally used to calculate the basis.

**Basis risk:** The risk that the value of a futures contract (or an over-the-counter hedge) will not move in line with that of the underlying exposure. Alternatively, it is the risk that the cash–futures spread will widen or narrow between the times at which a hedge position is implemented and liquidated.

**Basis swap:** Basis swaps are used to hedge exposure to basis risk, such as locational risk or time exposure risk. For example, a natural gas basis swap could be used to hedge a locational price risk: the seller receives from the buyer a *NYMEX* Division settlement value (usually the average of the last three days' closing prices) plus a negotiated fixed basis, and pays the buyer the published index value of gas sold at a specified location.

**Benchmark crude:** Synonymous with "reference crude" or "marker crude". A crude oil whose price is used as a reference against which other crudes are priced. Because of their liquidity, the NYMEX light sweet crude oil and IPE Brent crude oil futures contracts are used as global benchmarks. Dubai crude is widely used as a benchmark for Middle Eastern crudes, especially for sale to Asian markets.

**Bid:** An expression indicating a desire to buy a commodity at a given price; opposite of *"offer"*.

**Bilateral energy trading:** Trading whereby two parties (for example, a generator and a supplier) enter into a contract to deliver electricity at an agreed time in the future.

**Bilateral netting:** An agreement between two counterparties to offset the value of all in-the-money contracts with all out-of-the-money contracts, resulting in a single net exposure amount owed by one counterparty to the other.

**Biodiesel:** A renewable fuel synthesized from soybeans or other oil crops, or animal tallow that can substitute for petroleum diesel fuel.

**Biofuels:** Liquid fuels and blending components produced from *biomass* (plant) feedstocks; used primarily for transportation.

**Biogas:** A medium *Btu* gas containing methane and carbon dioxide, produced from the anaerobic decomposition of organic material in a landfill. Also called "biomass gas".

**Biomass:** Non-fossil material of biological origin constituting a renewable energy resource. Included in Wood and Waste.

**BOE:** Barrel-of-oil equivalent, a standard unit measure for oil and natural gas.

**Brent Blend crude oil:** a blend of crude oil from various fields in the East Shetland Basin in the U.K. The crude is used as a benchmark for the pricing of much of the world's crude oil production.

**Btu (British thermal unit):** A standard unit for measuring the quantity of heat energy equal to the quantity of heat needed to raise the temperature of 1 pound of water by 1 degree Fahrenheit at or near 39.2 degrees Fahrenheit. The Btu is a convenient measure by which to compare the energy content of various fuels.

**Buying hedge:** Buying futures contracts to protect against a possible price increase of cash commodities that will be purchased in the future. At the time the cash commodities are bought, the open futures position is closed by selling an equal number and type of futures contracts to those that were initially purchased.

**California Environmental Quality Act (CEQA):** A California law that sets out the process for public agencies to make informed decisions on discretionary project approvals. The process helps decision-makers to determine whether any environmental impacts are associated with a proposed project. It requires that environmental impacts associated with a proposed project be eliminated or reduced, and that air-quality mitigation measures be implemented.

**Cap-and-trade:** A policy that allows large amounts of emissions from a group of sources to be controlled at a lower cost than if the sources were regulated individually. The approach first sets an overall cap (or maximum amount of emissions per compliance period) that will achieve the desired environmental effects. Then, authorizations to emit, in the form of emission allowances, are allocated to affected sources, with the total number of allowances within the cap.

**Carbon dioxide ($CO_2$):** A colorless, odorless, non-poisonous gas that is a normal part of Earth's atmosphere. Carbon dioxide is a product of fossil-fuel combustion as well as other processes. It is considered a greenhouse gas as it traps heat (infrared energy) radiated into the atmosphere and thereby contributes to the potential for *global warming*. The global warming potential of other *greenhouse gases* is measured in relation to that of carbon dioxide, which by international scientific convention is assigned a value of one (1).

**Carbon dioxide equivalent:** The amount of carbon dioxide by weight emitted into the atmosphere that would produce the same estimated radiative forcing as a given weight of another radiatively active gas. Carbon dioxide equivalents are computed by multiplying the weight of the gas being measured by its estimated *global warming* potential. "Carbon equivalent units" are defined as carbon dioxide equivalents multiplied by the carbon content of carbon dioxide (e.g., 12/44).

**Carbon intensity:** The amount of carbon by weight emitted per unit of energy consumed. A common measure of carbon intensity is weight of carbon per *British thermal unit (Btu)* of energy.

**Carbon offsets:** Most commonly used in reference to the output of *carbon sequestration* projects in the forestry sector, or the output of any climate change mitigation project.

**Carbon sequestration:** The process of fixing atmospheric carbon dioxide in a *carbon sink* through biological or physical processes.

**Carbon sink:** A reservoir that absorbs carbon dioxide released as a pollutant from another part of the carbon cycle. Oceans and forests are the largest absorbers of carbon dioxide.

**Cash contract:** A sales agreement for either immediate or future delivery of the actual product.

**Cash settlement:** Transactions generally involving index-based futures contracts that are settled in cash based on the actual value of the index on the last trading day, in contrast to those that specify the delivery of a commodity or financial instrument.

**CBOT:** The Chicago Board of Trade.

**Certified Emission Reductions (CERs):** A technical term for the output of *CDM* projects, as defined by the *Kyoto Protocol*.

**Clean Development Mechanism (CDM):** Established under Article 12 of the *Kyoto Protocol*; the goals of the CDM are to promote sustainable development in developing countries while allowing industrialized countries to earn emissions-reduction credits from their investments in *GHG*-reduction projects in developing countries.

**Climate change:** A term used to refer to all forms of climatic inconsistency, but especially to significant change from one prevailing climatic condition to another. In some cases, "climate change" has been used synonymously with the term "*global warming*"; scientists, however, tend to use the term in a wider sense inclusive of natural changes in climate, including climatic cooling.

**Closing price:** The last price paid for a commodity on any trading day.

**CME:** The Chicago Mercantile Exchange.

**Colonial pipeline:** The on-land pipeline system connecting U.S. Gulf Coast refineries to Southeast and Atlantic Coast markets. The main artery runs from Deer Park, Texas, to Linden, NJ.

**Combined cycle:** An electricity-generating technology in which electricity is produced from otherwise-lost waste heat exiting from one or more gas (combustion) turbines

**Commodity:** An article of commerce or a product that can be used for commerce. In a narrow sense, products traded on an authorized commodity exchange. The types of commodities include agricultural products, metals, petroleum, foreign currencies, and financial instruments and indices, to name a few.

**Commodity Exchange Act (CEA):** The U.S. federal act that provides for federal regulation of futures trading.

**Commodity future:** A futures contract on a commodity. Unlike financial futures, the prices of commodity futures are determined by supply and demand as well as the cost-of-carry of the underlying. Commodity futures can, therefore, either be in contango (where futures prices are higher than spot prices) or *backwardation* (where futures are lower than spot).

**Commodity swap:** Commodity swaps enable both producers and consumers to hedge commodity prices. The consumer is usually a fixed payer and the producer a floating payer: if the floating-rate price of the commodity is higher than the fixed price, the difference is paid by the floating payer, and vice versa. Usually only the payment streams, not the principal, are exchanged, although physical delivery is becoming increasingly common.

**Commodity Futures Trading Commission (CFTC):** Established in 1974 to oversee U.S. commodity exchanges.

**Conference of Parties (COP):** The meeting of parties to the *United Nations Framework Convention on Climate Change*.

**Contracts for differences (CFDs):** Long-term U.K. electricity swaps agreed bilaterally, generally between generators and electricity supply companies, and referenced to prices in the Electricity Pool for England and Wales. The U.K. government announced in late 1998 that it planned to replace the Pool system with a three-tier market. A short-dated swap agreement used to minimize the basis risk between the daily published

Platt's quote for dated or physical Brent in a specific time window in the future and the forward price quote for a specific month (15-day market).

**Convergence:** A term referring to cash and futures prices tending to come together (i.e., the basis approaches zero) as the futures contract nears expiration.

**Crude oil:** A full-ranging hydrocarbon mixture produced from a reservoir after any associated gas has been removed. Among the most commonly traded crudes are *Brent Blend, West Texas Intermediate (WTI)* and Dubai.

**Default:** The failure to perform on a futures contract as required by exchange rules, such as a failure to meet a margin call or to make or take delivery.

**Delivery:** The transfer of the cash commodity from the seller of a futures contract to the buyer of a futures contract. Each futures exchange has specific procedures for delivery of a cash commodity. Some futures contracts, such as stock index contracts, are cash-settled.

**Derivative:** A financial instrument, traded on or off an exchange, the price of which is directly dependent upon the value of one or more underlying securities, equity indices, debt instruments, commodities, other derivative instruments, or any agreed upon pricing index or arrangement. Derivatives involve the trading of rights or obligations based on the underlying product but do not directly transfer property. They are used to hedge risk or to exchange a floating rate of return for a fixed rate of return.

**Derivatives:** A specialized security or contract that has no intrinsic overall value, with its value based on an underlying security or factor as an index. A generic term that, in the energy field, may include options, futures, forwards, etc.

**Differentials:** Price differences between classes, grades, and delivery locations of various stocks of the same commodity.

**Discounting:** Reducing future costs and benefits to reflect the time value of money and the common preference of consumption now rather than later.

**Distributed generation:** A system that involves small generation capacities located on a utility's distribution system for the purpose of meeting local (substation level) peak loads and/or displacing the need to build additional (or upgrade) local distribution lines.

**Downstream:** A relative term, which indicates greater removal from origins than some point of reference. For example, a petrochemical plant which cracks naphtha lies downstream from a refinery. Money made by marketing products constitutes downstream profits compared to earnings on crude sales. The opposite of "upstream".

**Early crediting:** Allowing crediting of emissions reductions achieved prior to the start of a legally imposed emissions-control period. These credits can then be used towards compliance, once a regulatory system is in place.

**Emissions:** Anthropogenic releases of gases to the atmosphere. In the context of global climate change, they consist of radiatively important *greenhouse gases*.

**Emissions reduction units (ERUs):** A technical term for the output of *JI* projects, as defined by the *Kyoto Protocol*.

**Emissions trading:** A regulatory program that allows companies the flexibility to select cost-effective solutions to achieve established environmental goals. With emissions trading, companies can meet established emissions goals by: (a) reducing emissions from a discrete emissions unit; (b) reducing emissions from another place within the facility; or (c) securing emissions reductions from another facility. Emissions trading encourages compliance and financial managers to pursue cost-effective emissions-reduction strategies and provides incentives to emitters to develop the means by which emissions can be reduced inexpensively.

**Energy demand:** The requirement for energy as an input to provide products and/or services.

**Energy efficiency (EE) programs:** Demand-side management programs that are aimed at reducing the energy used by specific end-use devices and systems, typically without affecting the services provided. These programs reduce overall electricity consumption. Examples include energy-saving appliances and lighting programs; high-efficiency heating, ventilating and air-conditioning systems or control modifications; and energy-efficient buildings.

**Exchange for physicals:** A transaction generally used by two hedgers who want to exchange futures for cash positions. Also referred to as "against actuals" or "versus cash".

**Exercise:** The process by which the holder of an option makes or receives delivery of futures contracts of the underlying futures market.

**Exercise price:** The price at which the futures contract underlying a call or put option can be purchased (if a call) or sold (if a put). Also referred to as "strike price".

**Exit:** The point at which a trader closes out of a trade.

**FAS 133:** The standard for financial reporting of derivatives and hedging transactions was adopted in 1998 by the U.S. Financial Accounting Standards Board to resolve inconsistent reporting standards and practices. It went into effect at most companies at the beginning of 2001.

**Federal Energy Regulatory Commission (FERC):** Housed in the U.S. Department of Energy but considered to be an independent regulatory agency responsible primarily to Congress.

**Forex market:** An over-the-counter market where buyers and sellers conduct foreign-exchange business.

**Forward contract:** A cash contract in which a seller agrees to deliver a specific cash commodity to a buyer sometime in the future. Forward contracts, in contrast to futures contracts, are privately negotiated and are not standardized.

**Forward curve:** Represents the price at which buyers and sellers purchase and sell allowances in forward settling transactions. Forward market prices decrease more than five years beyond the spot vintage, due to regulatory uncertainty.

**Forward-rate agreements (FRAs):** Cash payments are made daily as the spot rate varies above or below an agreed-upon forward rate and can be hedged with Eurodollar futures.

**Fossil fuel:** A general term for buried combustible geologic deposits of organic materials, formed from decayed plants and animals, that have been converted to crude oil, coal, natural gas, or heavy oils by exposure to heat and pressure in the Earth's crust over hundreds of millions of years.

**Future volatility:** A prediction of what volatility may be like in the future.

**Futures contract:** A legally binding agreement, made on the trading floor of a *futures exchange*, to buy or sell a commodity or financial instrument sometime in the future. Futures contracts are standardized according to the quality, quantity, and delivery time and location for each commodity. The only variable is price, which is discovered on an exchange trading floor.

**Futures exchange:** A central marketplace with established rules and regulations where buyers and sellers meet to trade futures and options on futures contracts.

**Gas oil:** European and Asian designation for No. 2 heating oil and No. 2 diesel fuel.

**Global warming:** An increase in the near surface temperature of the Earth. Global warming has occurred in the distant past as the result of natural influences, but the term is today most often used to refer to the warming some scientists predict will occur as a result of increased anthropogenic emissions of *greenhouse gases*.

**Greenhouse gases (GHGs):** Some greenhouse gases occur naturally, trapping heat in the atmosphere (such as water vapor, carbon dioxide, methane, nitrous oxide, and ozone) and their atmospheric levels are increased by human activity. The *Kyoto Protocol* addresses the control of atmospheric levels of six GHG: carbon dioxide, methane, nitrous oxide, hydrofluorocarbons (HFCs), perfluorocarbons (PFCs), and sulfur hexafluoride (SF6).

**Grid:** The layout of an electrical distribution system.

**Heat content of a quantity of fuel, net:** The amount of usable heat energy released when a fuel is burned under conditions similar to those in which it is normally used. Net heat content is also referred to as the lower heating value. *Btu* conversion factors typically used by the Energy Information Administration represent gross heat content.

**Heavy crude oil:** Has an API gravity lower than 28 degrees. The lower the API gravity, the heavier the oil.

**Hedge fund:** A mutual fund involving speculative investing in futures, swaps and options.

**Hedger:** An individual or company owning or planning to own a cash commodity — corn, soybeans, wheat, U.S. Treasury bonds, notes, bills etc. — and concerned that the cost of the commodity may change before either buying or selling it in the cash market. A hedger achieves protection against changing cash prices by purchasing (selling) futures contracts of the same or similar commodity and later offsetting that position by selling (purchasing) futures contracts of the same quantity and type as the initial transaction.

**Hedging:** The practice of offsetting the price risk inherent in any cash market position by taking an equal but opposite position in the futures market. Hedgers use the futures markets to protect their business from adverse price changes.

**Historic volatility:** How much a contract price has fluctuated over a period of time in the past; usually calculated by taking a *standard deviation* of price changes over a time period.

**Hydrocarbon:** An organic compound containing only carbon and hydrogen. Hydrocarbons are what comprise petroleum products, natural gas, and coal.

**Implied volatility:** The volatility computed using the actual market prices of an option contract and one of a number of pricing models. For example, if the market price of an option rises without a change in the price of the underlying stock or future, implied volatility will have risen.

**Intergovernmental Panel on Climate Change (IPCC):** Was established in 1988 by the World Meteorological Organization and the United Nations Environment Program. It surveys worldwide technical and scientific literature, publishing assessment reports. Widely accepted as the most credible source on climate change.

**International Petroleum Exchange (IPE):** London oil exchange which has futures and options contracts in Brent Blend crude oil and gas oil, and a futures contract in U.K. natural gas. The IPE and the New York Mercantile Exchange announced merger discussions in November 1998 but these fell through. The IPE was bought by the Intercontinental Exchange (ICE) and recently changed its name to ICE Futures.

**ISDA Master Agreement:** The International Swaps and Derivatives Association (ISDA) over-the-counter derivatives master agreement was drawn up by the New York-based trade association in 1987 and revised in 1992. The agreement is commonly used for contracts in various energy derivatives markets, especially the U.S. gas market.

**Jet fuel:** A refined petroleum product used in jet aircraft engines. It includes both kerosene-type and naphtha-type jet fuel.

**Joint implementation (JI):** A bilateral agreement between two entities to complete a GHG-mitigation project. The investor is an industrialized nation required to reduce emissions under the *United Nations Framework Convention on Climate Change*. JI may be able to provide credit for emissions abatement to the investor at a lower cost than domestic abatement.

**Kyoto Protocol:** An international agreement struck by 159 nations attending the Third *Conference of Parties* (COP) to the *United Nations Framework Convention on Climate Change* (held in Kyoto, Japan, in December 1997) to reduce worldwide emissions of greenhouse gases. On February 16, 2005, this treaty came into effect, binding 35 industrialized countries to cut *GHG* emissions to an average of 5% below 1990 levels.

**Limit order:** An order to buy or sell when a price is fixed.

**Limits:** The maximum number of speculative futures contracts one can hold as determined by the Commodity Futures Trading Commission and/or the exchange upon which the contract is traded. Also referred to as "trading limit". The maximum advance or decline from the previous day's settlement permitted for a contract in one trading session by the rules of the exchange.

**Liquidity (liquid market):** A characteristic of a security or commodity market with enough units outstanding to allow large transactions without a substantial change in price.

**Load management:** Steps taken to reduce power demand at *peak load* times or to shift some of it to off-peak periods. This may be with reference to peak hours, peak days or peak seasons. Air-conditioning usage, the primary element affecting electricity peaks, is the prime target for load management efforts.

**Long hedge:** Buying futures contracts to protect against a possible price increase of cash commodities that will be purchased in the future. At the time the cash commodities are bought, the open futures position is closed by selling an equal number and type of futures contracts to those that were initially purchased. Also referred to as a *"buying hedge"*.

**Marked to market:** At the end of each business day the open positions carried in an account held at a brokerage firm are credited or debited funds based on the settlement price of the open positions that day.

**Market-based pricing:** Prices of electric power or other forms of energy determined in an open market system of supply and demand under which prices are set solely by agreements as to what buyers will pay and sellers will accept.

**Market maker:** A broker or bank continually prepared to make a two-way price to purchase or sell for a futures, options or swaps contract.

**Market risk:** The uncertainty of returns attributable to fluctuation of the entire market.

**Montreal Protocol on Substances that Deplete the Ozone Layer:** This protocol was adopted in Montreal in 1987. It was adjusted in London (1990), Copenhagen (1992), Vienna (1995), Montreal (1997) and Beijing (1999). The protocol controls the consumption and production of chemicals containing bromine or chlorine that destroy stratospheric ozone.

**Naphtha:** A generic term applied to a petroleum fraction with an approximate boiling range between 122° and 400° Fahrenheit.

**National Environmental Policy Act (NEPA):** The environmental law that establishes federal energy policy, sets goals, and provides means for carrying out the policy in the U.S. It is a national policy for promoting efforts to prevent or eliminate damage to the environment and biosphere, and for establishing a Council on Environmental Quality.

**National Futures Association (NFA):** An industry-wide, industry-supported, self-regulatory organization for futures and options markets.

**Negawatt:** A megawatt of power avoided or saved from use on the energy grid.

**Nitrogen oxides (NOx):** Major air pollutants produced by agricultural and industrial activities, and the burning of fossil fuels and solid wastes. Nitrogen oxides (which include nitrous oxide ($N_2O$), one of the six GHGs listed in the *Kyoto Protocol*) can contribute to the formation of photochemical ozone (smog) and impair visibility, and have proven health consequences.

**Non-attainment area:** Any area that does not meet the national primary or secondary ambient air-quality standard established by the U.S. Environmental Protection Agency for designated pollutants, such as carbon monoxide and ozone.

**NYMEX:** New York Mercantile Exchange, the world's largest energy futures exchange.

**Offer:** An expression indicating a desire to sell a commodity at a given price; opposite of *"bid"*.

**Option:** A contract that provides the right but not the obligation to buy or sell a specified amount of a security within a specified time period.

**Over-the-counter market (OTC):** The largest derivatives market in energy is in the over-the-counter market. The majority of these contracts are traded bilaterally between companies and largely under a bilateral

*ISDA Master Agreement*. OTC trades can be cleared via *NYMEX* and the Intercontinental Exchange.

**Peak load:** The highest electrical demand within a particular period of time. Daily electric peaks on weekdays occur in the late afternoon and early evening, usually between 4 and 7p.m. in the winter and noon to 8p.m. in the summer. Annual peaks occur on hot summer days.

**Position:** A market commitment. A buyer of a futures contract is said to have a long position and, conversely, a seller of futures contracts is said to have a short position.

**Position limit:** The maximum number of speculative futures contracts that can held as determined by the *Commodity Futures Trading Commission* and/or the exchange upon which the contract is traded. Also referred to as "trading limit".

**Position trader:** An approach to trading in which the trader either buys or sells contracts and holds them for an extended period of time.

**Price limit:** The maximum advance or decline from the previous day's settlement permitted for a contract in one trading session by the rules of the exchange. According to the Chicago Board of Trade rules, an expanded allowable price range set during volatile markets.

**Purchasing/long hedge:** Buying futures contracts to protect against a possible price increase of cash commodities that will be purchased in the future. At the time the cash commodities are bought, the open futures position is closed by selling an equal number and type of futures contracts to those that were initially purchased. Also referred to as a "buying hedge".

**Reference price:** In an energy derivatives contract, the settlement price of the contract based on a particular location or particular blend of the commodity.

**Renewable Energy Credits (RECs):** Also known as "green tags" or "tradable renewable certificates", these credits are traded in both the regulatory and voluntary markets. The voluntary REC market is driven by demand for green energy.

**Renewable energy sources:** Energy sources that are naturally replenishing but limited in flow. They are virtually inexhaustible in duration but limited in the amount of energy that is available per unit of time. Renewable energy resources include biomass, hydro, geothermal, solar, wind, ocean thermal, wave action, and tidal action.

**Renewable Portfolio Standards (RPS):** U.S. regulations mandating that a certain amount of a state's electricity must be derived from generation using such resources as wind, solar, biomass and tidal energy, and methane from waste.

**Reportable positions:** The number of open contracts specified by the U.S. Commodity Futures Trading Commission (CFTC) when a firm or individual must begin reporting total positions by delivery month to the authorized exchange and/or the CFTC.

**Risk (implied):** In which the formula produces the percentage overbought/oversold for a contract using the price, a moving average and the option's implied volatility.

**Risk management:** Control and limitation of the risks faced by an organization arising from its exposure to changes in financial market variables, such as foreign exchange and interest rates, equity and commodity prices or counterparty creditworthiness

**Risk measurement:** Assessment of a firm's exposure to risk.

**Seasonality:** All energy futures markets are affected to some extent by an annual seasonal cycle or "seasonality". This seasonal cycle or pattern refers to the tendency of market prices to move in a given direction at certain times of the year.

**Selling short:** Selling a security and then borrowing it for delivery with the intent of replacing it at a lower price. In futures trading, selling short is to assume the responsibility of the seller rather than the buyer in the establishment of the futures contract between parties.

**Settlement:** The price at which all outstanding positions in a stock or commodity are *marked to market*. Typically, the closing price.

**Settlement risk:** The risk that arises when payments are not exchanged simultaneously.

**$SO_2$ allowance trading:** The centerpiece of the U.S. Environmental Protection Agency's (EPA) Acid Rain Program.

**Sour/sweet crude:** Refers to the degree of a given crude's sulfur content. Sour refers to high sulfur and sweet to low sulfur.

**Spark spread:** The difference between the price of electricity sold by a generator and the price of the fuel used to generate it, adjusted for equivalent units. The spark spread can be expressed in $/MWh or $/mmBm (or other applicable units).

**Speculator:** A market participant who tries to profit from buying and selling futures and options contracts by anticipating future price movements. Speculators assume market price risk and add liquidity and capital to the futures markets.

**Spike:** A sharp rise in price in a single day or two.

**Spot:** Usually refers to a cash market price for a physical commodity that is available for immediate delivery.

**Spot prices:** The price at which a commodity is selling at a particular time and place.

**Spread:** A trade in which two related contracts/stocks/bonds/options are traded to exploit the relative differences in price change between the two.

**Spreading:** The simultaneous buying and selling of two related markets in the expectation that a profit will be made when the position is offset.

**Standard deviation:** A measure of the fluctuation in a stock's monthly return over the preceding year. The positive square root of the expected value of the square of the difference between a random variable and its mean.

**Strike price:** The price per unit at which the holder of an option may receive or deliver the underlying unit; also known as the *exercise price*.

**Strips:** An option strategy in which an investor buys one call and two puts on the same underlying security with the same exercise price and expiration date.

**Sulfur dioxide (SO$_2$):** A pungent, colorless, gas formed primarily by the combustion of fossil fuels, it becomes an air pollutant when present in large amounts.

**Swap:** An agreement whereby a floating price is exchanged for a fixed price over a specified period. It is an off-balance-sheet financial arrangement, which involves no transfer of physical energy; both parties settle their contractual obligations by means of a transfer of cash. The agreement defines the volume, duration and fixed reference price. Differences are settled in cash for specific periods — monthly, quarterly or six-monthly. Swaps are also known as contracts for differences and as fixed-for-floating contracts.

**Swaption:** An option to purchase (call option) or sell (put option) a swap at some future date.

**Swing producer:**  A company or country which changes its crude oil output to meet fluctuations in market demand. Saudi Arabia is seen as the world's major swing producer as it deliberately limits its crude oil production in an attempt to keep supply and demand roughly in balance.

**Technical analysis:**  Technical analysis is based on the presumption that price takes into consideration all factors that could influence the price of the commodity. It is therefore broader than fundamental analysis, which looks at supply and demand. Past price movements can be analyzed for indication of future commodity-price movements.

**Technical rally:**  A short rise in commodity futures prices within a general declining trend. Such a rally may result from bargain hunting by market participants or because technical analysts have noticed a particular support level at which the commodity price is expected to increase.

**Time value:**  The amount of money options buyers are willing to pay for an option in anticipation that, over time, a change in the underlying futures price will cause the option to increase in value. In general, an option premium is the sum of time value and intrinsic value. Any amount by which an option premium exceeds the option's intrinsic value can be considered time value.

**Trading limit:**  See *position limit*.

**Underlying futures contract:**  The specific futures contract that the option conveys the right to buy (in case of a call) or sell (in the case of a put).

**United Nations Framework Convention On Climate Change (UNFCCC):** The international treaty unveiled at the United Nations Conference on Environment and Development (UNCED) in June 1992. The UNFCCC commits signatory countries to stabilize anthropogenic (human-induced) *greenhouse gas* emissions at "levels that would prevent dangerous anthropogenic interference with the climate system". The UNFCCC also requires that all signatory parties develop and update national inventories of anthropogenic emissions of all greenhouse gases not otherwise controlled by the *Montreal Protocol*. Out of 155 countries that have ratified this accord, the United States was the first industrialized nation to do so.

**Upside/downside risk:**  A short forward position taken without an offsetting long physical position in the underlying commodity is said to have upside risk. This means that the trader is speculating that the price of the commodity will decline. A long forward position taken without an offsetting short physical position in the underlying commodity is said to have downside risk, which means that the trader is speculating that the price of the commodity will increase.

**Value-at-risk (VaR):** Within a portfolio, this is the worst loss expected to be suffered over a given period of time with a given probability. The time period is known as the holding period and the probability is known as the confidence interval. Value-at-risk is not an estimate of the worst possible loss, but the largest likely loss. For example, a firm might estimate its VaR over 10 days to be $100 million, with a confidence interval of 95%. This would mean there is a one-in-twenty (5%) chance of a loss larger than $100 million in the next 10 days.

**Vintage year:** The first year an emissions allowance can be used for compliance purposes.

**Volatility:** A measure of the variability of a market factor, most often the price of the underlying instrument. Volatility is defined mathematically as the annualized *standard deviation* of the natural log of the ratio of two successive prices; the actual volatility realized over a period of time (historic/historical volatility) can be calculated from recorded data.

**Volume:** The number of purchases and sales of futures contracts made during a specified period of time; often the total transactions for one trading day.

**Weather derivatives:** Forward instruments used to hedge against or speculate on the weather. Virtually all of the instruments are based on degree-days, though precipitation swaps and sunshine options are among other possible instruments.

**West Texas Intermediate (WTI):** U.S. crude oil used as a benchmark for pricing much of the world's crude oil production.

**Wind energy:** The kinetic energy of wind converted into mechanical energy by wind turbines (i.e., blades rotating from the hub) that drive generators to produce electricity.

**Yield curve:** A chart in which the yield level is plotted on the vertical axis and the term to maturity of debt instruments of similar creditworthiness is plotted on the horizontal axis. The yield curve is positive when long-term rates are higher than short-term rates. However, yield curve is negative or inverted.

# 1 Setting the Stage for Collision or Convergence

As we approached the year 2005, one key question on the minds of corporate Europe was "What effect will the new dynamic of a pan-European emissions market have on the energy markets and industry?" With the rest of the world watching closely, on January 1, 2005 the European Union Emissions Trading Scheme (EU ETS) came into being. The fourth dimension of energy markets was born. Prior to this, traders and energy buyers only had to focus on the price of the fuel, quality of material, delivery time and location. Now, the cost of emissions from the use of that fuel also had to be taken into account in the whole cost equation.

Industry and traders alike could no longer depend on the simple arithmetic of oil, gas, coal and power prices to determine the "best deal". From this point onwards, energy producers, industry and traders had to examine the emissions cost of their energy production/source as a key component of their financial decision-making. Now, faced with alternative fuel sources, a company might find that the notionally cheaper source might, in fact, prove the more expensive once the cost of emissions generated by that fuel are taken into account.

What we have witnessed since the launch of the EU ETS is a convergence, an embracing of emissions trading and its uses as a commercial advantage, as a marketing tool — as in the case of green, carbon-neutral taxi firms being launched in England — and as a mechanism which helps firms finance the upgrading of technology to beat emissions-reduction targets and claim the attendant financial benefits by selling excess emissions credits.

Before going any further, let us clarify what we mean by "emissions trading". Technically speaking, emissions trading is a market-based approach to reducing levels of pollution. It was developed to help reduce pollution at a lower overall cost for pollution emitters ("emitters"). Since its invention in the late 1960s, it has mostly been used to deal with different kinds of air pollution, although it has also been used with water pollution. According to economists, the advantages of effective emissions trading are that it allows emitters flexibility in choosing how to address their pollution-reduction obligations; it encourages the use of the most economically efficient pollution-reduction measures, thus allowing emitters to save money while placing the minimum possible burden on the economy as a whole; and it encourages innovation in finding less expensive ways to reduce pollution.

Interestingly, soon after the launch of the EU ETS, with gas prices in Europe soaring to record highs in mid 2005 (in line with escalating international oil prices which reached close to US$70 a barrel in September 2005), the European power-generation community started burning more coal than ever before. This was because the cost of coal plus the emissions cost was still cheaper than burning natural gas or oil for electricity production. This drove an increase in demand for emissions credits and a surge in price which saw emissions credits rise from around €5 per MT of carbon dioxide ($CO_2$) at launch to over €30 within seven months. The substantial rise in the value of emissions credits started to give a large economic pay-back to those industries covered by the scheme because the credits are transferable, tradable instruments which could be sold at a premium to help subsidize the purchase of cleaner energy technologies or to upgrade plants to reduce emissions.

So where did this approach to emissions reductions — creating a market mechanism that forces industry to cut emissions by a set amount over time while providing economic incentives to do so — come from?

In the late 1960s, John Dales, a Canadian economist, developed the idea of using tradable emissions rights as a way to reduce the economic costs of pollution control. Several emissions-trading programs have been put into place since then, and it may come as a shock to some to hear that the earliest scheme was put in place in the

United States. The largest of these schemes is the American Acid Rain Program for sulfur dioxide ($SO_2$) emissions from electricity generators, which was started in 1995. This system has so far been regarded as a success: reductions targets have been met and sometimes exceeded, and reductions costs have been lower than they were under other pollution-reduction regimes.

The energy industry (encompassing oil, gas and power producers) is the world's leading emissions polluter but is set to become the leading supplier of environmental solutions because it's good for business. Today, as carbon intensity continues to grow while time to stabilize carbon dioxide and other greenhouse-gas (GHG) emissions is increasingly limited, the industry is at a turning point on global warming. This issue goes way beyond the Kyoto Protocol, which initially operates only for the period 2008 to 2012 (although discussions on arrangements for the period beyond 2012 are already under way), and will engage all countries in greenhouse-gas reductions over the next century.

The oil industry has the financial strength, intellectual capital and global presence to provide these global solutions. BP (with its "De-carbonization of fuel" strategy), Shell and Chevron Texaco have already taken the lead but other companies are not far behind. The carbon footprint of the major oil companies is complex and ever changing as a result of factors that include ever-evolving oil and gas production profiles, new pipeline transportation, refining and marketing, storage, and their growing involvement in the power industry. Therefore, the solutions will come from within the industry and include more efficient, environmentally benign technology but also basic changes in standard industry practices. Industrial best practices will now have a proactive environmental component, because it makes financial and commercial sense.

Environmental issues are now framed as corporate financial issues. Greater financial disclosure of corporate environmental risks, including climate change, has brought environmental issues in from the periphery to the forefront of corporate fiduciary responsibility. Increasingly, the environmental performance and the financial performance of companies are intertwined.

This also influences how consumers use energy and has an impact on automobile manufacturers, electric utilities, building owners, commercial banks and insurance companies.

Automakers are increasingly concerned about carbon dioxide emissions per vehicle and utilities now pay more attention to cutting their greenhouse-gas and other air emissions. Oil and gas companies are increasingly concerned about their emissions as production, refining, transportation and distribution liabilities and we have seen in Europe oil majors investing in what is called "carbon capture" and storage techniques, where carbon dioxide is captured from oil fields or from power stations and fed back in to the ground, sometimes back in to the oil fields.

Bank share valuations could fall if they lack adequate risk-management strategies for carbon, and several banks such as JPMorgan Chase have now enunciated new environmental lending policies with teeth. Insurance and reinsurance companies are at the forefront of confronting and addressing financial risks arising from, for example, catastrophic crop failures as a result of climate change, and health-related risks arising from linkages between climate change and infectious disease. These new financial risks for insurance and reinsurance companies may actually prompt them to drop coverage for certain companies. These new risks are beginning to prompt change and the creation of environmental markets.

The future promises more financial disclosure about potential liabilities. Indeed, Innovest Strategic Investors, the green Moody's, has already shown that companies perceived to be more environmentally aware are also more financially successful.

The EU ETS has had a positive effect on industry and its strategy towards emissions reductions by focusing attention on emissions as a potential financial liability which, if not handled properly, could run into many hundreds of millions of euros for some companies. If managed properly, however, the strategy promises substantial rewards for those achieving faster reductions than required, with the emissions credits above and beyond a firm's requirements being sold at a profit.

The EU ETS is an example of how market-based solutions through emissions trading are undoubtedly the way forward for the energy industry and energy-intensive industries. Environmental financial products for $SO_2$, which causes acid rain, and nitrogen oxides (NOx), which cause urban smog, began in the U.S. in 1995 and 1999, respectively. These pollutants were reduced through "cap and trade" mechanisms which are also now part of the Kyoto Protocol. Despite general perceptions to the contrary, emissions trading was made in America, and proposed by the U.S. delegation at the Rio Climate Convention Treaty in 1992. Today, we have a US$10 billion environmental financial market for $SO_2$ and NOx. The carbon markets are using the same template developed by the U.S. under the auspices of the first Bush Administration and proposed by the Environmental Defense Fund (now called Environmental Defense), an environmental group based in New York, with the implementation of the Clean Air Act Amendments of 1990. Contrary to the widespread perception that the U.S. is doing nothing on global warming, environmental law in America continues to focus on more stringent regulation of emissions reductions. In fact, in March 2005 the Clean Air Interstate Rules (CAIR) were passed to reduce $SO_2$ and NOx emissions by 2015 by a further 70% and 65% respectively — once again, the most exacting standards in the world. Furthermore, the U.S. is now looking to implement the first emissions-trading rules for mercury, another known toxin. It is the energy industry that bears the brunt of this clean up. Trading mechanisms have been proven to work and also be cost effective.

The U.S. has one of the most advanced emissions-trading markets in the world, trading US$3 billion in notional-value $SO_2$ allowances each year as prices rose to over $800 per ton in the spring of 2005. It also has the most advanced nitrogen oxide (NOx) markets in the world, with allowances trading at up to US$40,000 per ton during the summer of 2004 in the Houston/Galveston area, which has the worst air pollution non-attainment in America and has to reduce its NOx levels by 80% in 2008. Additionally, the California RECLAIM market for Southern California air quality has had active $SO_2$ and NOx markets as well. Such market-based solutions are now being embraced by several green hedge funds trading in $SO_2$, NOx, carbon and renewable-energy credits, as well as by emitters. After all, emissions trading is also about speculation.

## Europe begins its regime

Signed in December 1997, the Kyoto Protocol is the international agreement intended to reduce emissions of greenhouse gases (especially $CO_2$, methane and CFCs) in developed countries. The Protocol requires, for example, that the European Union reduce its emissions by 8% below 1990 levels by 2012, which equates to a reduction of 340 million tons of $CO_2$ emitted into the atmosphere.

The emissions-trading scheme started in the 25 EU Member States on January 1, 2005 and, after the launch value of approximately €5 per MT of $CO_2$, it rose quickly to a high of around €30 in mid

2005. If we take an average value of €20 per MT of $CO_2$ emission credits, the EU trading scheme was handling emissions credits worth €6.8 billion. A key aspect of the EU scheme is that it allows companies to use credits from Kyoto's project-based mechanisms, joint implementation (JI) and the clean-development mechanism (CDM) to help them comply with their obligations under the scheme. This means the system not only provides a cost-effective means for EU-based industries to cut their emissions but also creates additional incentives for businesses to invest in emissions-reduction projects in developing nations such as China and India, and in South America and Africa. In turn, this spurs the transfer of advanced, environmentally sound technologies to other industrialized countries and developing nations, giving tangible support to their efforts to achieve sustainable development.

The launch of the EU ETS and the implementation of the Kyoto Protocol in February 2005 have provided a wake-up call to corporate America. Multinational corporations in the U.S., Canada and around the world are starting to realize that they have compliance difficulties in many locations. The consensus emerging in the U.S. is that a climate-change regime will be in place in the next two to three years.

The issues of environmental financial liabilities and the emergence of climate-change risk have made U.S. companies extremely nervous about proceeding in market development with such near-term uncertainty and potential impact to their bottom line. In December 2004, Fitch Ratings issued the first ratings agency report on emissions trading, and with emissions trading now clearly on the balance sheet, clarity is starting to come to the issue of climate change in the U.S.

The long-term impact of these market-based solutions has been to reduce pollution in a cost-effective manner and accelerate the introduction of more environmentally benign technologies. It has also given industry time to implement new, cleaner technology and fuel sources, with minimal economic disruption to the capital-intensive energy industry, the agricultural industry and other industrial sources of pollution. The markets have actually created concrete and measurable emissions reductions for American business, although the news media turns a blind eye to it.

Emissions-trading markets are not true commodity markets in that they are "cap and trade", which means that emissions are ratcheted down over time. For the U.S. $SO_2$ markets, this involves a 35-year regime of reductions and more stringent standards until the year 2030. For $CO_2$ and other greenhouse-gas reductions, we will need a 100-year program that engages the entire world and sets quantifiable long-term benchmarks to reduce emissions. Implementation of the Kyoto Protocol is a modest first step to global emissions reductions, but the larger question is whether there will be significant $CO_2$ reductions in the next two decades to meet carbon stabilization in the atmosphere. The reality is that the entire world is in this for the long haul. There is no quick technological fix as long as the world is addicted to fossil fuels, whose consumption continues to rise. That habit is not going to change, as has been evidenced in the past year with record oil, coal and natural-gas consumption, despite higher prices. We need a climate-change regime that will aggressively reduce global carbon intensity, including both stationary and mobile sources, accelerate technology transfer and increase energy efficiency. The U.S. will lead in this effort.

Already, commodity $CO_2$ used for enhanced oil recovery in Texas and Wyoming is now married to carbon sequestration efforts in those states. The use of naturally depleted geologic formations is being pushed forward by the oil industry and the U.S. Department of Energy. Again, unknown to most of the world, the U.S. is leading in these green efforts.

In the United Kingdom, British Petroleum (BP) announced in early 2006 that it will remove $CO_2$ from natural gas out of the North Sea before burning it in an onshore power station, and then, using existing pipeline, transport the $CO_2$ gas back out to sea down in to a nearby depleted oil field.

Turning to mobile sources of pollution, hybrid gasoline/electric vehicles that reduce $CO_2$ tailpipe emissions and increase fuel economy are now being embraced by the U.S. public as well as other nations. In California, tailpipe emissions will be regulated in 2009, with these regulations subsequently being adopted in New York and other states, despite legal challenges from the automobile industries. Once again, these will be the first such standards in the world. We also have many energy-efficiency devices that reduce building loads from both commercial and residential buildings, again leading to a reduction in greenhouse-gas emissions.

What has been lacking in America is the mandate of the federal government. This is now beginning to change. Federally mandated standards are needed to create fungible commodity markets so that the rules bring a realistic financial value to emissions reductions, rather than the US$1–2 per ton shown on the Chicago Climate Exchange. The point is that both the $SO_2$ and NOx programs are mandated and have financial penalties for non-compliance. The low carbon prices of today reflect the market valuation of "voluntary" standards. Companies would rather sit on their carbon inventories today as prices will surely appreciate tomorrow.

Another driver behind the greenhouse-gas (GHG) market is that we now have institutional shareholders forcing corporations to acknowledge the environmental risk on their books. This has been done mostly by pension funds and is similar to the strategy that proved quite effective in tobacco litigation. There are also several litigation efforts to get the U.S. federal government to change its present oppositional position.

Nevertheless, global environmental markets are beginning, with GHG trades valued at about US$2 billion in notional value so far. The European trading scheme that started in January 2005 traded more than 49 million metric tons of $CO_2$ equivalent in its first six months.

The European program is a company-to-company cap-and-trade program, and the tradable unit is EU allowances. We have seen over three million tons traded on the Chicago Climate Exchange, with more than 80 companies participating, and carbon trading at less than US$2 per ton. However, many larger trades, including a one-million ton trade by electric utility Entergy in December 2004, have been traded on the over-the-counter (OTC) bilaterally traded market (directly traded between market counterparts). And we have seen the emergence of several green hedge funds that will actually trade carbon and renewable-energy credits speculatively.

## The banks step in

As well as the usual suspects such as electric utilities, oil companies and automakers, financial houses will be needed as market makers to ensure that these environmental financial markets work more effectively. Today, Morgan Stanley is the largest $SO_2$ emissions trader in North America, and now Goldman Sachs has a 4,000 MW portfolio of renewable-energy projects with its recent purchase of Zilkha Energy. Wall Street can ramp up for emissions trading very quickly, having both the talent and the balance sheet to make markets. In London, Barclays Capital, Calyon Financial, Rabobank and others are making a concerted effort to make carbon markets in Europe. We are witnessing a market transformation similar to developments in the oil market in the late 1970s; that is, opaque price discovery and little liquidity. But the good news is that this time it is happening all over the world at the same time. We are now positioned for the beginning of a liquid spot market instead of the one-off trades that have occurred up until now. On April 22, 2005, the European Climate Exchange, sister of the Chicago Climate Exchange, was launched.

## Where we are going in the U.S.

Today, 28 different U.S. state greenhouse-gas programs are in place or taking shape. We are seeing shareholder pressure. We are seeing U.S. multinational companies worried about double environmental standards in the U.S. and the rest of the world. The federal government will now have to act, and it will move faster than imagined as the EU and Japan start out on the learning curve of environmental financial markets. The U.S. is now into its eleventh year of action in this area and, contrary to uninformed public perceptions, the fact is that more stringent standards are being implemented for $SO_2$ and NOx. It is only a matter of time before the carbon regime takes place, and that will be sooner rather than later. Already U.S. utilities are moving forward since they are the most severely affected by this. But the economic pain will be shared and this will not be as disruptive as claimed. Every American wants clean air and clean water. A small price for human health is not much of a sacrifice for a country that gobbles up 20 million barrels of oil per day and has over 900,000 MW of peak capacity. The surprise to many will be that, as the emissions markets continue to roll forward, many companies will bite the bullet and make the necessary investment in new, cleaner, energy-efficient technology. This means that less coal will be used to produce the same energy, and it will be gasified coal. Just as hybrid cars use less fuel and reduce emissions, so will new power-generation equipment. It will boost investment in an under-invested sector and create jobs.

The U.S., with its entrepreneurial culture, risk capital and knowledge base in trading, is still well positioned to lead in developing environmental financial markets. This may be the best thing that has happened to America, as new jobs are created in emissions trading, clean technology and energy efficiency. At today's high prices, it's now or never.

It is now a critical time for the emissions-trading sector, and the next 10 to 15 years will throw up signals that will induce both optimism and pessimism. These might include:

- Threats to human survival posed by global climate change and the spread of infectious disease
- New technologies in the generation and management of renewable energy
- Growth in relevant financial products and increasing interest from major financial players and investment banks such as Goldman Sachs, AIG and others, who are quietly entering the emissions and renewables space
- Growing financial liabilities driven by the climate issue
- The reality that the stabilization of emissions is a long-term target
- Elements supporting growth in greenhouse-gas (GHG) emissions markets, such as potential fungibility of its derivatives, growth in GHG emission levels, increased public perception, and increased liabilities of potential shareholder lawsuits related to GHGs.

State-level Renewable Portfolio Standards (RPS), which mandate a percentage of energy that must be generated from renewable sources, provide a driver for renewable-energy markets, augmenting solar-panel power generation's 30% annual market growth and wind energy's 40% annual growth. Financial products for energy efficiency ("negawatts") are emerging.

GreenTrading™, the triple convergence of GHG, renewable energy and negawatt markets, could be become a US$3 trillion commodity market opportunity over the next 20 years. Admittedly, though, its development will require greater liquidity, standardization and indexed construction, market making by major players and cross-border trading.

Out of all that has been said to introduce the scope and huge scale of emissions markets, the risks, the opportunities, and the potential rewards, one thing is certain: despite possible lack of clarity in how emissions controls and the markets built around them will evolve beyond Kyoto's current 2012 limit, emissions markets have arrived. They are here to stay, their industry reach will get broader and broader and, as a result, they will undoubtedly continue to become an increasingly key focus for global energy markets and industry.

# The Birth of the Global Emissions Market

**2**

In 1898, Swedish scientist Svante Ahrrenius warned that carbon dioxide emissions could lead to global warming. It was not until the 1970s, however, that scientists' growing understanding of the earth's atmosphere brought this previously obscure field of science to wider attention and it was not until the late 1980s that any international agreements came into force.

The first such agreement addressing the issue of the destruction of the ozone layer came in September 1987 through the Montreal Protocol, which was noted as a landmark international agreement designed to protect the stratospheric ozone layer. In Montreal, 24 nations signed a treaty that most observers had thought would be impossible. Some years later, the Montreal Protocol on Substances That Deplete the Ozone Layer was characterized by the heads of the World Meteorological Organization (WMO) and the United Nations Environment Programme (UNEP) "as one of the great international achievements of the century".

Although it did not address emissions such as carbon dioxide (which came later under the Kyoto Protocol), the Montreal agreement undoubtedly put the earth's atmosphere and global warming at the top of the international political agenda and aligned countries from all over the world on this crucial issue. This paved the way for discussions that led to the 1992 Rio meeting discussed later in this chapter.

The Montreal Protocol stipulated that the production and consumption of compounds that deplete ozone in the stratosphere — chlorofluorocarbons (CFCs), halons, carbon tetrachloride, and methyl chloroform — were to be phased out by 2000 (2005 for methyl chloroform). Scientific theory and evidence suggest that, once emitted into the atmosphere, these compounds could significantly deplete the stratospheric ozone layer that shields the planet from damaging UV-B radiation. UNEP prepared a Montreal Protocol Handbook that provides additional detail and explanation of the provisions. The publication *Thematic Guide on Ozone Depletion and Global Environmental Change*, produced by The Center for International Earth Science Information Network (CIESIN), presents an in-depth look at causes, human and environmental effects, and policy responses to stratospheric ozone depletion (see www.ciesin.org). Under the Montreal Protocol, the basic phase-out schedule for CFCs in developed countries is as follows: 35% reduction in 2004, 65% reduction in 2010, 90% reduction in 2015, 99.5% reduction in 2020, and 100% phase-out in 2030. The final 0.5% after 2020 is to be available only to service existing refrigeration and air-conditioning equipment. Developing countries will freeze CFC consumption at 2015 levels (maximum) in 2016, and phase it out completely by 2040.

Given the threats to life that have been averted through this landmark treaty, few would challenge the WMO and UNEP's appraisal of the importance of the Montreal Protocol.

Ozone, whose existence was unknown until 1839, has been characterized by the world's scientific community in general as probably the single most important chemically active trace gas in the earth's atmosphere, without which life as it currently exists could not have evolved. The Montreal Protocol, by phasing out certain chemicals, preserved the stratospheric ozone layer that absorbs harmful ultraviolet radiation from the sun. Depletion of this thin gaseous shield — which, if compressed to the planet's surface, would be no thicker than gauze — would have incalculable impacts on human, animal and plant cells, as well as on climate and ecological systems.

The development of data and arguments over greenhouse gases, CFCs and the earth's atmosphere and links to global warming/climate change brought together international scientists, United Nations groups and leading politicians and triggered debate. This then led to the next stage — the so-called Earth Summit, held in Rio in 1992.

## Back in America: The Clean Air Act Amendments of 1990

Before we talk about Rio, it would be useful to review developments in the U.S. where, in 1990, important amendments to the Clean Air Act were introduced. The Act had started life in 1956 in response to London's great smog of 1952. Congress passed the Act in 1963. This was followed by the Clean Air Act Amendment in 1966, the Clean Air Act Extension in 1970, and further Amendments in 1977 and 1990. Numerous state and local governments have enacted similar legislation, either implementing federal programs or filling in locally important gaps in federal programs.

The importance of the 1990 Amendments was that they contained proposals for emissions trading, added provisions for addressing acid rain, ozone depletion and toxic air pollution, and established a national pollution-permits program.

There is a general misconception that Europe invented emissions trading, yet it was the U.S. that created the legislation to kick-start emissions trading in 1990, prior to the introduction of the Kyoto Protocol.

Although the 1990 Clean Air Act Amendments are federal law and cover the entire country, the individual states do much of the work to implement them. For example, it is the state air-pollution agencies that hold hearings on permit applications by power or chemical plants and impose fines on companies that violate air-pollution limits.

Under this law, the Environmental Protection Agency (EPA) sets limits on how much of a pollutant can be in the air anywhere in the U.S. This ensures that all Americans have the same basic health and environmental protections. The law allows individual states to have stronger pollution controls, but establishes a benchmark below which they are not allowed to fall.

The law recognizes that it makes sense for states to take the lead in implementing the Act, because pollution-control problems often require special understanding of local industries, geography, housing patterns, and so forth.

In consultation with the public, through hearings and opportunities to comment, states have to develop state implementation plans (SIPs) that explain how they will fulfill their obligations under the Act. Each SIP is submitted to the EPA for approval. Where an SIP proves unacceptable, the EPA can assume responsibility for implementing the Act in that state.

Through the EPA, the U.S. government assists the states by providing scientific research, expert studies, engineering designs and money to support clean-air programs.

### Interstate air pollution

Air pollution often travels from its source in one state to another state. In many metropolitan areas, people live in one state and work or shop in another; air pollution from cars and trucks may spread throughout the interstate area. The 1990 Clean Air Act provides for interstate commissions to develop regional strategies for reducing interstate air pollution.

### International air pollution

Neither does air pollution respect national borders. The 1990 law covers pollution that originates in Mexico and Canada and drifts into the U.S., and vice versa. Further detail on the various state-level trading schemes for greenhouse gases can be found in Chapter 4.

## The Rio Earth Summit: An international framework on climate change

Greater scientific understanding arising from research and the Montreal treaty led to a series of intergovernmental conferences focusing on climate change in the late 1980s and early 1990s. In 1990, the Second World Climate Conference called for a framework treaty on climate change. Sponsored by the WMO, UNEP and other international organizations, this conference featured negotiations and ministerial-level discussions involving 137 states and the European Community.

The Framework Convention on Climate Change was one of two binding treaties opened for signature at the United Nations Conference on Environment and Development (UNCED) in 1992. Since its adoption at the "Earth Summit" in Rio de Janeiro, the United Nations Framework Convention on Climate Change has been the centerpiece of global efforts to combat global warming. It has also been one of the international community's most essential tools in the struggle to promote sustainable development.

The treaty, also known as the Climate Convention, addressed potential human-induced global warming by having the participating countries pledge themselves to seek "stabilization of greenhouse-gas concentrations in the atmosphere at a level that would prevent dangerous anthropogenic interference with the climate system".

Though this was stated only in general terms, the Climate Convention parties did agree to attempt to limit emissions of GHGs, mainly $CO_2$ and methane ($CH_4$).

As the treaty was just a framework convention, this meant that specific commitments to target emission levels were not included. However, it did support a number of principles later included in the Climate Change Convention. These were: climate change as a "common concern of humankind", the importance of equity, the "common but differentiated responsibilities" of countries at different levels of development, sustainable development and the precautionary principle (that is, where there are threats of serious or irreversible damage, a lack of scientific certainty should not be used as a reason for postponing cost-effective measures to prevent environmental degradation).

Although signed at UNCED, the Climate Convention was negotiated through a separate process under the Intergovernmental Negotiating Committee (INC) for the Framework Convention on Climate Change. The text was adopted at New York on May 9, 1992, opened for signature at Rio de Janeiro in June 1992, and thereafter at United Nations Headquarters from June 20, 1992 to June 19, 1993. On December 21, 1993, Portugal became the fiftieth state to ratify the Climate Convention, thus fulfilling the minimum requirement for the treaty to come into force, which happened on March 21, 1994.

## The environmental challenge

To give policy makers and the general public a better understanding of what researchers had learned, in 1988 the United Nations Environment Programme (UNEP) and the World Meteorological Organization (WMO) established the Intergovernmental Panel on Climate Change (IPCC). The IPCC was given a mandate to assess the state of existing knowledge about the climate system and climate change; the environmental, economic and social impacts of climate change; and possible response strategies.

The IPCC released its First Assessment Report in 1990. Approved after a painstaking peer-review process by hundreds of leading scientists and experts, the Report confirmed the scientific basis for climate change. It had a powerful effect on both policy makers and the general public and exerted a strong influence on negotiations on the Climate Change Convention in 1992.

## IPCC findings

The IPPC found that humanity's emissions of greenhouse gases are likely to cause rapid climate change. Carbon dioxide is produced when fossil fuels are burned, and its effects intensify when carbon-dioxide-absorbing forests are cut down. Methane and nitrogen oxides are released as a result of agricultural practices, changes in land use and other causes. Chlorofluorocarbons (CFCs) and other gases also play a role in trapping heat in the atmosphere. By thickening the atmospheric "blanket" of greenhouse gases, mankind's emissions are upsetting the energy flows that drive the climate system.

Climate models predicted that the global temperature would rise by between 1°C and 3.5°C by 2100. This projection was based on emissions trends at that time (circa 1990) and contains many uncertainties, particularly at the regional level. Because the climate does not respond immediately to greenhouse-gas emissions, it will continue to change for hundreds of years after atmospheric concentrations have stabilized. Meanwhile, rapid and unexpected climate transitions cannot be ruled out. Although many scientists still dispute whether greenhouse gases from the burning of fossil fuels are creating this situation, with some arguing that volcanoes emit much more greenhouse gases than human activities, climate change is real, and is happening during our lifetime. Mankind has a responsibility to take whatever action it can to slow down disruptive and destructive climate changes that could affect our way of life and, ultimately, threaten our survival.

Climate change will have powerful effects on the global environment. In general, the faster the climate changes, the greater will be the risk of damage. If current trends continue, the mean sea level is expected to rise some 15–95 cm by 2100, causing flooding and other damage. Climate zones (and thus ecosystems and agricultural zones) could shift towards the poles by 150–550 km in the mid-latitude regions. Forests, deserts, rangelands and other unmanaged ecosystems could become wetter, drier, hotter or colder. As a result, many will decline or fragment, and individual species will become extinct.

Human society will face new risks and pressures with some instability to global food production, with some regions possibly experiencing food shortages and hunger. Water resources will be affected as precipitation and evaporation patterns change around the world. In the winter of 2004/2005 the United Kingdom, for example, received only 70% of its normal rainfall and is expecting drinking-water rationing in the summer of 2006. This may become an increasingly common situation across Europe and other parts of the Western world.

Physical infrastructure will be damaged, particularly by a rise in sea levels and by extreme weather events, which may increase in frequency and intensity in some regions. Economic activities, human settlements and human health will experience many direct and indirect effects, with the poor being the most vulnerable to the damaging effects of climate change.

People and ecosystems will need to adapt to the future climate regime. Past and current emissions have already ensured that there will be some degree of climate change in the 21$^{st}$ century. Adapting to these effects will require a good understanding of socio-economic and natural systems, their sensitivity to climate change, and their inherent ability to adapt. Many strategies are available for promoting adaptation.

Stabilizing atmospheric concentrations of greenhouse gases will require a major effort. Based on current trends, the growth in emissions of carbon dioxide and other greenhouse gases is expected to result in the equivalent of a doubling of pre-industrial $CO_2$ concentrations in the atmosphere by 2030, and a trebling by 2100. Stabilizing global $CO_2$ emissions at their current levels would postpone $CO_2$ doubling to 2100. Emissions would eventually have to fall to less than 30% of their current levels if concentrations were to be stabilized at doubled $CO_2$ levels sometime in the 22$^{nd}$ century. Such cuts would have to be made despite growing populations and an expanding world economy.

After the Convention was adopted in Rio, the Intergovernmental Negotiating Committee (INC) that drafted it continued its preparatory work, meeting for another six sessions to discuss matters relating to commitments, arrangements for the financial mechanism, technical and financial support to developing countries, and procedural and institutional matters. The INC was dissolved after its eleventh and final session in February 1995, and the Conference of the Parties (COP) became the Convention's ultimate authority.

The Convention required the Conference (COP-1) to review whether the commitment of developed countries to take measures aimed at returning their emissions to 1990 levels by 2000 was adequate for meeting the Convention's objective. The Parties agreed that new commitments were indeed needed for the post-2000 period. They established the Ad Hoc Group (AGBM) to draft "a protocol or another legal instrument" for adoption at COP-3 in 1997.

The IPCC's Second Assessment Report was adopted soon after a meeting in Berlin in December 1995. The Report was reviewed by some 2,000 scientists and experts worldwide and came to the conclusion that "the balance of evidence suggests that there is a discernible human influence on global climate". However, the Report did much more — for example, confirming the availability of various cost-effective strategies for combating climate change.

The COP held its second session (COP-2) in July 1996, with ministers releasing a declaration emphasizing the need to accelerate talks on strengthening the Climate Change Convention and endorsing the Second Assessment Report "as currently the most comprehensive and authoritative assessment of the science of climate change, its impacts and response options now available". They further stated that the Report "should provide a scientific basis for urgently strengthening action at the global, regional and national levels, particularly action by Annex I (industrialized) countries to limit and reduce emissions of greenhouse gases".

## COP-3: Kyoto

The Kyoto Protocol, as it became known, was ratified in December 1997 by all major countries except for the U.S. It covered, amongst other things, the sharing of information on greenhouse gases between developed nations.

The 1996 review of national communications from developed countries revealed that carbon dioxide accounted for 80.5% of total greenhouse-gas emissions from developed countries. Fuel combustion was confirmed as the most important source of $CO_2$. With the 33 countries included in the review accounting for around

63% of global $CO_2$ emissions in 1990, this seemed to confirm that carbon dioxide was the most important greenhouse gas resulting from human activities. That is why emissions-reduction schemes and cap-and-trade schemes adopted around the world had $CO_2$ at the top of the list.

## The Kyoto Protocol, 1997

The Kyoto Protocol (see Appendix A) was negotiated by more than 160 nations in December 1997, its aim being to reduce net emissions of certain greenhouse gases (primarily carbon dioxide). Each of the participating developed countries was required to decide how to meet its respective reduction goal during a five-year period, 2008–2012.

The Protocol requires that industrialized countries agree to limit their greenhouse-gas emissions in this period at an average of 5.2% below their 1990 emission levels. The resulting assigned amount (measured at a national level in AAU or Assigned Amount Units) is based on six types of greenhouse gas: carbon dioxide ($CO_2$), methane ($CH_4$), nitrous oxide ($N_2O$), hydrofluorocarbons (HFCs) (also covered by the 1987 Montreal agreement), perfluorocarbons (PFCs) and sulfur hexafluoride ($SF_6$).

The emissions-reduction targets vary from country to country but, on average, an 8% reduction is required across the European Union, with a 7% reduction for Japan.

Countries were divided into two categories, which determined what controls were placed on them and the emission targets expected of them.

Broadly these categories are as follows:

- Annex I countries — industrialized countries, incorporating the European Union, Switzerland, Canada, Hungary, Japan, Poland, New Zealand, the Russian Federation, Ukraine, Norway, Australia and Iceland.
- Non-Annex I countries — developing countries, whose emission constraints/controls are much less strict that those of Annex I countries.

Under the Kyoto Protocol, each Annex I country receives a budget of AAUs for the period 2008–2012. Each can decide how it will use its

AAU allowance, either selling them or carrying them over to the next commitment period.

This flexibility is not just a matter of politics but a very practical requirement that enables countries to cope with unexpected climate or economic changes within the designated period.

## The U.S. opts out

Under the Kyoto Protocol, the U.S. would have had to agree to reducing emissions by around 6%. It chose to opt out.

In a study entitled "Impacts of the Kyoto Protocol on U.S. Energy Markets and Economic Activity", the Energy Information Administration (EIA), an independent statistical and analytical agency in the U.S. Department of Energy, projected that meeting the U.S. targets under the Protocol would call for significant market adjustments. Among its findings were the following:

- Reductions in $CO_2$ emissions would result in the use of between 18% and 77% less coal than projected in the EIA Reference Case in 2010, particularly affecting electricity generation, and between 2% and 13% less petroleum, mainly affecting transportation.
- Energy consumers would need to use between 2% and 12% more natural gas in 2010 and between 2% and 16% more renewable energy, and extend the operating life of existing nuclear units.
- To achieve these ends via market-based means, in 2010 average delivered energy costs (in inflation-adjusted 1996 dollars) must be between 17% and 83% higher than projected.

No wonder then that the U.S. opted out of ratifying the Kyoto Protocol in 2001. The U.S. defended its position on economic grounds and in the light of the absence of targets for developing countries. It would be unfair to say that the U.S. is doing nothing about emissions reductions; far from it. As outlined earlier, it was operating GHG trading schemes many years prior to the 2005 EU ETS came into force. These state-level climate policies, including regional exchange of $CO_2$ allowances, are discussed in more detail in Chapter 4.

## Emissions-reduction mechanisms under the Kyoto Protocol

The mechanisms are meant to create a platform for international co-operation on emissions and allow countries that have ratified the Kyoto agreement to undertake emissions-reduction projects in other countries or purchase or otherwise acquire emission allowances from other countries to help with compliance with their obligations.

The three mechanisms are:

- Clean Development Mechanism (CDM projects)
- Join Implementation (JI schemes)
- International emissions trading.

## Joint Implementation and the Clean Development Mechanism: An Overview

The Kyoto Protocol provides participating countries with a number of flexible instruments for achieving their reduction commitments. The Netherlands was the first country in the world to use Joint Implementation and the Clean Development Mechanism.

JI and CDM are project-related, meaning that they are linked to a specific project to reduce emissions. For example, this may entail the creation of a wind-farm power facility which has an emissions-reduction benefit. In Brazil, for example, such emissions credits have been generated under CDM schemes in which the investor who created the wind farm under the oversight of the United Nations was able to have the emissions reduction accredited, approved and certified. This enables the investor to take this emission reduction in Brazil over to the European Union emissions-trading scheme, for example. Such investments in energy projects are of interest to the host country because they contribute to sustainable economic growth without an increase in emissions. This example is just one of many projects that might not have been achieved without carbon finance being made available under the Kyoto Protocol and the JI/CDM structures, without which there just would not have been an incentive for investors to venture to this or other regions and help develop reduced-emission or zero-emission power plants.

JI is aimed at countries that also have a reduction obligation under Kyoto, mainly Central and Eastern Europe. CDM focuses on developing countries such as Brazil that don't have reduction obligations.

## What are carbon credits?

Carbon credits are acknowledgements of the achievement of reductions of emissions of greenhouse gases as a result of a project / an investment. One carbon credit is given for one ton of $CO_2$ equivalent (carbon dioxide equivalent).

In JI, carbon credits are officially called Emission Reduction Units (ERUs). In the CDM, they are called Certified Emission Reductions (CERs). You will also see the term 'ton $CO_2e$', which is the same as a carbon credit, ERU or CER.

Under CDM, Annex I countries or authorized entities in Annex I countries can obtain Certified Emission Reductions by investing in emissions-reduction projects in a developing country. CERs can be registered and saved for compliance with current Kyoto commitments or banked for later periods.

The JI mechanism encourages emissions reductions through the implementation of projects by one Annex I entity — be it a bank, power company, oil company or government — in another Annex I country. The investor can receive an agreed number of Emission Reduction Units for the investment against payment of a negotiated price. A project can qualify for the generation of ERUs under the JI mechanism only if reductions are additional to business-as-usual and can only be generated from 2008.

**Figure 2.1:**   Carbon credits and how they work

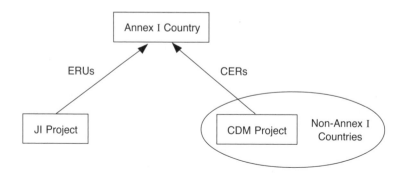

It is important to note that, unlike a CDM, both participants must be Annex I parties and thus have an emissions-reduction target set by the Kyoto Protocol. Examples of JI and CDM projects are noted in Chapter 4.

In the European Union context, an industrial site where there are potential emissions-reduction projects under the JI framework can only be accepted for JI if that site is not already part of the EU ETS.

## The compliance aspects of the Kyoto mechanisms

The control regime for the Kyoto Protocol is very strict and to prevent a country from overselling its AAUs it must maintain at least 90% of its assigned amount (reserve compliance level). This is the minimum level of emissions credits the country must maintain; anything below this level cannot be traded out to other countries.

Some market observers are concerned that this compliance reserve of 90% could affect the cross-border trading of credits. For example, let's say a British company has a contractual commitment to transfer an allowance to a Russian company, but the United Kingdom has fallen below its minimum compliance level. In this case, the British company might find that it is not able to transfer the allowance. This is something companies must check is being addressed in any cross-border trading agreements.

Where a country drops below the minimum reserve level, it is given 30 days to restore the reserve to its required minimum level by buying/acquiring credits from another country's AAUs, or through CER or ERU schemes.

However, if at the end of the commitment period and on completion of a formal review, a country is found not to own enough emission credits to comply with the Kyoto agreement, it would be given 100 days to make up the shortfall. If then this shortfall has still not been corrected, the country would be forced to make up this difference in the second commitment period (that is, the shortfall would roll over) and it would suffer a very punitive penalty of 30% additional allowance. This could create huge problems for that nation's firms who have individual allowances for emissions, since the country as a whole would be barred from international emissions trading.

# 3 Green Trading Schemes

"Green trading" is a term that was coined several years ago to capture the value of the convergence of the capital markets and the environment. It encompasses all forms of environmental financial trading including carbon dioxide and other greenhouse gas (GHG) reductions, sulfur dioxide (acid rain) and nitrogen oxide (ozone), renewable energy credits and negawatts (value of energy efficiency). All of these emerging and established environmental financial markets have one thing in common: making the environment cleaner by either reducing emissions through using clean technology or not using energy through the use of financial markets. Sometimes, it is possible to do both, as in reducing emissions and reducing energy usage by moving to cleaner technology. Green trading is one mechanism to accelerate this environmentally beneficial change.

The financial value of all of these environmental benefits is determined by the trading markets. The quaint notion that we are trading pollution is actually an over-simplification of the need of markets to create financial incentives to reduce pollution and accelerate more efficient and environmentally benign technology transfer. For example, in the well-established U.S. sulfur dioxide ($SO_2$) and nitrogen oxides (NOx) markets, we have seen market-driven changes in the past few years. As coal burning increased as a result of a rising demand for electricity and a decreasing supply of natural gas, the emissions-trading markets responded in kind. The price of emissions allowances rose to over US$800 per ton for sulfur dioxide and US$40,000 for NOx. Sulfur dioxide credits in the 11-year-old market had never risen above $225 per ton before. This financial penalty for increasing emissions accelerated the emergence of new technology into the coal-burning power-generation space that was previously uneconomic. During the past year, at least 20 coal-gasification facilities have either been announced or are in planning. In the previous year there were none. The benefit of gasification technology is that it not only reduces $SO_2$ and NOx emissions but it also reduces carbon dioxide emissions. The technology also increases coal-burning efficiency from 30% to over 70%, meaning that less coal will be needed to produce the same amount of electricity. This efficiency benefit is often overlooked by environmentalists, economists and policy makers, who tend to view the energy-supply picture as static, with ever-increasing energy demand. Basically, we will be using less energy, and it will be cleaner forms of energy as a result of market-based incentives coupled with financial penalties for non-compliance. These are not voluntary markets but markets with a government mandate. They have been proven to work and to be cost effective. They are essentially the template for the Kyoto Protocol.

Another venue for green trading has been in the renewable-energy area, where wind, solar and biomass markets are accelerating commercially as a result of the monetization of "renewable-energy credits", as they are called in the U.S. Today, 19 states have or are developing a renewable portfolio standard (RPS) that is jump-starting markets to take advantage of "green power" programs that are now popular with consumers. There are more than 600 such programs, where consumers willingly pay more for green power. The renewable-energy projects in these states are able to bank-finance their development and create a revenue stream of green credits that reduce the cost of capital; in effect, creating "green finance".

As fossil-fuel prices remain high throughout the remainder of this decade as a result of under-investment, and as global energy demand continues to increase, clean technology will become a more attractive economic choice for deployment in global markets. Energy and environment issues are becoming increasingly interlinked in such a way that rising demand is accelerating the need for clean technology solutions. Green trading is the financial mechanism that allows markets to meet that goal of global deployment of new, cleaner technology to meet rising demand for electricity, transportation, heating and cooling applications. What used to be expensive and un-commercial is rapidly being transformed into economic solutions to global environmental problems. Green trading is the mechanism to create these market-based incentives, and their application is global as developing economies such as China, India and Russia are moving forward on both emissions-trading initiatives and clean-technology applications.

Emissions-trading markets are not true commodity markets as they are "cap and trade", which means that emissions are ratcheted down over time. For the U.S. $SO_2$ markets, this involves a 35-year regime of reductions and more stringent standards until the year 2030.

The Kyoto implementation program that began on February 16, 2005 is a modest first step to global emissions reduction but is happy to look at the minutiae rather than the obvious bigger picture; that is, the reality that the entire world is in this together for the long haul.

For the past two years, corporate America has been trying to figure out the business case for GHG reductions. The business case is fairly simple: either pay less now or pay more later. Most companies are now beginning to analyze their risks and realize that there is a global issue here and that they have got to do something about it. This is especially true of U.S. multinational companies who have one set of standards in the U.S. and another in the EU. They don't want double environmental standards and are beginning to agitate for change in the U.S. federal position on GHGs. Environmental financial risk is rising as an issue in corporate America, with emissions trading offering a cost-effective solution to reducing pollution.

Global environmental markets are beginning to take hold, with GHG trades valued at about US$2 billion in notional value to date. The emissions-trading scheme that started in the 25 EU Member States in January 2005 saw more than 49 million tons traded in the period to July 31, 2005, with over 10 million tons traded in July alone.

## The fourth dimension of energy trading

The European program is a company-to-company cap-and-trade program, and the tradable unit is EU allowances. Prices have risen dramatically since the beginning of trading in January 2005, with prices for carbon ton equivalent (that is, $CO_2$ per metric ton or

$CO_2/MT$) holding steady at €25 for most of the second half of the year.

As mentioned earlier, the price moved from €5 to almost €30 but the sharp increase in oil prices (and, in turn, gas prices) in 2005 made coal burning in power production more cost effective, even after paying for the higher cost of emissions. Let's say, for example, that a coal-fired power plant produces roughly 0.9 MT of carbon dioxide per megawatt hour (MWh) of electricity generated, whereas a natural-gas turbine plant only produces around 0.4 MT. But with oil prices at US$66 per barrel and natural-gas prices in Europe (which are closely correlated to oil prices) moving higher as a result of stronger oil prices, the burning of coal for power production started to look cheaper, despite the higher emission levels. Emissions-credit prices lagged behind oil prices, thus enabling an arbitrage between the price of coal and that of natural gas, and emissions-credit costs could be locked in by traders. This is what we term "the fourth dimension of energy trading".

Before emissions trading began, energy trading was difficult enough, having to take into account such things as transmission restrictions for power lines, insufficient transport to move oil where it was needed, bad weather, *force majeure*, terrorism, OPEC headlines, seasonality and volatility. Now, the fourth dimension has been added to this already complex trading universe. While the old rule of "buy low, sell high" may not be exactly true, buying the cheapest fuel around is only a good deal if the trade remains profitable after the addition of the emissions cost of that fuel.

The EU system is open to cooperation with compatible schemes in other countries that have ratified the Protocol. This has the potential to enlarge the market for trading.

Focused initially on big industrial emitters, which produce almost half of the EU's $CO_2$ emissions, the scheme gives European and foreign-owned businesses based in the EU a "first-mover" advantage through the invaluable early experience they are gaining. As a result of the mandatory monitoring and reporting of emissions, companies are, for the first time, establishing $CO_2$ budgets and carbon-management systems. Because $CO_2$ has a price, companies are engaging the ingenuity of their engineers to identify cost-effective ways to reduce their emissions, both through improving current production processes and investing in new technologies. As a result of the EU carbon market, a range of new businesses is emerging: carbon traders, carbon-finance specialists, carbon-management specialists, carbon auditors and verifiers. New financial products such as carbon funds are entering the market.

While emissions trading has the potential to involve many sectors of the economy and all the greenhouse gases controlled by the Kyoto Protocol, the scope of the ETS is intentionally limited during its initial phase while experience of emissions trading is built up. Consequently, during the first trading period, from 2005 to 2007, the ETS covers only $CO_2$ emissions from large emitters in the power- and heat-generation industry and in selected energy-intensive industrial sectors: combustion plants, oil refineries, coke ovens, iron-and-steel plants and factories making cement, glass, lime, bricks, ceramics, pulp and paper. A size threshold based on production capacity or output determines which plants in these sectors are included in the scheme. Even with this limited scope, more than 12,000 installations in the 25 Member States are covered, accounting for around 45% of the EU's total $CO_2$ emissions or about 30% of its overall greenhouse gas emissions. The scheme will be reviewed around mid 2006 to allow fine-tuning in the light of experience gained and to consider whether it should be extended to other sectors, such as chemicals, aluminium and transport, and to other greenhouse gases.

**Figure 3.1:** Sources of greenhouse gas emissions in the EU (2001)

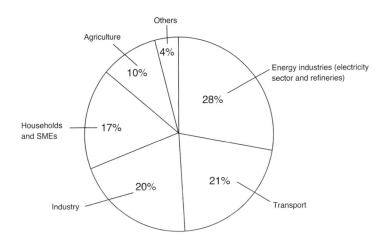

*Source:* European Environment Agency

In America, we have seen three million tons traded on the Chicago Climate Exchange (CCX), with more than 80 companies participating, and carbon trading at about US$1.50 per ton. Many larger trades are taking place on the U.S. OTC company-to-company market, including Entergy's one-million-ton trade mentioned earlier. In the U.S., we are getting an increase in activity from the marriage of $CO_2$ injection for enhanced oil recovery and emissions trading. Companies are generating carbon credits through the capture and storage of $CO_2$ by putting it back into the ground and, in some cases, using it as a gas injection to increase the pressure in old oil fields where the field pressure maybe getting low.

The capture and storage of $CO_2$ in the ground is known as "carbon sequestration" and this technology is facilitating the trading of millions of tons of carbon. On top of all of this, in the U.S. and the EU we have seen the emergence of green hedge funds which will actually trade carbon speculatively.

## How does emissions-trading work?

There are many different designs for emissions-trading systems, but they display common characteristics. A regulating body, such as a government or industry association, decides on a target for the maximum amount of pollution allowed for a group of emitters over a given period of time. In order for emissions trading to work, this target has to be less than the amount of pollution these emitters would emit in a "business-as-usual" situation — otherwise they would have no incentive to reduce their emissions.

Some form of tradable permit (also called an "allowance" or a "credit") is created, equivalent to a set volume of emissions, and emitters are required to hold permits for all of their emissions. A measurement and enforcement system is set up to ensure that emitters have permits for these emissions, and to penalize those who don't. Finally, a number of permits equal to the target set by the regulating body is divided up among the emitters, either by auction or according to reductions targets set for each emitter or type of emitter.

Since the total number of permits in the system covers less than the amount of emissions the emitters would have normally emitted, there will be a shortfall of permits. Each participant will then face a choice: either reduce their emissions, or find enough permits to cover all of their emissions. Some emitters will face higher reduction costs than others, which creates a market opportunity. Emitters with low reduction costs will be willing to reduce their emissions more, so that they can sell their permits at a profit to emitters with higher reduction costs. Emitters with higher reduction costs will want to buy these permits, as long as the cost is less than the cost of reducing their own emissions.

The term "domestic emissions-trading system" (DET system) is used to distinguish between national-level systems and international trading systems. Under the Kyoto Protocol, international emissions trading is allowed between nations who have signed the Kyoto agreement.

In countries with DET systems, emitters are able to buy credits from emitters in other countries. For this reason, most nations that have ratified the Protocol are creating DET systems to allow emitters access to these "emission credits".

## How does emissions trading save money?

The cost of reducing pollution is often different for each pollution emitter. Emissions-trading systems are set up to allow emitters with high reduction costs to save money by buying pollution reductions from emitters with lower reduction costs. At the same time, emitters with low reduction costs are able to reduce their compliance costs by making a profit on extra reductions.

For example, imagine a situation where the government tells two emitters that they must each reduce their emissions by 10%. To keep the example simple, we will imagine that each polluter is producing 100 tons of pollution per year, which means that they must each reduce their emissions to 90 tons of pollution per year. Because of differences in the activities and equipment of each emitter, however, their reduction costs per ton of pollution are different. It will cost Polluter A $150 for each ton of reductions it achieves, whereas it will cost Polluter B $50/ton.

|  | Polluter A | Polluter B | Total |
|---|---|---|---|
| Required emissions reduction | 10 tons | 10 tons | 20 tons |
| Cost of emissions reductions | $150 per ton | $50 per ton |  |
| Total cost of reductions | $1,500 | $500 | $2,000 |

If each polluter reduces by 10%, they will spend $2,000 in total (Polluter A: $150/ton × 10 tons + Polluter B: $50/ton × 10 tons). If, however, the two polluters are in an emissions-trading system, Polluter A can pay Polluter B to reduce by an additional 10 tons, instead of reducing its own emissions. The total amount of emissions reductions will stay the same, at 20 tons, but the total cost of the reductions will be reduced, as long as Polluter B charges a price that is less than Polluter A's reduction cost of $150/ton. This example assumes that Polluter B asks for $75 per ton of reductions, making the total cost of the reductions $1,000 (Polluter A: $75/ton × 10 tons + Polluter B: $50/ton × 20 tons – payments of $75/ton × 10 tons).

| | Polluter A | Polluter B | Total |
|---|---|---|---|
| Required emissions reduction | 10 tons | 10 tons | 20 tons |
| Cost of emissions reductions | $150 per ton | $50 per ton | |
| Amount of emissions reduced | 0 tons | 20 tons | 20 tons |
| Emissions reductions purchased ($75.00 per ton) | 10 tons | 0 tons | |
| Total cost of purchased reductions | $750 | $0 | |
| Payments received for reductions | $0 | $750 | |
| Total cost of reductions | $750.00 | $1,000 – $750 = $250 | $1,000 |

In this example, the total amount of reductions has stayed the same, but the overall cost of the reductions has dropped by half.

Two points should be kept in mind about how this works in a real emissions-trading system. First of all, because a large number of emitters will be trading in the system, the market will set the price of reductions. Secondly, emitters will find that their reductions cost per unit will gradually increase as they reduce more and more.

## The development of a liquid spot market in emissions

We are now positioned for the beginning of a liquid spot market similar to the power and gas markets, with more spot trading, high volumes, price indices, and advanced brokerage, rather than one-off trades. We will also see a growth in carbon finance.

The aggregate size of green trading markets belies their growth trajectory. We estimate that the total notional value today is over US$10 billion and rising. This includes not only annual trade in $SO_2$ and NOx allowances, carbon trading and renewable-energy trading but also all outstanding trades. Breaking that down further, we see a carbon market of roughly US$2 billion and growing, an $SO_2$ market of US$8 billion, and the remaining markets of under US$1 billion. We anticipate that these markets will be over US$100 billion by 2010.

## What's ahead in the U.S.?

The evolving regulatory landscape is still an open issue. On the horizon, there are more states with both renewable portfolio standards (RPS) and GHG-reduction systems taking shape. What should not be overlooked, however, is that what we saw in the U.S. $SO_2$ program may well be repeated in GHG and in renewables. That is, so many states started to put together their own $SO_2$ regulations that companies operating in a multi-state environment finally said to the federal government that they wanted some consistency in the regulation. In effect, companies asked for federal regulation, which resulted in the 1990 amendments to the federal Clean Air Act and the first successful emissions-trading program in $SO_2$. Similar developments have occurred in the NOx market and such action will undoubtedly happen again for GHG markets.

The GHG markets are beginning to take off because the European market is able to draw on the U.S. experience and on the talent available in the U.S. financial and energy-trading community. In this way, the markets will create fungible commodities that can be traded between states and across borders.

# Background on U.S. emissions trading

As the international leader in developing and regulating air pollution, the U.S. has adopted an evolutionary approach to air-pollution management, with both the experience and the availability of new technology driving the change in strategies and the improvements in air quality. One of the more recent innovations is "emissions trading", which has resulted in the most mature and advanced environmental financial markets in the world.

The goal of the emissions-trading program is to reduce emissions in a flexible manner that increases efficiency and reduces costs. The underlying principle is that the cost of emissions reductions varies from facility to facility. Some facilities may be able to reduce emissions more than the required amount at a cost that is lower than other facilities covered by the program. Participants, especially those with lower costs and costs that are below the market price, can choose to reduce emissions below the required levels and sell that differential to those that have higher emissions-reduction costs.

Begun in 1995 with the aim of reducing both sulfur dioxide (a primary cause of acid rain) and nitrogen oxide (which attacks the ozone layer), the U.S. emissions-trading programs are based on a total volume of allowed emissions (in contrast to actual emissions, which are higher than the allowed amount) and a cap-and-trade program to achieve that volume. Under cap-and-trade, allowances or "rights to pollute" equal in number to the volume of allowed emissions are allocated to market participants. Each allowance is a permit to release one ton of the specified emission into the air and has a vintage, determined by the first year that they are usable for compliance. For each ton of pollutant discharged, the emitter must expend one allowance, which is then retired and cannot be used again. Any remaining allowances can be sold, traded or banked for future use. If a source of air pollution does not have sufficient allowances to cover its emissions, it can buy allowances in the open market. Non-compliance results in government sanctions, including fines. But the market sets the actual price.

The long-term impact of the system will be to reduce pollution in a cost-effective manner and accelerate the introduction of more environmentally benign technologies in the U.S. and throughout the world. This is designed to cause minimal economic disruption to the capital-intensive energy industry and other industrial sources of pollution. It would build on and extend new financial markets where "trading pollution", as environmentalists like to call it, would actually create concrete and measurable emissions reductions for American business and, in the process, create jobs for Americans. The fact is that with a cap-and-trade regime, emissions are reduced over time, but it gives industry that time to comply with the law and invest in new technology.

However, we need to begin a regime that will aggressively reduce global carbon intensity for both stationary and mobile sources, accelerate technology transfer, and increase energy efficiency. The irony is that the technology exists today to get the job done. We already have integrated gas combined-cycle, clean-coal technology, which is rapidly commercializing. We have hybrid vehicles which reduce both tailpipe emissions and increase fuel economy and are now accepted by the American buying public. We have many energy-efficiency devices that reduce building loads from both commercial and residential buildings and make them "green".

Emissions trading is a major mechanism to accomplish many of these goals. The ability to monitor and certify verifiable reductions is already in place through both third-party certification companies and geo-positioning satellites and remote sensing devices. For the past few years, corporate America has been trying to figure out the business case for greenhouse gas reductions. The business case is fairly simple: either pay less now or pay more later as the financial value of the emissions rises over time. So we have companies beginning to analyze their risk and realize that there is a global issue here and that they have got to do something about it. Some companies such as AEP, Cinergy and Southern California Edison are already stepping forward voluntarily in anticipation of mandatory laws and are demanding that federal standards be implemented.

Another driver behind the GHG market is that we now have institutional shareholders forcing corporations to acknowledge the environmental risk on their books. Shareholder pressure and financial risk concerning future liabilities to companies is driving this issue forward. Pension funds are largely responsible for this and their strategy is similar to that adopted in relation to tobacco litigation.

Acid rain used to be a large problem in the eastern U.S. but the introduction of market-based solutions to reduce air emissions created a mature financial market for the environment that has addressed the problem successfully. This approach to reducing sulfur dioxide emissions in the U.S. became the template for Kyoto and all emissions-trading schemes throughout the world. This mechanism was truly made in America and has shown the best partnership of the public and private sectors. The government, through the EPA, sets the standards for reducing air emissions on an annual basis and an auction is held at the Chicago Board of Trade. The markets then trade the emissions allowances. Over the past 10 years, the level of emissions has been reduced and more sources of emissions have been incorporated into this very effective program. Today, the market — not the government — signals the price of compliance, and the price is currently over US$700 per ton.

This same experience has been applied to NOx trading, which began in 1999. Today, 22 states are in the program.

Once again, using the markets to attain required air-quality standards works. Recently, in Houston, Air Products and Chemicals introduced a market-based solution to attain compliance with regulations governing ozone reductions for the power, oil refining and petrochemical industries. By creating a private market, industry can meet achievable reductions in emissions in a short time period. In this case, an 80% reduction is needed by 2008. In the summer of 2004, markets in Houston/Galveston traded NOx credits for as high as US$40,000 per ton. Once again, the market price is creating innovations and investment in plant and equipment. It is a movement away from the previous "command and control" regulatory strategy to a more market-centric approach to solving air-quality problems.

Since carbon dioxide constitutes about 80% of greenhouse gas emissions, most of the focus on market development has been on carbon trading with a view to reducing $CO_2$ emissions. While carbon markets today amount to only about US$2 billion, estimates are that this will be a US$100 billion market or higher by 2010, which makes for real money and real financial trading. The U.S. actually stepped in first with the launch of the Chicago Climate Exchange (CCX) in September 2003. Today, it has more than 70 companies signed up on a voluntary basis and many others are starting to look seriously at self-imposed caps. These markets are currently trading at between US$1–2 per ton. It's the start of the U.S. market but, so far, lacks the engagement of Wall Street banks and large energy companies as market makers. For example, Morgan Stanley is now the largest emissions trader in the U.S. sulfur dioxide market, and achieved that position in just two years. The fact is that Wall Street and corporate America can ramp up quickly when the rules are in place to trade carbon dioxide effectively. Today, many individual states are following innovative and diverse approaches to reducing emissions of greenhouse gases and collaborative state GHG registries have been proposed. However, multi-jurisdictional registries create multiple reporting requirements, multiple registries and multiple trading regimes. This situation is a disincentive for business to take early action. Harmonized standards will be more cost effective for many companies and encourage voluntary reporting. They will accelerate the fungibility of carbon dioxide as a commodity which will, like the oil markets, trade globally.

Registries help companies deal with state, regional, national and international GHG trading schemes. Industries need standardized measurement methodologies to facilitate trading as well as for reasons of transparency. The integrity function of registries is that they allow GHG credits to become commodities with certifiable rules, measurement auditing and reporting requirements. They are the precursor for commodity markets but not markets in themselves. Markets will address performance, delivery and price risks and hedging needs as they mature.

## The position in Europe

Most of the attention today is on the EU ETS which began on January 1, 2005. Multiple industries are covered in this program.

The Europeans embraced the experience and knowledge available within the U.S. emissions markets, and are taking it a step further. The first phase, from 2005 to 2007, covers $CO_2$ only and includes power generators, the cement industry, steel and chemicals, with 13,000 sites affected. A wide array of industries with varying degrees of control costs will be covered and that should make for a good market. The European program is a company-to-company cap-and-trade program, following the U.S. market model, and the tradable unit will be EU allowances.

## Renewable-energy trading in the U.S.

Renewable-energy credits (RECs) are becoming a reality as well. The Texas, California and Massachusetts REC markets have been extremely active and we are starting to see real market growth, with 19 states now implementing RPS. As more states adopt renewable-energy credit programs and RPS, many more trades will occur. There is also demand on the voluntary side, with many active green-power marketers meeting that supply. There are also state purchase mandates that include renewable-energy procurement programs in which some federal agencies are participating.

Generally, the market drivers for RECs are the same as for renewable energy or green power. These drivers include green-pricing programs for utilities, competitive green-power marketing, state renewable portfolio standards and purchase mandates, and electricity information disclosure. In some instances, REC trading is given added impetus by a requirement that RECs be used for compliance with certain programs. Further, particularly in carbon markets, RECs may be used to claim greenhouse gas reductions.

Currently more than 600 utilities in 34 states offer their customers an option to buy green power as a premium product, at a slightly higher price than the standard rate for electricity. This does not mean, however, that green power is available to all consumers in those states.

The market for renewable-energy certificates, both separate from and bundled with electricity, is expanding as renewable-energy mandates and voluntary demand for green power grow. The number of wholesale and retail marketers of RECs is growing too, while the infrastructure — in the form of generally accepted protocols and REC tracking systems — continues to develop.

The application of RECs in emissions-trading markets, however, is in its infancy and much policy work remains to be done (and practical experience gained) to ensure that renewable energy has an opportunity to participate in those markets. At present, it appears that the value of RECs is higher in energy markets than in GHG-emissions markets, though this could change as emissions markets become better established. Government mandates, in the form of renewable portfolio standards, are driving the continuing development of the renewable-energy market.

# The way ahead

The regulatory landscape is still evolving. On the horizon, there are now more states with RPS (19 states in total) and GHG-reduction systems (28 in states in total).

Green trading markets are now entering the "hockey stick" phase, so called because the growth of the market is in the shape of a hockey stick — pretty flat at the beginning followed by a very sudden rapid exponential growth, which represents the curved shape of the end of a hockey stick. This "hockey stick" shape is a term used in the energy and emissions markets and worth noting.

This year (2006) promises to bring us the financial market acceleration that has been expected for many years. Despite all the press on the EU ETS and the implementation of Kyoto, the U.S., with its entrepreneurial culture, risk capital and knowledge base in trading, is still well positioned to lead the development of environmental financial markets.

# Green markets: A global snapshot

Green markets are now more than 10 years old and are rapidly evolving into full-fledged markets, with large and diverse numbers of participants. The oldest is the sulfur dioxide ($SO_2$) market, which began operations in 1995. The successes of the $SO_2$ market have exceeded the expectations of most participating in its design, an outstanding achievement for what is essentially a government-sponsored program. As a result, the principles of emissions-trading markets were extended to nitrogen oxides and greenhouse gases, while a corollary market has developed for renewable-energy credits. Each of these markets is dynamic and is evolving to accommodate more participants and to increase the efficacy of measures to improve the environment.

# Mature markets: Sulfur dioxide

The sulfur dioxide emissions-trading market is the most sophisticated emissions-trading market in the world and one of the oldest. The $SO_2$ market is also the most liquid of all environmental markets. $SO_2$ has been actively traded daily in spot and forward markets since the inception of the market and can now be traded on regulated futures markets. The annual value of $SO_2$ trades is US$3 billion.

Other "green" trading markets tend to emulate the successful $SO_2$ market. Generally, analysts agree that emissions trading has contributed to significant cost savings in achieving $SO_2$ reductions. A modest estimate of total savings from using $SO_2$ trading vis-à-vis command-and-control solutions is 44%. Costs have been one-quarter to one-half of what was originally estimated. These benefits derive from the flexibility that trading systems give firms in complying with their obligations, particularly in changing markets, such as the restructuring of the power industry.

In the U.S., the 1990 acid rain initiative specified that 1980-level $SO_2$ emissions were to be reduced by 8.5 million tons by 2000. The North American $SO_2$ Allowance Program had two phases. Phase I began in 1995 and required 110 older coal-fired power plants to reduce emissions by 3.5 million tons per year. Phase II began in 2000 and was expanded to incorporate 3,200 units, including all fossil-fuel power plants generating over 25 MW of electricity. The "cap" was reduced by five million tons of $SO_2$ and a more stringent allowance allocation was applied. The annual allowances issued in the second phase will eventually reduce total annual emissions to 8.95 million tons. A new program, the Clean Air Interstate Rule (CAIR), which incorporates cap-and-trade provisions, came into effect in March 2005. Under CAIR, the EPA expects $SO_2$ emissions to be reduced by a further 70% in the 28 affected eastern states. Given the tight standards, emissions trading can be expected to increase over time, adding to market liquidity.

The cap-and-trade provisions of the law and regulations give affected sources the flexibility to find the lowest-cost means to meet the requirements by choosing from a portfolio of options — switching fuels, installing emissions-reduction technology, changing operations or purchasing allowances. If the number of tons of emissions exceeds the number of allowances held in the unit's account when the accounts are settled at the end of the year, the owners/operators of the source must pay a fine.

After years of prices below US$200 per allowance, prices began to rise dramatically in November 2003 and exceeded US$600 per ton in July 2004. By March 2005, prices exceeded US$700 per ton. Along with higher prices, volatility increased substantially and bid-ask spreads increased. A major driver in higher allowance prices is the declining size of the bank of allowances, unused allowances carried over from previous years, and the introduction of the new targets under the CAIR. At its peak, the number of banked allowances exceeded 11.6 million, but by the end of 2003 this had declined to 7.9 million tons. In addition, higher natural gas and low-sulfur coal prices limited the flexibility to switch fuels profitably and helped to make allowances more valuable.

The $SO_2$ market is not a true commodity market because it is the creation of the government, which imposes a cap on the market. Nevertheless, the program design exemplifies many of the principles of a well-functioning market. Under the rules of the Environmental Protection Agency, an $SO_2$ allowance is a verifiable property right that can be tracked on the EPA's allowance tracking system (ATS). Straightforward verification, based on monitoring equipment at each site, helps to keep transaction costs low.

The market has been liquid, with a large number of participants, none of whom have a large market share, and substantial numbers of banked allowances that have facilitated trading. Several companies provide price-transparency and risk-management services. To date, trades between two parties have dominated the market. Companies collect information about these bilateral trades and publish indices of $SO_2$ prices. These companies include Cantor Fitzgerald (www.emissionstrading.com), Evolution Markets (www.evomarkets.com), Energy Argus (www.energyargus.com) and Platts (www.platts.com).

At the time of writing, the $SO_2$ market is in a state of dynamic change, marked by a declining volume of banked emissions, higher prices, greater price volatility, plans to possibly double the number of plants with emissions-control equipment, and new, tighter standards. The Chicago Climate Exchange (CCX) and the New York Mercantile Exchange (NYMEX) have responded to the uncertainty generated by these factors by creating $SO_2$ futures markets to increase liquidity and market efficiency. NYMEX kicked off trading in late 2005, while CCX has begun trading its Sulfur Financial Instrument (SFI). Acceptable allowances that qualify as a SFI are current and prior-year vintage allowances and allowance vintages for the first year subsequent to the calendar year of the contract expiration. The SFI contract has a minimum of 25 tons of sulfur dioxide emission allowances at US$1 per ton, or US$25 per contract. The allowances are transferred within the EPA's allowance tracking system. The success of the $SO_2$ emissions market can be measured in many ways. Emissions have been significantly reduced; costs have been lower than expected; compliance has been virtually 100%; and administrative costs are far lower than they are for command-and-control programs. Building on this success, the U.S. implemented emissions-trading schemes for NOx.

## Maturing markets

The NOx emissions-trading program has been in effect for only a few years, but it is already a vigorous market. The largest volume NOx emissions market is the outcome of EPA's NOx Budget Trading (NBT) program and affects much of the eastern part of the country. (NOx markets are regional because NOx is often transported long distances and is a precursor to the formation of ozone (smog), a pollution problem that tends to be regional in scope.) The first compliance period for the NBT ended on May 1, 2003, by which time approximately 1,000 units in 11 states and the District of Columbia were required to reduce NOx emissions. In the second compliance period, beginning on May 31, 2004, the NBT (commonly referred to as the "NOx SIP call") was expanded to cover an additional 11 states and a total of 2,600 sources.

Like the $SO_2$ emissions-trading program, the NOx NBT is a cap-and-trade program with a tradable instrument, the NOx emission allowance, that must be verified and registered with the EPA. NOx emission allowances can also be banked. However, because of the regional impact of NOx and the difficulties in reducing ozone, the NBT has several features that are different from the $SO_2$ trading market. First, the compliance period covers May to September, the period when ozone is most likely to form. Second, states have critical responsibilities in implementing the NOx trading program, including responsibility for allocating the allowances across sources. And third, the NOx program covers industrial sources and oil and natural-gas units, in addition to fossil-fuel-fired power-generation units covered by the $SO_2$ program.

NOx emissions trading covers multiple years (vintages). Prices for 2003 vintage allowances traded at US$5,000 per ton in October 2002 and rose to US$8,000 (the market peak to date), before falling below US$3,000 per ton. Prices for 2004 vintages were less volatile because a mild 2003 summer enabled banked allowances to be carried over. Prices have been higher for the 2005 and 2006 vintages, reflecting uncertainty about the amount of technology that will be installed in time for the respective ozone seasons and the number of banked emissions that will be carried forward. Prices for the 2005 vintage have generally been above US$3,000 per ton and as much as US$4,000 per ton since the low price point in the spring of 2003. Prices for 2005 vintage averaged US$3,586 in January 2005. Prices for 2006 vintage allowances have tended to be several hundred dollars lower than prices for 2005 vintages.

## Emerging markets: Carbon dioxide and greenhouse gases

For $CO_2$ and GHG markets, 2005 is likely to be a watershed year. In February 2005, the Kyoto Protocol came into force, more than seven years after it was established. With Russia's ratification in November 2004, countries that account for over 60% of the total 1990 carbon dioxide emissions have now ratified the Protocol. They include the members of the European Union, Japan, New Zealand, Canada, Russia and most of the countries known as the "economies in transition" (the countries that used to be "behind the Iron Curtain"). The U.S. and Australia have not ratified the Protocol, but are nonetheless pursuing programs to reduce GHG emissions.

Under the Kyoto Protocol, countries can use emissions trading to lower the overall cost of reducing GHGs to meet the Protocol targets. As outlined earlier, the Protocol provides three flexible mechanisms for trading among countries: an international emissions-trading regime allowing industrialized countries to trade carbon permits in the international market; JI trading among industrialized countries and the economies in transition; and the CDM, which permits developing countries that are not parties to the Protocol to sell emissions reductions to Annex I countries.

In anticipation of the Protocol coming into force, GHG markets expanded. In 2002 and 2003, the transitional JI economies and developing CDM countries dominated emissions-credit transactions, with 60% of global transactions in 2002 and 91% in the first three quarters of 2003. Point Carbon estimates that JI and CDM markets represented 60% of the total value of transactions in 2004, with the Netherlands taking the lead. In May 2000, the Dutch began procuring carbon credits from the non-industrialized JI countries and later expanded their program to include purchases from CDM countries. In addition, the Netherlands, governments in several other countries (including Japan, Austria, Spain, Finland, Canada, Norway, Belgium, Italy, Luxembourg, Denmark and Sweden) and several companies have authorized third-party funds, from the World Bank and private banks, to purchase GHG credits from JI and CDM projects. Private companies are also developing and marketing carbon credits from JI and CDM projects.

The JI and the CDM markets were the largest until a clear shift in the market occurred in 2004 as the EU countries prepared to implement the EU ETS, a program adopted to reduce the cost of Kyoto compliance by trading permits of carbon dioxide. The ETS officially started on January 1, 2005, but an estimated eight million allowances for forward transactions were traded in the brokered market by mid December 2004. Trades on the European market have been increasing, with the volume of forward $CO_2$ trades exceeding one million tons during the first week of 2005. In March 2005, when a spot market was put into place, this figure was approaching one million tons per day.

The European Commission estimated that adopting the EU-wide trading scheme would reduce the costs of attaining its emission targets by at least 20% if it covered the energy-supply sector only, and by as much as 34% if the program was expanded to include all sectors (including agriculture, transport, households, services, and so on). The estimated benefits of the EU-wide trading system are in addition to those likely to be generated by individual country programs, which are in various stage of development. Denmark and the United Kingdom implemented GHG markets several years ago. Other countries are also developing national markets.

The EU ETS market is estimated to be worth US$15 billion per year. An estimated 100 million tons of carbon credits were traded in 2004, with a value at that time of US$360 million (in today's EU ETS market that would be closer to US$2.5 billion in value). In the new EU market, prices peaked in the over-the-counter market at above €13 per ton in the first weeks of 2004, but fell to €6–8 per ton in the early days of 2005. By the end of March 2005, prices exceeded €14 per ton. Who could have expected then that prices were going to hit close to €30 per ton?

Prices in the JI and CDM markets range from €3.5 to €4.9 per $CO_2$/MT equivalent, and even in 2005 were still only around €5.

Despite their respective decisions not to ratify the Kyoto Protocol, Australia and the United States have GHG-emissions programs in place. The Australian GHG Abatement Scheme, which began in January 2003, is a mandatory program affecting NSW electricity retailers and other parties. In the U.S., states are leading the way for GHG programs. California has developed an extensive registry and is considering mandatory GHG reductions. The Northeast States, with observers from the Mid-Atlantic States and the eastern Canadian provinces, are developing the Regional Greenhouse Gas Initiative (RGGI), and Massachusetts and New Hampshire have state-level emissions-trading rules pending. Oregon has a carbon-offset fund that enables voluntary reductions.

Voluntary company initiatives are also driving GHG markets. CCX is a voluntary program with over 40 members, over half of which are private companies that emit GHGs. CCX members initially agreed to reduce their emissions to 4% below the 1998–2001 baseline by 2006. Cumulatively, the members have exceeded this target in the first compliance year (2003) by 8%. In separate efforts, Entergy, DuPont and other U.S. companies have purchased Verified Emissions Reduction (VERs) credits to meet their self-imposed GHG emissions-reduction targets.

## Renewable-energy credits

Essentially, renewable energy is energy produced from a resource that is naturally regenerated over a short time period, incorporating the wind, sun, flowing water, biomass or geothermal means. Renewable-energy power-generation technologies are the fastest growing in terms of new capacity, reflecting improvements in technology, lower costs, and greater value for the benefits associated with renewable energy. From a cost and price-risk perspective, renewable energy has high capital but low operating costs and thus offers cost and price certainty, in contrast to the uncertainty surrounding increasingly volatile fossil-fuel prices.

When renewable energy displaces energy produced from fossil fuels — oil, natural gas and coal — it confers numerous benefits. Environmentally, renewable energy typically reduces to zero GHGs and other emissions that are harmful to the environment and human health. Renewable energy can also confer energy-security benefits when it displaces imports of oil and natural gas from unstable regions of the world or when it is generated locally in lieu of energy taken from transmission grids that are vulnerable to interruptions.

The principle mechanism for trading the benefits of renewable energy is the renewable-energy credit (REC). RECs, also known as "green certificates", are the currency of trade in RPS programs. RPS programs require electricity wholesalers and retailers to include a specified proportion of electricity generated from renewable resources in their sales portfolio. They must demonstrate annually that they have sold the minimum amount of renewable energy specified in the RPS. All RPS programs permit the sellers to generate the required volume of renewable energy from generating facilities that they own, but some programs also permit sellers to purchase credits from other renewable-energy producers in the form of RECs. RECs reflect the volume of energy generated (typically measured in kWh) and the attributes (that is, the specific value of benefits described above) associated with the generation.

Experience indicates that market-based mechanisms such as RECs are likely to be the most efficient and cost-effective means for achieving robust renewable-energy development. Expansion of the RECs market will increase efficiency by lowering the costs of renewable energy and its attributes and by enabling the development of the lowest-cost renewable-energy resources, regardless of their physical proximity to customers. As the standardization and trading of RECs increases, centralized exchanges to help buyers and sellers manage risks are likely to progress. Exchanges can also reduce transaction costs, increase liquidity, provide credit clearing, and permit hedging with futures and options.

In the U.S., 19 states (including the District of Columbia) have enacted RPS programs. Of these, 12 permit trading in RECs across states with comparable RPS regulations and interchangeable RECs. Some U.S. power pools are supporting RECs trading within and between states. For example, California Energy Commission and the Western Governors' Association are jointly developing the Western Renewable Energy Generation Information System (WREGIS) to track and register renewable-energy generation and certificates region wide.

In Europe, the Netherlands has an RPS, with a 10% renewable-energy target for its energy portfolio by 2020, and a green certificate scheme. Under this green certificate program, renewable-energy generators receive the certificates and are permitted to sell them to consumers inside or outside the country. Among other REC activities in Europe, the EU Joint Research Center has launched an Internet-trading project to design and test a system to trade renewable-energy credits.

Numerous other programs complement RPS programs by promoting the development of renewable energy and, ultimately, growth in renewable-energy markets. Growth in the markets is expected to enable technology developers and facility operators to reduce costs and thereby help to expand the deployment of renewable energy. Programs that promote renewable technologies will also help to augment the renewable-energy supply and availability of RECs to trade, thereby increasing liquidity of the RECs market.

In the U.S., incentives to spur the development of renewable energy vary widely and include government and private financial incentives such as the Federal Production Tax Credit; state-sponsored renewable-energy funds that have to date supported more than 700 MW of renewable capacity additions and have the potential to triple the capacity; programs that enable consumers to choose to purchase green power and that are available now to more than 50% of U.S. electricity customers; and green-pricing programs that give customers the option of paying more for their electricity to support investments in renewable energy.

Several European governments offer incentives for investment in renewable energy. The Netherlands, for example, has supported investment through such instruments as feed-in tariffs, direct subsidies, investment incentives and benefits charges.

## Negawatts

While we concentrate on $SO_2$, NOx, GHG and renewable-energy markets, we cannot neglect two other emerging markets that will have trading mechanisms. These are the negawatt or energy-efficiency market and the mercury-trading markets.

The concept of "negawatts", which measures energy reduced rather than energy produced, has been around for decades, but state-of-the-art technology is now making it more convenient and economic. The key to today's negawatt markets is "demand response", a system of technologies that enables utilities and customers to engage in contracts to curtail power consumption when power loads and prices are high. Not generating electricity reduces pollution, fuel consumption, capital for underutilized peaking equipment, and their associated costs.

The Peak Load Management Alliance states that demand-response benefits — in addition to the cost savings and system reliability — include:

- Market efficiency — when customers receive price signals and incentives, usage becomes more aligned with costs.
- Risk management — demand response provides a program through which customers can manage their electricity needs to avoid high costs and to ensure that electricity is available when needed.
- Environmental — through demand response, production from less-efficient power plants is reduced, often resulting in a reduced impact on the environment. Demand response also can reduce or defer new plant requirements.
- Customer service — customers welcome a program that allows them to be more directly involved in how, when and at what price they use electricity from the grid. In this age of choice, demand response provides customers with greater control over their energy bills.
- Market power mitigation — when customers have choice, they are less vulnerable to prices set by a power supplier and conditions that lead to tight supplies and/or transmission constraints.

Several regional transmission grid operators and some companies, including the New England Independent System Operator (ISO-NE), the New York Independent System Operator (NYISO), the PJM interconnection (PJM), and the California Independent System Operator (CAISO), have instituted demand-response programs. PJM program participants, for example, have the choice of two options: a Day-Ahead Option or a Real-Time Option. The program offers electricity users the opportunity to provide load reductions in exchange for a payment based on hourly wholesale electricity prices.

Participation is fully voluntary and retail customers can participate in the program through any existing PJM member. In the Day-Ahead Option, participants submit load-reduction bids (of at least 100 kW) into the day-ahead energy market. Participants whose bids are accepted are paid for their load reductions based upon the day-ahead, hourly electricity market prices. In the Real-Time Option, participants can decide at any time to provide load curtailments (with one hour's notice to PJM), and receive payment based on the real-time electricity price. The program became effective on June 1, 2002, and will remain in effect until December 1, 2007.

## Mercury

On March 15, 2005, the EPA in the U.S. issued the world's first mercury-control rules affecting air emissions. The Clean Air Mercury Rule aims to permanently cap and reduce mercury emissions from coal-fired power plants. The rule establishes "standards of performance" limiting mercury emissions from new and existing utilities. In the first phase, due by 2010, emissions will be reduced by taking advantage of "co-benefit" controls — that is, mercury reductions achieved in the process of reducing $SO_2$ and NOx emissions. With the new rule will come a new emissions-trading market.

# 4 Global Trading Schemes

## The U.S. markets

Environmental financial markets developed through the U.S. acid-rain program but actually had precursors in the gasoline programs of the 1970s. But it is the $SO_2$ program that has now been brought forward as a template for all market-based emissions-trading schemes. The efficacy of the program is unsurpassed as a means of achieving environmental remediation in a cost-effective manner. More recently, there have been a number of water-rights trading schemes emerging in the U.S. West to deal with water problems there, revealing another environmental application for trading schemes. But it is the sulfur dioxide trading program targeted to reduce acid rain that has proven to be the most workable and cost-effective scheme to date.

## The problem and its solution

As the international leader in regulating and managing air pollution, the U.S has adopted an evolutionary approach to air pollution, with experience and the availability of new technology driving the change in its strategies and the improvements in air quality. One of the more recent innovations is emissions trading, which has resulted in the most mature and advanced environmental financial markets in the world.

Federal involvement in combating air pollution began in the 1950s, but it was not until 1970 that a public consensus on the need for stricter approaches resulted in tough laws and regulations, as expressed in the Clean Air Act (CAA) Amendments of 1970. For the next 20 years, command-and-control approaches imposed by these and subsequent amendments dominated U.S. strategy. The 1970 Amendments emphasized strict deadlines for compliance, imposing New Source Performance Standards (NSPS), National Ambient Air Quality Standards (NAAQS), and standards for hazardous emissions and emissions from motor vehicles. The NSPS imposed strict regulations governing emissions from new stationary sources (primarily fossil-fuel plants).

The NAAQS set goals for the highest permissible levels of particulates, sulfur oxides, carbon monoxide, nitrogen oxides, ozone, hydrocarbons and lead in the ambient air — with primary attention given to protecting public health and secondary attention to protecting the environment. The U.S. Environmental Protection Agency had the responsibility to establish the standards and the means for attaining them. States had the responsibility to establish State Implementation Plans, issue permits and enforce them. The EPA was not required to consider technical feasibility or the cost of compliance as it imposed the standards.

In the end, the 1970 Amendments proved overly ambitious; the nation did not achieve the standards by the deadlines. In the CAA of 1977, Congress extended the compliance deadline and, in 1990, again amended the Act to solve problems of the past and deal with new issues. Most of the changes continued or expanded command-and-control approaches (approaches such as the NSPS, which specified the best technology or a maximum level of emissions for a given plant) to achieving cleaner air. However, in 1990 Congress also introduced a more flexible and cost-effective means to reduce emissions under the Acid Rain Title — emissions trading.

Today, the U.S. emissions-trading market is valued at US$6 billion annually, primarily reflecting the value of the sulfur dioxide market that began in 1995, with contributions from the NOx emissions program that went into effect in 1999. As highlighted in the previous chapter, the Administration proposes to extend emissions trading to include mercury. The goal of these programs is to reduce emissions in a flexible manner that increases efficiency and reduces costs.

# Ten years of SO$_2$ emissions trading

The SO$_2$ Allowance Program is the most liquid of all environmental markets. SO$_2$ actively trades daily in spot and forward markets and, more recently, on regulated futures markets.

The SO$_2$ allowance program has been a success. Resources for the future estimates that the benefits of the SO$_2$ allowance program through 2000 exceed the economic costs by a reasonable order of magnitude. Analysts have generally agreed that emissions trading has contributed to significant cost reductions in achieving SO$_2$ reductions. Costs are one-quarter to one-half of what was originally estimated. A modest estimate of total savings from emissions trading relative to command-and-control solutions is 44%. This estimate takes into account falling fuel and technology prices, the increased availability of western coals and the development and use of technologies not anticipated in 1990 when the Acid Rain Program was conceived.

Under the program, affected power plants receive one allowance for each metric ton of sulfur they are entitled to emit. In contrast to command-and-control approaches that often specify technology and/or the specific plant that must reduce emissions, the power generators have the flexibility to choose both the plants where they will reduce the emissions and the methods for achieving the emissions targets: they can switch fuels, install pollution-control equipment, shut down, or purchase allowances. The allowances can be bought, sold or banked (that is, saved for future years if not used). If the number of tons of emissions exceeds the number of allowances held in the unit's account, the owners/operators of the source must pay a fine.

This flexibility, including emissions trading, has contributed a significant share of the savings, in part because it accelerates the introduction of efficient means to reduce pollution. In Phase I of the two-phase program, which began in 1995, about half of the emissions reductions were achieved through fuel switching, an option that was not always available under previous regimes. Trading resulted in innovation in organizational approaches, in the organization of markets, and through experimentation in individual units. Allowance trading also helped firms to respond to electricity restructuring, enabling them to find low-cost means of complying when faced with competitive pressures. In addition, emissions trading facilitated the timing of firms' investments and their ability to hedge unexpected events such as equipment outages or high prices for low-sulfur fuel.

Phase I required 110 older, coal-fired, power plants to reduce emissions by 3.5 million tons per year. Each affected plant was allocated allowances equal to an implied rate of 2.5 pounds $SO_2$/mmBtu multiplied by the average of fossil-fuel consumption from 1985 through 1987 (expressed in million Btus).

Phase II began in 2000 and the number of affected sources was expanded to 3,200 units, including all fossil-fuel power plants generating over 25 MW of electricity. The "cap" was reduced by five million tons of $SO_2$ and a more stringent allowance allocation was set at an average 1.2 pounds $SO_2$/mmBtu fuel output for all affected plants. The 1990 Acid Rain Title specified that 1980 $SO_2$ emissions were to be reduced by 8.5 million tons by 2000. The annual allowances issued in the second phase will eventually reduce total annual emissions to 8.95 million tons. When Phase II began, firms had banked 11.6 million tons of sulfur dioxide emission allowances, which eased the transition to the significant decrease in allowed emissions in Phase II.

## The evolution of $SO_2$ prices

During Phase I, prices were below forecasts, ranging from a low of US$66 per allowance in 1996 to a high of US$210 in 1999. During Phase II, prices remained below US$200 for most of the period through 2003. In November 2003, prices surpassed US$200 per ton and have since stayed above that level, exceeding US$600 per ton in July 2004 and US$700 per ton in March 2005. Along with prices, volatility increased substantially and bid-ask spreads increased. (See www.evomarkets.com)

Several factors are likely to have contributed to the recent higher prices. For a start, EPA rules proposed in January 2004 indicate that the government intends to significantly tighten the emissions cap, as required by existing law. At the same time, the bank of allowances has declined. At its peak in 2000, the number of banked allowances exceeded 11.6 million tons, but by the end of 2003 it had declined to 7.9 million tons, a volume that was approaching levels not seen since 1997. This tightened the emissions markets and also helped drive prices higher.

While the declining size of the bank of emissions held by companies for later use and tighter emission standards are critical factors in price increases, several recent changes in demand-side

**Figure 4.1:**   Reported monthly prices for transactions in U.S. EPA SO₂ allowances

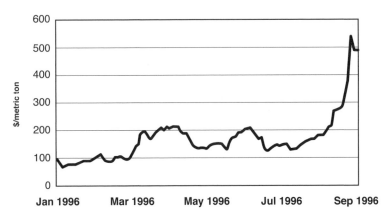

*Source:* CCFE

factors have probably also contributed to escalating prices. Most visible were natural-gas prices which, in late 2004, were 13–15% higher than they were in late 2003, which in turn were 25% higher than in late 2002. Even though the Acid Rain Program has a direct effect on electricity-generating plants fueled by natural gas, these plants have minimal emissions compared to their coal-fueled counterparts, which has therefore contributed to the achievement of the $SO_2$ emissions cap. But, as natural-gas prices rose, some generators shifted back to coal and expended allowances to offset the additional emissions. Further, significantly higher prices for low-sulfur coal in 2004 created incentives to use lower-priced high-sulfur coal, where available, and expend allowances.

## $SO_2$ market design and attributes

The EPA succeeded in getting broad participation in the program through careful market design that exploited the efficiencies of the market. The design contains several attributes that are critical to a successful market:

- Standardization of the "commodity" — $SO_2$ trading is not a true commodity market, because it is a government-mandated market, based on cap and trade. Nevertheless, the market behaves like a commodity market in that it has a single unit of trade, a ton of $SO_2$ emissions, defined by the government.

- Verifiable property rights — Establishing ownership rights is the first step in taking advantage of market efficiencies. The $SO_2$ emissions-trading program established a system of property rights for depositing sulfur dioxide into the atmosphere. The law established the entitlement to pollute and authorized the EPA to establish a program that issues the permits complete with a serial number to track the vintage and trading history, records ownership, and validates the trades through continuous emissions monitoring. Each property right is conferred in the form of a traceable permit. The EPA's Allowance Tracking System (ATS), an electronic system that is open to the public, facilitates monitoring and verification. The EPA posts all transfers on the Internet. In turn, market participants have the assurance that their investment in emissions rights is a legally recognized action and that they are protected from cheating.
- Straightforward and enforceable penalties — The Clean Air Act and the administrative design help to expedite enforcement. Failure to achieve the required target results in an automatic penalty. The penalty was set at US$2,000/ton in 1990 and is adjusted each year for inflation.
- Low transaction costs — Low transaction costs help to make a market more efficient and reduce the barriers to participation. Transaction costs include the costs necessary to validate an emission, identify and negotiate with a trading partner, and ensure compliance under any resulting contract. The emissions-trading program has reduced transaction costs for the government and companies. For example, the size of the EPA's allowance staff is a fraction of the size of staff managing other regulatory programs. Despite low government staffing for oversight, compliance in the first six years has effectively been 100%.

The EPA uses continuous monitoring at each of the affected facilities as a standard means for measuring that the emission has been released; that is, that the permit has been expended. Data is transmitted electronically and the EPA uses its ATS database to track allowances, which are then issued on a vintage-year basis from 2000 to 2030. For each ton emitted, one ton is retired in the ATS.

Private participation in the market indicates the effectiveness of the design.

- Large number of participants and low market concentrations — A large number of participants, with none dominating the market, indicates that the market is behaving competitively. Over time, the $SO_2$ market participants have become more heterogeneous, starting initially with affected utilities and expanding to include emissions brokers and the brokerage arms of major investment banks. As shown in Figure 4.2 below, in the first 11 months of 2004, 14 participants accounted for around 65% of the trades, with the single largest participant, Morgan Stanley Capital Group, accounting for some 13.5% of the trades. To date, most $SO_2$ transactions have been bilateral. As futures markets grow,

**Figure 4.2:** Top participants in $SO_2$ OTC market: January–November 2004

| Company | Gross Trades | % of Total |
|---|---|---|
| Morgan Stanley Capital Group | 2,121,295 | 13.47% |
| Millennium Environmental Group | 828,923 | 5.26% |
| American Electric Power Service | 818,165 | 5.19% |
| Dominion Energy Marketing | 808,007 | 5.13% |
| PSEG Energy Resources & Trade | 775,279 | 4.92% |
| Kansas City Power & Light Company | 746,373 | 4.74% |
| Cinergy Services | 688,277 | 4.37% |
| Southern Electric Company | 676,205 | 4.29% |
| Arizona Public Service Company | 660,580 | 4.19% |
| JP Morgan | 539,196 | 3.42% |
| Constellation Energy | 513.995 | 3.26% |
| PPL Generation | 498,622 | 3.16% |
| TXU Company | 485,007 | 3.08% |
| Mirant Americas Energy Marketing | 406,117 | 2.57% |

*Source:* CCX (www.chicagoclimateexchange.com/mktdata)

trades cleared on exchanges are likely to represent an increasing share of the market.

- Liquidity — Liquidity helps to ensure that a market is competitive and therefore efficient. From its inception, the $SO_2$ program has involved large numbers of allowances, beginning with 8.8 million tons in 1995 and peaking at 9.9 million tons in 2000. The number of allowances traded and their percentage of the total pool of allowances tended to increase in Phase I, as companies gained experience with trading and tighter caps came into effect. As shown in Figure 4.3 below, in Phase II, trading volumes exceeded Phase I levels through 2003 when an average of 10.4 trades per day, averaging 4,600 tons each, were reported to the EPA.

- Transparent prices — Price transparency helps all market participants judge whether the market is operating efficiently. Transparency has evolved with the $SO_2$ markets.

OTC brokers trade spot and forward trades for credit vintages for the period through 2030. Private entities provide price transparency

**Figure 4.3:**    Annual Volume of Commercial $SO_2$ Allowance Transfers

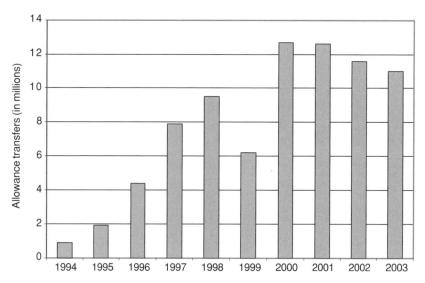

*Source:* US EPA

and risk-management services. Several companies, including Cantor Fitzgerald (www.emissionstrading.com), Evolution Markets (www.evomarkets.com), Energy Argus (www.energyargus.com) and Platts (www.platts.com), collect information about bilateral trades and some publish indices of $SO_2$ prices. The market has been liquid, with a large number of participants (none of which has a large market concentration) and substantial numbers of banked allowances that facilitated trading.

More recently, CCX, the world's first multi-national and multi-sector marketplace for the reduction and trading of greenhouse-gas emissions, has enhanced price transparency through its sulfur futures market. NYMEX established $SO_2$ futures market in June 2005.

In addition, the EPA publishes the prices paid in its annual auction. Starting prices are at a fixed price of US$1,500 per allowance (adjusted yearly for inflation).

The EPA auction sells allowances from the Special Allowance Reserve (approximately 2.8% of the total allowances), starting with the highest bid price and continuing until all allowances are sold or the pool of bids is exhausted. Bidders send sealed offers containing information on the number and type of allowances desired and the purchase price to the Chicago Board of Trade (CBOT), no later than three business days prior to the auctions. Each bid must also include a certified check or letter of credit for the total bid cost. The spot allowance auction transacts allowances that are to be used in that same year, and the advance auction sells allowances that can be used for compliance seven years after the transaction date, although they can be traded earlier.

Once the Special Allowance Reserve is exhausted, private holders are then allowed to offer their allowances, which are sold starting from the lowest-priced allowances. Private allowance holders must ensure that the vintage of their allowances is for the year in which they are offered, for any previous year, or for seven years in the future. If sources need more allowances than they can obtain in the annual auctions, they may use banked allowances or they purchase them on the $SO_2$ market.

- Risk Management — Opportunities to hedge prices at low cost can help market participants manage the risks associated with price volatility and improve market efficiency. As the

$SO_2$ market matures, risk-management options are becoming increasingly important. After years of relatively steady prices in the range of US$150 to US$210, prices rose dramatically in late 2003 and price volatility increased throughout 2004, as shown in Figure 4.4 below. Volatile prices can make it difficult to plan, reducing the efficiency of price formation and the efficiency of the $SO_2$ market.

As 2006 begins, the $SO_2$ market is in a state of dynamic change, marked by a declining volume of banked emissions, higher prices, greater price volatility, and plans to possibly double the number of plants with emissions-control equipment and address increasingly tighter standards. The CCX and NYMEX have responded to the uncertainty generated by these factors by creating $SO_2$ futures markets to increase liquidity and market efficiency. The futures markets offer participants the ease, transparency and standardization of an organized exchange as well as credit clearing. The ability to purchase futures will augment the ability to manage risk through options contracts, which several brokerages have offered in recent years. The options typically allow purchasers to specify an exercise deadline and strike prices. The options provide an alternative method to limit ("hedge") future allowance costs.

**Figure 4.4:**  Day-to-day changes in $SO_2$ allowance prices, October 2003 — November 2004 ($/ton)

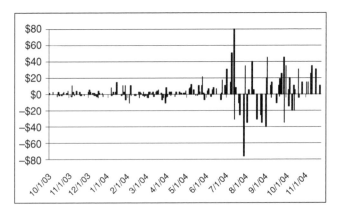

*Sources:* Amerex, Ameren

The NYMEX Board approved an $SO_2$ futures trading market which began trading in early 2005. The provisions of the rules for these futures contracts deliver the emissions allowances bought or sold for future delivery at the EPA's Allowance Tracking System. Detailed specifications can be found at the NYMEX website (www.nymex.com).

The Chicago Climate Futures Exchange (CCFE), a subsidiary of CCX, launched a futures market in December 2004 (see Figure 4.5 below). The unit of trade for the futures market is the Sulfur Financial

**Figure 4.5:** SFI Futures conracts

| Salient Features of CCFE® Sulfur Financial Instrument® Futures Contracts | |
|---|---|
| Contract Size | 25 tons of sulfur dioxide emission allowances |
| Minimum Tick Increment | $1.00 per ton = $25.00 per contract; Daily Price Limits to be specified by exchange rules |
| Symbol | SFI |
| $SO_2$ Allowances Eligible for Delivery | $SO_2$ allowances transferred in the EPA Allowance Tracking System. Allowances acceptable for delivery are: current and prior-year vintage allowances and allowance vintages for the first year subsequent to the calendar year of the contract expiration. |
| Expiration Cycle | Six quarterly contracts listed plus out-year December expiration contracts. Initial listing: <br><br> March '05    December '05    December '06 <br> June '05    March '05    December '07 <br> September '05    June '06    December '08 |
| Nearby Expiration Month Speculative Position Limits | 10,000 contracts, equivalent to 250,000 tons |
| Delivery Procedure | Delivery of eligible $SO_2$ allowances via USEPA Allowance Tracking System as per exchange instructions. |
| Regulatory Authority | CCFE® is regulated by the Commodity Futures Trading Commission. |

*Source:* CCX

Instrument (SFI). SFIs are based on emission allowances used for compliance with the Clean Air Act of 1990.

The success of the $SO_2$ emissions market can be measured in many ways. Emissions have been significantly reduced; costs have been lower than expected; compliance has been virtually 100%; and administrative costs are far lower than they are for command-and-control programs. Building on this success, the U.S. adopted an emissions-trading scheme for NOx, as outlined in the following section.

## NOx market

The largest NOx trading program, the NOx Budget Trading Program, commonly referred to as the NOx SIP Call or NOx NBP, came into effect in 2003 and affects most of the eastern states.

The NOx SIP Call is designed to attain the National Ambient Air Quality Standard for ground-level ozone. The SIP Call does not require that any specific sources be limited in their NOx emissions, but only that the entire state meet its overall emissions-reduction targets through its State Implementation Plan. (Information on other EPA-mandated NOx control programs can be found at: www.epa.gov/airmarkets/cmprpt/nox03/noxreport03.pdf)

Similar to the $SO_2$ Allowance program, the NOx NBP uses trading and market forces to reduce the marginal cost of emissions abatement. The program allocates each affected source fewer allowances than its baseline emissions output and then gives the operator the flexibility to reduce emissions at some or all of the facilities or purchase additional allowances to cover the emissions that exceed the allocated allowances.

The map in Figure 4.6 indicates the geographical scope of the NOx SIP Call which, unlike the $SO_2$ program, is regional rather then national. The first compliance period under the NOx program began on May 1, 2003. The affected states were Massachusetts, Connecticut, Rhode Island, New York, New Jersey, Pennsylvania, Maryland, Delaware, and the District of Columbia. These states had already significantly reduced emissions under the Ozone Transport Commission's (hereafter, "the Commission") cap-and-trade program, summarized in Box 4.1 below. The Commission's jurisdictions were required to reduce their NOx emissions by 35–40% relative to 2002 levels. Because the NOx program's target was similar to the one the

**Figure 4.6:**  NOx SIP Call region

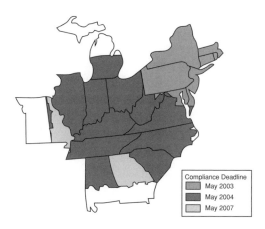

*Source:* EPA

states had adopted in the Commission's program, it superseded the commission's program.

In the second compliance period, Alabama, Illinois, Indiana, Kentucky, Michigan, North Carolina, Ohio, South Carolina, Tennessee, Virginia and West Virginia began participating in the NBP. Sources in the 11 additional states were required to control NOx to the same level as the sources in the nine jurisdictions affected in 2003; that is, at 0.15 pounds NOx/mmBtu for electricity-generating units.

The implementation of the NBP expanded the number of sources covered by the Ozone Transport Commission's program from 1,000 to 2,600 under the NBP rules. In addition, the number of allowances expanded from 140,000 to more than 500,000 per year. Under the Commission's program, electricity generators achieved an average emission level of 0.22 lbs./mmBtu by 2002. For the NBP, electricity generators were allocated allowances based on an average 2007 emission level of 0.15 lbs./mmBtu and industrial sources were required to reduce emissions by 60% by 2007.

**Box 4.1:**   The Ozone Transport Commission's cap-and-trade program

The U.S. Environmental Protection Agency and the regional participants designed the Ozone Transport Commission's cap-and-trade program to reduce NOx emissions in the Northeast States during summertime. Participating states were Maine, New Hampshire, Vermont, Massachusetts, Connecticut, Rhode Island, New York, New Jersey, Pennsylvania, Maryland, Delaware, the northern counties of Virginia, and the District of Columbia. In 1994, the Commission adopted a memorandum of understanding to achieve regional emissions reductions of NOx. States had the authority to determine which sources could opt into the program and which sources should be awarded early-reduction allowances for taking NOx reductions before the program began in 1999.

The EPA and the participating Commission states and stakeholders designed the NOx cap-and-trade program together to reduce emissions and to develop a consistent plan across all participating states. The two organizations jointly developed model rules that covered program applicability, control period, emissions limitations, monitoring record keeping and electronic reporting requirements. Each participating state was then required to develop its own plan that was consistent with the model rules, allowing for easy emissions-trading transactions across states and uniform enforceability. The emissions caps became effective in two separate stages; one on May 1, 1999 (219,000 tons) and the second on May 1, 2003 (143,000 tons). The implementation of the NBP in May 2003 superseded the Commission's May 1, 2003 deadline.

The Ozone Transport Commission had several design features that were carried into the NOx program:

The control period was May through September, to coincide with the months when NAAQS for ozone are usually exceeded.

The program covered large electricity-generating units with a rated output of 15 MW or more. (Under the NBP, the minimum rated output is 25 MW.) Other affected sources included all fossil-fuel-fired boilers, sources with indirect heat exchangers with a maximum rated heat capacity of 250 MMBtu/hour, and sources included at the state's discretion.

At the end of each control period, each emission source was required to document and show that actual emissions did not exceed its allowances.

The EPA required large emitters to continuously monitor emissions, and certified monitoring systems measured all emissions. Smaller emitters could more simply estimate emissions. Allowances and transactions were recorded in the EPA NOx Allowance Tracking System.

Any participating state had to identify budget sources for funding its program, properly allocate NOx allowances within its borders, and assure that each source complied with all requirements of the program.

Like the $SO_2$ emissions-trading program, the NOx Budget Trading Program is a cap-and-trade program. The EPA has standardized the allowance and created property rights that can be verified, traded and banked. The EPA's tracking system enables verification and helps to keep transaction costs low. Federal penalties are fixed at three allowances per excess ton of emissions and states have the authority to impose additional penalties.

The NOx program differs from the $SO_2$ program in several ways, however. The differences are driven by the nature of the pollutant, the diversity of sources, and the experience gained in implementing the $SO_2$ emissions-trading program.

- May-to-September ozone control period — Unlike the $SO_2$ program that covers emissions year-round, the NOx program is effective during the summer months of May through September, known as the "ozone control period". These are the five months when the presence of sunlight and heat causes most ozone or smog to be formed from oxides of nitrogen (NOx) and volatile organic compounds. Reducing such emissions helps to reduce ozone and its adverse effects on public health, forests, agricultural crops, building and monuments.
- State responsibilities — States have critical responsibilities in implementing and enforcing the NOx program. States were given emissions budgets to allocate to sources, to maintain their own accounts and to set aside allowances for new projects or to address specific goals. (For example, several states allocate NOx allowances to energy-efficiency and renewable-energy projects. The allowances act as an incentive to spur development by enabling the projects to

sell the NOx allowances and generate revenue.) In addition, the EPA set up the Compliance Supplement Pool, which provided extra allowances to help states comply with the SIP Call program during the first two years without affecting the reliability of the electricity supply. Within states, allowances were distributed to sources on the basis of demonstrated need or as a reward to those who implemented early reductions. Allocations of NOx allowances occur under differing schedules in different states. Some states are allocating streams of five vintage years or longer (for example, 2003–2007), while others have allocated a year at a time, with allocations made several years in advance of the affected year.

- November compliance deadline — The deadline for effecting NOx trades is November 30. On that date, the EPA closes all accounts in the NBP and determines whether each unit was in compliance during the prior ozone season. In contrast, the compliance date for $SO_2$ trading is March 1 of the year following the compliance year.

- Industrial boilers and oil- and gas-fired electricity-generating units — Like the $SO_2$ program, the NOx program targets large coal, oil and natural-gas electricity-generating units. However, it also includes other major coal, oil and natural-gas burning units, including large industrial boilers, turbines and combined cycle units. As shown in Figure 4.7 below, about 62% of the units covered by the NBP are in the $SO_2$ program; another 25% are oil- and natural-gas-fueled units not covered in the $SO_2$ program, with the remainder being, typically, industrial units.

- Banking — The NBP does allow for the banking of allowances, but "progressive flow control" was built into the trading system to prevent too many banked allowances being used in one time period. The flow-control measure is triggered when 10% of the total allowances for the next year's budget are banked. The EPA calculates the "flow control ratio" by dividing 10% of the total budget by the number of banked allowances. This ratio then indicates the percentage of banked allowances that a source can deduct from its account in a ratio of one allowance/ton. If the remaining banked allowances are to be used, then they are discounted and deducted at a rate of two allowances/ton.

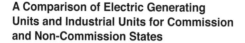

**Figure 4.7:** Units affected by the NBP

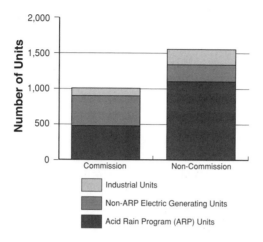

**A Comparison of Electric Generating Units and Industrial Units for Commission and Non-Commission States**

*Source:* EPA

- Auction — The EPA does not conduct an NOx emissions auction.

## Benefits of NOx trading

Because the NBP system has been in effect for less than three years, most of the demonstrated benefits of the NOx emissions-trading system to date have come from the Ozone Transport Commission's emissions-trading program described earlier. Between 1990 (the baseline year for the Acid Rain Program and other Clean Air Act requirements) and 2000 (with two years of trading under the Commission's program), the Commission's jurisdictions had reduced their emissions by 55%. After three years of trading, the Commission's states had further reduced emissions by 33% from 2000 levels and by 70% from baseline levels by 2003. In total, the EPA/Commission's progress report found that, by 2002, sources covered by the NOx Budget Program had reduced emissions by 280,000 tons during ozone season. Moreover, the program demonstrated high compliance

— virtually all of the sources affected by emissions targets in 2003 held sufficient allowances to cover their emissions. Among the seven sources that had allowance deficiencies, the total deficit was 75 allowances.

As shown in Figure 4.8 below, the non-Commission/NBP states had achieved only a 27% reduction from the 1990 base by 2000 and an approximately 50% reduction by 2003. They thus have to achieve a significantly higher percentage of reductions by 2007 than the Commission states and, therefore, have tighter budgets for the NBP.

## The evolution of NOx prices

Prices for NOx emission allowances saw a rapid increase in the early years of trading and have proved to be more volatile than prices in the early years of the $SO_2$ program. NOx emissions trading covers multiple years (vintages), with current-year vintages showing the

**Figure 4.8:**    Regional baselines, trading budgets and 2003 NOx emissions

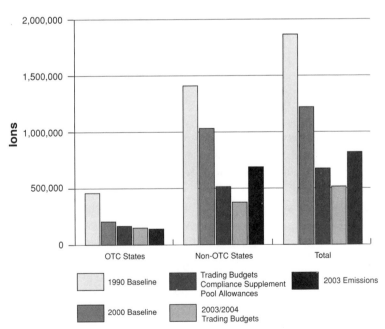

*Source:* EPA (Ozone Transport Commission)

greatest price volatility because weather and total power generation can have a dramatic effect on allowance prices. Prices for 2003 vintage allowances traded at US$5,000 per ton in October 2002 and rose to US$8,000 (the market peak to date), before falling below US$3,000 per ton. Prices for 2004 vintages were less volatile, because a mild 2003 summer enabled banked allowances to be carried over. Prices for the 2005 and 2006 vintages have been higher, reflecting uncertainty about the amount of technology that will be installed in time for the respective ozone seasons and the amount of banked emissions that will be carried forward. Prices for the 2005 vintage have generally been above US$3,000 per ton and as much as US$4,000 per ton since the low price point in the spring of 2003. Prices for 2005 vintage averaged US$3,586 in January 2005. Prices for 2006 vintage allowances have tended to be several hundred dollars lower than for 2005 vintages (See Figure 4.9 below).

The underlying drivers of these price fluctuations have not been clearly determined, but several factors seem important. First, like any new market, the NOx trading program faced considerable initial uncertainty about participants' behavior (for example, the likelihood of hoarding or the willingness to invest). The 2002 market was not aware of the number of equipment retrofits that were under way that would reduce emissions in subsequent years. Second, relative fuel prices can be a factor. In February 2003, a spike

**Figure 4.9:** Vintage-year NOx allowance prices by month of sale

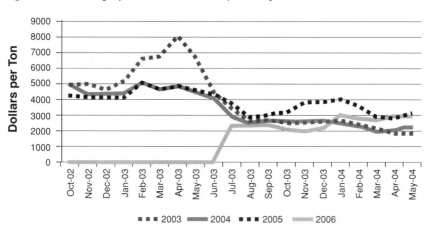

*Source:* EPA

in natural-gas prices helped to spur allowance prices because the market feared that sustained higher natural-gas prices would cause Northeastern generators to switch to oil, which in turn would increase demand for allowances. Similarly, higher sustained natural-gas prices may have influenced the higher prices for 2005 and 2006 vintage allowances in early 2005.

Third, weather and total electricity generation can have a dramatic effect on the value of allowances. As summer temperatures rise, more electricity is generated and more allowances are likely to be used. The effects of weather and higher generation are intensified because the additional generating units brought on line to meet the higher electricity demand are likely to be older units that have higher emission rates which, in turn, cause them to consume more allowances per unit of electricity produced. For example, after the price run-up in the spring of 2003, a mild summer softened demand for summer 2003 allowances and prices fell on the previous year.

Fourth, banking can have an effect. Prices for 2004 and 2005 vintages fell along with the 2003 vintage allowance prices as the market became aware of the number of banked allowances that would be carried over. Fifth, individual company decisions can be reflected in the market. The supply of 2004 allowances was plentiful, because distressed companies and companies installing retrofit equipment sold 2004 allowances to raise cash. In contrast, prices for 2005 vintage have seldom been below US$3,000 and usually exceed 2006 prices, which probably reflects perceptions about the progress of individual companies' plans for installing NOx retrofit control equipment.

## Efficiency of the NOx market

Though young, the NOx market has many of the attributes of an efficient market as evidenced by the number and concentration of participants, its liquidity, price transparency and risk-management opportunities.

The NOx program is a relatively liquid environmental market and routinely trades on a daily basis. Allowance-transfer activity itself is divided into three categories: transfers to or from the state as allowance allocations or allowance surrenders; transfers within a company or between related entities (holding-company transfers to an operating subsidiary, for example); and transfers between separate economic entities, which are considered "economically significant trades". Trading volumes between separate economic entities have been increasing since trading began. Transfer among separate economic entities comprised about 40% of the total transfers within or between commercial entities in 2003. As each year passes, additional companies are entering into trades. Liquidity is likely to increase with the addition of a NYMEX NOx contract in 2005.

In 2004, commercial trading in the U.S. NOx SIP Call program from January–October was 200,936 tons, with a total of 1,641 trades. The highest trading volume was for the 2004 vintage (43% of the total volume traded); the 2005 vintage represented 24% of the volume traded. When the number of 2004 vintage allowances traded (86,000) is compared to the total number of available allowances (and using the simplified assumption that only one trade occurred per allowance), trading in the first nine months of 2004 represented approximately 13% of the total allowances available in 2004.

Several brokerage firms, including Evolution Markets, Natsource and Cantor Fitzgerald, report NOx allowance prices. Platts publishes weekly and monthly brokers' emission-price indices.

Many different transaction structures are available for trading, including immediately settled, forward settled, swaps, and option transactions. Increased option-trading activity reflects increasing liquidity in the market and historical price volatility. The NOx options-trading market heated up as the 2004 ozone season began. Evolution Markets has found that one-month volatility for 2004 ranged from 5% to 130% and the implied one-month volatility has ranged from a low of 32% to 65% in the October 2002 to June 2004 period. Customers tend to prefer affordable call options that provide upside price protection. Option "collars" and "fences" are also available for those wanting to avoid paying option premiums. Weather-indexed NOx options offer participants an even lower cost alternative, especially for volumes of NOx production associated with significant deviations from normal summer weather patterns.

Despite its complexity and short life, the NOx emissions-trading program has resulted in significant emissions reductions. The program has broad support and has encouraged lawmakers to consider expanding its application to another pollutant, mercury.

## EPA action on coal burning

The size and importance of the $SO_2$ and NOx markets is growing again. In March 2005, the Administration took the next steps to further reduce $SO_2$ and NOx emissions and to initiate a program of mercury control. While it was hoped that these actions could be effected under the Clear Skies legislation, deadlock in the Senate committee has so far prevented legislative action. Delays in passing Clear Skies led the EPA to adopt new $SO_2$ and NOx rules as part of the Clean Air Interstate Rules (CAIR) in March 2004.

The CAIR mandate the largest reduction in air pollution since the Clean Air Act Amendments of 1990. The EPA believes that they will reduce $SO_2$ emissions by a further 70% and NOx emissions by 60% in the 28 affected Eastern states. These reductions are likely to be more costly to achieve than those implemented to date. With the additional reductions required and the likely higher costs of control, emissions trading is expected to be vigorous.

Within days of the release of the CAIR, the EPA also issued the first ever rules to control mercury.

The Administration would prefer legislation to implement multi-pollutant controls because this would provide more certainty for companies. It first proposed comprehensive legislation, the Clear Skies program, in 2002. The delays in passing the legislation reflect strongly differing opinions on which emissions should be affected and the means for controlling them. The President's proposal covered $SO_2$, NOx and mercury. In particular, the Senate was deadlocked on whether to include greenhouse gas emissions. All proposals include emissions trading for $SO_2$ and NOx, but stakeholders have been divided on whether mercury should be reduced through a similar program.

While the U.S. is not participating in the Kyoto Protocol, trading in greenhouse gas emissions is occurring there.

## The EU's emissions scheme

The EU Emissions Trading Scheme (EU ETS) began in January 2005 in 25 EU member states and is mandatory for certain industries across Europe with emissions above a certain threshold.

Building on the market mechanisms created under the Kyoto Protocol to the 1992 United Nations Framework Convention on

Climate Change (UNFCCC) — joint implementation (JI), the clean development mechanism (CDM) and international emissions trading — the EU has developed the largest company-level scheme for trading in carbon dioxide emissions, making it a world leader in this emerging market.

The incentive to reduce emissions became sizeable during the course of 2005, as the value of one metric ton of $CO_2$ emissions started the year at around €5 per metric ton, and by July had hit a high close to €30 per metric ton. In Phase 1 of the EU trading scheme there is a natural cap on prices at €40 per metric ton, which is the level of the fine that will be applied at the end of 2007 to any company that does not have sufficient emissions credits to cover its validated emission levels.

The 15 states that made up the EU until its enlargement to 25 countries on May 1, 2004 are committed to reducing their combined emissions of greenhouse gases by 8% from 1990 levels by the end of the Protocol's first commitment period between 2008 and 2012. This overall target has been translated into differentiated emissions-reduction or limitation targets for each state (see Figure 4.10). The 10 new member states are not covered by the EU target but, in most cases, have their own reduction targets of 6% or 8% under the Protocol. They are full participants in the EU trading scheme.

By combining the emissions-trading scheme with CDM and JI, the EU is underlining its commitment to realizing the advantages that the Kyoto mechanisms offer as a supplement to significant domestic action by industrialized countries to reduce their emissions.

The ETS has been established through binding legislation proposed by the European Commission and approved by all EU Member States and the European Parliament. The scheme is based on six fundamental principles:

- It is a cap-and-trade system.
- Its initial focus is on $CO_2$ from big industrial emitters.
- Implementation is taking place in phases, with periodic reviews and opportunities for expansion to other gases and sectors.
- Allocation plans for emission allowances are decided periodically.
- It includes a strong compliance framework.
- The market is EU-wide but taps emissions-reduction opportunities in the rest of the world through the use of

CDM and JI, and provides for links with compatible schemes in third countries.

The scheme may be expanded to incorporate aviation and shipping. We will look at this in more detail in Chapter 9. An initial attempt by EU ministers to bring aviation into emissions trading at the end of 2005 failed after U.S. authorities threatened legal action if it was going to apply emissions trading to U.S. airlines landing and taking off in EU airspace, citing an American law that made it illegal for a foreign government to tax an American airline. The U.S. viewed emissions schemes as a form of indirect taxation in the context of airlines.

At the center of the emissions-trading scheme in the EU is the common trading "currency" of emission allowances. One allowance represents the right to emit one metric ton of $CO_2$. Member States have drawn up national allocation plans for 2005–2007 which give each installation in the scheme permission to emit an amount of $CO_2$ that corresponds to the number of allowances received. Decisions on the allocations are made public.

The limit or cap on the number of allowances allocated creates the scarcity needed for a trading market to emerge. Companies that keep their emissions below the level of their allowances are able to sell their excess allowances at a price determined by supply and demand at that time.

Those facing difficulty in remaining within their emissions limit have a choice between taking measures to reduce their emissions, such as investing in more efficient technology or using a less carbon-intensive energy source, or buying the extra allowances they need at the market rate, or a combination of the two, whichever is cheapest.

This ensures that emissions are reduced in the most cost-effective way. Most allowances are allocated to installations free of charge — at least 95% during the initial phase and at least 90% in the second phase from 2008 to 2012. Though only plants covered by the scheme are given allowances, anyone else — individuals, institutions, non-governmental organizations or whoever — is free to buy and sell in the market in the same way as companies.

After each calendar year, participating entities must surrender a number of allowances equivalent to their verified $CO_2$ emissions in that year. These allowances are then cancelled so they cannot be used again. Those installations with allowances left over can sell them or bank them for the future.

**Figure 4.10:** EU ETS emission allocations

| Member State | CO$_2$ allowances in million tonnes | Installations covered | Kyoto target |
|---|---|---|---|
| Austria | 99.01 | 205 | −13% (*) |
| Belgium | 188.8 | 363 | −7.5% (*) |
| Czech Republic | National allocation plan yet to be assessed | | −8% |
| Cyprus | 16.98 | 13 | − |
| Denmark | 100.5 | 362 | −21% (*) |
| Estonia | 56.85 | 43 | −8% |
| Finland | 136.5 | 535 | 0% (*) |
| France | 469.53 | 1 172 | 0% (*) |
| Germany | 1 497.0 | 2 419 | −21% (*) |
| Greece | National allocation plan yet to be assessed | | +25% (*) |
| Hungary | 93.8 | 261 | −6% |
| Ireland | 67.0 | 143 | +13% (*) |
| Italy | National allocation plan yet to be assessed | | −6.5% (*) |
| Latvia | 13.7 | 95 | −8% |
| Lithuania | 36.8 | 93 | −8% |
| Luxembourg | 10.07 | 19 | −28% (*) |
| Malta | 8.83 | 2 | − |
| Netherlands | 285.9 | 333 | −6% (*) |
| Poland | National allocation plan yet to be assessed | | −6% |
| Portugal | 114.5 | 239 | +27% (*) |
| Slovak Republic | 91.5 | 209 | −8% |
| Slovenia | 26.3 | 98 | −8% |
| Spain (**) | 523.7 | 927 | +15% |
| Sweden | 68.7 | 499 | +4% (*) |
| United Kingdom | 736.0 | 1 078 | −12.5% (*) |
| **Total so far** | **4 641.97 (**)** | **9 089 (**)** | |
| **Approximate percentage of estimated overall total** | **ca. 70%** | **ca. 70%** | |

(*) Under the Kyoto Protocol, the EU-15 has to reduce its greenhouse gas-emissions by 8 % below 1990 levels during 2008–12. This target is shared among the 15 Member States under a legally binding burden-sharing agreement (Council Decision 2002/358/EC of April 25, 2002). The 10 Member States that joined the EU in May 2004 have individual targets under the Kyoto Protocol with the exception of Cyprus and Malta, which as yet have no targets.

(**) Figures do not include some Spanish installations for which allocations are in preparation.

Those that have not produced enough allowances to cover their emissions will have to pay a dissuasive fine for each excess metric ton of $CO_2$ they have emitted. In the initial phase, the penalty is €40 per ton, but from 2008 this will rise to €100.

## The ETS transaction registry and the global registry

Allowances are not printed but held in accounts in electronic registries set up by Member States. The European Commission has set out specific legislation for a standardized and secured system of registries based on UN data-exchange standards to track the issue, and the holding, transfer and cancellation of allowances. Provisions on the tracking and use of credits from JI and CDM projects are also included. The registries system is similar to a banking system which keeps track of the ownership of money in accounts but does not look into the deals that lead to money changing hands.

The system of registries is overseen by a central administrator at EU level who, through an independent transaction log, checks each transaction for irregularities. Any irregularities have to be remedied before a transaction can be completed. The EU registries system will be integrated with the international registries system used under the Kyoto Protocol.

The registry is a web-based application. The website homepage must have a public area and a secure area. The public area allows visitors to apply for a new account or to view publicly available reports. The secure area permits existing account holders to access their accounts using (as a minimum) a password and log-in identification number (countries have the option of putting in place additional security measures).

In order to apply for a new account, operators, individuals and organizations must complete an online registration process and also submit various documents as proof of identification. After verifying the various documents, the Registry Administrator informs the CITL (the EU transaction log) and the ITL (an Independent Transaction Log which keeps track of global emissions-credit transfers under the Kyoto Protocol).

The ITL is currently being developed for the United Nations Framework Convention on Climate Change (UNFCCC) Secretariat, which was adopted by governments in Rio de Janeiro in May 1992, and will be linked in to the existing and operational CITL which checks EU ETS credit transfers, as outlined in Figure 4.11 below.

These registries can be regarded very much like a bank where, instead of cash, emissions units are held. It should be made clear that they are not trading platforms or exchanges so cannot be used to trade. Account holders only use the registries to complete trades (take or make a delivery at the end of a trading session).

There are two key types of trade in emissions units. The spot market, as the name suggests, requires immediate delivery of units. Account holders therefore have to ensure that they use the registry to transfer units in or out of their accounts at the end of each day's trading. The forward or futures market rarely results in delivery of any emissions-trading units. This is because contracting parties often trade out of their market positions. However, periodically account holders must use the registry to make or take delivery of their units.

The nature of trading contracts (for example, terms and conditions) is determined by the market and is independent of the registry.

The ETS was the first in the world to recognize the emissions-reducing effects of JI and CDM projects in developing countries for

**Figure 4.11:**   Emissions-trading registries

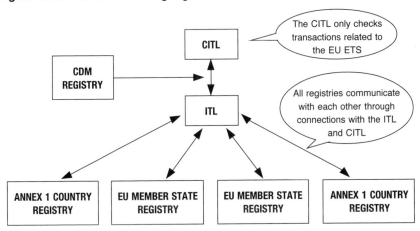

The ITL will be activated just before the start of international emissions trading under the Kyoto Protocol in 2008. Prior to that only the CITL will be operational, and will only check transactions relating to the EU ETS.

*Source:* Defra, UK

its own cap-and-trade scheme; that is, it recognizes most of these credits as being equivalent to its own emission allowances: 1 ETS Allowance = 1 CER = 1 ERU.

This has encouraged European firms with emissions exposures to invest in emissions-reducing projects in developing nations and receive an emissions benefit within the ETS. (See Chapter 2 for more details on the JI and CDM schemes).

JI and the CDM enable developed countries that have binding emissions-reduction or limitation targets under the Kyoto Protocol to undertake emissions-saving investments in third countries and credit these savings towards their own emission targets.

The CDM covers projects in developing nations without an emission target under the Protocol. Reductions since 2000 are potentially eligible to receive credits from CERs (certified emission reductions) under the European ETS.

JI applies to projects in other industrialized countries and countries with economies in transition that have agreed to an emission target and will yield credits known as "emission reduction units" (ERUs) once the first Kyoto commitment period starts in 2008.

Following are some practical examples of how the system works:

- **Landfill project in Costa Rica (October 2005)**
  The Rio Azul landfill gas-to-energy project was registered as a CDM project by the UNFCCC and is the first of its kind in Costa Rica. The project will use the landfill gas from a municipal landfill site in the city of San José. CERs totaling 1,560,835 tons $CO_2$ equivalent are expected over the 10-year crediting period.

- **JI projects for the Netherlands (July 2005)**
  The Netherlands intends to sign six JI contracts for the purchase of emissions reductions. The total number of carbon credits to be contracted will be 3.58 million ERUs and 0.93 million AAUs (Assigned Amount Units, of which the first recorded deal was in December 2002, whereby the Republic of Slovakia sold Kyoto allowances to Sumitomo Corporation of Japan). The average price is €5.13 per ton $CO_2e$. In previous tenders, 17 projects, with a total amount of 11.6 million tons $CO_2e$, have been contracted.

- **Wind-energy project in China (June 2005)**
  The Huitengxile Windfarm Project has been registered as a CDM project by the UNFCCC. It is the first CDM project activity hosted in China and the first wind-energy project of the 10 registered CDM projects by the UNFCCC. The project is located at Huitengxile, Inner Mongolia Autonomous Region, and involves the installation of 22 turbines providing a total of 25.8 MWe (megawatt electrical — a term that refers to power produced as electricity).

The total amount of CERs is expected to be 514,296 tons $CO_2$ equivalent over the 10-year crediting period.

Further details of these and other projects are available from www.carboncredits.nl. As these examples show, the EU scheme is encouraging investors to participate in the rapidly emerging market for JI and CDM projects which promote the transfer of environmentally sound technologies that help the host countries meet their sustainable development goals.

For EU companies covered by the scheme, the recognition of JI and CDM credits increases the range of options available for meeting their emissions targets, improves the liquidity of the market and potentially lowers the price of allowances, thus further reducing their compliance costs.

As the above examples illustrate, countries as well as individual companies are looking for emissions-reduction credits through JI and CDM to help meet their targets under the Protocol. It is worth noting that CERs and ERUs can be used within the EU ETS *independently* of the Kyoto Protocol. In fact, EU Member States can allow operators of installations that fall under the EU ETS to use CERs from 2005 onwards.

However, after 2008 CERs and ERUs can be used towards their emissions targets in line with installation-level import caps. Technically, the use will occur through the issuance and immediate surrender of one EU emissions allowance (EUA) in exchange for one CER or ERU. This implies that CERs and ERUs will not be able to be exchanged for EUAs for trading purposes since the equivalent EUA would immediately be surrendered for compliance.

What is rather interesting is that the Linking Directive, the EU directive (Directive 2004/101/EC of the European Parliament dated October 27, 2004) that permits companies operating in the EU ETS to use credits from the Kyoto Protocol project mechanisms, does not specify a cap on the import of CERs during the first EU ETS trading period (2005–07). It does, however, leave the decision on whether or not to use CERs towards compliance in the hands of the individual member states. The volume of credits imported might hence be dictated by the number of issued CERs that will be available during that period. However, the European Union has been taking note of the very large number of potential CERs being generated in the market and, as of first quarter 2006, has started to talk about reconsidering limits on how many credits can be imported into the EU ETS.

At the time of writing, it was still the case that from 2008–12 operators in the EU ETS can use CERs and ERUs up to a percentage of the allocation to each installation. This figure is to be specified by each member state in its national allocation plan (NAP), which sets out the emissions targets due to fall on industry, taking into account supplementary requirements of the Kyoto Protocol that insist that the buying of credits from overseas is "supplemental" to domestic action.

So far, carbon credits from nuclear facilities and land use, land-use change and forestry (LULUCF) projects are not allowed to enter the EU ETS. The review of the EU ETS scheduled for mid 2006 may consider whether to allow the import of LULUCF credits up to 1% of the EU ETS allocation from 2008.

One of the main issues surrounding the use of JI credits in the EU ETS is the danger of double counting; that is, that the same emissions-reduction measure generates ERUs and frees up EUAs at the same time. In this respect, three categories of JI projects can be distinguished:

- First, JI project activities that take place in installations that fall under the EU ETS. Such activities, which directly reduce or limit an installation's emissions, can only sell ERUs if an equal number of EUAs are cancelled by the operator of that installation.

  This means that the operator of an EU ETS installation that hosts a JI project needs to surrender an EUA for each ERU that is issued. It therefore needs to make sure that the installation receives an adequate allocation of EUAs in line with the baseline specified for the JI project, in order to honor any ERU sales agreements it has already signed. If such a project has not yet been approved as a JI project before the allocation plans have been finalized, the project needs to demonstrate that the EU ETS, which falls under the Acquis Communautaire* that governs the entry of accession countries to the EU ETS, would not provide a sufficient incentive to reduce the emissions claimed by the applicant JI project. This might be the case if the expected EUA prices in the EU ETS are too low to make the investment economically viable, and if it can be demonstrated that ERU prices are high enough to provide an incentive for the proposed JI emissions-reduction investment which would otherwise not be implemented.

- Second, emissions-reduction activities such as grid-connected renewable-energy projects or energy-efficiency projects that indirectly reduce the emissions of installations covered by the EU ETS may only sell ERUs if an equal number of EUAs is cancelled from the national member state's registry. To that extent, member states will probably have to set up a reserve pool of EUAs corresponding to the expected number of ERUs to be issued and transferred. This reserve pool means that installations that fall under the EU ETS will get fewer EUAs.

- The third category is emissions-reduction activities that do not directly fall under the EU ETS and do not indirectly limit or reduce emissions from installations within the EU ETS. Examples of such projects include methane-capturing from landfills, NOx-reduction projects, non-grid-connected renewable-energy projects and energy-efficiency projects. Projects from this third category are not affected by the Linking Directive and can be developed "as usual" as long as they are additional to the Acquis Communautaire.

---

* The Acquis Communautaire is, basically, the entire body of European laws, including all the treaties, regulations and directives passed by the European institutions as well as judgments laid down by the Court of Justice, which must be adopted, implemented and enforced by any country planning to join the European Union. As well as changing national laws, this often means they must set up or change the necessary administrative or judicial bodies which oversee the legislation.

# 5 Market Mechanisms for Reducing Emissions

For carbon dioxide ($CO_2$) and greenhouse gas (GHG) markets, 2005 was a watershed year, a key turning point in the history of market mechanisms for the reduction of emissions. In addition to the Kyoto Protocol coming into force in February, the agreement on climate change reached at the G8 summit in July gave further impetus to action on reductions in $CO_2$ emissions and GHGs. It acknowledged climate change as a serious and long-term challenge and agreed an action plan that recognized the importance of financing the transition to cleaner energy. It also contained a commitment to use "market-based policy frameworks" such as the EU ETS. The key here is that market-based mechanisms are considered to be an effective way to provide confidence to industry in the value of investments it makes in its business and industrial processes in order to achieve emission reductions.

## Greenhouse gases

Increasing concentrations of GHGs from human activity such as the burning of fossil fuels and industrial pollution are believed by many to be contributing to global climate change. The theory is that GHGs trap infrared radiation emitted from the earth's surface and raise temperatures. Global temperatures over the past century have risen 1°C, and they continue to rise. Higher temperatures could have far-reaching and profound effects on temperature-sensitive forms of life and on the planet's ice caps, sea levels and precipitation patterns.

The gas believed to be making the single largest human contribution to the greenhouse effect is carbon dioxide ($CO_2$) and the largest source of $CO_2$ emissions is the burning of fossil fuels. The other five greenhouse gases related to human activities covered by the Kyoto Protocol are methane ($CH_4$), nitrous oxide ($N_2O$), hydrofluorocarbons (HFCs), perfluorocarbons (PFCs), and sulphur hexafluoride ($SF_6$).

Because $CO_2$ is the dominant GHG, one metric ton of carbon dioxide equivalent (t $CO_2e$) has become the currency of emissions reduction and trading. Reductions in the other gases covered are converted into carbon dioxide equivalents based on their believed contribution to global warming relative to carbon dioxide. In general discourse, the unit of trade is commonly referred to as $CO_2$ and the market is called the carbon market.

**Figure 5.1:**   Global temperature changes (1880–2000)

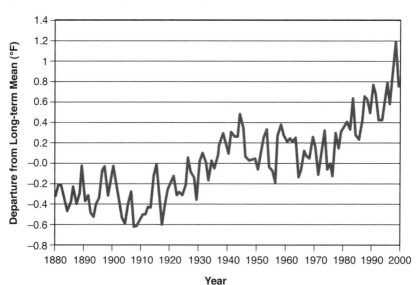

*Source:* U.S. Environmental Protection Agency (EPA), 2004.

# The Kyoto Protocol — The framework for international emissions trading

Concerns about potential climate change have been the subject of worldwide debate for at least 25 years, beginning with the first international conference on climate change in 1979. In June 1992, more than 150 countries signed the United Nations Framework Convention on Climate Change (UNFCCC) at a UN conference — the so-called Earth Summit — held in Rio de Janeiro, Brazil. The UNFCCC set out a framework for action aimed at stabilizing atmospheric concentrations of greenhouse gases to avoid "dangerous anthropogenic interference" with the climate system and spelled out commitments for different groups of countries.

Under the Convention, most of the responsibility for achieving the reductions in GHGs is assigned to the Annex I countries, industrialized countries which include the members of the Organization for Economic Co-operation and Development (OECD) and the countries referred to as the "economies in transition" (EITs), formerly known as the Iron Curtain countries. EITs include the Russian Federation, the Baltic States, and several Central and Eastern European States. The UNFCCC also established the Conference of Parties (COP), the supreme body for decision-making and implementation of the Convention. In general, the COP meets annually, with a defining number assigned to each meeting. Thus, the meeting held in December 2004 in Buenos Aires, the tenth, is referred to as COP-10.

At COP-3, held in Kyoto in December 1997, 160 countries adopted the text of the Kyoto Protocol. In the ensuing year, 84 countries signed the Protocol, affirming their commitment to seek ratification of the Protocol in accordance with their national constitution and laws. Article 25 of the Protocol specified that the Protocol would take effect 90 days after two conditions were met: (1) at least 55 countries (Annex I and developing countries) had ratified it; and, (2) the Annex I countries that ratified would represent at least 55% of the total 1990 GHG emissions for Annex I parties. Developing countries were encouraged to ratify the Protocol. Those that did not were not permitted to sell emissions reductions to the industrialized countries, as described below.

The conditions set out in Article 25 were not met until November 2004, when Russia ratified the Protocol and brought the total volume of GHG emissions of the ratifying Annex I countries to 61.2%. The

Kyoto Protocol thus became effective on February 16, 2005. More than 125 countries, including many developing countries not included in Annex I, have ratified the Protocol and are participating in its programs.

The U.S. and Australia — which together account for 38.2% of total 1990 GHG emissions for Annex I countries — have not ratified the Protocol and are unlikely, therefore, to be participating in emissions trading under the Kyoto umbrella. Nevertheless, as discussed in later sections of this chapter, both countries are pursuing programs to reduce GHG emissions and to utilize emissions trading.

The Kyoto Protocol strives to reduce the concentration of GHGs in the atmosphere by prescribing a schedule of emissions-reduction targets for the Annex I countries. Overall, the Annex I countries agreed to reduce their collective emissions of six greenhouse gases by at least 5% below 1990 levels between 2008 and 2012 (the first commitment period). Annex B of the Kyoto Protocol sets country-by-country reduction targets for this period. The target or maximum amount of emissions (measured as the equivalent in carbon dioxide) that a party to the agreement may emit over the commitment period is known as a party's "assigned amount". Countries from the developing world have no such targets and no actions for the years after 2012 have been agreed, although the issue was discussed at the COP-10 meeting in Buenos Aires.

To achieve their Kyoto targets, Annex I countries must put in place domestic policies and measures to reduce GHGs. The policies and measures for achieving the emissions-reduction commitments include command-and-control methods, voluntary programs and emissions trading. Individual governments and businesses have programs in place or are considering options such as energy-efficiency standards, investment in alternative-fuel and emissions-reduction technologies, and legislation and regulations to cap emissions. The European Climate Change Program (ECCP), the goal of which is to identify and develop all the necessary elements of a European strategy to implement the Protocol, is considering and implementing a broad range of options. In addition to emissions trading, these include generating electricity from renewable energy sources, voluntary commitments by automobile producers to reduce $CO_2$ emissions by 25% and proposals to tax energy products.

Emissions trading is a critical Kyoto strategy for reducing emissions. Based on the experience with sulfur dioxide and nitrogen oxide trading in the U.S., GHG emissions trading holds the potential to increase overall compliance with required emissions-reduction targets and lower the total costs of compliance. As discussed earlier in this book, emissions trading is a market-based regulatory system that provides flexibility in the means to comply.

In general, renewable-energy technologies such as wind and solar technologies, methane-reduction technologies such as landfill and coal-bed methane recovery projects, and industrial projects that reduce one of the six GHGs recognized in the Protocol are candidates for generating emissions reductions for trade. Parties may also offset their emissions by increasing the amount of greenhouse gases removed from the atmosphere by so-called carbon sinks. The eligible sink activities include forest restoration, the planting of forests, and the management of crop and grazing land. Greenhouse gases removed from the atmosphere through eligible sink activities generate credits known as "removal units" (RMUs).

Under the Protocol, emissions trading can occur within and between countries. The Kyoto Protocol employs three "flexibility mechanisms" to enable flexibility in compliance: emissions trading, joint implementation (JI) and the clean-development mechanism (CDM), as described earlier and in more detail in Box 5.1 below. The flexibility mechanisms provide a hybrid system for trading, based partially on cap-and-trade within and among Annex I countries under the emissions-trading mechanism and partially on the ability of Annex I countries to import emissions reductions derived from investments in JI and CDM countries. While the country governments officially own the emissions and are responsible for achieving the targets, governments, companies and non-governmental organizations (NGOs) engage in activities to reduce emissions and participate in the emissions-trading market.

The Kyoto Protocol also provides a framework for market design and enforcement of its provisions. The Protocol has enabled the standardization of the commodity (one metric ton of $CO_2e$ or carbon dioxide equivalent) for emissions trading. The Protocol requires that Annex I countries develop and maintain registries to provide transparency, reduce transaction costs and enable enforcement. Separate mechanisms are being developed to approve JI and CDM transactions. The foundations of the emissions-trading market are in the Kyoto Protocol implementation and enforcement requirements, described in Box 5.2, which provide verifiable property rights, help to reduce transaction costs, promote transparency, and provide for enforceable penalties.

**Box 5.1:**   Kyoto Protocol flexibility mechanisms: Alternative means for trading GHG emissions

1.   Under emissions trading, an Annex I country may transfer emission credits known as "assigned amount units" (AAUs) to another Annex I country that finds it more difficult or costly to meet its emissions target. The emissions-trading program is a cap-and-trade program, with many characteristics of the U.S. sulfur dioxide and nitrogen oxide trading programs discussed in Chapter 3.

2.   Joint implementation (JI) also involves transfers of emissions credits between Annex I countries. The difference is that one Annex I country may obtain credits from another Annex I country by investing in a project that reduces emissions in the territory of another. The investor counts the resulting emissions reduction units (ERUs) against its own target. In practice, joint implementation projects are most likely to take place in economies in transition, where there tends to be more scope for cutting emissions at low cost.

3.   The Clean-Development Mechanism (CDM) brings the developing countries into the trading framework. Annex I countries may implement projects (in developing countries) that reduce emissions and use the resulting certified emissions reductions (CERs) to help meet their own targets. The CDM aims to reduce the costs of compliance for the industrialized countries and to help developing countries achieve sustainable development and contribute to the ultimate objective of the UNFCCC.

*Source:* United Nations Framework Convention on Climate Change (UNFCCC)

## The EU Emissions Trading Scheme (ETS)

To date, the EU has the most fully developed carbon-emissions-trading market. In January 2005 the EU launched the first inter-country emissions-trading scheme in the world as a means to reduce carbon dioxide emissions and comply with the Kyoto targets. Estimates are that the EU market is worth US$15 billion annually, about five times the size of the U.S. sulfur dioxide market. The EU ETS illuminates the likely benefits of emissions trading and how the Kyoto flexibility mechanisms are being implemented.

**Box 5.2:** Kyoto Protocol: Implementation and enforcement requirements

The underlying effectiveness of the emissions-trading process is based on Kyoto requirements. Annex I parties will submit annual emissions inventories and regular national communications under the Protocol, both of which will be subject to in-depth review by expert review teams. The review teams have the mandate to highlight potential compliance problems — known as "questions of implementation" — and refer these to the Compliance Committee if parties fail to address them. Parties must also establish and maintain a national registry to track and record transactions under the mechanisms. As an added monitoring tool, the secretariat keeps an independent transaction log to ensure that accurate records are maintained. It will also publish an annual compilation and accounting report of each party's emissions and its transactions over the year. All information, except that designated as confidential, will be made available to the public. (There are safeguards in place to limit what type of information may be designated as confidential.)

The Protocol's compliance system gives "teeth" to its commitments. It consists of a Compliance Committee, composed of a plenary, a bureau, and two branches: a facilitative branch and an enforcement branch. As its name suggests, the facilitative branch aims to provide advice and assistance to parties, including "early warning" that a party may be in danger of not complying, whereas the enforcement branch has the power to apply certain consequences on parties not meeting their commitments. If a party fails to meet its emissions target, it must make up the difference in the second commitment period and pay a penalty of 30%. It must also develop a compliance action plan and its eligibility to "sell" under emissions trading will be suspended.

*Source:* UNFCC

The European Climate Change Program provides the framework for the EU nations to meet their Kyoto Protocol obligations. In its first steps to implement the Kyoto Protocol, the EU allocated its 15 member states the emissions-reduction target of 8% it had agreed to in the Protocol, as shown in Figure 5.2 below. Under this allocation, known as the "burden-sharing agreement", the wealthier states agreed to reduce emissions at rates that were greater than the 8%

**Figure 5.2:** Burden-sharing agreement (BSA) distributes GHG reduction targets across EU-15

| Member State | 1990 | 2001 | BSA |
|---|---|---|---|
| Germany | 1216.2 | 993.5 | −21.0 % |
| UK | 747.2 | 657.2 | −12.5 % |
| France | 558.4 | 560.8 | 0 % |
| Italy | 509.3 | 545.4 | −6.5 % |
| Spain | 289.9 | 382.8 | 15.0 % |
| Netherlands | 211.1 | 219.7 | −6.0 % |
| Belgium | 141.2 | 150.2 | −7.5 % |
| Greece | 107.0 | 132.2 | 25.0 % |
| Austria | 78.3 | 85.9 | −13.0 % |
| Finland | 77.2 | 80.9 | 0 % |
| Sweden | 95.9 | 70.5 | 4.0 % |
| Denmark | 69.5 | 69.4 | −21.0 % |
| Portugal | 61.4 | 83.8 | 27.0 % |
| Ireland | 53.4 | 70.0 | 13.0 % |
| Luxembourg | 10.9 | 6.1 | −28.0 % |
| **EU15** | **4204.0** | **4108.3** | **−8%** |

Total GHG emissions (MtCO$_2$e) in 1990 and 2001 and reduction targets for 2008–2012

*Source:* EEA, 2003

average, and thus created opportunities for the less-wealthy EU members to grow. When the 10 additional members joined the EU in 2004, their emissions-reduction commitments under the Kyoto Protocol were brought into the EU framework.

In March 2000, the European Commission produced a Green Paper examining how a GHG emissions-trading scheme could be used within the EU to facilitate compliance with Kyoto. The paper concluded that the EU could reduce the cost of meeting the 8% emissions-reduction target by one-third (€3 billion in 1999 prices) if it employed a regional trading scheme in addition to emissions-trading schemes at the individual member-state level.

Other benefits flow from the EU's regional trading scheme, too:

- It enlarges the pool of emissions to be traded and enables the inter-country market to create a single "European" price for emissions traded within Europe. Together, these factors increase the market's liquidity.
- A regional trading scheme lowers transaction costs by relying on one trading system and one regulatory framework (rather than a set for each of the 25 EU member states). In other words, a single large system creates economies of scale.
- The EU's experience with trading in 2005 through 2007 will better prepare it for the international emissions-trading scheme intended to be launched by 2008 under the Kyoto Protocol — perhaps giving it a leading edge.

In light of these substantial benefits, in July 2003 the European Parliament formally approved a directive to establish an emissions-trading scheme (ETS) for GHGs, to be launched in January 2005. Issues related to its scope, sectors covered, and allowance-allocation procedures were resolved in intensive negotiations between the European Parliament, the European Commission and representatives from the EU member states. The first phase of the EU ETS will run from January 1, 2005 to December 31, 2007, with a second phase that will coincide with the first commitment period of the Kyoto Protocol, from January 1, 2008 to December 31, 2012. All 25 EU member states can participate in the emissions-trading program.

While the EU has worked to ensure compatibility between its scheme and Kyoto's international scheme, the first phase will implement only part of the Kyoto commitment. The first phase of implementation covers only $CO_2$, because emissions of that gas are most easily and accurately monitored and have one of the greatest effects on global warming. The first phase covers around 12,000 specific installations (plants) in specified sectors (see Chapter 3).

Among countries, dramatic differences in the structure of industry and the sources of power generation will affect how the allocations are made, as Figure 5.3 below indicates. For example, fossil-fuel-based power generation dominates the emissions profile for Denmark, whereas metals production dominates the Austrian

**Figure 5.3:**   Share of emissions by sector covered by the EU ETS for EU-15 in Year 2001

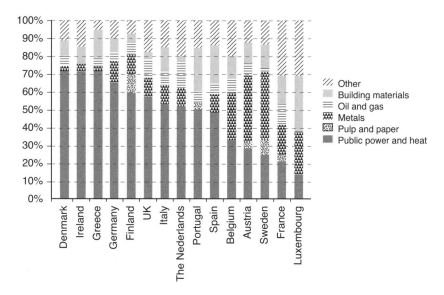

Sources: Eurostat and Point Carbon (www.pointcarbon.com)

profile. Because of these differences, these countries will establish the allocations for each installation through their respective national allocation plans (NAPs).

### National Allocation Plans and the Linking Directive

Under the EU burden-sharing agreement, each member state has an overall target for its national emissions, as shown in Figure 5.4 below.

Under the EU ETS, each member state designates a portion of its target to the installations within its borders, with the remainder usually being addressed via alternative national energy and environmental policies. In general, member states must comply with common criteria mandated by the ETS Directive. Figure 5.5 below illustrates the volume of EU GHG emissions through 2002 and the reductions necessary to achieve the 8% reductions targeted for 2008–2012. Overall GHG emissions were only slightly above the targeted line of reductions, even though carbon dioxide emissions are a major component of overall GHG emissions and were 101.6% of base-year levels in 2002. By focusing on carbon dioxide emissions

**Figure 5.4:**  Emissions-reduction targets for EU member states 2005–2007

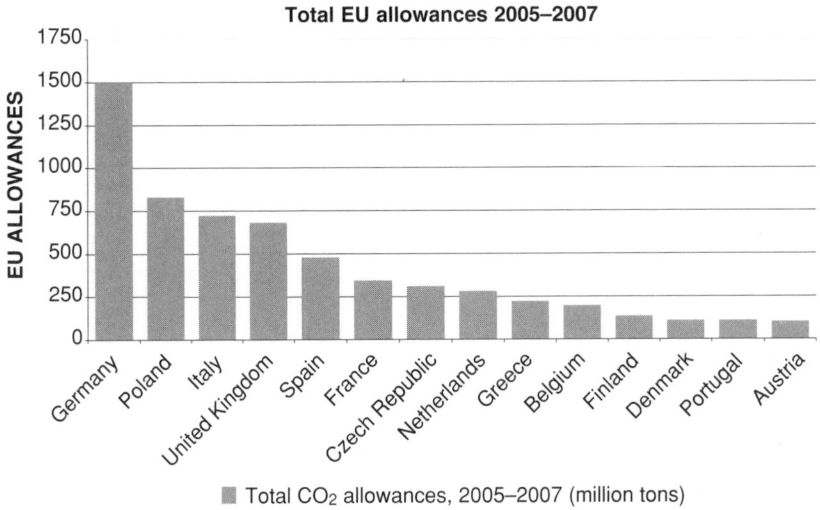

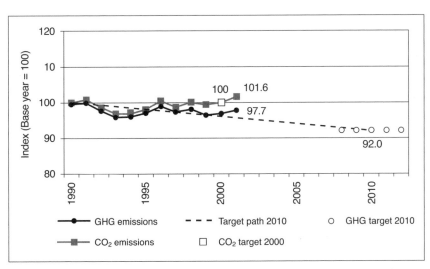

**Total EU allowances 2005–2007**

Total $CO_2$ allowances, 2005–2007 (million tons)

*Source:* Mark Woodward, IPE/ICE Futures, February 2, 2005

**Figure 5.5:**  Total EU GHG emissions in relation to the Kyoto target

*Source:* European Environment Agency (EEA), 2003

in the 2005–2007 period, the EU is likely to make considerable strides in reducing total GHG emissions, increasing the likelihood that it will meet the 2008–2012 targets for the first commitment period.

At least 90% of the EU allowances will be distributed to plants at no charge, but countries have the option of auctioning up to 5% of the 2005–2007 allowances and up to 10% for the period 2008–2012. The auctions, if implemented, will enable market participants to purchase allowances and will help to establish prices. Member states had to submit their national allocation plans for 2005–2007 for review and approval by the European Commission by March 31, 2004. Negotiations for the 2008–2012 NAPs will begin in 2006.

In addition, under the EU's Linking Directive, carbon-emissions credits from JI and CDM projects established under the Kyoto Protocol can be imported into the EU ETS. As a result, emissions from four mechanisms, all representing one ton of carbon dioxide equivalent, will be traded in the ETS, as shown below:

| International Emissions Trading Scheme (IET) | Assigned Amount Units (AAUs) |
|---|---|
| EU Emissions Trading Scheme (EU ETS) | EU Emissions Allowance (EUAs) |
| Joint Implementation (JI) | Emissions Reduction Units (ERUs) |
| Clean Development Mechanism (CDM) | Certified Emissions Reductions (CERs) |

The IET and EU ETS are cap-and-trade programs derived from the Kyoto Protocol emissions-trading mechanism. Most JI projects are taking place in Eastern and Central Europe. The JI credits (ERUs) are generated from individual projects that are separate from the plants covered by cap-and-trade. The CDM credits (CERs) are also project-based and have no relationships to emissions-reduction targets since CDM projects are found in developing countries that are not subject to Kyoto targets. The Linking Directive doesn't specify a cap on the import of CERs during the first EU ETS trading period; individual member states have the option, but are not required, to use CERS or ERUs towards compliance. From 2008 onwards, CERS and ERUs can be used up to a yet-to-be-determined percentage of the allocation to each installation.

*Pricing carbon*

During the first half of 2005, EU ETS prices were quite volatile because of the uncertainties associated with a new market combined with the rise in global oil and gas prices. This created a rush into the emissions markets as power generators sought to trade the arbitrage between the combined cost of coal and the required emissions credits to generate power (called "the Dark spread") versus the cost of oil or gas and the required emissions credits to generate power. Traders had to get used to the convergence of emissions and energy markets: the fourth dimension of energy trading had arrived (see Chapter 3). The price of EU allowances at the start of 2004 was around €13; by early 2005, the price for EUAs applicable to the 2005 trading period had fallen to around €6–8 per ton of carbon dioxide, with prices rising in the middle of 2005 to close to €30 per ton. By the end of 2005 key market participants, including energy producers and oil majors, seem to have adjusted to the new fourth dimension of oil, gas, coal, and power markets. The market fundamentals and technical indicators monitored by traders started to drive prices as liquidity and market efficiency began to improve in the underlying emissions-credits market.

On the topic of liquidity, the supply of allowances is actually determined by reduction targets and the individual national allocation plans of member states. Demand is driven by many long- and short-term uncertainties. In the longer term, the ability of each plant and country to achieve its targets will be determined by the overall economic growth, changes in economic structure, the availability of technology to reduce $CO_2$ emissions, and other factors. In the short term, weather, the capability to switch fuels and the influence of relative energy prices will be critical to the rate at which the allowances are retired.

Prices for ETS emissions reductions have been significantly higher than the price of project-based emissions reductions and are likely to remain that way. CERs and ERUs are typically priced €3–6 per ton of $CO_2$ equivalent. The reason that they tend to be steeply discounted vis-à-vis EUAs is that the risks of creating and delivering an emissions reduction from a developing country or EIT are substantially higher than from a cap-and-trade program among industrialized countries with well-established regulatory, industrial and financial systems. To the extent that CERs and ERUs are brought into the ETS, the overall cost of GHG reductions will be lower and, consistent with the UNFCCC and Kyoto Protocol goals, the less-wealthy countries will benefit from cleaner development.

**Figure 5.6:**    2005 EUA carbon price and volumes

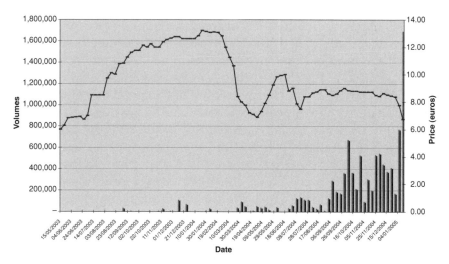

*Source:* Peter Koster, European Climate Exchange, London, February 2, 2005

## Assessment and outlook for the ETS

The EU's launch of the first large-scale, regional emissions-trading program is a tremendous political achievement, and it marks the realization of a decade-long effort to design and implement a cross-border market mechanism to serve an environmental goal. In addition, the inclusion of carbon dioxide emission credits from JI and CDM projects further reflects government and business initiatives to use market mechanisms to meet emissions-reduction goals. These initiatives also prepare the way for an international scheme.

But a venture that includes 25 participating countries, covers multiple industrial sectors and 12,000 point sources, and has a short timeframe for implementation, poses significant challenges. The varying strengths of environmental institutions across the heterogeneous EU further complicate implementation and create concerns about the potential equity and environmental integrity implications.

Many EU countries are not yet on track to meet Kyoto's binding targets, and only a handful have launched domestic schemes. The financial costs of developing a regional emissions-trading market and meeting its reduction target will be significant for the EU as a whole. Successful implementation will require all member states to become familiar with the market fundamentals of emissions trading and the design elements of the EU's program, including the allowance-allocation process and monitoring and compliance issues. The EU and national governments will have to sustain major commitments to engaging in the coordination and cooperation needed to help all parties come up to speed.

But some countries, such as Germany and the U.K., are well on track to meet Kyoto targets, as shown in Figure 5.7 below. In the U.K., the switch from coal to natural gas in the early 1990s reduced

**Figure 5.7:**  Distance-to-target indicators under the EU burden-sharing agreement

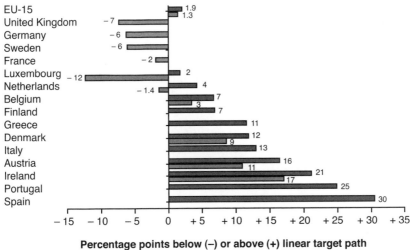

Percentage points below (–) or above (+) linear target path

■■ DTI 2002        □ DTI 2002 with use of Kyoto mechanisms

**Note:**  The distance-to-target indicator (DTI) measures the deviation of actual emissions in 2002 from a (hypothetical) linear path between base-year emissions and the burden-sharing target for 2010. A positive value suggests an under-achievement and a negative value an over-achievement by 2002. The DTI is used as an early indication of progress towards the Kyoto and Member States' burden-sharing targets. It assumes that the Member States meet their targets entirely on the basis of domestic policies and measures. Therefore, for those Member States in an advanced stage of implementing Kyoto mchanisms a second DTI estimate is presented, showing the additional effects of the use of these mechanisms in 2002.

*Source:* EEA, 2004

carbon emissions dramatically and accounted for a significant portion of the emissions reductions. In Germany, the eastern states brought into the country by reunification contributed a large 1990 base of emissions that have subsequently disappeared in the economic restructuring that has occurred in the last decade. In contrast, countries like Spain, Portugal and Ireland have been among the fastest-growing economies in the EU and therefore have been increasing their GHG emissions. They will need specific policies to reduce emissions and can expect to be active buyers of emission credits.

A number of Central and Eastern European countries that have experienced economic restructuring and downturns since the 1990s now have emissions levels lower than their 1990 levels. Their compliance under Kyoto should exact little if any financial cost, and their excess emission allowances could make them net sellers under the emissions-trading program.

Overall, the cross-border aspect of the EU ETS delivers economic and environmental gains, and its balance of mandates and incentives is serving as a powerful environmental policy instrument. It is also promoting a vigorous, new environmental financial market that builds on the U.S. experience with sulfur dioxide and nitrogen oxide markets, as discussed in earlier chapters. Most of all, the ETS provides a model for other countries and regions on how to implement emissions-trading schemes to comply with the Kyoto Protocol.

## Emissions trading in specific EU countries

Some countries initiated emissions-trading programs before the ETS was under way. Denmark was the first EU member state to start a domestic carbon-trading scheme. The government allocated emissions permits to electricity-generating facilities based on their levels of emissions between 1994 and 1998. The goals were to:

- limit domestic $CO_2$ emissions to 21% of 1990 levels by 2008–2012
- prepare for Denmark's participation in the Nordic electricity market
- guide implementation of the flexible Kyoto mechanism in the future.

The Danish government is also hoping its domestic carbon-trading scheme will provide incentives for producing electricity with more environmentally friendly technologies.

The United Kingdom launched its own voluntary emissions-trading scheme in 2002, with a national emissions-reduction target of 20% below 1990 levels. The government has offered economic incentives to companies that participate: they receive an 80% discount on the Climate Change Levy, a tax on industrial and commercial energy consumption. Over 434 inter-company trades were recorded in 2002, for a total of 2.48 million tons of $CO_2$ equivalent. Other European countries, including the Netherlands, Switzerland, Germany, Norway and Sweden, are designing their own domestic emissions-trading programs.

The Netherlands has piloted a number of JI programs to help companies fund projects that invest in renewable energy and energy efficiency in developing and Central and Eastern European countries. In May 2000, the Dutch Ministry of Economic Affairs offered a regional emissions-trading scheme called the Emission Reduction Unit Procurement Tender (ERUPT) program. Through this program, the government has been able to buy reductions in GHG emissions (carbon credits) from private projects located in economies in transition to meet its own targets. In addition, it issued separate tenders to purchase carbon credits from developing countries (CERUPT), which are not Annex I parties to the Kyoto Protocol.

## Non-EU countries

Up until the implementation of the ETS, the majority of emissions-reduction transactions involved sales from transitional economies and developing countries. Sizeable buyers such as the Dutch procurement funds (CERUPT/ERUPT) and the World Bank Prototype Carbon Fund (PCF) have been the principal purchasers of CERs and ERUs.

The share of all emissions-reduction sales involving JI and CDM projects rose from 38% to 60% in 2002, and to 91% over the first three quarters of 2003. The majority of these are in Latin America, Asia (particularly India and China), and former Soviet Union countries such as Russia and Ukraine. Fewer transactions have involved projects in the poorer countries of Asia and Africa. This raises challenges to find means to expand the reach of the Clean

Development Mechanism to the poorer countries to ensure that the mechanism operates more equitably. Given the importance of the CDM to the countries that host such projects and to the industrialized countries that need their lower-cost carbon credits, substantial effort is being committed to expanding the relevance of the mechanism in poorer countries.

The U.S. and Australia, unlike other Annex I countries, did not ratify the Kyoto Protocol; nevertheless, both have programs under way to reduce GHG emissions. In Australia, the New South Wales GHG Abatement Scheme began in January 2003. The only regional emissions-trading scheme in Australia, it imposes mandatory GHG emissions-reduction targets on all New South Wales electricity retailers and other parties. Participants can trade abatement certificates to meet their requirements. Transaction volumes in this market have been low so far, with prices ranging from A\$6–7/tCO$_2$e (equivalent to US\$3–4).

In the United States, the individual states are leading the way. California has a well-developed registry system that is tracking emissions and reductions. Oregon has a carbon-offset investment fund that purchases emissions reductions. Massachusetts and New Hampshire have taken steps to develop cap-and-trade systems which are currently in the rulemaking stage, determining the structure of the trading system. Under the Regional Greenhouse Gas Initiative, eight Northeastern states are developing a regional GHG market, with CO$_2$ emissions from the electricity-generation sector its first target. A model rule that each state can adapt was issued in April 2005, with a regional registry system to follow in 2006 or 2007 and a regional cap-and-trade system further down the road.

Independent of state initiatives, voluntary programs and commitments from individual companies characterize the current U.S. market environment, which is largely buyer-driven. A few companies, such as Entergy and DuPont, have been the primary source of demand for Verified Emissions Reduction credits, which are credits transacted in voluntary programs. These and other companies are voluntarily participating in programs such as the EPA Climate Leaders, the U.S. Department of Energy Climate Challenge, and the Chicago Climate Exchange (CCX) to gain experience with emissions trading and to demonstrate their commitment to reducing emissions.

The CCX is a self-regulating exchange based on voluntary but legally binding commitments by its members, who currently number over 40. Only members can trade credits through CCX's electronic exchange, and they can trade emissions-reduction credits derived from projects in Canada, the U.S., Mexico and Brazil. Trading began in December 2003. Although volume has been limited, final prices have been around US$0.98 for the 2003 vintage and US$0.84 for the 2005 vintage. (Vintage is the year in which the emission reduction occurs.)

Because the U.S. and Australia are not parties to the Kyoto Protocol, their emission reductions are not recognized under the Protocol or the EU ETS. Thus, U.S. and Australian emissions-reduction credits cannot be exported to the ETS and are excluded from the bulk of the international emissions-trading markets.

## Prospects for progress

While GHG markets are emerging, the future of the Kyoto Protocol remains uncertain. The real financial costs of, and obstacles to, Annex I countries meeting their emissions-reduction commitments have yet to fully materialize, and Kyoto's failure to designate binding emissions-reduction targets for developing countries, especially China and India, constitutes a major weakness that must be rectified.

These uncertainties will directly affect the development of Kyoto's international regime. The EU is eager to establish talks on the future of global emissions regulation after 2012, the end of the current Kyoto Protocol target period, and preliminary talks, led by the United Kingdom, began towards the end of 2005. The EU hopes to negotiate more stringent targets for industrial nations and possible targets for developing nations. But the U.S. and a coalition of developing countries remain strongly opposed, clouding the prospects for progress.

# Overview of the Carbon Exchanges

The EU did not invent emissions trading, despite what the European news media have said. As we have seen, the U.S. began trading emissions for sulfur dioxide in March 1995 under the oversight of the U.S. EPA, and added NOx trading in 1999 as a federal program.

Emissions trading was made in America, and proposed by the U.S. delegation at the Rio Climate Convention Treaty in 1992. The U.S. has the most advanced emissions-trading markets in the world, trading US$3 billion in notional value $SO_2$ allowances each year as current prices have touched US$800 per ton. It also has the most advanced NOx markets in the world, with allowances trading at up to US$40,000 per ton last summer in the Houston/Galveston area. Also the RECLAIM market for southern California air quality has active $SO_2$ and NOx markets. These market-based solutions are now being embraced by several green hedge funds trading $SO_2$, NOx, carbon and renewable-energy credits, as well as by emitters. After all, emissions trading is also about speculation.

At present, credits for GHG emissions are traded in nine notable exchanges/markets, all of which, with the exception of the European Union Emissions Trading Scheme, are commercial exchanges.

- The Chicago Climate Exchange (CCX), which opened on December 12, 2003

- The Chicago Climate Futures Exchange, a CCX subsidiary, which opened on December 10, 2004
- NYMEX, the New York Mercantile Exchange — based in New York and London (U.K.)
- The European Union Emissions Trading Scheme (EU ETS), which opened on January 1, 2005
- The European Climate Exchange (ECX), a CCX subsidiary based in London, which opened on April 22, 2005
- Nord Pool, which began trading and clearing European Union Allowances (EUA) on November 2, 2004
- Powernext, the power and carbon exchange in France
- EEX, the energy exchange in Germany
- EXAA, the Austrian energy exchange

Participants in these markets include the following:

- companies that want to buy emissions allowances to achieve compliance
- companies that want to sell their own surplus allowances for profit
- municipalities and other units of government
- financial institutions that trade for profit
- private individual investors
- projects that have been created under the Kyoto Protocol.

These markets are similar to the U.S. $SO_2$ and NOx markets discussed earlier. Together they demonstrate that cap-and-trade schemes are an effective tool for helping individual parties achieve their emissions-reduction targets and for achieving overall reductions in emissions — in both regulated and unregulated markets. This chapter sketches the origins and development of these markets and explains how they operate.

# Chicago Climate Exchange (www.chicagoclimatex.com)

## *Mission and origins*

The CCX is a voluntary but legally binding GHG emissions-trading program intended to encourage and develop the institutions and skills needed to manage GHG emissions in the absence of government regulation and to demonstrate that companies will reduce emissions voluntarily. Its mission is to "provide members from the private and public sectors with cost-effective methods for reducing their greenhouse gas emissions by building and operating a market-based emissions-reduction and trading program that is flexible, has low transaction costs, is environmentally rigorous and rewards environmental innovation".

The Exchange grew out of a feasibility study conducted in 2000 by Northwestern's Kellogg Graduate School of Management and Environmental Financial Products under a grant from the Joyce Foundation in Chicago. The study concluded that a pilot program for a North American trading market was feasible for unregulated emissions. In August 2001, another grant permitted the researchers to examine how a market could be created. Forming an advisory board and recruiting firms to help develop market rules were among the principal tasks. On December 12, 2003, CCX began continuous electronic trading of GHG emission allowances.

## Membership

While participation in the CCX is voluntary, many members have joined in order to publicly express their commitment to environmental values — both in terms of corporate social responsibility and to demonstrate the responsible management of environmental risks that could give them a competitive advantage. Participation also motivates members to increase their energy efficiency and learn how to manage emissions better — lessons likely to be useful if federal and/or state governments do regulate GHG emissions.

CCX members act as buyers (usually companies or municipalities that emit GHG gases); sellers, who have emissions offsets; and traders, who help provide market liquidity.

CCX offers four classes of membership:

- Members, who emit GHGs from facilities within North America
- Associate Members, who have small or no direct GHG emissions but commit to CCX compliance by offsetting business-related emissions
- Participant Members are offset providers who are project owners or implementers, registered aggregators, or parties selling exchange offsets, or liquidity providers who are trader groups, brokers or market makers

- Exchange Participants, who are non-U.S. parties that have an account for acquiring traded allowances.

As of March 2005, CCX had 72 members. Over 40% were liquidity providers.

### Emissions-reduction targets

All CCX members have committed to reducing their $CO_2$ emissions by 4% below their average 1998–2001 baseline by 2006, with a 1% reduction increase each year beginning in 2003. Total $CO_2$ target reductions for 2003 were set at 223,860,259 metric tons, using a baseline average of 226,121,473 metric tons. But CCX members reduced emissions to 205,970,919 metric tons in 2003 — 8% beyond their targets for the first compliance year. Only two members did not meet their targets.

Companies can meet their targets by physically reducing their own emissions on site; by purchasing allowances from other members of the exchange; and by purchasing credits from offsetting projects such as landfill and agricultural methane sequestration in soils and forest biomass, as explained below

### Units of trade and data management

While, technically, CCX covers the six GHGs listed in the Kyoto Protocol only $CO_2$ is monitored and offset through CCX. All trades, measurements, price quotes and reporting on CCX are in metric tons of $CO_2$ equivalents. All other gases are converted into metric ton $CO_2$ equivalents based on the 100-year Global Warming Potential (GWP) established by the Intergovernmental Panel on Climate Change. The GWP permits comparison of how much heat each GHG traps in the atmosphere. The $CO_2$ equivalent number is the ratio of heat trapped by one unit mass of the gas to that of one unit mass of $CO_2$ over a specified period of time

To standardize trades, CCX developed the Carbon Financial Instrument, equivalent to 100 metric tons of $CO_2$. The Instrument comes in two forms:

- Exchange Allowances (XAs), issued to both Exchange and Associate Members according to their baseline emissions for carbon sequestration in forests and reductions in electricity use.

- Exchange Offsets (XOs), issued by other mitigation projects registered with CCX by Participant Members. Exchange Offsets are always issued after $CO_2$ reduction has occurred and the requisite documentation has been presented. Initially, eligible projects included the following:

  - landfill-methane destruction in the U.S.
  - agricultural-methane destruction in the U.S.
  - carbon sequestration in U.S. forestry projects
  - carbon sequestration in U.S. agricultural soils
  - fuel switching, landfill-methane destruction, renewable energy, and forestry projects in Brazil.

All Carbon Financial Instruments are recorded in a registry maintained by CCX with a designated annual vintage and can be banked from year to year. Reporting is done quarterly. To help increase price transparency, data have recently been added to Bloomberg, the global data vendor, making the data accessible to non-CCX members.

CCX is also making efforts to work with other groups towards harmonizing measurements and audits for the market as a whole. CCX members can now submit data for use in the World Economic Forum's Global Greenhouse Gas Register, as long as they also submit relevant data on indirect emissions and emissions from jurisdictions not covered by CCX. Global harmonization of all these conflicting standards for greenhouse gases is the crux of the problem preventing a global fungible greenhouse gas regime from coming into place.

### How the CCX manages trades

The CCX Electronic Platform is open for trades from 10am to 12:30pm (Central Standard Time), Monday through Friday. The National Association of Security Dealers, a private-sector regulator of the U.S. securities industry, audits members' baselines and annual emissions and regulates the CCX Trading System, monitoring for fraud and market manipulation.

- *The Electronic Trading Platform*: Trading occurs only on this platform, and only account-holding CCX members are eligible to trade on it. The platform is a price-transparent market, with all order sizes, market depth and a market ticker viewable at all times. Trades can be executed on the open market, with exchange clearing or bilateral trades negotiated privately apart from the platform.

- *The Clearing and Settlement Platform*: This platform processes transactions from the Electronic Platform, to net out positions and produce payment instructions. The Clearing and Settlement Platform also provides daily statements to members.
- *The CCX Registry*: In conjunction with the two platforms, this creates real-time data for all account holders.

## Price and volume

Because CCX is a voluntary program, prices and trade volumes are lower than they would be in a regulated market. But prices per metric ton of $CO_2$ reached US$2 in the fourth quarter of 2004, a marked increase over the third-quarter average of US$0.96. Similarly, fourth-quarter trading volume constituted 40% of the total trading volume to date, an increase from 15.7% of total volume in the third quarter.

**Figure 6.1:**   CCX 2004 vintage prices and volumes

| 1.  CCX Carbon Financial Instruments — Market Data March 2005 | | | | | | |
|---|---|---|---|---|---|---|
| Vintage | Open | High | Low | Last | Chg | Volume |
| 2003 | $1.61 | $1.61 | $1.52 | $1.52 | −0.10 | 3,400 |
| 2004 | $1.60 | $1.61 | $1.54 | $1.54 | −0.08 | 4,000 |
| 2005 | $1.60 | $1.60 | $1.50 | $1.50 | −0.12 | 14,700 |
| 2006 | – | – | – | $1.65 | – | – |

Price units: Per metric ton of $CO_2$
Volume units: Metric tons of $CO_2$
Change: Based on previous month's last traded price

*Source:* Chicago Climate Exchange

**Figure 6.2:** Current prices

**Carbon Financial Instrument (CFI) daily price limits**

| April 4, 2005 | | | | |
|---|---|---|---|---|
| **Product** | **Contract** | **Basis** | **Minimum** | **Maximum** |
| CCX CFI | Vintage 2003 | $1.50 | $1.27 | $1.73 |
| CCX CFI | Vintage 2004 | $1.50 | $1.27 | $1.73 |
| CCX CFI | Vintage 2005 | $1.50 | $1.27 | $1.73 |
| CCX CFI | Vintage 2006 | $1.50 | $1.27 | $1.73 |

Prices quoted in metric tons of $CO_2$.
1 Carbon Financial Instrument (CFI) is equivalent to 100 metric tons of $CO_2$

*Source:* Chicago Climate Exchange

**Figure 6.3:** CCX monthly volume in metric tons

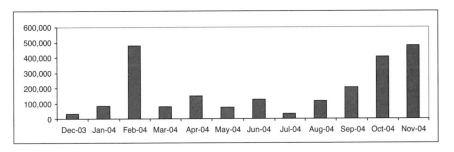

*Source:* Chicago Climate Exchange

# Chicago Climate Futures Exchange (www.chicagoclimatex.com)

In late 2004, CCX developed a subsidiary called the Chicago Climate Futures Exchange. On December 10, 2004, that exchange launched Sulfur Financial Instruments which standardized and cleared futures contracts for trading sulfur dioxide ($SO_2$) emissions allowances. $SO_2$, a regulated emission, has been traded over the counter since 1990. As a futures contract, Sulfur Financial Instruments are designed to help manage price risk and fluctuation of $SO_2$ allowances in conjunction with over-the-counter trades. Contracts are for 25 tons of $SO_2$ emission allowances, which has been criticized by industry participants as being too small and which, they say, should be 100 tons. In June 2005 the New York Mercantile Exchange launched sulfur dioxide and nitrous oxide futures, with contract sizes of 100 tons and 10 tons, respectively. Both contracts are listed for 36 consecutive months forward, starting with the August 2005 contract. These will be physically settled through the EPA's Allowance Tracking System.

# NYMEX (www.nymex.com)

While the impact of global climate change poses a significant market challenge for both the energy and agricultural industries, these industries have incredible market opportunities in renewable energy and emerging green financial markets. The U.S. has been the leader in establishing liquid environmental-trading markets for sulfur dioxide since 1995 and for NOx since 1999, and now has the opportunity to introduce financial futures for these commodities. Greenhouse gases offer a global opportunity for creating carbon as a fungible commodity in much the same way as has happened for crude oil. The New York Mercantile Exchange, with its dominance as the energy futures exchange, its clearinghouse function and brand recognition, has the opportunity to become the premier green exchange. The market opportunity is US$3 trillion, with environmental financial contracts touching all NYMEX fossil-fuel contracts in oil, gas, power and coal. Since all its energy futures contracts are touched by emissions, it seems likely that it will also extend its trading platform to both carbon trading and renewable energy as those markets mature. The exchange never likes to be the first mover and would rather see trading volumes and market liquidity before entering the market. This is unlike the ICE Futures markets (formerly the International Petroleum Exchange), which is moving forward with its ECX venture to trade carbon.

# The European Union Emissions Trading Scheme

As described in the previous chapter, the EU ETS is a cap-and-trade program designed to reduce GHG emissions in compliance with Kyoto Protocol targets.

The EU ETS is organized around two timeframes that correspond with those of the Kyoto Protocol. Its goal is to reduce $CO_2$ emissions to 8% below 1990 levels by the start of the 2008–2012 time period, and to achieve this at the lowest possible cost and with the greatest possible efficiency. The scheme is designed to achieve the lowest possible abatement costs. As described in detail in Chapter 4, the ETS permits both Joint Implementation and Clean Development Mechanism projects.

The EU must lower emissions by 8% overall. The percentage reductions assigned to each country aren't sensitive to scale, so it's necessary to look at the tons of $CO_2$ that must be reduced to determine where the primary buyers will come from. Larger, more-developed countries like Germany and Italy will share the bulk of actual reductions. The fact that a large share of the burden falls on relatively few countries makes accurate competitive pricing all the more important to guarantee reaching overall EU targets.

Under the umbrella of the EU ETS several exchanges have emerged to offer a trading platform for trading spot and futures/forward markets in European emissions credits. The scheme is not itself a trading platform. Therefore, private ventures have come forward to offer them. In the rest of this chapter, we take a detailed look at some of the more noteworthy European exchanges, all of which offer trading in ETS credits.

# The European Climate Exchange
# (www.europeanclimateexchange.com)

## The players

While the EU ETS has set the ground rules for carbon dioxide emissions reductions for the EU, the reality is that several exchanges have sprung up to participate in the actual trading scheme. One is the European Climate Exchange (ECX), a subsidiary of the Chicago Climate Exchange. It was launched on April 22, 2005 and has created a venture in which its trades will use both the electronic technology and the clearing mechanism of the IntercontinentalExchange's

ICE Futures (formerly the International Petroleum Exchange), the second-largest energy-futures exchange in the world. The ICE Futures exchange went totally electronic on April 7, 2005 and closed its floor-trading operation. This turned out to be a good move with volume increasing, a move watched closely by its arch competitor, NYMEX, which launched a London trading floor in September 2005, only to close floor trading and go electronic in the first quarter of 2006.

The significance of this is that NYMEX is not only the predominant global energy-futures exchange but has a very successful OTC clearing operation through Clearport and, since June 2005, includes $SO_2$ and nitrous oxide futures contracts. NYMEX could also clear carbon dioxide contracts in the U.S. as well as in Europe and take the credit and counterparty risk.

The ECX offers carbon financial instruments (CFIs) to companies all over the world. ECX CFIs are advanced, low-cost and financially guaranteed tools for trading emission allowances issued under the EU ETS.

ECX products are listed by ICE Futures and traded on ICE Futures' electronic platform, offering a pan-European platform for carbon emissions trading with standard contracts and clearing guarantees provided by LCH.Clearnet.

More than 50 leading businesses, including global companies such as ABN AMRO, Barclays, BP, Calyon, E.ON UK, Electrabel, Fortis, ICAP, Morgan Stanley and Shell, have signed up to trade ECX products.

The ECX has agreed to cooperate with France-based Powernext to give participants access to both ECX's futures and Powernext's spot contracts on a single screen.

The ECX was selected because many emitters are members of the IPE. ECX trades made on the Interchange are executed and financially guaranteed by London Clearing House's LCH.Clearnet Limited, eliminating the need for a third-party credit-risk-management program.

Futures contracts are traded on ECX. A futures contract is an agreement on the part of the buyer and the seller that calls for the seller (called "the short") to deliver to the buyer (called "the long") a specified quantity and quality of an identified commodity, at a fixed time in the future, at a price agreed to when the contract is first entered into. For the ECX CFI futures contracts traded on ICE Futures, the underlying market is the EU ETS. ECX CFIs have the normal characteristics of futures contracts and are financially guaranteed by the LCH.Clearnet.

Each instrument futures contract is for 1,000 tons of $CO_2$ emissions; the minimum price per ton is €0.05 and each contract is for a minimum of €50. Eligible emissions contracts are delivered to EU member-state registry accounts with IPE. Contracts are quarterly for the first time period of the EU ETS and annual for the second period. EU ETS accepts Certified Emissions Reductions (CERs), which come from CDM projects under the Kyoto Protocol, but for regulatory and logistical reasons does not allow trading in CERs.

Commodity markets need simplicity to engender replication of trade and they need focused liquidity. The complexities involved in implementing the Kyoto Protocol cannot be overemphasized. Getting these markets to work is a major challenge, and the proliferation of exchanges in Europe could be an impediment to market liquidity. It may be that the ECX has the best chance of achieving market liquidity because of its link to the ICE. ECX is working with EU member states with the largest emissions — France, Germany and the U.K. — to develop smooth reporting of allocations and efficient trade clearing

Both the CCX and the ECX have developed standardization and verification protocols on open exchange platforms through the creation of the Carbon Financial Instrument and partnerships with other exchanges. While CCX paves the way for North America's as-yet unregulated emissions trading, ECX provides market consolidation that will lower the marginal cost of abatement for parties required to reduce emissions.

Early signs of success for the ICE (IPE) and ECX venture were reported on October 6, 2005. Emissions Market and ECX/ICE (IPE) both achieved record volumes the previous day, with the ECX celebrating over 2.3 million tons of carbon dioxide traded on the IPE. It was reported that 2,312,000 tons were traded through ECX CFI futures contracts on the IPE — 857,000 ECX CFI futures contracts traded on the electronic platform with a further 1,455,000 tons in OTC trades registered for clearing via the IPE's EFP facility.

## Using futures contracts to hedge risk

Hedging is the act of taking equal and opposite positions in the cash and futures markets to protect a cash-market position against loss arising from price fluctuation. It is frequently referred to as a

**Figure 6.4:** Daily closing prices for EU ETS and volumes for delivery on 1$^{st}$ December 2005

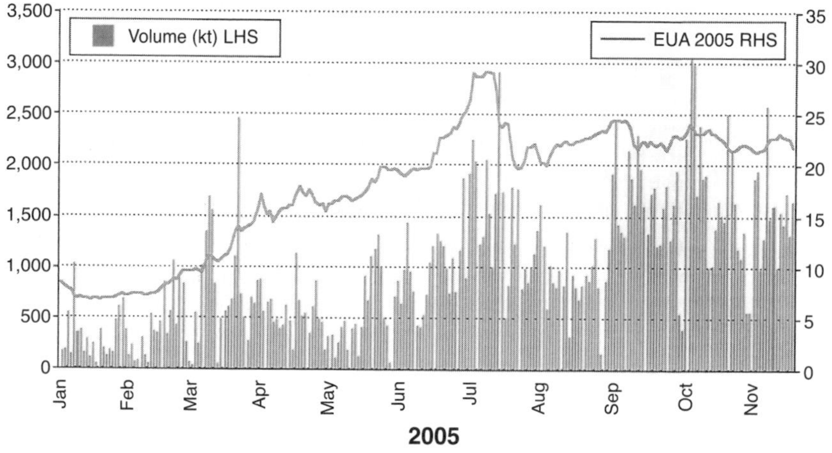

Source: Point Carbon

temporary substitute for a purchase or sale. In anticipation of buying or selling the cash commodity, the hedger buys or sells futures contracts.

Because the cash and futures prices tend to rise and fall together, the futures market provides the medium for commodity owners and users to hedge against adverse price risk. With opposite positions in the cash and futures markets, price losses in one market will be approximately offset by gains in the other.

There are two types of hedges: the buying, or "long", hedge, and the selling, or "short", hedge. In a buying hedge, futures contracts are bought in anticipation of a later purchase in the cash market. A buying hedge is used by individuals to protect against an increase in the price of the cash commodity that they will buy (or expect to buy) at a future date.

The selling hedge is used by those who are trying to protect against declines in the price of a commodity they own or will produce for sale at a later date. For example, if an energy company has sold futures contracts against its emissions-allowance inventory, it has established opposite positions in the cash and futures markets. It is long in the cash market because it owns allowances, and it is short in the futures market because it has sold futures contracts. If prices decline, the hedger will realize a lower price in the cash market when it sells the allowances. However, this loss will be offset by the profit realized when it buys back the futures contract at a lower price.

## Nord Pool (www.nordpool.com)

ECX is not the only exchange participating in the EU ETS. The Nordic Power Exchange (also known as Nord Pool) started trading and clearing European Union Allowances (EUA) on March 1, 2005 when national registries were listed. The EUA forward contracts listed on Nord Pool will have physical delivery. Nord Pool Clearing will act as counterparty in all exchange trades, guaranteeing cash settlement of the contracts. Nord Pool will use its Power Click technology platform, which it has installed with many of its customers across Europe. Nord Pool is the most successful electricity-futures exchange in the world and also clears OTC contracts but, compared to ECX and Powernext, has struggled to capture trading volume as quickly as the competition.

## Powernext (www.powernext.fr)

Powernext Carbon offers an organized spot market enabling exchange of allowances and non-compliance risk management.
This market is based on four principles:

- straight-through process from transaction to delivery
- price transparency
- non-discriminatory access to the market and complete anonymity for participants
- guarantee of transaction performance based on a settlement mechanism which secures payment and quota delivery.

On December 14, 2004, Caisse des Dépôts, Euronext and Powernext signed a letter of intent to pool their expertise in setting up a spot market of carbon dioxide equivalent tons. Under this arrangement, Powernext operates Powernext Carbon market, authorizes members, provides a continuous trading platform and lays down the market rules. A department of Caisse des Dépôts — separate from the function of Registry — manages the delivery-versus-payment (DVP) mechanism and acts as intermediary, guaranteeing the payment and delivery commitments agreed by members while trading. Euronext is involved in developing the model and lends its authority to the project.

Powernext Carbon is a spot market of carbon dioxide equivalent tons quoted in euros. These contracts are governed by the French commercial law for trading in goods (in this case, "movable property") and are not covered by provisions applicable to markets for financial instruments.

As of November 22, 2005, there were 30 active members in Powernext's Carbon Market, as shown below in Figure 6.6.

At the beginning of the trading session members have a trading limit comprising their current cash balance (as determined at 5pm the previous day) plus any authorized overdraft, as determined in accordance with the cash account agreement. They also have a delivery limit; that is, the total quantity of allowances recorded on the allowance account by CDC between 9am on the day in question and 8pm on the previous day.

If a member uses a settlement bank, the latter has a trading limit whereas the member has his own limit, known as the "member limit".

Trading is a two-phase process. First, participants submit bids, or asks, via their orders, which specify a given quantity and price. When one order is matched with an opposite order from another member, a transaction is created. This generates a delivery instruction, on receiving which the Caisse des Dépôts controls the limit of the

**Figure 6.5:**   The Powernext Carbon contract

| Contract Description | |
|---|---|
| Product | European Union Allowance |
| Place of delivery | EU-25 (on condition that national registries are interfaced with the DVP system) |
| Trading unit | Ton of $CO_2$ equivalent |
| Price tick | 0.01 € |
| Nominal | 1 lot = 1,000 tons |
| Quotation mode | Continuous via Global Vision |
| Trading hours | 10:00 am to 3:00 pm Continental European Time (CET) on business days |

**Figure 6.6:** Membership of Powernext's Carbon Market

|  | 30 active members on 22 November 2005 | Start Date |
|---|---|---|
| 1 | ACCORD ENERGY LIMITED | 24 June 2005 |
| 2 | CARBON CAPITAL MARKETS | 24 June 2005 |
| 3 | ELECTRABEL SA | 24 June 2005 |
| 4 | ENDESA TRADING SA | 24 June 2005 |
| 5 | GASELYS | 24 June 2005 |
| 6 | GREENSTREAM NETWORK LTD | 24 June 2005 |
| 7 | SNET | 24 June 2005 |
| 8 | SOCIETE GENERALE SA | 24 June 2005 |
| 9 | TOTAL GAS AND POWER LIMITED | 24 June 2005 |
| 10 | BGC INTERNATIONAL | 01 July 2005 |
| 11 | VELCAN ENERGY | 11 July 2005 |
| 12 | NOVOSZAD & WINZER OEG (CLIMATE CORPORATION) | 19 July 2005 |
| 13 | UNION FENOSA GENERACION SA | 22 July 2005 |
| 14 | IBERDROLA GENERACION SAU | 27 July 2005 |
| 15 | BNP PARIBAS | 29 July 2005 |
| 16 | RWE TRADING GMBH | 4 August 2005 |
| 17 | ENDESA GENERACION SA | 11 August 2005 |
| 18 | DUBUS SA | 24 August 2005 |
| 19 | TOTSA TOTAL OIL TRADING SA | 7 September 2005 |
| 20 | COMPAGNIE DE CHAUFFAGE INTERCOMMUNALE DE L'AGGLOMERATION GRENOBLOISE | 16 September 2005 |
| 21 | CLIMATE CHANGE MARKETS LIMITED | 27 September 2005 |
| 22 | AARE-TESSIN LIMITED FOR ELECTRICITY (ATEL) | 3 October 2005 |
| 23 | ENEL TRADE S.p.A. | 4 October 2005 |
| 24 | NUON ENERGY TRADE WHOLESALE N.V. | 6 October 2005 |
| 25 | BARCLAYS BANK Plc | 20 October 2005 |
| 26 | AEM TRADING Srl | 25 October 2005 |
| 27 | SAGACARBON | 3 November 2005 |
| 28 | VICAT | 10 November 2005 |
| 29 | EDISON TRADING S.p.A. | 17 November 2005 |
| 30 | SVD 9 (newly VEETRA, subsidiary of Dalkia, energy division of VEOLIA ENVIRONMENT) | 22 November 2005 |

buyer's cash account or that of his settlement bank in the amount of the transaction and the limit of the seller's allowance account in the volume of allowances of the transaction. At this stage, the Caisse des Dépôts makes a commitment to transfer the allowances to the buyer's account and the cash to the seller's account. The trade is rejected if the buyer does not have sufficient funds or if the seller does not have sufficient allowances.

Once the trade is validated, the Caisse des Dépôts completes the process by transferring allowances from the seller's account to its transit account and from its transit account to the buyer's account.

The trade is delivered once the CITL (The European Commission system that keeps track of emission-credit transfers and acts as a central registry for keeping legal records of such transfers) sends official notice that the transfer is complete. This triggers the debiting of the buyer's cash account and crediting the Caisse des Dépôts's transit cash account and the seller's cash account in the amount of the transaction.

## EEX (www.eex.de)

In October 2005, the European Energy Exchange AG (EEX) launched futures trading in EU emission allowances, having adopted the required changes of the rules and regulations the previous month, thus paving the way for the $CO_2$ Derivatives Market. The newly listed European Carbon Futures are denominated in 1,000 EU emission allowances of the first and/or second trading period. The tradable maturity is the month of December for each of the following years, up to and including 2012. EEX had already introduced a spot market for emission allowances in March 2005.

These futures will enable the trading participants to hedge prices of emission allowances, with the EEX clearing house assuming the counterparty risk. The EEX also offers clearing of futures transactions concluded over the counter between counterparties. Within the framework of this so-called OTC clearing, EEX cooperates with several renowned brokers and wishes to repeat the success achieved in OTC clearing of futures transactions in German electricity.

The EEX operates a spot and a derivatives market for energy and energy-related products and, with 128 trading participants from 16 countries, boasts the highest number of trading participants and the biggest turnover in Europe. In addition to electricity and futures

**Figure 6.7:**   EEX contract specifications for futures on EU Allowances

| ISIN-Code/WKN/ Exchange Code/ Name | | | | |
|---|---|---|---|---|
| | DE000A0E4PX2 | A0E4PX | F1PE | First Period European Carbon Future |
| | E000A0E4PY0 | A0E4PY | F2PE | Second Period European Carbon Future |

| | |
|---|---|
| **Object of the Contract** | Delivery and acquisition of EU Allowances<br>— for the three-year period beginning on January 1, 2005 (First Period European Carbon Future) and<br>— for the five-year period beginning on January 1, 2008 (Second Period European Carbon Future) |
| **EU Allowance** | Permits to emit one ton of carbon dioxide or one ton of a carbon dioxide equivalent within the meaning of the directive 2003/87/EC from October 13, 2003 and of the national regulations based on said directive, which are kept by a national register within the meaning of art. 19 and which can be transferred within the scope of the said directive (EU Allowance).<br><br>Third Country permissions within the meaning of art. 25 of the directive can be put on a par by the Exchange Management Board with EU Allowances, if these are absolutely equal to EU Allowances. Emission Reduction Units (ERU) and Certified Emissions Reductions (CER) are not equal to EU Allowances. |
| **Contract Size** | 1,000 EU Allowances |
| **Pricing** | Two decimal digits after the point; this corresponds to €0.01 per EU Allowance |
| **Minimum Price Fluctuation** | €0.01/EU Allowances, this corresponds to €10 per contract |
| **Tradable Delivery Periods** | — First Period European Carbon Future: December 2006 and December 2007<br>— Second Period European Carbon Future: Each December of the years 2008 to 2012 |
| **Last Trading Day** | The penultimate exchange day of each November. |

**Figure 6.7:**  *Continued*

| Delivery Day | On the second settlement day after the last trading day. i.e the first exchange day in December. |
|---|---|
| DEHSt Account | EEX AG keeps an account in trust for all trading participants at the national register (DEHSt) which has the effect that the respective trading participants own proportionate part of the total stock of EU Allowances recorded in this account. |
| Fulfillment | Fulfillment is carried out by means of transferring the EU Allowances within the internal inventory accounts of EEX AG and of the changes in the proportionate part of the total stock of EU Allowances in the account at DEHSt kept in trust by EEX AG.<br><br>Upon the payment of the purchase price, the buyer of a Future Contract on emission allowances purchases on the delivery day the corresponding proportionate part of the total stock of EU Allowances which are booked in the account of EEX AG at DEHSt. The seller of a Future Contract on emission allowances transfers his corresponding proportionate part of the total stock, which is booked in the account of EEX AG at DEHSt. |
| Removal | Every co-holder of the total stock of EU Allowances in the account of EEX AG at DEHSt is entitled to demand the transfer to an account to be specified by the trading participant at a suitable national register of EEX on the second exchange day after said request at any time, however, no later than as of March 31, 2008 for the first trading period starting on January 1, 2005 and no later than as of March 31, 2013 for the second trading period starting on January 1, 2008 |

options on electricity, trading in $CO_2$ emission allowances commenced in March 2005. The range of services provided by EEX is complemented with related services such as the joint clearing of exchange transactions and over-the-counter transactions (OTC clearing).

# EXAA (www.exaa.at)

Austria's electricity market was fully liberalized on October 1, 2001. Just one year later, the gas market was also opened up, making Austria one of the front-runners in the process of liberalizing energy markets in the European Union. EXAA (Energy Exchange Austria), located in Graz, is an essential component of the new market system in Austria. EXAA's shareholders comprise the Vienna Stock Exchange (Wiener Börse AG) as the commodity exchange, system providers and electricity utilities.

With its fully electronic trading platform, the Austrian Energy Exchange ensures easy access for all market players. Small electricity utilities, as well as big electricity traders and industrial consumers, can enjoy the advantages of trading at the exchange via the Internet. Naturally, this is not limited to Austrian market participants. In general, it is readily available to any company that wants to take an active part in the European electricity market. In the future, EXAA also intends to address neighboring regions, especially EU-candidate countries from Southeastern Europe.

With the primary goal of ensuring transparency in the organization of the Austrian electricity market, spot trading was introduced according to plan and officially launched on March 21, 2002.

EXAA extended its portfolio of products traded by adding $CO_2$ Emission Certificates in June 2005. (The EU directive 2003/87/EG allows trading with emission allowances.)

According to the Austrian emissions certificate law (*Emissionzertifikategesetz*), carbon emissions allowances are considered as goods, which enables the trading of those certificates at EXAA as a commodity exchange.

In fact, across most of the world $CO_2$ and other emission credits are considered to be assets which could be applied in repo finance structures to obtain cheaper secured lending from banks.

As in the energy market, EXAA guarantees as a central counterparty (the central counterparty assumes the financial risk of default by sellers and buyers and guarantees the anonymity of deals concluded) the fulfillment of all open positions. Furthermore, it guarantees the physical delivery of the certificates.

Eight participants kicked off the market, including companies which are affected by the Kyoto Protocol. Electricity utilities, such as the Swiss Energiegesellschaft Laufenburg AG (EGL) and the

Österreichische Elektrizitätswirtschafts-AG (VERBUND), have been members at the EXAA energy spot market for a long time. Remarkably, two affected Austrian industrial companies, Tondach Gleinstätten AG and the glass manufacturer D. Swarovski & Co., will take part in trading.

At EXAA, $CO_2$ Certificates that are used for covering emissions in the current pre-Kyoto trial period from 2005 to 2007 (EUAs) are traded. The auction takes place on Tuesday each week. As well as the proven trading system from the EXAA Energy Market, the new trading engine for $CO_2$ certificates uses Internet communication.

## So many emissions, too many exchanges?

In addition to these exchanges that have introduced greenhouse gas emissions trading, another new venture, Climex, is planning to list contracts based on carbon dioxide emissions in Amsterdam. This operation forms part of a comprehensive Dutch initiative to trade carbon, renewable-energy certifications and nitrogen oxide emissions. NewValues is behind this initiative and is backed by Rabobank, the transmission-system operator Tennet, consultancy Ecofys and several other Dutch companies. All trades will clear through APX B.V., the Amsterdam Power Exchange, to reduce credit and delivery-performance risk.

In these efforts there may be echoes of the earlier launching of a number of electricity exchanges in Europe, most of which failed to gain liquidity. It seems likely that most of these new exchanges, too, will either fail or consolidate. Perhaps the early signs are already being seen in, for example, the alliance of Powernext and ECX to allow their respective countries to trade on the same platform.

The focus of attention should be on the ECX, as it is linked to a liquid energy-futures exchange (IPE) and may rank alongside EEX for German trading. Despite all the rhetoric about a United States of Europe, it seems that the EU member nations are drifting towards their individual nationalistic tendencies. The failing of the EU was to create a single regional greenhouse gas, renewable-energy, and emissions-trading platform. That may be what arises from all these currently fragmented efforts. Only a $CO_2$ emissions-trading scheme was created, with separate country-specific renewable-energy programs. The U.K.'s renewable obligation certificates, for example, encouraged power producers in the U.K. to generate a certain amount of "green energy" and compensated them for meeting targets but fined them for failing.

It would have been better to create a pan-European renewable-energy scheme alongside the pan-European Emissions Trading Scheme, as part of an integrated European energy policy.

The Russia-Ukraine gas-supply dispute in the winter of 2005 shocked EU energy ministers into action, triggering active discussion on the topic of an integrated energy policy across Europe. This may give rise to an opportunity to discuss the integration of renewable-energy policy across Europe with emissions reductions and emissions trading. Watch this space during 2006/2007 as the EU energy ministers are certainly taking pan-European energy security and policy very seriously. We may still have borders on maps in Europe, but economically and in energy terms there are no borders. We are all increasingly integrated and cannot allow even one part of the EU to fail in its energy policy.

# Carbon Collides with Power — The European Experience

## 7

Prior to the development of carbon markets ($CO_2$ emissions), whenever electricity suppliers raised their power prices it was standard practice for them to blame high oil and gas prices for their actions. Now, however, emissions trading in Europe has radically transformed the economics of the electricity-generation business.

The U.K. gives us a clear example of this transformation. There, the gas, power and energy sector was the first to liberalize and is considered one of the most liberalized in Europe.

If we index the price movements of heavy fuel oil, crude oil (ICE Brent), coal (Amsterdam-Rotteram-Antwerp), Zeebrugge Gas, and UK Power, as shown in Figure 7.1, crude oil prices rose during 2004 and 2005, and so did U.K. Power prices. However, the gas price did not follow this upward trend. In fact, it remained pretty stable in relation to oil prices.

We can conclude, therefore, that something new made spot power prices move.

What pushed power prices higher? Well within a year of the official introduction of the EU ETS in January 2005, carbon ($CO_2$

125

**Figure 7.1:**   Fuel price movements, indexed (100) to January 2004

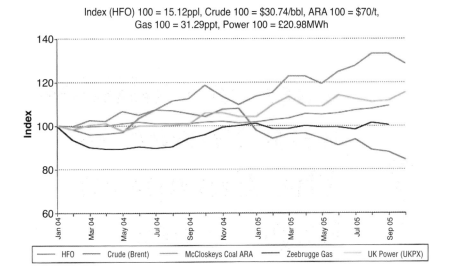

Index (HFO) 100 = 15.12ppl, Crude 100 = $30.74/bbl, ARA 100 = $70/t,
Gas 100 = 31.29ppt, Power 100 = £20.98MWh

*Source:* The McCloskey Group

emissions) had hit the power industry as the fourth dimension of the energy business.

Just as the use of "Dark" (coal to power) and "Spark" (gas to power) price spreads had been established as the standard approach to examine power-generation profitability, $CO_2$ emissions trading came along to collide with the power industry, changing everything.

The cost of emissions, like that of fuel costs, is now taken into account when determining power-station profitability. Ultimately, it determines the merit order of a plant; that is, the order in which a power company will call upon that plant to operate subject to demand and power prices. For every MWh of electricity it produces, the generator must be able to provide corresponding carbon-emission permits. The number of permits needed, of course, depends on how the MWh was generated. Coal-fired power stations produce roughly twice as much $CO_2$ emissions for each MWh produced as a gas-fired power station.

In the U.K., the majority of $CO_2$ emission allowances granted to power producers use a factor of carbon emissions of 0.947 for coal-fired power stations and 0.411 for gas-fired power stations. It is generally accepted that an average coal-fired plant operates at 36% efficiency, emitting 0.9 tons of $CO_2$ per MWh of electricity generated, whilst a gas-fired plant, with 49% efficiency, emits around 0.45 tons.

As a result, coal's usual wide price advantage over gas is drastically reduced since it must use more carbon credits per MWh, leaving the spark spread (the power produced from burning gas) much more profitable than the dark spread from coal-fired stations.

All of this is due to the EU ETS, which is designed to discourage power production from heavy carbon-emitting power plants. The mechanism of the EU ETS cap-and-trade scheme should mean that the most carbon-efficient generation sources run first and, indeed, this appears to be what is happening.

With carbon emissions playing such a key role now in determining power prices and the cost of producing power across Europe, how are the forward markets for emissions developing? What tools are becoming available for trading and how far forward can these instruments be traded in order to lock in carbon-adjusted "dark and spark" spreads?

There are five futures exchanges operating in Europe which actively trade in emissions-credits contracts. However, based on volumes recorded for the period January through September 2005, the OTC market is almost three times the size of the largest futures exchange volume.

Traders in the OTC market use three contract agreements: ISDA, IETA and EFET, which are discussed in detail in Chapter 8. The reason we mention it here is that the existence of three master trading agreements for the same underlying EU ETS emissions contract, combined with credit limits, has at times restricted the ability of firms to trade with one another during the last few years.

In addition to the OTC market, there are two key futures exchanges — the European Climate Exchange and Nord Pool — as discussed in Chapter 6. These have provided clearing services for counterparties, thus getting around the usual bilateral credit issues and avoiding problems arising when traders do not having master agreements in place to enable them to trade. These clearing mechanisms have undoubtedly improved market liquidity, especially in the forward market, with markets being made at the end of 2005 for 2008 prices in EU ETS emissions contracts.

Many key participants expect growth by 2007 to be double that of 2005. But traders and users of the market alike are asking themselves what is going to happen in Phase II of the scheme, from 2008 and beyond.

The true price for the emissions contracts in 2008 will very much depend on the balance between the actual oil, gas and coal prices at the time, the weather conditions endured during the intervening winters, and the supply side of emissions credits within the EU ETS. In addition to this, the penalty for non-compliance in Phase II increases to €100 per MT from the Phase I penalty of €40 per MT, giving a further financial incentive for companies to buy up more emissions than they need. There is a lot of talk in the marketplace that many CDM projects under the Kyoto Protocol — principally from India and China, and from South American and other developing countries — may swamp the European and other Kyoto-linked cap-and-trade schemes, putting pressure on carbon prices.

It's worth pointing out that the international regulatory organizations such as the United Nations-based UNFCCC or the European Commission, which created the GHG industry, have not established the markets in which Kyoto allowances or European allowances can trade. The decision was always to let the marketplace create its own solutions, as discussed in Chapter 6.

Thus, the UNFCCC, the Kyoto Protocol, the Marrakech Accords, the European Emissions Directive (EED) and the EU ETS *do not* specify what a tradable emissions contract should look like. The Kyoto Protocol and the EED set the parameters that define the carbon commodity that is being traded, but *do not* prescribe how that commodity should be traded in practice. Participants in any OTC deals or exchange-traded contract should therefore check carefully that the contract suits their specific purpose as it may be different every time they trade.

Concerns over delivery dates in the non-standardized emissions contracts for the EU ETS were evident in Europe in December 2005. The reason for this was that the OTC contracts settled in the markets on December 21, meaning that a firm short December 1, 2005 could not cover via buying on the ECX on exchange futures contracts, which in turn led to a noticeable price differential developing between the 2005 ECX contract and the 2005 OTC contract.

This was an issue for the market because, although there is no requirement that delivery of allowances should take place on any particular date, a convention is emerging in the market that allowances for a given year will be delivered on December 1 of that year.

With regard to the future evolution of the emissions markets, a look at recent developments in commodity markets can give some idea of what to expect.

Generally, the evolution of commodity markets has tended to followed a pattern. In very general terms, the spot trade, or short-term contracts for a specified quantity of the commodity to be delivered at a specified time, usually starts out as a marginal activity, accounting for around 10% of trade. This is often tolerated by mainstream producers and consumers only to balance fluctuations in supply and demand.

The consequence is an increase in the volume of trade taking place in the spot market. By the time spot trade reaches about 25% of total trade, typically three things happen in a commodity market:

- Spot trade contracts become standardized because traders do not want to draft new documents every time they deal and because it minimizes risk if detailed trading terms are back-to-back between suppliers and their customers.
- Spot prices become more transparent.
- Publications start to report those prices, arranged into indexes reflecting trade at the most active locations, or hubs, for physical trade.

Factors that have held prices rigid in the past no longer hold sway. Even when long-term contracts persist, counterparties begin to assess their economic performance against a new transparent spot benchmark. Frequently, to keep long-term business relationships in place, the counterparties to such deals change the pricing mechanics of their contracts to reflect a spot index and the price of the physical production becomes sensitive to spot prices.

The market becomes more volatile since price volatility, once confined to a low-volume spot market, now spreads through the whole commodity.

Volatility in the commodity price has to be managed to prevent risk to business. The more companies that enter the spot market to manage price risk, the more significant the spot volume becomes, soon outstripping the volume of physical production. This attracts market makers and speculators and the volume of trade continues to increase.

The next step in the market evolution is usually where a futures market is developed. This is not a universal model but it fits the experience of the international oil market and the European gas and power markets. In the case of oil, the external shock that caused the long-term oil contract structure to break down was the 1970s oil shock that followed the crisis in Iran. This encouraged spot trade, from which price volatility, price indexation and the entry of financial participants into the market flowed. In the case of European gas and power, it was the European gas and electricity directives that provided the catalyst for change in the markets. Although the starting point for the emissions "commodity" market has been very different, it is now developing along the same path as other commodity markets.

So, unlike oil, gas and power, the emissions market did not start with long-term contracts, but with a volatile forward contract. The physical market came later, with the opening of national emission registries to track the transfer of allowances. This coincided with the launch of a number of competing futures exchanges, as discussed in Chapter 6.

The forward market in emissions contracts in Europe has been trading since 2003, although the risk of trading in the forward market in its early days was rather high due to the fact that the regulatory process, in particular the ratification of the Kyoto Protocol, was not yet fully in place.

Although the risk has changed since the ratification of Kyoto and the launch of the EU ETS, the terms that are agreed between traders remain the same. These are:

- The price in euros per ton of $CO_2$
- The quantity (number of allowances)
- The vintage (for example, 2005, 2006, 2007, or 2005–2007, or Phase II 2008 onwards)
- The timing of delivery (for example, December 1, 2005, or March 1, 2006)
- The timing of payment, which can be:
  a. immediate settling: within up to about five days, the price, multiplied by the number of allowances, is paid to the seller, subject to agreement on credit terms
  b. forward-settlement transactions: within an agreed number of days after delivery.

There is no standard contract size in the OTC forward market. When the contract started trading, it did so in small lots of 5,000 to 10,000 tons at a time. Now that the market is more established, trades are normally 25,000 to 100,000 tons.

During most of 2004 and 2005 very little business was executed in the forward market in the 2008–2012 period (Phase II) but trades started becoming more common at the end of 2005. All Phase I credits expire at the end of 2007, except for French and Polish allowances, which are bankable into the Phase II period.

**Figure 7.2:** Market liquidity, OTC and exchanges in European Emissions Allowances (contracts)

| 2005 | OTC | ECX/ICE | Nord Pool | Powernext | EEX | EXAA | Exchange Total | Total |
|---|---|---|---|---|---|---|---|---|
| Jan | 6,385,000 | | | | | | | 6,385,000 |
| Feb | 7,795,000 | | 371,000 | | | | 371,000 | 8,166,000 |
| Mar | 15,058,000 | | 1,065,000 | | 109,000 | | 1,174,000 | 16,262,000 |
| Apr | 14,515,000 | 370,000 | 1,664,000 | | 35,500 | | 2,069,500 | 16,584,500 |
| May | 8,647,000 | 1,076,000 | 1,092,000 | | 36,210 | | 2,204,210 | 10,851,210 |
| Jun | 13,113,000 | 6,325,000 | 4,007,000 | 124,000 | 317,398 | 7,500 | 10,780,898 | 23,893,898 |
| Jul | 13,410,000 | 11,090,000 | 2,900,000 | 676,000 | 330,025 | 28,150 | 15,024,175 | 28,434,175 |
| Aug | 6,750,000 | 5,633,000 | 3,461,000 | 567,000 | 342,961 | 32,658 | 10,036,619 | 16,786,619 |
| Sep | 28,935,000 | 17,931,000 | 2,883,000 | 643,000 | 216,219 | 29,390 | 21,702,609 | 50,637,609 |
| Total | 114,608,000 | 42,425,000 | 17,443,000 | 2,010,000 | 1,387,313 | 97,698 | 63,363,011 | 177,971,011 |

*Sources:* Point Carbon (for OTC), the exchanges.

# 8 Legal Agreements for Emissions Trading

As discussed in earlier chapters, the Kyoto Protocol has brought into effect the framework for global emissions-reduction schemes. Within national schemes and international schemes such as the EU ETS any company, with or without its own emission allowance and target, can buy and sell spot-market emission and forward contracts with one another and on various exchanges set up to facilitate this.

In 2005 all documentation on emissions trading (futures/forwards/OTC) revolves around contracts developed by three main trade groups: the European Federation of Energy Traders (EFET); the International Emissions Trading Association (IETA); and the International Swaps Dealers Association (ISDA, which is widely utilized in the OTC energy-derivatives market). Not surprisingly, the EFET is mostly used in Europe, where as many utility companies also use its gas and electricity trading agreements.

JI and CER agreements (as discussed in Chapters 2 and 4) tend to be conspicuous by their absence, as the first CDM/CER transaction was only provided in October 2005 and the agreement used by both parties had not been made public at the time of writing. Joint Implementation agreements only come into effect in the second phase of the EU ETS from January 2008. In principle, the legal structure of JI and CDM agreements should only really differ on the issue of delivery, as many JI agreements will be between governments and municipalities and will probably have to tone down the delivery default terms in the CDM agreement.

The websites of the following bodies may be useful in providing more information in this regard:

European Federation of Energy Traders (www.efet.org)
International Emissions Trading Association (www.ieta.org)
UN Framework Convention on Climate Change (www.unfccc.int).

Copies of the EFET Allowances Appendix and IETA master agreement can be found in Appendix B and Appendix C, respectively, while the ISDA is explained in greater detail later in this chapter.

For the purposes of this chapter, we take a look at these three key master agreements and ask the questions: What should I be looking out for? What are the key differentiators between the general terms and conditions of these contracts from a commercial standpoint?

Please note: anyone looking to utilize one of these contracts should take independent professional legal advice before entering into an emissions-trading agreement.

## The major agreements

The major agreements pertaining to international emissions trading (outside the U.S.) between individual entities, be they oil companies, power companies or speculators in the market, are:

- The European Federation of Energy Traders ("EFET") Allowances Appendix (Version 2.0, published July 2005) to the EFET General Agreement Concerning the Delivery and Acceptance of Electricity (Version 2.1 published December 2000).
- The International Emissions Trading Association ("IETA") Emissions Trading Master Agreement for the EU Scheme (Version 2.1, published June 2005).
- The International Swaps and Derivatives Association ("ISDA") form of Part [6] to the Schedule to an ISDA Master Agreement (either the 1992 or 2002 version) for EU Emissions Allowance Transactions and the form of Confirmation of OTC Physically Settled EU Emissions Allowance Transactions (Short Form) (published June 2005).

# Legal basis risk

Before going into detail on the actual master agreements themselves, it's worth pointing out that the difficulty with having three sets of agreements in the market is that if a trader buys using one set and sells using another, the differences between the buy and sell provisions open up a legal "basis risk" (the concept of basis risk is discussed in more detail in Chapter 11) for the trader.

In other words, there is a risk of loss for the trader/company concerned with respect to such detailed items as the failure to deliver emissions credits, the buyer's replacement costs, market disruption events, tax and netting of transactions.

The financial players, like banks, prefer to use the ISDA terms because they are familiar with them and because they already have ISDA master agreements in place with a wide range of market participants such as the oil and gas companies, with whom they have been dealing over a long period of time to manage oil and gas price risk.

The power sector, which contains a number of very large players who are necessary to provide market liquidity, prefer the EFET terms, because they too have EFET master agreements already in place from their history of managing power price risk.

The IETA terms have been designed specifically for the emissions market and are more straightforward agreements.

Given that the emissions market is a market created by regulation, one of the most significant terms under the three sets of master agreements in use is a provision covering what happens if there is a change to the rules of the EU ETS. If parties enter into a transaction to buy or sell emissions allowances and then the EU ETS changes substantially, the basis of the deal may be called into question. IETA and EFET have specific provisions to deal with this eventuality; ISDA does not, although these circumstances may well qualify as what ISDA terms "a market or settlement disruption event".

Under the IETA terms, either party can call for a renegotiation of the mechanics of the deal with a fallback to an independent expert determination. There is no change to the liability for risks and costs. EFET places obligations on the parties to attempt to comply and to negotiate amendments that allow them to do so up to any financial limit that is negotiated in advance in the master agreement.

ISDA provides that if the EU ETS is abandoned completely, the transaction can similarly be abandoned and no further payments are made. Moreover the seller has to refund any payments already made by the buyer.

From a trading perspective this is a drawback. For example, if an installation were to sell some or all of its allowances in the market, it could use the revenue to invest in emissions-reduction technology, which would mean that it would need fewer allowances for compliance purposes. If the EU ETS was then abandoned, the installation would have to refund the money to the buyer, although it would already have been spent on the new technology. The installation would then probably have to borrow to make the refund and would be left with a project that would not have passed corporate investment hurdle rates had it not been for the provisions of the EU ETS.

## EFET

EFET comprises 75 members from 18 European countries and represents most of the European electricity- and gas-trading entities. These member companies, which include the wholesale energy-trading units of most major European utilities, have a keen interest in the emissions-trading scheme and the underlying compliance responsibilities established by the various EU Directives on greenhouse gas emissions as part of the European Climate Change Programme, in accordance with the Kyoto Protocol.

## IETA

The IETA is an international organization of major companies whose goal is to ensure that the objectives of the United Nations convention on climate change and, ultimately, climate protection are met. It also ensures that the tools available include effective systems for trading in GHG emissions by businesses in an economically efficient manner, while maintaining social equity and environmental integrity. IETA currently has more than 100 members.

## ISDA

The ISDA is the global trade association representing participants in the privately negotiated derivatives industry, a business covering swaps and options across all asset classes (interest rate, currency, commodity and energy, credit and equity). ISDA was chartered in 1985 and today numbers over 670 member institutions from 47 countries on six continents. These members include most of the world's major institutions which deal in, as well as being leading end-users of, privately negotiated derivatives. The membership includes associated service providers and consultants.

Since its inception, ISDA has pioneered efforts to identify and reduce the sources of risk in the derivatives and risk-management business. Among its most notable accomplishments are developing the ISDA Master Agreement; publishing a wide range of related documentation materials and instruments covering a variety of transaction types; producing legal opinions on the enforceability of the netting out of payments and receipts due between two counterparts and collateral arrangements; securing recognition of the risk-reducing effects of netting in determining capital requirements; promoting sound risk-management practices, and advancing the understanding and treatment of derivatives and risk management from public policy and regulatory capital perspectives.

The key elements of the three agreements cover:

- Failure to deliver/accept emissions credits
- Payments
- Netting of settlements
- *Force majeure*
- Changes made to the actual emissions-allowance trading scheme
- Business/banking day for the purpose of delivery.

## Failure to deliver emissions credits under a trading agreement

All three framework agreements offer a one-day grace period on failure to deliver emissions credits under a trade. ISDA gives one delivery business day, which is triggered if notice of failure to deliver is served by the buyer. IETA contracts give one delivery banking day, again only if notice is served by the buyer. Only the EFET agreement does not require the buyer to serve notice terminating a transaction before liability for covering the buyer's replacement cover costs kicks in.

The ISDA provides for the buyer's replacement costs to be paid on the first succeeding business day. The IETA provides for the buyer's replacement costs to be paid on or before the third banking day following receipt of such written notice of termination from the buyer.

Generally, "replacement cost" is equal to the market value of undelivered allowances plus default interest. (It's worth noting that both the IETA and EFET trading agreements allow for incidental cost recovery, but not the ISDA Master Agreement.)

The EFET provides for the buyer's replacement cover costs to be paid on or before the fifth business day after the delivery date or following receipt of an invoice, whichever is the later.

All three frameworks include wording to protect sellers of allowances against failure to accept credits by a buyer. If this happens, the seller can cancel the delivery and charge the buyer for any replacement costs and default interest.

## Payments under emissions-trading agreements

It is important to specify the agreed payment date in your contracts with other counterparties since only the EFET agreement actually states a fallback clause if parties to a contract do not specify a preferred payment date for their emissions trading with one another.

The ISDA and IETA contract frameworks allow parties to choose whether the payment date will be the fifth business day following the later of the delivery date and the invoice date or the later of the twentieth day of the month following the end of the month in which the delivery date occurs or, if this day is not a business day, the first following business day and the fifth business day following the invoice date. No fallback is provided, so it is important that the counterparties agree on this before trading begins. However, under an EFET agreement the contract defaults to a payment cycle of either the twentieth day of the calendar month or, if this is not a business day, the first business day following or the fifth business day following receipt of an invoice.

## Netting of settlements

The ISDA Master Agreement does not allow parties to avoid the application of physical settlement of delivery obligations under emissions trades. This will come as no surprise to those who are familiar with ISDA's (www.isda.org) big efforts with netting agreements for all the markets in which it is involved. It has spent a lot of time and money around the world obtaining legal opinions on its netting agreements in as many jurisdictions as possible. ISDA membership is mainly representative of the world's major financial institutions and banks and they have been at the forefront of reducing as much as possible the credit exposures to trading counterparties through the use of enforceable legal netting agreements. They have done this for two important reasons. Firstly, banks are very conscious of capital employed and capital at risk in their business because of regulators and the way banks have to make the best use of their capital. Secondly, the key area handled by netting agreements is the prevention of "cherry picking" by receivers for a bankrupt firm. Say, for example, Company "A" owes US$500,000 to Company "B", which has since gone into receivership. However, Company "B" actually owes Company "A" US$1 million. Receivers force Company "A" to pay up the US$500,000 dollars it owes Company "B" before they consider paying the US$1 million Company "B" owes Company "A". Several banks and financial institutions found themselves in situations like this when Enron went bankrupt in 2001.

All the framework agreements covered by this chapter allow for the netting of deliveries of allowances where delivery is on the same delivery business day (or banking day for IETA contracts) and where delivery is to occur between the same pair of trading accounts and is of the same allowance type and compliance period (compliance period refers to the Kyoto Protocol compliance period).

## Force majeure

The IETA and EFET agreements provide separate methodologies for calculating termination payments following a *force majeure* than for other termination events. ISDA does not make this distinction, applying the same calculation method for all such events..

The IETA and EFET contracts allow parties to choose between the market-quotation and loss-payment methods in calculating *force majeure* termination payments. The 1992 ISDA Schedule has the same provision, but under the 2002 ISDA the method for calculating termination payments is the close-out amount. If the contract falls under the 1992 ISDA Master Agreement, termination payments are to be calculated by obtaining at least three quotes from the market. The 2002 ISDA does not specify the number of quotations to be obtained.

The IETA and EFET agreements require parties to obtain five quotations when using the market-quotation method.

The other key thing to note is that the IETA contract provides a fallback position that *force majeure* termination payments will not apply unless specified by the parties. The EFET does not have such a provision.

Under the IETA and EFET agreements, if a *force majeure* event takes place the first party to hear of it is obliged to notify the other in writing. Each party then provides the other with a non-binding estimate of the extent and expected duration of the *force majeure* event and its impact on the performance of transactions. Obligations with respect to the relevant emissions-allowance transaction would be suspended during the *force majeure* and affected parties are expected to use reasonable endeavors (as defined in the law of contract in the jurisdiction to which the agreement is subject) to overcome the situation.

The point at which a contract in *force majeure* can be terminated by either party is the same under each of the three arrangements; that is, where a *force majeure* continues for a period of nine days (delivery business days for ISDA/EFET and delivery banking days for IETA), or continues for three days prior to any end-of-phase reconciliation deadline (if sooner). IETA does not allow for termination when a *force majeure* continues up to reconciliation deadline; only the end-of-phase reconciliation deadline.

Under the IETA and EFET, all *force majeure*-affected transactions are terminated by written notice to the other party. The ISDA, on the other hand, allows for a party to terminate separately the relevant emissions-allowance transactions affected by the settlement-disruption event/*force majeure*. In other words, it gives added flexibility in that it allows for the termination of contracts on an individual basis, rather than as a whole.

## Changes to allowance-trading scheme

Since the structure of emissions-trading schemes is fixed through international regulations and protocols, the IETA, EFET and ISDA trading-agreement frameworks do not take into consideration possible changes to the allowance-trading scheme itself. The ISDA Master Agreement does at least consider what action parties should pursue if the trading scheme is abandoned/halted altogether. If this were to happen, then both parties can terminate the transactions under the trading scheme with written notice, with no further payments required. The seller will refund to the buyer any amount paid in connection with the transactions, together with interest at market rates.

## Business/banking day for the purpose of delivery

Unless there is a clear definition of what counts as a business day or a banking day, this can lead to difficulties in the event of a settlement dispute.

The definitions within the three agreement frameworks under discussion here are as follows:

*ISDA*

- The delivery business day as defined in respect of a European Union Emissions Allowance trade is any day which is not a Saturday or Sunday on which commercial banks are open for general business in both the seller's and the buyer's delivery business day location.
- The delivery business day is taken to be between 9am and 5pm, Central European Time.

*IETA*

- The delivery banking day (the IETA equivalent of a banking day) is defined as any day (other than a Saturday or Sunday) on which commercial banks are open for general business in both the seller's and the buyer's delivery banking day location.
- For EU Emissions trades, the delivery banking day is taken to be between 9am and 5pm, Central European Time.

*EFET*

- The delivery business day as defined for allowance transactions in Europe is any day which is not a Saturday or Sunday on which commercial banks are open for general business at the location of the two parties to the agreement.

- The delivery business day to is taken to be between 9am and 5pm, Central European Time.

The EFET and IETA agreements were formulated in more recent years with the emissions markets specifically in mind. The ISDA agreement, however, has been around since the 1990s and has been adopted widely by financial institutions and the banking industry. Financial traders and funds use ISDA for all over-the-counter energy markets, including the oil, power and gas markets. Although it is true to say that EFET is the primary contract used under the EU ETS, ISDA remains at the forefront of global trading. As we noted earlier, the 2002 version of the ISDA agreement is different from the earlier version, and which version is used can affect certain key business areas, even for emissions trading.

## The ISDA agreements: A comparative review

In 1992, the ISDA Master Agreement revolutionized the documentation and legal contract process surrounding swaps trading across all markets, including energy. The 1992 version remains the more popular and is widely used in energy-trading markets (especially oil price-index swaps).

ISDA agreements are made up of two important parts: the standard ISDA Master Agreement 2002 and the ISDA Schedule to the Master Agreement (see Appendix D). The Schedule is the part that is negotiated between counterparties and contains information such as procedures on settlement, early termination, default, netting arrangements (if any), and banking details for both parties to the Master Agreement.

The majority of crude oil, petroleum products, and power and gas OTC derivatives such as swaps and options, (that is, derivatives that are money-settled, also referred to as cash-settled, and do NOT involve any physical delivery of the commodity) use the 1992 ISDA Master Swaps Agreement Multicurrency, Cross-border version. In addition to this, counterparties in the market generally use this Master Swaps agreement with 1993 ISDA Commodity Derivatives definitions and the 2000 supplement to the 1993 ISDA Commodity Derivatives definitions available from the ISDA organization (www.isda.org).

ISDA's 2003 Operational Benchmarking Survey found that the use of master agreements has been steadily increasing. ISDA members reported that signed master agreements are in place with around 92% of their OTC derivatives counterparties, compared to around 90% in 2002 and 85% in 2001 (www.isda.org).

Developments in markets and derivatives disasters, such as the collapse of Enron, prompted a major review of the ISDA Master Agreement. In January 2003, the ISDA issued its first full revision of the 1992 Master Agreement (Multicurrency, Cross-border version). The product of several months' consultation and amendment, the 2002 Master Agreement (ISDA 2002) builds upon and amends many of the provisions of its predecessor. Not many companies have yet adopted ISDA 2002, but it is slowly being introduced by energy-market participants. It is important therefore to understand the key differences between the two versions.

## The ISDA Master Agreement

An ISDA agreement is a voluminous document containing 14 sections covering such things as definitions, interpretation, governing law and jurisdictions, obligations, default and termination events, contractual currency, transfers, and so on.

ISDA produces a number of useful publications to help business managers understand the meanings of the contract sections of its agreements. These include:

- *1993 ISDA Commodity Derivatives Definitions*: These definitions are designed to facilitate the documentation of commodity transactions under the 1992 Master Agreements. Sample forms of confirmation are included.
- *2000 Supplement to the 1993 ISDA Commodity Derivatives Definitions*: The Supplement is an update of the 1993 ISDA Commodity Derivatives Definitions (the "1993 Definitions"), which many participants in the OTC commodity-derivatives markets have incorporated into existing confirmations or other agreements. As is the case with the 1993 Definitions, the Supplement is designed for use by participants in the markets for commodity-derivatives transactions in documenting cash-settled commodity swaps, options, caps, collars, floors, and swaptions or such other cash-settled commodity-derivatives transactions as the parties desire.

The Supplement includes additional commodity reference prices for energy, metals and paper and adds significantly to the number of commodity reference prices set out in the 1993 Definitions and includes the Commodity Reference Price Framework from the 1993 Definitions, which facilitates the definition of a commodity reference price that is not set out in the Supplement.

- *2000 ISDA Definitions and Annex*: This is what the majority of players in the energy market are using at the moment, although this may change in the not-too-distant future.

### Pre-confirmations and long-form confirmations

Banks and financial institutions aim to have ISDA agreements negotiated and signed off within three months, although it can often take between three and six months to put an ISDA in place. Because of this, counterparties often trade with one another while negotiations are still taking place. Although most risk-management policies prohibit any trading before an agreement has been reached, the commercial need to trade sometimes takes precedence. But trading without an agreement does add considerable legal risk and in such circumstances it may be better to use what is termed a "pre-confirmation" or a "long-form confirmation".

A "pre-confirmation" states the terms of the derivatives transaction and choices of provisions that would appear in the ISDA Master Agreement. The idea behind this is to commit counterparties to this wording before the agreement is signed. However, a tightening of risk-management policies over documentation and trading before the signing of an ISDA agreement means these are becoming less common.

These days, "long-form confirmations" are far more frequently used. (They get their name from the fact that they usually consist of about nine feet of telex roll or fax paper.) Basically, this is a one-off derivatives contract for a specific deal which covers all the main eventualities. This type of confirmation is probably best for dealing with entities which are not regular trading partners and so do not warrant the legal cost of creating an ISDA. It can also be helpful in situations in which an ISDA agreement is not yet in place but where there is an urgent need to trade. "Long-form" contracts should be used for short dated "plain-vanilla" derivatives, with a counterpart in a familiar jurisdiction.

## ISDA documentation processing

When entering into an ISDA agreement, one of the counterparties will usually take the initiative and send its standard ISDA Schedule draft wording for the other party to review and comment on. As mentioned earlier, the ISDA Master Agreement itself is not open to change; the ISDA Schedule is the negotiated document.

Prior to negotiation on terms, the respective credit departments must first process the counterpart details and pass the details of internally approved credit terms to their legal departments, which need this for inclusion in the ISDA Schedule. This also determines whether Credit Support Annexes are required.

Before rushing into the expense of processing legal documentation with a new OTC counterpart, it is useful to check the memorandum and articles of association of the counterparty's organization. These are known as the "M and As" and provide the legal incorporation details of the organization, specifying what business functions it can carry out and sometimes what it is prohibited from doing. It is very important to check that there is nothing in the M and As of the firm that prevents it from entering into OTC derivative contracts with other companies. If the M and As are satisfactory, then both parties should be ready to put together an ISDA agreement.

Although the ISDA Master Agreement is a standard document, there are areas of it which give rise to different types of risk for counterparties and are therefore often areas of negotiation in the Schedule. (Remember that the Schedule is where counterparties make the choices of how certain areas of the Master Agreement will affect their derivatives transactions.) These areas are as follows:

(The following notes refer to ISDA 1992, which is still the key agreement offered by energy counterparties at the time of writing.)

- Legal risk
  *Section 1(b) Inconsistency:* Where there is any inconsistency between the ISDA Master Agreement text and the ISDA Schedule, the Schedule will prevail. Also, if there is any conflict between a Confirmation and the ISDA Master and the Schedule, the Confirmation will prevail. This can contribute to operational risk, so trade confirmations must be issued correctly.

*Section 1(c) Single agreement:* If trades are closed out, this section ensures that the values of all trades between the two counterparties are calculated and netted off against each other, so that only one payment is required between the two counterparties. This prevents "cherry picking" where, if a company has gone bankrupt, the liquidator can call in payments on trades that are profitable for the bankrupt client, but refuse to pay out on trades which are not profitable. For example, imagine that counterparty A and counterparty B do two derivatives trades, with counterparty A making US$2 million on one deal (it is a zero-sum game, so counterparty B is losing US$2 million), and on the other deal counterparty B is making US$1.5 million (with counterparty A losing US$1.5 million). In this situation, if counterparty B went bankrupt and Section 1(c) was not in place (because it had been deliberately excluded via the wording in the ISDA Schedule), then counterparty A could end up being forced to pay to counterparty B US$1.5 million (even though the net position is that counterparty B owes counterparty A US$500,000). The single-agreement concept reinforces the position that a liquidator cannot do this. It collapses and nets out the entire portfolio of derivatives trades into one single payment due to one counterparty or the other.

*Section 5(a) Events of default:* This covers a party's failure to make any payment or delivery under Section 2 of the Master Agreement which covers the counterparty's obligations. In the past, the energy industry adopted a grace period of three days, but this is increasingly being shortened to just one day. The section also covers credit-support default, misrepresentation, default under specified transactions (we look at this in more detail in Appendix E), cross default, bankruptcy, merger, illegality and credit event upon merger.

*Section 7 Transfer of the agreement:* Normally, counterparties are not allowed to transfer the ISDA Agreement or any rights and obligations under it without written consent from the other party. There are a few exceptions to this rule but these are rare instances where a counterparty wants to transfer the agreement to avoid an "event" (for example, illegality, a tax event, or certain cases surrounding a merger) and a counterparty transfers the close-out money payable to it by a defaulting counterparty to another firm.

*Section 8 Contractual currency:* This protects counterparties from foreign-exchange losses on settlement and close-out payments.

*Section 9(d) Miscellaneous (remedies cumulative):* When a party is faced with the counterparty defaulting, it should not forget that the termination of derivatives trades is not the only course of action. It can leave the trades open or even sue for damages, if it chooses to do so.

*Section 13 Governing law and jurisdiction:* The majority of energy-derivatives trades under ISDA outside the United States, even with American companies, are conducted under English Law and the jurisdiction of the English courts. Under ISDA there is a choice between English Law and English Courts or State of New York Law and the jurisdiction of the courts of the State of New York and the U.S. District Court located in the borough of Manhattan in New York.

- Counterparty risk
  *Section 5 Events of default and termination events:* This is examined from a practical standpoint in Appendix C.

- Market risk
  *Section 6 ISDA Master Agreement:* This covers early termination, especially with automatic early termination. We look at this in the ISDA Schedule example in Appendix E.

- Documentation risk
  *Section 4 Agreements:* This covers the agreement on what documents the counterparties agree to provide one another (for example, company certificates of incorporation, copies of licenses and renewals). It also covers an agreement that in some cases counterparties must maintain certain licenses and also pay any stamp duty taxes on any agreements, and so on.

- Payment on settlement risk
  *Section 2:* This key area is where counterparties agree on details of how payments are to be made, how netting is

performed, and provisions protecting counterparties against withholding-tax deductions.

## Trading before an ISDA is signed

If a trade does take place prior to an ISDA being signed between the two counterparties (which is not advisable unless there are considerable commercial pressures to put a hedge on very quickly), then the Trade Confirmation sent out will normally state that both counterparties to the deal must use "best endeavors" (a legal term as to the amount of effort used to achieve an agreement) to enter into an ISDA agreement. The Confirmation usually states that the derivatives trade is subject to the terms of an ISDA Master Agreement without a Schedule; that is, that it is basically un-amended.

The lack of a Schedule, though, means that the two counterparties cannot make their own choices over key issues in the Master Agreement. These issues would include choices over what triggers automatic early termination of derivatives deals; payment netting and methods; what happens in the event of one of the counterparties merging with another company; termination currency; tax representations (regarding withholding taxes on settlement payments); credit support (any parent companies willing to support the credit exposure on the derivatives trades); and which entities are included in Specified Entities (the other companies that are included in the agreement for the purposes of triggering a default).

The biggest risk for an organization if it trades without an ISDA Agreement is that if the other counterparty goes into bankruptcy or liquidation, a liquidator could end up "cherry picking" any profitable deals.

## ISDA Master Agreement Schedule

The ISDA Master Agreement Schedule basically states which sections of the Master Agreement will be in force between the two parties to the agreement and is thus often the center of much discussion and negotiation. Although ISDA Schedules will differ slightly from one another in commercial terms, there are still key parts that turn up again and again.

The ISDA Schedule is always executed (signed off) on the same date as the Master Agreement it refers to. If an organization updates a Master Agreement Schedule at a later date and it has some OTC derivatives currently outstanding under its old agreement, it is common practice for energy-trading companies to backdate the new ISDA Schedule agreement so that old transactions are covered by the updated ISDA Schedule.

The Schedule is made up of the following core sections:

- Termination provisions
- Tax representations
- Agreement to deliver documents
- Miscellaneous provisions
- Other provisions.

## The main differences between ISDA 2002 and the ISDA 1992 Master Agreements

Although ISDA 2002 and ISDA 1992 are similar in many ways, substantial revisions have been made to some of the more fundamental provisions of ISDA 1992, particularly relating to default events, as set out below:

- *Failure to pay or deliver*: A failure to pay or deliver must be remedied within one local business day (or one local delivery day in the case of deliveries) of notice of such failure being given to the relevant party in order to avoid an event of default. ISDA 1992 allowed a grace period of three local business days.
- *Breach of agreement; repudiation of agreement*: ISDA 2002 incorporates a new subsection giving rise to an event of default if a party disaffirms, disclaims, repudiates, or rejects, in whole or in part, or challenges the validity of, the Master Agreement, any confirmation or any transaction evidenced thereby. This subsection is similar to, and is in addition to, the credit-support default under 5(a)(iii)(3) of ISDA 1992 in respect of credit-support documents.
- *Credit-support default*: The failing or ceasing of any security interest granted by a party or a credit-support provider to the other party pursuant to a credit-support document can give rise to an event of default.

- *Default under specified transaction*: This section has been amended to separate (i) defaults in making payment on the last payment or exchange date (or any payment on an early termination), (ii) defaults in making any delivery, (iii) any other defaults (other than delivery) and (iv) disaffirming, disclaiming, repudiating, rejecting, or challenging the validity of a specified transaction. Delivery default and other defaults require the subsequent liquidation or acceleration of obligations under the relevant specified transaction (in respect of all defaults excepting delivery) or all transactions outstanding under documentation applicable to that specified transaction (in respect of delivery default only). Final-payment default allows a grace period of one day but requires no further knock-on effects in order to constitute an event of default. Each of the defaults, except for final-payment default, now refer expressly to a default under any credit-support arrangement relating to a specified transaction as being capable of giving rise to an event of default under this heading. The definition of specified transaction under ISDA 2002 expressly excludes transactions under the Agreement.
- *Cross-default*: The first paragraph of this event of default has been amended to clarify that the threshold amount relates to the size of the aggregate principal amount of the agreements or instruments in respect of which there has been a default, event of default, and so on. While this is probably what was intended by ISDA 1992 as well, there was perhaps room for debate as to whether the threshold amount applied to the size of the specified indebtedness or the size of amounts involved in the default.
- *Bankruptcy:* Although the provisions are largely the same in ISDA 2002, there have been changes made to the applicable grace periods. Where a party institutes, or has instituted against it by a regulator, supervisor, or any similar insolvency officer, insolvency or bankruptcy proceedings, it would appear that an event of default will arise immediately, without reference to any grace period or the entering of any judgment. Where proceedings are instituted against it by any other entity, such proceedings can give rise to an event of default if either (i) they are not dismissed within 15 days or (ii) judgment is entered. The grace period under ISDA 1992 was 30 days. Also a reduction in grace period has been

made with respect to circumstances where a secured party takes steps to enforce its credit security.

- *Termination events*: The principal differences between the termination events in ISDA 1992 and ISDA 2002 are the expanded section concerning illegality and the inclusion of *force majeure*. Unlike its predecessor, ISDA 2002 does not make express reference to a change in law or interpretation and merely requires that the illegality be due to an event or circumstance (other than any action taken by a party or, if applicable, a credit-support provider of such party) occurring after a transaction has been entered into. The subsection dealing with illegality of a transaction has been changed to make it clear that the illegality should affect the office through which payments and deliveries are effected in respect of a transaction, and that the ability to take receipt of payments and deliveries is also included. The subsection dealing with illegality in respect of a credit-support document has been restricted to cover only obligations to make or receive payments or deliveries or compliance with any other material provision of the affected credit-support document.

- *Force majeure:* ISDA 2002 includes a provision dealing with *force majeure*. It is basically like the optional "Impossibility" provision, which was suggested within the user's guide to ISDA 1992. *Force majeure*, like illegality, has been made office-specific and expressly includes the ability to take receipt of deliveries and payments as well as the ability to make them. Of potential concern to counterparties to the ISDA 2002 is the expansion of *force majeure* to include not just circumstances where performance is pretty much impossible, but also where the affected trading office is prevented from performance or where performance is impracticable. Like illegality, *force majeure* can arise in respect of a transaction or in respect of a credit-support document. The principal difference between the operation of *force majeure* and illegality is that it requires not only that the relevant cause be out of the control of the affected office, party, or credit-support provider but will only apply if such office, party, or credit-support provider could not overcome the prevention, impossibility, or impracticability having used reasonable efforts such as would not require such party etc. to incur more than incidental losses. In other words, the party has to work hard to ensure that it really cannot get around the problems it faces.

- *Credit Event upon Merger:* This termination event has been amended in two ways: first, by a redrafting of the section by reference to separate designated events (the first of which being the equivalent ISDA 1992 termination event), the inclusion of an express requirement to take account of any credit-support document and by the expanding of the equivalent ISDA 1992 wording to include the transfer of a substantial part of a party's assets, as well as reorganization, reincorporation, and reconstitution; and second, by the addition of two, new, designated events. The first of these is the acquisition of an ownership interest in a party by any person, related to an entity enabling such person to control that party. The second is the making by a party of any substantial change in its capital structure by means of the issuance, incurrence, or guarantee of debt or the issue of either (i) preferred stock or other securities convertible into debt or preferred stock, or (ii) an ownership interest in that party. These new designated events were not previously included in the ISDA 1992 and do seem open to a fairly broad interpretation.

- *Deferral of payments:* ISDA 2002 introduces deferral provisions which will be effective upon the occurrence of an illegality or *force majeure*. The new provisions defer any payment or delivery obligations under a transaction affected by illegality or *force majeure* so that such obligation does not become due until the earlier of (i) the first local business day (or local delivery day in the case of deliveries) after the applicable waiting period, and (ii) the date on which the event or circumstance giving rise to the illegality or *force majeure* ceases to exist. The waiting periods are set out in ISDA 2002 as three local business days in respect of illegality and eight local business days in respect of *force majeure*. However, this will be reduced to zero in each case in respect of illegality or *force majeure* affecting credit-support documents where delivery or payment is actually required on the relevant day.

- *Close-out netting — early termination:* Although the principal difference between the early-termination provisions of ISDA 1992 and ISDA 2002 is the differing method of valuation, there are a number of other changes, many of which build upon the newly expanded illegality and the newly introduced *force majeure* termination events.

- *Rights to terminate contracts:* The provisions relating to the right to terminate following an event of default are unchanged, as are the provisions relating to the right to terminate following a termination event (save for the exclusion of illegality from the list of termination events giving rise to an obligation to transfer or reach agreement). ISDA 2002 contains two new provisions that relate solely to illegality and *force majeure*. Unlike the other termination events, except in certain limited circumstances, either party may designate an early termination date in respect of all or less than all affected transactions. If one party serves notice terminating less than all affected transactions, the other party may respond, designating the same early-termination date in respect of all affected transactions. In the case of illegality and *force majeure* affecting credit-support documents, only the non-affected party can serve an initial notice terminating either all or less than all affected transactions. However, if less than all affected transactions have been terminated, the affected party does have the right to respond with a designation of an early-termination date in respect of all affected transactions.
- *Payments on early termination:* Unlike ISDA 1992, ISDA 2002 only permits parties to use the close-out amount valuation method. The mechanics of arriving at an early-termination amount owing once the close-out amount is established are similar in operation to calculating an amount owing on an early-termination date once a settlement amount has been determined in accordance with the second method and market quotation election under ISDA 1992. The early-termination amount will generally be equal to the sum of the close-out amount determined by the determining party (or half the difference between the close-out amounts determined by each party in the case of a termination following a termination event with two affected parties) and any unpaid amounts owing between the parties.
- *Set-off:* This provision is included for the first time within ISDA 2002, although it is substantially similar to the suggested "Set-off" provisions in the user's guide to ISDA

1992. The effect of the provision is to enable the non-defaulting party or non-affected party (provided that all outstanding transactions are affected transactions) in circumstances where there is one such party to elect that any early-termination amount owing be reduced to the extent of any other amounts owing between the parties. In order to satisfy the requirement for mutuality between the parties in order for set-off to apply, ISDA 2002 also incorporates a representation that parties are dealing as principals in respect of all transactions.

- *Office multi-branches:* The provisions dealing with multi-branch arrangements have been expanded in ISDA 2002. Counterparties are expressly prevented from having recourse to the head office of a multi-branch party in respect of deliveries or payments deferred in accordance with the provisions of ISDA 2002 following an illegality or *force majeure* for so long as those deliveries or payments are so deferred. New deeming provisions have also been included whereby a party will be deemed to have entered into a transaction through its head office, unless otherwise specified in the applicable confirmation or agreement between the parties.

In operations relating to ISDA-based swaps deals, the most interesting development is in the area of confirmations. While this may appear to be just a technical difference between ISDA 2002 and ISDA 1992, it is really worth noting that while confirmations can finally now be executed and delivered by counterparties via e-mail, the actual agreement to the trade can only be executed and delivered by counterparties via fax or secure electronic messaging systems (for example, Swift — which ISDA 2002 appears to differentiate from e-mails). Notices or other communications in respect of events of default, termination events and early termination may not be given by either e-mail or electronic messaging system.

# 9 Green Power Trading: Developments and Opportunities

## Renewable-energy trading

Renewable energy is naturally regenerated over time from sources such as the wind, sun and water and from geothermal and biomass sources. Among electricity-generating technologies, those powered by renewable energy are the fastest growing. And the future of renewable energy is bright. With economic growth, energy demand continues to rise. In the world's single largest energy-consuming country, the U.S., energy consumption is now growing at approximately 2% per year, which is slightly faster than the population growth, which currently stands at around 1.5%. Developing countries have even larger needs for energy resources. Among these are the large and densely populated countries of India and China, whose rapidly increasing energy needs have caused fossil-fuel prices — principally those of coal, oil and natural gas — to rise.

Renewable energy confers numerous benefits for the environment and human health, energy security, and economic and political stability. It does not have the adverse environmental and health effects associated with the emissions produced when burning fossil fuels. Given the volatility of fossil-fuel prices, renewable energy may provide more predictable costs, because most of the cost of renewable energy is in the capital needed to construct the project. Thereafter, the resource itself (water, sun, wind, waste or geothermal reservoir) is mostly free. Increased use of renewable energy would disperse energy resources, reducing reliance on the complex infrastructure used to transport fuels and electricity and central power plants (including nuclear facilities) that are vulnerable to terrorism. To the extent that renewable energy is dispersed and easier to site than traditional energy resources, it can reduce delays in developing energy resources. Further, growth in renewable-energy generation and in REC markets can create jobs, with biomass and wind plants bringing new revenue to farmers and rural communities. Renewable energy may also help to reduce oil imports, particularly when it displaces traditional hydrocarbon-based transportation fuels such as diesel and gasoline with the introduction of bio-diesels and ethanol produced from crops.

While interest in renewable energy is generally increasing, costs have been and continue to be a major barrier to its wider use. In some situations, wind, biomass and solar applications can be competitive with energy produced from fossil fuels. But, in most situations, improving cost competitiveness is considered the single most important factor limiting expanded use of renewable technologies. Experience with other technologies teaches us that to reduce costs, more renewable-energy facilities must be built. More technology must be deployed to gain experience with the technologies and find means to reduce the costs involved.

## Increasing market penetration

Governments and non-governmental organizations have numerous programs to reduce the cost of renewable energy and increase its market penetration. These programs include financial incentives (income-tax credits, property- and sales-tax exemptions, loan and special grant programs, industry recruitment incentives, accelerated depreciation allowances, and grants) and technology research and development programs.

More recently, consumers have been provided with the means for directly supporting the deployment of renewable energy through increased market penetration for renewable energy. The options now open to consumers include:

- Green-power markets —Today, more than 50% of all U.S. consumers have an option to purchase some type of green-power product; that is, electricity produced from renewable energy, from a retail electricity provider. Today, there are over 350 utility green-power programs.
- Green pricing — Some utilities offer their customers the option of paying more for their electricity to support the installation of renewable-energy facilities.

While customer-based schemes, especially green marketing, are growing and have contributed to the increased use of renewable energy, states (and some foreign governments) have found the rate of adopting renewable energy too slow. In the U.S., 18 states and the District of Columbia have adopted RPS to accelerate the penetration of renewable technologies, as shown in Figure 9.1.

**Figure 9.1:**   Adoption and spread of U.S. renewable portfolio standards

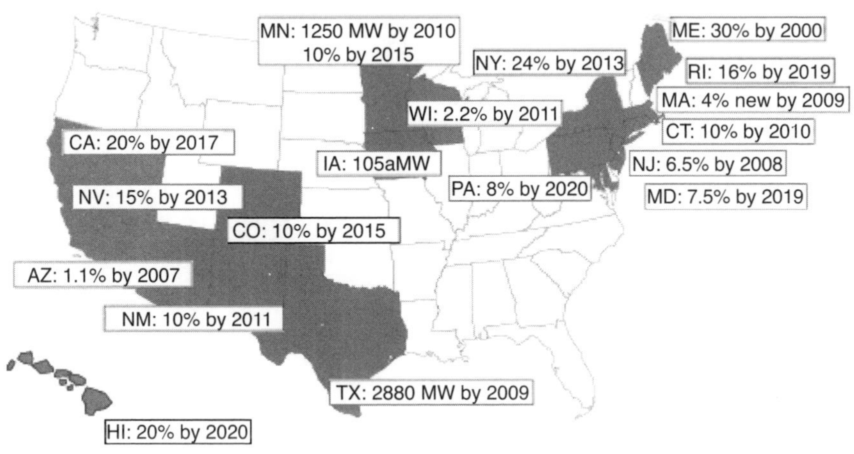

MN: 1250 MW by 2010 10% by 2015
NY: 24% by 2013
ME: 30% by 2000
RI: 16% by 2019
WI: 2.2% by 2011
MA: 4% new by 2009
CA: 20% by 2017
CT: 10% by 2010
IA: 105aMW
PA: 8% by 2020
NJ: 6.5% by 2008
NV: 15% by 2013
MD: 7.5% by 2019
CO: 10% by 2015
AZ: 1.1% by 2007
NM: 10% by 2011
TX: 2880 MW by 2009
HI: 20% by 2020

*Source:* NREL (www.eere.energy.gov/greenpower/resources/pdfs/37388.pdf)

RPS are a form of command-and-control regulation. Over time, the standards serve to maintain or increase the quantity of renewable energy in the system.

A renewable portfolio standard reflects the overall renewable-energy goal defined by policy makers. Standards are expressed in terms of a fixed amount of renewable energy delivered as a percentage of total electricity sales, and include schedules for achieving compliance and penalties for non-compliance. Standards typically specify the renewable resources eligible for inclusion in the program. Goals are defined in one of two ways: *capacity* to generate renewable energy, or *energy* actually delivered. The capacity approach rewards participants for investing in renewable energy, whereas the energy approach rewards the investor for performance — the delivery of renewable energy.

When the standard is based on energy delivered, the utility or retailer can have several options for supplying the renewable energy: it can own the generation equipment and produce its own green electricity; it can buy green electricity from another supplier; or, in some cases, it can buy the benefits of renewable energy by purchasing renewable-energy certificates (RECs). RECs (pronounced "recks") are a market-based approach to increasing renewable-energy production that can provide the greatest amount of renewable power for the lowest price and that create an ongoing incentive to drive costs down. Of the states that have adopted RPS in the U.S., 14 are using RECs to achieve their goals.

A REC represents all environmental attributes of one megawatt-hour (MWh) of electricity generated from a renewable source. These attributes can be sold separately from the underlying physical electricity generated from the source. RECs are also referred to as "green tags" in some jurisdictions.

Trading occurs in both mandatory and voluntary REC markets. In North America, only Texas and Massachusetts formally recognize renewable-certificate trading as part of mandatory renewable portfolio standards.

Other states are moving toward similar programs: the New England Power Pool (NEPOOL) and the Pennsylvania–New Jersey–Maryland (PJM) pool host a number of programs and renewable portfolio standards are also being developed in California and New York.

# Texas

RECs are part of the state's electric deregulation requirements. The Texas RPS came into effect in January 2002. The program mandates that 2,000 MW (about 3% of total state usage) of new renewable capacity be built in Texas by 2009. Electricity generators are granted RECs in direct proportion to the number of MWh of renewable energy (hydro, wind, solar and biogas) they produce.

All retail electricity providers are required to hold RECs based on the level of their annual retail electricity sales in the state. RECs are valid for a period of three years.

# Massachusetts

The Massachusetts RPS define renewable-energy sources as solar, wind, ocean/wave/tidal, fuel cells, landfill methane, and low-emission biomass. Electricity from such sources began to be generated after December 31, 1997. The RPS came into effect in 2003 and certificates have started trading. The cumulative minimum RPS requirement is 4% by 2009.

# New England Power Pool

Connecticut and Maine also have RPS requirements and permit retail electricity providers to achieve compliance using certificates from generation sourced anywhere in NEPOOL, or an adjacent power pool, provided that the power flows onto the NEPOOL grid.

In NEPOOL, certificates for each MWh of generation are created electronically on a monthly basis and tracked by a generation-information system. They are put into the system on a quarterly basis and there is a time lag of three to six months between when generation occurs and when the certificates can be traded.

Because Maine's RPS includes hydro generation in its definition of renewables, the certificate market is oversupplied since there is a significant percentage of hydro power in the state's energy mix.

In stark contract to this, in Connecticut the RPS requirements apply only to competitive retail electricity suppliers, restricting compliance-driven demand for certificates. The state has established two classifications of renewable generation:

- Class I — solar, wind, new sustainable biomass, landfill gas, fuel cells
- Class II — waste-to-energy facilities, biomass facilities not included in Class I, certain approved hydro facilities.

The RPS currently require at least 7% for combined Class I and II, with at least 6% from Class I alone by 2009.

In Vermont, in April 2005 the State Senate passed a bill authorizing the implementation of an RPS set at 3% by 2006, and a tradable REC system.

## PJM

In PJM, the most advanced state is New Jersey, where recognition of pure attribute trades and the establishment of a market for certificates has emerged. Currently, by March 1 of each year since the scheme's inception in 2002, each electric-power supplier or basic generation-service provider files an annual report with the Board of Public Utilities. The state has established two classifications of renewable generation:

- Class I — solar, photovoltaic, wind energy, fuel cells, geothermal technologies, wave or tidal energy; and methane gas from landfills or a biomass facility, provided that the biomass is cultivated and harvested in a sustainable manner
- Class II — produced at a resource-recovery facility or hydro-power facility (with a maximum design capacity of 30 MW or less).

The current RPS requirements are 2.5% for Classes I and II combined, with a target of 4% from Class I by 2012.

## California

California passed its RPS in September 2002, requiring sellers of retail electricity to increase their purchase of renewable energy by 1% per year, up to a maximum of 20% by 2017. This will almost double the state's reliance on renewable-energy resources.

In the remainder of this chapter, we will examine the nature of markets for renewable-energy credits, their development and the means to participate in them.

# Renewable-energy credits

## Using the marketplace to achieve environmental goals

As discussed in previous chapters, market-based approaches provide the flexibility to find the most efficient and cost-effective ways to reduce target pollutants. For example, the use of emissions-trading mechanisms for sulfur dioxide in the U.S. resulted in program costs that were far less than predicted and initial rates of pollution reduction that were faster than predicted.

Building on the concepts of emissions trading, competitive trading in renewable-energy credits (RECs) has emerged. RECs — which are also referred to as "green tags", "green tickets", "TRCs" (tradable renewable certificates) and "TRECs" (tradable RECs) — are created simultaneously with renewable-electricity generation. A REC represents the "green" portion of energy produced from renewable sources.

The mechanism of RECs is illustrated in Figure 9.2. A generator that produces electricity from renewable resources produces two products — electricity and the benefits or "attributes" associated with renewable energy displacing fossil fuels. The generator receives a certificate for the renewable energy from the central organization (government, regulator, companies, or non-governmental organization) overseeing the renewable market. The renewable-energy certificate, which is sold in units of electricity generated, tracks the ownership of the green portion of the energy produced. The generator can sell the electricity and the REC separately, with each product producing a separate revenue stream. Thus, the generator is likely to receive more by selling the renewable-energy certificate in addition to the electricity than the electricity alone.

Like emissions allowances, RECs are fungible. They therefore help buyers and sellers overcome some of the physical, economic and market barriers to renewable energy. Developing renewable-energy resources provides many challenges. RECs address the physical and economic issues that arise from an uneven distribution of renewable resources across geography and wide variations in the

**Figure 9.2:** The mechanism of RECs

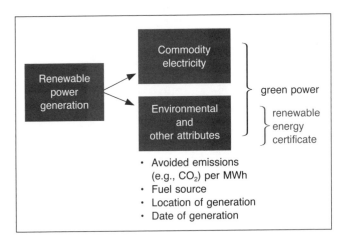

*Source:* WRI, 2004

quality of the resources that dramatically affect production costs. In the U.S., for example, geothermal resources are concentrated in the west and wind resources are particularly good on the Great Plains. RECs help to overcome this disparity, because they are physically unbundled from electricity and can therefore be "distributed" where electricity cannot be physically transmitted. For example, Hawaii has substantial geothermal resources but no way of transmitting the electricity produced off the islands. It can convert the green portion of the power generation to a REC and sell the benefits to Minnesota, which has no geothermal capacity.

RECs can also help utility companies and power generators find the lowest-cost means to comply with renewable portfolio standards. When another generator provides cheaper renewable-energy resources than a particular power generator can produce, then that more expensive generator can buy the REC rather than produce more expensive renewable energy required by the standards.

Wyoming may have substantially more wind resources and lower costs than New York. New York can buy the REC from a Wyoming wind generator, but the electricity itself is sold in Wyoming's local generation market. The ability to buy RECs also enables immediate compliance with renewable standards while giving retailers the time to carefully assess their options for investing in renewable-energy generation and to develop sound strategic plans.

Some "green pricing" programs even allow retailers to contain costs by employing RECs.

RECs also offer market benefits. Trading RECs helps consumers to enter the market through green pricing even when their utility does not own renewable-energy generators. Most advantageous is that selling green attributes separate from electricity, an instantaneous product that cannot be stored, helps to avoid the inherent complexity of energy trading. REC transactions can be conducted on a schedule independent of energy generation, enabling the maximization of seasonally generated renewable energy. Moreover, futures markets and derivative products (such as sell-and-buy options, futures, banking, and borrowing) that facilitate liquidity and risk management can emerge.

Market forces are likely to tie the price of RECs to the cost difference between generating electricity from renewable resources and generating electricity from conventional sources. Over time, RECs trading will lower the costs of renewable-energy attributes: competition within the market will ensure the lowest price and liquidity will facilitate further investment in renewable-energy generators. RECs will especially lower the costs of renewable-energy attributes for states and areas that do not have the most economical renewable-energy resources available within their region.

*RECs market participation*

New Zealand, Australia and the Netherlands have comprehensive renewable-energy programs and credit markets. Russia and China appear to be interested in implementing similar programs. The EU adopted a Renewable Energy Directive in 1991 as the basis for certificate trading within some member states and potentially across member states. Many European countries participate in the Association of Issuing Bodies (AIB) and the Renewable Energy Certificate System (RECS), which are international efforts to facilitate RECs trading. One of the most successful renewable-energy programs that incorporates RECs can be found in the Netherlands, as discussed in Box 9.1 below.

In the U.S., of the 18 states which have implemented RPS or mandatory programs, 14 allow the importation of bundled electricity and RECs from nearby states, while 12 permit unbundled transactions. (The U.S. Congress has considered several proposals for a national renewable portfolio standard, but no action has been taken.) Two of the largest mandatory programs are the Texas ERCOT

**Box 9.1:**   The Netherlands: A working example of a comprehensive renewable-energy program

The Netherlands offers an example of a comprehensive and efficient renewable-energy policy. Renewable energy represents 3.4% of total energy supply in the Netherlands. While windmills are icons of Dutch culture, most of the renewable energy is based on biomass. Wind represents only 0.7% of electricity production, although wind-based electricity generation is expected to increase.

The government has ratified the Kyoto Protocol and is committed to reducing its average GHG emissions by 6% between 2008 and 2012. As part of its cleaner-energy strategy, the government has adopted a plan to produce 10% of its energy from renewable-energy sources by 2020. A detailed action plan that specifies steps to attain a comprehensive and efficient renewable-energy program is expected to facilitate a robust renewable-energy market. The policies underlying the program are:

*Electricity market liberalization:* The Dutch liberalized their energy market and opened it to competition in 2001 by unbundling electricity production from retail sales and promoting the development of liquid and efficient markets. Ultimately, the goal is to privatize the utilities, which are currently owned by local governments. These initiatives enable energy markets to increase the potential for renewable energy by loosening constraints to market entry and possibly expanding the size of the geographic market area when utilities are combined.

*Financial incentives:* Another factor is support for renewable energy through a mix of instruments ranging from feed-in tariffs that increase the revenues for renewable generators, direct subsidies, fiscal investment incentives (tax exoneration), and a system-benefits charge used to finance renewable-energy investments.

*Research and development:* The government funds research and development for wind, solar, biomass, and heat pumps.

*Voluntary programs:* Dutch renewable-energy policy includes voluntary actions, such as agreements between utilities.

*Participation in international programs:* The Netherlands is an active participant in the Association of Issuing Bodies and the Renewable Energy Certificate System.

The first RECs program in the Netherlands was a voluntary program developed by EnergieNed, the Dutch association of electric utilities. The program, which included an electronic tracking system, began in 1998 and lasted for three years. From this emerged the Renewable Energy Certificate System, another industry-driven program. The policy employs a renewable-energy certificate scheme to verify and track electricity generated from renewable sources and trading. These green certificates are awarded to renewable-electricity generators, who can then sell them to consumers in any part of the country or to foreign customers who contract with suppliers or consumers in the Netherlands.

program, with sales of 2.9 million MWh in 2003, and the New England NEPOOL/GIS, with 5.8 million MWh of RECs sales in 2004.

RECs can also be the currency of voluntary programs. In 2003, RECs were the currency of exchange for 33% of green-pricing sales, up from 11% in 2002. Given the rapid growth in recent green-pricing sales (44% in 2003), the potential for RECs in this market is large. RECs are also used in governments' efforts to procure green energy for their own use. The U.S. Environmental Protection Agency and Government Services Administration, as well as state governments, have purchased RECs. The largest group of voluntary RECs purchasers is companies. They are purchasing about one million MWh annually and participate in programs such as Green-E, the EPA Green Power Partnership, and the World Resources Institute Green Market Development Program.

Ultimately, there is hope that RECs will also be formally recognized in emissions-trading programs. If they are, the emissions-reduction attribute associated with the REC could be traded in those markets.

RECs transactions take many forms involving utilities or direct retail sales by RECs marketers:

- Utilities purchase RECs to comply with renewable-energy standards.
- Utilities can also act as REC retailers when they are operating in competitive markets and must provide energy to all customers who do not select an alternative retailer.
- RECs retail marketers sell directly to customers, bypassing the local utility. Sometimes they sell electricity produced by

renewable energy and bundle the REC in the sale. At other times they may sell the REC only, either within the region where it was produced or nationally.

- RECs brokers structure transactions directly between interested REC buyers and sellers.

Most sales are for current years, but RECs are sold in forward markets where retailers make sales based on a future stream of RECs. Known as forward selling, this mechanism can create upfront revenue to defray the capital costs of a project.

From a legal perspective, the U.S. programs view a REC as a unit of trade for a single commodity, renewable energy. But many believe that the market for RECs can be expanded into a mechanism for selling and buying multiple *attributes* of a unit of renewable energy, such as the environmental and health benefits of reduced pollution or improved energy security.

The market value of the attributes of renewable-energy generation has become recognized even though extensive regulated markets don't yet exist.

## U.S. market performance

The U.S. RECs market is fragmented, with both compliance and voluntary markets. Among the 19 states which have RPS that enable or require compliance markets, the National Renewable Energy Laboratory (NREL — www.nrel.gov) has found that most activity to date has been in Texas, Massachusetts, Connecticut and Maine. Figure 9.3 shows a sample range of REC trading prices in compliance markets. These prices demonstrate a range that differs by a factor of 10 for lowest to highest prices and the approach to non-compliance penalties in two states, Connecticut and Massachusetts. Those differences are largely driven by the local costs of renewable energy. They are also influenced by supply-demand conditions, size of the purchase volume, vintage (year produced), and type of renewable energy (where there is a particularly large premium for solar energy). As RECs trading across state lines and between regions accelerates, the prices are likely to converge.

Opportunities in the existing compliance markets are large. According to NREL, the 14 compliance states currently need 13 million MWh of renewable-energy generation annually to fulfill

**Figure 9.3:** Sample range of REC trading prices in compliance markets

| | 2003 REC Trading Prices ($/MWh) | Jan–Oct 2004 REC Trading Prices ($/MWh) | Non-compliance Penalty ($/MWh) |
|---|---|---|---|
| Connecticut (Class I) | 37–48 | 35–48 | $55 |
| Maine/CT Class II | N/A | 0.65–0.70 | $55 (CT) |
| NJ (PJM) Class I | 4–6.50 | 6.50–7.50 | $50 |
| NJ (PJM) Class II | 2–4.50 | 4.25–5 | $50 |
| Massachusetts (New) | 21–40 | 40–49 | $51 |
| Texas | 10–14 | 11–15 | $50 |

*Sources:* Evolution Markets and Cantor Fitzgerald

their RECs requirements. It is not clear that this volume of generation is actually occurring; so far, only eight million MWh of RECs have been identified. The compliance market must increase by between three and five times to deliver 45 MWh of RECs to meet requirements of the programs that exist today. In dollar terms, the 2004 potential value (defined by requirements, not actual performance) was US$137 million and the 2010 value will be US$608 million. Implementation of RPS in other states will only add to these estimates.

According to NREL, voluntary markets are smaller than mandatory markets, with approximately three million MWh of sales in 2003, but are growing rapidly. As shown in Figure 9.4, prices vary by a factor of 100, but that is primarily because solar RECs trade at a premium. Lawrence Berkeley Laboratory and NREL have estimated that the voluntary green-power market (three-quarters of which depends on voluntary RECs trading) could grow at an annual rate as low as eight million MWh or as high as 61 million MWh by 2010. Based on an estimated current market value of between US$15 million and US$45 million, the market value could grow to a likely value of between US$100 million and $300 million.

What these estimates mask is the value of RECs relative to emission allowances. As shown in Figure 9.5, a single REC has a value that is many times the current U.S. prices for emissions.

**Figure 9.4:**  Sample range of REC trading prices in voluntary markets

|  | Wind | Solar | Biomass | Small Hydro |
|---|---|---|---|---|
| California | 1.75–2.00 |  | 1.50 |  |
| WECC | 1.25–7.50 | 30.00–150.00 | 1.50–3.50 |  |
| Central | 2.00–5.50 |  | 1.50 |  |
| PJM | 15.00–17.00 | 80.00–200.00 | 4.00–5.00 |  |
| New York | 15.00–16.00 |  | 6.00 |  |
| NEPOOL | 35.00 |  | 45.00 | 5.00 |
| SPP | 2.50–5.00 |  |  |  |
| Southeast |  |  | 3.50 |  |

*Sources:* Evolution Markets and GT Energy (data for July 2003 through October 2004).

**Figure 9.5:**  The value of RECs in their impact on energy value

**Allowance values**

| Application | Emissions Value | Energy Value |
|---|---|---|
| $CO_2$ | $1.45/ton | $0.87/MWh |
| NOx | $3,000/ton | $2.25/MWh |
| SOx | $700/ton | $4.20/MWh |
| Compliance RECs | Not applicable | $5–$45/MWh |
| Voluntary RECs | Not applicable | $5–$15/MWh |

*Source:* Evolution Markets

# The mechanics of RECs markets

As with any tradable asset, trading creates flexibility and liquidity within the market. Yet efficient trading relies on well-established market procedures. As discussed in Chapter 3, the U.S. sulfur dioxide and nitrogen oxide markets have benefited from clear government procedures and auxiliary trading mechanisms provided by the private sector. For RECs, a set of standardized procedures does not exist — the property rights, standardization of contracts, procedures for verifying resources and trades, and terms of trade are still evolving. As the market matures, it will become more liquid, efficient and cost-effective.

A system to track RECs ownership is also critical. A network at a national or international level can create a closed-loop system for buying and selling RECs. It is important that states do not count renewable energy towards a standard within one state and then sell RECs essential to any renewable-energy market to parties outside that state. As shown in Figure 9.6, power pools (wholesale energy markets with regional transmission networks that may include one or more states) are using their infrastructure and industry experience to create a market for RECs and to track trading.

The Texas and New England power pools are already supporting REC trading within and between states. Recently, the Western Governors' Association (WGA), which represents the governors of 18 states and three U.S. islands in the Pacific, called for the development of a single, independent institution in the Western

**Figure 9.6:** Regions with REC tracking systems in operation or development

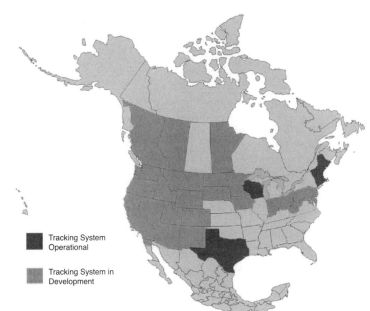

*Source:* Center for Resource Solutions

United States to issue, track and verify renewable-energy generation certificates. Recognizing the benefit of collaboration and the power of REC trading to promote the development of renewable energy, in July 2003 California's Energy Commission and WGA agreed to jointly develop the Western Renewable Energy Generation Information System (WREGIS) to register and track renewable-energy generation and certificates across the region.

The European Commission Joint Research Center has launched an Internet trading project to design and test a reliable, universal, open, inexpensive system to trade RECs. The project is intended to demonstrate the feasibility of using meters and the Internet for verification. Internet trading is tremendously efficient, and electronic integration of supply-and-demand options should result in the lowest costs. If this project succeeds, it will probably lead to extensive Internet trading of RECs.

Each state is defining the characteristics of its RECs; ultimately, the goal is to standardize the REC and the property right it represents to facilitate trading. The liquidity of markets will grow as the definition of what constitutes a REC becomes more standardized. The emergence of systems like WREGIS will facilitate these efforts.

Verification mechanisms are being developed. Verification can be achieved in several ways. Regulators review the utility's contracts to ensure that RECs are transferred to the utility. They audit utilities to verify that REC purchases meet demand served. In voluntary markets, Green-E$^R$ (administered by the Center for Resource Solutions) and EcoPower$^{SM}$ (administered by the Environmental Resources Trust) certify the RECs.

In addition, international organizations including the Association of Issuing Bodies (AIB) and the Renewable Energy Certificate System (RECS) are addressing the mechanics of RECs. RECS, whose members include most European countries and countries from other parts of the world, aims to satisfy the international need for an adequate certificate system on renewable energy and reduce the fragmentation of markets. RECS is working towards facilitating new products that use its certificates and stimulate the redemption of certificates. It is also promoting the harmonization of mandatory demand. Important elements in this discussion are the implementation of guarantees of origin; accepting the principle of green reciprocity; and monitoring the import and export of renewable energy based on guarantees of origin/RECS certificates.

# The future of RECs markets

As in any market, buyers and sellers of RECs will be exposed to the risks of imperfect information, poor performance and opportunism. Uncertainty can be reduced through user-friendly REC trading markets and making information on prices available to the public. Standardized trades through central exchanges with publicly posted prices can further reduce transaction costs and market uncertainties. To manage these risks, buyers and sellers will often try to discover market prices. As the market grows and more buyers and sellers enter, the potential for hedging with futures and options will allow traders to manage their risks appropriately and stabilize prices. With a growing market will come the increased involvement of insurance companies and financial institutions concerned about energy security, and the volatility of fossil-fuel prices will also drive market expansion and renewable-energy development.

# Renewable obligations in the U.K.

The Renewables Obligation (RO) was introduced in April 2002 and requires all licensed electricity suppliers in England and Wales to supply a specified proportion of their electricity sales (3% in 2002–2003 rising to 15.4% in 2015–2016) from a choice of eligible renewable sources.

Suppliers have to demonstrate compliance with their target each year by either surrendering one Renewable Obligation Certificate or ROC (pronounced "Rock") to the U.K.'s electricity regulator — OFGEM, the Office of Gas and Electricity Markets — for each MWh of its obligation, or paying a "buy-out price" of £30 (adjusted annually by RPI) to OFGEM for each MWh of its obligation.

A supplier will typically comply through a combination of both; that is, surrendering some ROCs and paying some buy-out.

A ROC is proof that electricity has been generated from an accredited renewable generation plant. Each ROC represents the generation of 1 MWh of renewable electricity and can be traded separately from the underlying electricity.

Electricity suppliers have an incentive to comply by purchasing ROCs as, if they get the pricing right, it is a lower cost-compliance option than paying the buy-out. In addition, it is beneficial for some suppliers to be seen to be meeting their renewables targets by buying green certificates, rather than just paying a fine for failing to meet their targets.

The buy-out payments made to OFGEM go into a communal pot and are re-distributed to the suppliers in proportion to the number of ROCs they have surrendered in the relevant compliance period — a "recycling payment". The true value of the ROC is therefore derived from the avoided fine plus the amount of the recycling payment. Suppliers, generators and traders all speculate on the amount that this payment will be worth. However, only ROCs surrendered by suppliers (and not those held by generators) will be eligible for this payment.

A concern though was that the level of ROC-eligible generation for the compliance year ending March 31, 2004 was only around 1.7%, according to the Renewable Power Association (RPA). This was well below the required 4.3% quota for the second compliance period, indicating that most suppliers are going to be unable to meet their quotas. The increase in the RO quota from 3% in 2003 (fiscal year) to 4.3% in 2004, combined with the lack of renewable-generation capacity, is predicted to lead to an increase in the price of ROCs for the second compliance period (CP2). The ROC Price Marker, published by Platts (www.platts.com), suggests that ROC values could be as high as £56.75.

This, though, is the least of the concerns for U.K. power generators as the market as a whole faces power shortages that will arise from the decommissioning of older power stations (including nuclear) being planned for the near future. U.K. politicians are faced with the harsh reality that the only power source which can, within the time and the emissions controls required, replace the planned losses in power production and cover the expected increase in power consumption is more nuclear power plants. That the prime minister, Tony Blair, mentioned this at the 2005 annual conference of the Labour Party merely underlines the seriousness of the situation.

The U.K. Department of Trade and Industry (DTI) issued a Renewables Obligation (Amendment) Order 2003 Statutory Consultation in August 2003, outlining a number of changes proposed by the DTI. The majority of the changes were technical adjustments to ensure that the Obligation works as originally intended, but there were also significant changes proposed for the co-firing rules. These included extending the period for which the co-firing of biomass in coal-fired power stations is eligible for ROCs to 2016 (co-firing currently ends in 2011), and changes to the usage of energy crops in the co-firing process.

Following the consultation period, the DTI announced the results in December 2003. The changes were as follows:

- Co-firing under the Renewables Obligation is to be extended to allow longer for an energy-crop market to develop to serve biomass operations at co-fired stations.
- The existing caps on the proportion of electrical output from any one plant that can come from co-firing will be adjusted downwards to better ensure that co-fired ROCs do not flood the ROC market. These are firm limits.
- Fossil-fuel stations will be allowed to convert to biomass without refurbishment, which should lead to an increase in electricity produced under the RO using biomass.

Co-firing with biomass that attracts ROCs will change as follows:

- Any biomass can be co-fired until March 31, 2009, with no minimum percentage of energy crops.
- At least 25% of co-fired biomass must be energy crops from April 1, 2009 until March 31, 2010.
- At least 50% of co-fired biomass must be energy crops from April 1, 2010 until March 31, 2011.
- At least 75% of co-fired biomass must be energy crops from April 1, 2011 until March 31, 2016. Co-firing ceases to be eligible for ROCs after this date.

To balance the above changes and reduce the risk of flooding the ROC market with co-firing ROCs, thereby affecting ROC prices and investor confidence adversely, it is proposed that the 25% cap on an individual supplier from April 1, 2006 should be changed to 10% from April 1, 2006 until March 31, 2011 and 5% from April 1, 2011 until March 31, 2016.

## Dutch green certificates

The process of liberalization of the Dutch green-electricity market was introduced in July 2001 to facilitate transparent trading in renewable electricity. This marked the introduction of the Dutch green-certificates scheme, which replaced the green-label system that had been in place since 1998.

Wind turbines, biomass plants (including incinerators), solar-power plants and hydropower plants of below 15 MW all qualify for renewable certificates under the scheme. From January 1, 2002, imported renewable electricity was also eligible to apply for Dutch green certificates.

The certificates are issued by the Green Certificates Body, which was founded by TenneT, the national grid-operator.

Partial exemption from the energy tax only applies to renewable electricity in possession of a green certificate. On the demand side, consumers are free to choose their energy supplier. They pay an additional tariff when they buy green electricity but, in return, are partially exempted from the energy tax. For end-users, the green electricity is, on average, as expensive as regular electricity. The Dutch green-electricity market has shown strong growth, and presently includes approximately 1.8 million households (25% of the total).

Under the EU Renewable Electricity Directive, the Netherlands accepted an indicative renewable-energy target of 9% of total electricity consumption by 2010, and in 1995 the government established a long-term target of 10% of final energy consumption (equivalent to approximately 17% of total electricity consumption at that time) from renewable generation by 2020.

## Italian green certificates

In September 2001, the European Union Council of Ministers and the European Parliament adopted a directive on the promotion of electricity from renewable-energy sources in the internal electricity market. The EU target for total energy consumption by 2010 is 22%, and Italy's target is set at 25%. Italy's energy law, also known as the Bersani Decree, requires all energy producers and importers to ensure that 2% of all electricity supplied to the national market comes from renewable sources as of 2002.

The government can progressively increase the quota to meet the target. Eligible renewable-energy sources include solar, wind, hydro, biomass, waste, tidal, and geothermal sources. Suppliers can fulfill the obligation by buying tradable green certificates from entitled new renewable-energy plants (established or restructured after April 1, 1999), by building new renewable-energy plants, and by importing electricity from renewable-energy plants from countries with similar instruments on a reciprocal basis. Each green certificate represents an energy value of 100 MW or a multiple thereof. The national authority handling the scheme is the GRTN (Italian Transmission System Operator).

## Swedish green certificates

In May 2003, the Swedish green certificates — *Elcertifikat* — scheme was approved by the Swedish Parliament to encourage electricity production from renewable-energy sources. Plants producing electricity from wind, solar, wave, geothermal, and certain types of bio-fuel and hydroelectric power are entitled to certificates. Overall the target is to increase the production of renewable electricity by 10 TWh from the 2002 level by the year 2010.

To create demand for green certificates, a formal quota obligation is imposed on electricity suppliers and users. Customers can manage their own quota obligations, or the supplier can pass the cost of the certificates on to the customers through their electricity bills. For 2003, it was proposed that the proportion of renewable energy would be 7.4% of the electricity consumed or invoiced. By 2010, this will have increased to 16.9%. For the initial five years, a decreasing price guarantee is being offered to electricity generators in order to secure their market for certificates, from SEK60 per certificate in 2003 to SEK20 per certificate in 2007.

The Swedish Energy Agency monitors, analyzes and supervises the development of the electricity market, and Svenska Kraftnät, the national transmission company, issues the certificates and supervises their participation in the international Renewable Energy Certificate System.

# 10 What Risk? An Introduction to Managing Risk

Risk is the lifeblood of business. Without it, why would people support your profit margin? Properly managed businesses thrive and prosper from controlled risk that gives good shareholder returns. Unmanaged or poorly managed, a business may not last very long, particularly in the capital-intensive business of the energy industry and markets. The focus of this book is how to apply derivatives practically for trading or price-risk management (hedging) purposes. In the real world you cannot just write about or examine price-risk control on its own.

The mere use of derivatives in your organization can increase other risks which you must examine and that is why we promote a holistic approach to the creation of a price-risk management program.

Let's look at some of the other risks your organization probably faces already. These must be reviewed and properly controlled so that your price-risk management program or trading program using derivatives achieves its goal and does not create any unwanted or unplanned difficulties.

## What risks?

In order to teach others about risk, a few years ago we created a risk matrix, shown in Figure 10.1 below. The term "matrix" is used

**Figure 10.1:** The Risk Matrix

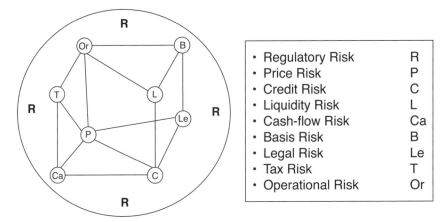

| | |
|---|---|
| • Regulatory Risk | R |
| • Price Risk | P |
| • Credit Risk | C |
| • Liquidity Risk | L |
| • Cash-flow Risk | Ca |
| • Basis Risk | B |
| • Legal Risk | Le |
| • Tax Risk | T |
| • Operational Risk | Or |

because the relationship between each risk is not a two-dimensional relationship. All the risks we will consider are interrelated and affect one another in varying degrees. Hence, you cannot approach price-risk management without reviewing the other risks your firm may face.

All the risks listed in Figure 10.1 will have a direct bearing on whether you need to manage your risk and, if you do, which derivatives and or markets you use, with whom and where you trade and how much you trade or manage, depending on operational risks.

For energy markets, regulatory risk has always been a major influence in long-term price movements, but for emissions markets, regulation created them out of thin air, so to speak. Emissions markets were created through legislation and as they develop there is always further regulatory risk that needs to be monitored closely, particularly for longer-term risk exposure and/or trading positions.

This chapter runs through the precise meaning of the various risks that need to be examined in a holistic manner. Risk is like energy, like a law of physics: you can neither create nor destroy it; it merely transfers from one type of risk to another. The key aim in risk management is to spread a concentrated risk out to other types of risks, making it more manageable, or to transfer risk to a type of risk in which you have stronger expertise within your company and outsource the management of risk you cannot handle yourself.

# Regulatory risk

This is the risk that market regulators, governments, international authorities (UNFCC, for example) and others introduce in controlling practices, law, specifications of materials (energy) and market design/ structure. It includes rules for changing existing regulations or adding new ones that affect the way companies can do business, which in turn affect future price trading in certain markets.

# Price risk

Also known as market risk, this is the risk of losing money when the price of the energy market you are trading in or exposed to moves against you. For example, as an electricity user you would lose money if the power price increased dramatically in a short space of time and you were unable to pass on these price increases in your own product or service cost to your customer. As a crude-oil producer you would lose money if the price of oil went down from current levels.

# Credit risk

This is the risk of financial losses arising from the default of the counterparty to a contract.

# Liquidity risk

In the context of this book, this is the risk of losses arising from a derivatives market becoming illiquid. For example, you may be speculating on the price of jet fuel going down, but a war breaks out in the Gulf and the price of jet fuel becomes very strong, very quickly. You had sold financial swap contracts on jet fuel and now need to buy them back to close-out your position. Because of the volatility in the oil markets during the war, many banks and oil traders will not give a bid or offer in the markets. So you could have a liquidity risk and not be able to close out your swaps contract. Even if you were able to do so, you might have done so at a large cost to your company.

It is very important to understand properly the derivatives market you use for speculation or price-risk management and to appreciate how big a position your company can place in such markets. Some of the biggest derivatives disasters have occurred because companies have either not realized or have ignored the dangers of liquidity risk. A prime example of this was the Metalgessellschaft (MG) incident on NYMEX in the mid nineties.

MG was carrying out "text book" hedging of long-term (ten years forward) physical deals using liquid spot-market futures contracts on NYMEX. The benefit of using NYMEX futures was that they were very liquid, with many hundreds of millions of barrels worth of contracts trading daily. However, liquidity risk still became apparent when MG's positions became too big for the marketplace. It had such a large position in the end that its hedging activities began to influence the market and the price. Prices began to move adversely against the company. In the end, its hedging program started to work against it and it built up a massive cash-flow risk. In the end, the company went broke.

## Cash-flow risk

This is the risk that your organization will have sufficient or indeed the correct currency to meet its derivatives obligations. In the MG example above, the company had profits from physical deals it had locked in with its customers 10 years in the future. However, since it was using spot futures on NYMEX every month, it had to settle and pay losses or receive profits on these futures contracts. In theory, everything would have been fine if it had been able to hold all the hedges for 10 years, as the cash-flow from its physical deals would have financed its futures position losses. However, MG could not support the losses that it had to finance with NYMEX in the prompt futures markets as the contracts expired (cash-flow prompt losses), and so it was forced to declare Chapter 11 bankruptcy.

With Korean Airlines in the late nineties it was a different story. Here the company did not have enough of the right currency. At one point, the Korean Won lost a lot of value against the U.S. dollar and, as jet-fuel trading in derivatives is carried out in U.S. dollars, Korean Airlines ended up losing money because it had not hedged (protected) its risk in the currency differential between the Won and the dollar.

## Basis risk

This is the risk of loss due to an adverse move or breakdown of expected differentials between two prices (usually of different products). In the context of price-risk management, it is used to describe the risk that the value of a hedge (using a derivative contract/structure) may not move up or down in sync with the value of the actual price exposure that is being managed. When conducting price-risk management, ideally you want to use a derivatives contract that has zero or the lowest basis risk with the energy price you need protection from. The larger the basis risk, the less useful the derivative is to you for risk-management purposes. The attraction of OTC swaps and options is that basis risk can be zero at times, as OTC contracts can often price against the same price reference as your physical oil. However, futures contracts (sometimes referred to as "on-exchange" derivatives) traded on exchanges like the International Petroleum Exchange (www.theice.com), NYMEX (www.nymex.com ) and the Tokyo Commodity Exchange (www.tocom.com) have all their pricing references and terms fixed in the exchange's regulations and so if their pricing reference does not match your underlying physical exposure, either you accept that basis risk or look for an OTC alternative. It's worth noting that the differences between these two different types of derivatives are becoming increasingly blurred as their two worlds converge. NYMEX, for example, now has a successful international clearing mechanism for OTC derivatives — called "Clearport™" — which clears them like futures contracts.

The Enron collapse in 2001 certainly added momentum to the credit concerns of OTC contracts which, 99% of the time, are traded bilaterally (traded directly between two corporate entities rather than via an exchange such as the IPE-ICE or TOCOM or NYMEX). Understanding what factors tend to trigger major market moves also helps us watch out for developments in basis risk. Just because basis risk is not present at the time of the original analysis of the correlations between the price of the chosen derivative contract for hedging and the physical energy exposure, does not mean that this will always be the case, particularly for long-term (over one year) hedging deals.

The main factors that tend to trigger major market moves are weather, political events, physical events and regulation.

Basis risk occurs when:

- physical material in one location cannot be delivered to relieve a shortage in another location
- a different quality of product cannot be substituted for an energy product in severe shortage (very much the case for pipeline gas and power markets if any problems occur with transmission networks)
- the time required to transport or produce an energy product is insufficient to reach the market in time to alleviate the shortage.

Basis risk can be broken down to the following key components, as described in Figures 10.2 through 10.4.

**Figure 10.2:**　Product Basis

- Product basis
  - This is the most important basis risk in the energy markets.
  - If there is a mismatch in quality, weight, or other specification, then the underlying product and the derivative contract are not 100% fungible/identical. Product basis risk is present to some degree.
  - In the energy markets there is a large number of products but only a few liquid hedging tools for the risk manager. As a result, energy price risk is only hedged in a limited number of liquid over-the-counter (OTC) and futures markets.
  - Even when the instrument/tool underlying price shows a strong historical correlation with the hedged product, if the relationship breaks down basis risks could emerge — for example, in times of high volatility; the Gulf War being a prime example of such a scenario.

**Figure 10.3:**　Time Basis

- Time basis
  - This is a common exposure in many markets.
  - In energy markets a time-basis exposure can be very dangerous, particularly when there is a sudden shift in demand or transportation problems occur. For example, a power generator in the U.S. is expecting stronger natural gas prices in the summer (due to additional use of air conditioning etc.). It hedges its position by buying the August contract in NYMEX Natural Gas Henry Hub futures. If a severe heat wave was to arrive early in summer, say in late June, then the price of July gas may become much stronger than the August price. August futures may not give adequate price risk cover against the July requirement.

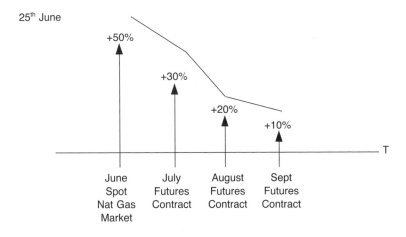

25<sup>th</sup> June

+50%

+30%

+20%

+10%

T

| June | July | August | Sept |
|------|------|--------|------|
| Spot | Futures | Futures | Futures |
| Nat Gas | Contract | Contract | Contract |
| Market | | | |

August Futures contract only rises by
20% whereas the spot June physical
Market "spikes" up by 50%

**Figure 10.4:** Locational Basis

- Locational basis
  - If you have a derivatives contract which prices against exactly the same specification of energy against which you are hedging price risk. But this energy (oil, gas, power, coal) is located in a different geographic region. From the physical energy you have exposure to, you have locational basis risk.
  - Localised supply/demand factors, political tension, grid problems or, in the case of hydrocarbons/gas, pipeline problems, in either the location used for pricing the derivatives contract or the location where the physical supply is located could make your derivatives contract a liability rather than a risk-reducing benefit.

  e.g.

European Gasoil — Singapore Gasoil

## Locational risk in action

A point of interest is that the International Petroleum Exchange of London, now called ICE Futures (www.theice.com), has a successful Brent Crude Oil futures contract. IPE Brent futures started in 1983, two years after the WTI (West Texas Intermediate) crude futures contract launched on the NYMEX. The NYMEX WTI was trading successfully, so why would people use the IPE Brent futures instead of WTI for hedging?

The answer is what has become known as the "Cushing Cushion", which gets its name from the major oilfield area of Cushing, Oklahoma, which fed into the oil pipeline network across America. This continues to add locational basis risk for anyone hedging international crudes (for example, West African, Brent, Mid East crude oils, Dubai, Tapis) with the WTI NYMEX contract. It is possible to hedge international crude oils with WTI NYMEX; WTI is a more liquid futures contract than Brent, so there are some liquidity advantages. However, from time to time (particularly in winter) the Cushing Cushion basis risk will arise. This is where WTI's crude price in the U.S. can act totally independently of international market prices. The two main causes of this situation arise when pipeline bottlenecks from the Gulf Coast prevent additional foreign crude from reaching the mid-continent refineries and when bad weather closes the Louisiana Offshore Offloading Point (LOOP), halting the offloading of foreign crude from carriers into the oil pipeline system. The first reaction of speculators and refineries that are dependent on oil in the pipeline system is to buy WTI NYMEX futures, sometimes resulting in WTI premiums of US$3 a barrel over the IPE Brent price.

## Mixed basis risk

Mixed basis risk occurs when an underlying position is hedged with more than one type of mismatch between the energy you are trying to price-risk manage and the pricing index reference of the derivatives instrument you are going to use.

For example, a January gasoil (heating oil) cargo might be hedged with a March jet kerosene swap, leaving both time and product basis exposures.

## How to assess basis risk

To assess basis risk, you need to ask yourself whether the hedging-tool pricing reference close to the product you are hedging has:

- the same oil spec
- the same physical location
- the same timing
- price correlation (three years' data is our suggestion)
- price causation (does a price change in one really influence a price change in the other? This is only relevant if the

pricing-index reference of your derivatives contract differs from your underlying physical energy.)

## Legal risk

This is the risk that derivatives contracts may be not be enforceable in certain circumstances. We will be looking at legal contract issues and negotiation pointers in later chapters (see also Chapter 8), but the most common concerns surround certain clauses on netting of settlements, on netting of trades or bankruptcy and the fact that liquidation of contracts may be unenforceable. As protection, you should obtain opinions on the effectiveness of ISDA and netting agreements. As we saw in Chapter 8, the ISDA has already published various opinions on many jurisdictions around the world.

## Operational risk

This is the risk of loss that may occur through errors and omissions in the processing and settlement of derivatives. Internal controls, alongside an appropriate back-office system (whether manual or computerized), should be employed to reduce this risk.

# 11 Risk-Policy Guidelines

If you buy or sell or are exposed to energy or emissions cost/price movements, at some point you will be at risk, so it makes sense to hedge.

We are talking about the kind of hedging that defends against volatility in price and gives increased certainty in the cost or profit of an exposure to the markets as required by your firm. The single biggest fact of energy and emissions markets today is that, as a result of deregulation, prices fluctuate wildly and, sometimes, unexpectedly.

In order to monitor the effectiveness of the use of energy derivatives properly and to control their use within your organization, it's important to have a clear policy for energy derivatives. Company shareholders are usually very demanding; in one way, they don't want companies to hedge away any of their upside profit potential, yet they also hate to see too much downside potential loss exposure. An energy consumer that implements a bad hedging strategy may end up paying high fixed prices for energy while its competitors pay lower spot prices.

So how does a company choose the correct hedging strategy? It's not easy. There are a huge number of options to consider, such as forward contracts with suppliers and derivative instruments to hedge price-risk fluctuations. Options, swaps, collars, futures and forwards are all techniques that must be investigated. In selecting the right strategy, an energy consumer must carefully assess its current and potential risks. An organization should not become involved in a product at significant levels until senior management and all relevant personnel (including those in risk-management, internal control, legal, accounting and auditing departments) understand the product and are able to integrate it into the organization's risk-measurement and control systems.

Before designing and implementing a risk-management program, senior management must perform a comprehensive risk assessment to determine all of the energy-price risks facing the company. The risk assessment examines the company's operations and should determine how much of a particular energy risk it either consumes or produces. The end result of the assessment should be a report that clearly states the entire set of energy price-risk exposures by energy type, location, volume and price-reference index. Using historical volatility data, a dollar amount that is at risk for the company each year can be calculated. Many financial institutions, such as banks, that are involved in energy-price risk management can do a lot of this assessment/analysis work on behalf of end-users and producers.

Once the assessment is complete, the company can begin the process of establishing its risk-management policies and procedures. Anyone who wishes to engage in the use of energy or emissions derivatives should understand the markets and be able to assess whether they are appropriate for the organization's trading or risk-management needs. There should be a clear segregation of duties, establishing market and credit-risk management functions with clear authority, independent of the front-office derivatives-trading function.

Answering a number of key questions can also help the company collect information to assist in the creation of its policy. First of all it is important to determine whether the organization is a consumer, a producer or a trader. If a producer, what products does it have in price risk and are these risks fixed or floating? Is the company trading or simply hedging, and what are its aims in doing so? Is its aim, for example, to mitigate a disaster-risk scenario, control overall price risk, or trade risk as a speculator?

Assessing the credit risk arising from derivatives activities will help determine whether there is too much exposure to any single counterparty, and whether the organization can utilize credit insurance. This risk can be reduced by broadening the use of multi-product master agreements with netting provisions.

Another point to consider is whether the company allows its traders to speculate as well as hedge. What is the total volume of energy available to hedge and/or trade? As a hedger, how much do you want or need to hedge?

When hedging, it's probably wise to look at up to 50% of exposure for general day-to-day hedging requirements. Any hedging over 50% of consumption or production volume is speculative and should only be considered as a rare pre-emptive measure ahead of a "disaster scenario" or, as we have seen in recent years, to protect against volatile near-term energy-market prices.

Another question to ask yourself is whether traders should be allowed to sell as well as buy options. (This can incur open exposures for companies if not done as part of a larger structure. Also in some derivative disasters, the sale of options has been used to generate cash flow to cover up losses elsewhere in a portfolio.)

Usually end-users will hedge around 10% to 30% of volumes around budget levels up to four years forward (due to the backwardation in the forward price curve at the time of writing), leaving an additional 50% to 70% (up to 100% total) for opportunistic hedging if levels come below budget levels closer to prompt.

Also, end-users should generally look to have another policy for hedging in times of extreme price movements, allowing the energy-procurement department or the dedicated risk-management department to act quickly to protect the firm against extreme price movements that might be seen in, say, times of war. For example, if you were an electricity consumer in the U.S. when power costs spiked to US$10,000 per MWh, you would have wanted to protect yourself before that happened, perhaps by up to 100%.

Answering such questions will help an organization to then look at the next step of putting together a risk-management policy. At this stage, further questions need to asked. For example, what types of derivatives should be used? Futures? Options? OTC? On-exchange? Swaps?

Normally, an organization should state in its risk-management policy (as a hedger) or derivatives-usage document (as a speculator) which types of derivatives can be used, in which markets they can be used and how far forward each type of derivative contract (futures, options, swaps) can be made in each market (for example, Singapore gas-oil, Dubai crude, Brent, fuel-oil Rotterdam).

For hedgers, such decisions will be based on how well the available energy derivatives markets correlate in terms of price (and causation relationship) with the underlying energy markets that are to be hedged and in which the organization has price-risk exposure. Once a list of possible energy derivatives has been selected to match its requirements, the organization must then review this with contract liquidity in mind. (This will require checking with brokers on the average daily volume, normal bid/offer spread gap, and the number of active counterparts.) If liquidity is bad, the organization may have to consider a proxy hedge — such as IPE Brent Futures to hedge Middle East crude exposure, for example. IPE Brent is not a Middle East crude contract, but it has high liquidity and has some price correlation with Middle East crudes. This might be used instead of the OTC Dubai or Oman swaps, which are much more closely linked with Middle East crude but whose price transparency and overall liquidity may not be good enough for some organizations.

For traders/speculators, this decision will be based upon liquidity of the energy-derivatives markets (volume and number of counterparts trading the market) and also the level of price transparency that exists. For a trader/speculator, the lack of price transparency can be an attraction, whereas for a hedger, price transparency is more important than liquidity. Liquidity is more important for a trader, who will normally wish to trade out/close out a position ahead of its expiry/settlement. An organization that is hedging will normally let derivatives contracts run their full term through to expiry as it is hedging an underlying energy-price risk. So, for a hedger, the ability to trade out/close out a derivatives position may be less of a concern. The price linkage between the derivative and the energy-price risk being hedged may be more important to the hedger than the liquidity of the market.

So much of the success of such moves will depend upon the ability of the operations department to manage the derivatives positions. Questions will need to be asked about whether the organization will require new IT infrastructure to process and manage these positions. Does it have the relevant skill sets or will training be required before the start of this activity? How will these derivatives positions be valued — against third-party forward curve assessment (Platts Forward Curve, for example) or broker quotes/dealer quotes? How often will these derivatives positions be valued — daily, weekly, monthly, quarterly?

If the company is a trader/speculator, what position limits will be set — volumetric/notional value? Will the limits be set by tenure and product? Which traders can trade what products and which types of derivatives can they trade? Who will be responsible for monitoring these positions and reporting any break in the organization's policy for derivatives usage? What reports will be produced to assist risk-monitoring/performance function — open position? market value? profit and loss? hedge-effectiveness reports (correlation analysis between the derivatives used for hedging and the underlying energy risk being hedged)? How often will these reports be produced? Who has to see them and sign them off as read?

Before the start of any activity, the organization must assess the operational risk of this new business, as well as the credit risk, market risks, legal risks, tax risks, and so on. Responsibility for ensuring that these risks are reviewed regularly should be clearly spelt out.

While this is certainly not an exhaustive list, all of these questions can assist an organization to start looking at policy decisions and to put together a short report on what it requires of its risk managers and traders. Accounts departments can also get a good idea of what type of accounting will be required, either as hedges or speculative trades. All of this information, together with feedback from relevant line managers, should then be presented to the board of directors/ management, which is responsible for creating a general policy and reporting structure for the organization.

Once the general policy has been formulated, line managers should be asked to fine-tune a more detailed risk-management guidebook on the use of derivatives for traders, operations staff and managers.

## Risk management of carbon emissions

In broad terms, emissions allowances as marketable instruments can be held for hedging current or future emissions exposures or for speculative purposes to benefit from expected changes in the market price of the allowance.

Shareholders of companies require, and firms should provide, clarity over whether the allowances are being held for hedging or speculative purposes, as the risk profile of the company and its balance sheet and financial results may be directly affected by these choices.

A company needs to be able to demonstrate for risk-management and accounting purposes whether it is buying emissions credits/allowances for hedging or speculative purposes required to meet future emissions exposure.

A clearly written operating and control-risk framework for carbon, backed up by credible management-information and related systems, enables a company to implement its emissions policy and provide whatever evidence is required to support it.

When formulating a risk-management policy for emissions, there are many factors to consider, some of which are different from those for energy markets. These could include:

- The financial objectives of the company (which may differ in emissions and energy markets)
- The predictability of production (and consequently GHG production)
- The extent to which movements in allowance prices can be absorbed within profit margins and how much risk the board of directors is willing to accept
- The extent to which the company can pass on the effects of movements in allowance prices to customers
- The extent to which competitors are able to absorb price fluctuations or pass them on to customers
- The volatility of allowance prices and subsequent price changes that may have on future cash flows (at the end of 2005, prices were already being traded in to 2008 for EU ETS $CO_2$ credits)
- The ability of the company to hedge the relevant exposures; that is, the availability of instruments such as derivative contracts to hedge exposure.

To enable the effective management of emissions risks, there needs to be an assessment of whether the existing data-collection mechanisms and reporting systems are sufficient for the company's needs. Prior to joining emissions schemes, large emitting companies may not have required truly accurate approaches to monitoring and recording the true level of their emissions. Now, having such accurate approaches is vital for proving to regulators that emissions levels have indeed been reduced.

# A sound framework for energy-market risks

The primary components of a sound risk-management process include a comprehensive approach to risk measurement, a detailed structure of derivatives-position limits and clear guidelines for governing risk taken by the company's officers. There also needs to be a strong information system for controlling, monitoring, reporting and aggregating risk, including that from energy-and-emissions trading positions. These components are fundamental to both derivatives and non-derivatives activities.

The underlying risks associated with derivatives activities, such as credit, market, liquidity, operations and legal risk, are not new to the energy-trading sector; it's just that their measurement and, in turn, their management can be more complex than for physical energy deals.

As is the case with all risk-bearing activities, the risk an organization takes in its derivatives activities should be properly supported by adequate working capital. The organization should also ensure that its capital base is sufficiently strong to support all derivatives risks on a fully consolidated basis and that adequate capital is maintained in all of its group entities engaged in these activities. This is even more important if an organization's subsidiaries or any of its affiliates are Specified Entities in any of its ISDA or other master trading agreements (see Chapter 8). Any default, perhaps on a loan or a derivative contract payment from one of its group companies, could affect its own trading position in the markets and see counterparties closing out its positions.

An organization's system for measuring the various risks of derivatives activities should be both comprehensive and accurate. Some key points on recording risk are set out below:

- Risk should be measured and aggregated across all derivatives activities to the fullest extent possible.
- An organization using derivatives should have a system in place that enables management to assess exposures on a consolidated basis.
- The risk-measurement system used (value-at-risk, for example) should be good enough to reflect accurately the multiple types of risks facing the organization. (This will vary depending on the types of derivatives used.)

- Risk-measurement standards should be understood by relevant personnel at all levels of the organization — from individual traders to the board of directors — and should provide a common framework for limiting and monitoring risk-taking activities.
- The process of marking derivatives positions to market (for fair-value accounting and management-control purposes) is fundamental to measuring and reporting exposures accurately.
- An organization speculating in OTC energy and other derivatives should have the ability to monitor credit exposures, physical and derivatives trading positions and market-price movements on a daily basis.

Stress testing of derivatives positions should also be included in any concise risk-management policy. Value-at-risk (VaR) can be a good system for clearly illustrating the U.S.-dollar risk an organization may take overnight within a certain level of confidence — a 95% confidence level, for example. That said, this only provides a prediction of a possible reality and does not reveal exactly what the reality will be. Therefore, stress testing alongside even a VaR system is both important and prudent for measuring the impact of market conditions, however improbable, that might cause market gaps, volatility swings, disruptions of major relationships or reduce liquidity. This should be conducted on a regular basis to check what the impact on the organization would be if a disaster situation occurred (for example, a large standard deviation move from normal market situations). Would it survive the cash-flow crunch?

Dealers should regularly perform simulations to determine how their portfolios would perform under market and operational (real-world) stress conditions. These simulations should reflect both historical events and future possibilities (the oil industry during the first Gulf War in the early 1990s provides a good real-life scenario to run through your system using historical data). Stress scenarios should include both abnormally large market swings and periods of prolonged inactivity. The tests should consider the effect of price changes on the mid-market value of the portfolio, as well as changes in the assumptions about the adjustments to mid-market (such as the impact that decreased liquidity would have on close-out costs).

It should be noted, too, that these same reports can help the company meet the requirements for derivatives accounting disclosures. (In this regard, it is advisable to adopt fair-value derivatives-accounting and disclosure practices such as FAS133 or IAS39.)

Ideally, such worst-case analysis should be conducted across the entire organization, taking into account the effect of unusual changes in prices and or volatilities. It should also look at "what if?" scenarios for market liquidity and for early-termination events under ISDA OTC derivatives arising from a key default of a large counterparty. These scenarios should include input from the organization's legal department to ensure that contingency plans for disaster scenarios are understood fully by all line managers.

For a risk-management process to be complete, these regular stress tests should not be limited to quantitative computation of potential losses or gains. They should really include more qualitative analyses of the action that management might take under particular "disaster" scenarios.

Wherever time permits, it is better to have a written policy for guidance on "what if?" scenarios. From these, contingency guidelines and plans outlining operating procedures and lines of communication, both formal and informal, can be put together. If an adverse event occurs, the panic that follows could cost more in terms of reputation and money lost than the original problem. With forethought and planning, such panic can be averted by adapting the contingency plans to suit the precise needs of whatever crisis might arise.

Even if the contingency plans are not an exact fit, they will make everyone focus on resolving the issue rather than simply dwelling on the problem and watching it grow.

## Trading controls

It may take a lot of man-hours and cash investment to achieve but a sound system of integrated limits and risk-taking guidelines can pay for itself many times over if implemented from the outset. It is an essential component of the risk-management process and is usually money well spent. Derivative-position control, risk-management reporting and subsequent action plans by management and traders alike is the first line of defense an organization has against internal fraud.

Such a trading/position-limit system should set boundaries for organizational risk-taking/risk-reduction through hedging and should also ensure that positions that exceed predetermined levels receive prompt attention. Market-risk limits must be decided based on factors such as management tolerance for low-probability extreme losses as opposed to higher-probability modest losses; capital resources; market liquidity; expected profitability; trader experience; and business strategy. (Market risk is best measured as "value at risk" using probability analysis based upon a common confidence interval — for example, two standard deviations — and time horizon — for example, a one-day exposure.)

Any position-control breach should trigger the creation of what is termed an "exception report", which should be reviewed on at least a daily basis. The system should be consistent with the organization's overall risk-management processes and with the adequacy of its capital position. Just because an organization is hedging rather than speculating does not mean it does not need position controls. It is important for management to ensure that the extent of hedging is within board-approved remits and policy.

If derivative-position limits are breached, such occurrences should be made known to senior management and the position should be reduced immediately or approval sought for the larger position from authorized personnel.

Having said that, position limits are not restricted to the size of position; they also include the types of derivatives and the energy products in which derivatives can be used by the organization. Clear details should be written into the risk-management policy and made available to traders. If the organization is also speculating, then the policy should also detail the size limits of positions based on tenure (how far forward contracts can be made). The organization may say, for example, that a trader can trade Naphtha Swaps up to six months forward but no further because of liquidity concerns.

## Position limits

In summary, the limits imposed on specific positions may be by:

- energy product/type — Dubai Crude, UK NBP Gas, Singapore Gas-oil 0.5%, New York Harbor Unleaded Gasoline, for example

- type of derivative — swaps, futures, options, exotic options
- tenure (the size and forward reach of the position) — Dubai Crude swaps two million barrels, one to six months forward and one million barrels seven to 12 months forward.
- division or office or group of offices/divisions
- individual trader.

An accurate and timely management-information system is essential to the proper operation of derivatives activities, and the more real-time the better. A system is only as good as the quality of the data going into it.

In speculative trading operations, the gross and net exposures should be reported, broken down by energy market and counterpart and showing the net position on each market and the overall VaR or other risk-measurement result across all markets. Such information, together with profit-and-loss statements, should be reported on at least a daily basis to managers who supervise but who do not themselves conduct trading activities (this is a necessary segregation of duties as part of the risk-control function).

End-users who use derivatives infrequently for long-term hedging are still advised to generate profit-and-loss (that is, fair-value marked-to-market) calculations of their hedge against underlying energy-market exposure to ensure that their hedge is effective and to see how it is performing at the close of business every day. Other position and disaster-scenario reporting may seem excessive, but we would not advise anyone against doing lots of reporting and assessment of cash-flow risk and risk reduction through hedging. In the end, though, it is up to the management of the organization to make a final choice as to what level of reporting seems appropriate to the company's level of derivatives usage.

Reporting on derivatives positions to higher levels of senior management and the board may occur less frequently but it should provide these individuals with adequate information to judge the changing nature of their organization's risk profile. After all, they are ultimately responsible to shareholders if anything goes wrong. For companies using derivatives for hedging long-term energy exposures and which do not frequently change their derivatives position, quarterly reporting to the board is probably sufficient in most cases. If an organization is changing or adding to its derivatives positions on a more frequent basis, then monthly reporting may be more prudent.

In the best of all possible worlds, an organization will implement a computerized risk-management system that can provide board members with a snapshot of the derivatives and, if applicable, physical energy portfolio, together with the resultant risk profile, at any given time. This should be backed up with a mandatory update to the board — perhaps every quarter or whenever appropriate to the organization's specific needs.

Risk-management information systems should ideally translate the measured risk for derivatives activities (combined with physical energy-trading activity, if applicable) from a technical and quantitative format to one that can be easily read and understood by senior managers and directors. Value-at-risk methodologies can be very useful in this situation as by their very nature they reduce risk down to a monetary value over a given time period within a certain range of probability.

It should go without saying that an organization should authorize only professionals with the required skills and experience to transact and manage the energy risks, as well as to process, report, control, and audit derivatives activities.

The derivatives portfolios of dealers should be valued based on mid-market levels less specific adjustments, or on appropriate bid or offer levels. Mid-market valuation adjustments should allow for expected future costs such as unearned credit spread, close-out costs, investing and funding costs, and administrative costs.

Any organization using derivatives should use a consistent measure to calculate on a daily basis the market risk of their derivatives positions and compare it to market-risk limits.

Dealers should periodically forecast the cash investing and funding requirements arising from their derivatives portfolios. The frequency and precision of forecasts should be determined by the size and nature of mismatches. A detailed forecast should determine surpluses and funding needs, by currency, over time. It should also examine the potential impact of contractual unwind provisions or other credit provisions that produce cash or collateral receipts or payments. There have been instances of currency problems for hedgers using derivatives, as we saw with the case of Korean Airlines in Chapter 10.

The market-risk manager — who is rarely involved in actual risk-taking decisions — should act as a catalyst for the development of sound risk-management systems and procedures, questioning whether results are consistent with those suggested by an analysis of value at risk. This role could be reinforced by having a suitably qualified end-user on the board to test the effectiveness of the company's risk-management or trading programs.

End-users should adopt (as appropriate to the nature, size, and complexity of their derivatives activities) the same valuation and market-risk management practices that are recommended for speculative traders. Specifically, they should consider regularly marking to market their derivatives transactions for risk-management purposes; periodically forecasting the cash investing and funding requirements arising from their derivatives transactions; and establishing a clearly independent and authoritative function to design and assure adherence to position and or risk limits set by the organization.

As they are hedging an underlying or future exposure to energy price, most end-users may not expect any significant change in the combined value of their derivatives positions and the underlying energy exposure. Even if this is expected to be the case, an end-user should establish hedge performance-assessment and derivatives / management-control procedures that are appropriate for their derivatives activities.

Speculative traders and even end-users who hedge using derivatives should measure both their current exposure, which is the replacement cost of derivatives transactions (their market value), and their potential exposure, which is an estimate of the future replacement cost of their derivatives transactions. This should be calculated using probability analysis based upon broad confidence intervals (say, two standard deviations) over the remaining terms of the transactions. This will enable them to calculate the current and future replacement costs of derivatives should a counterparty default now or in the future.

Any credit risk on derivatives, and all other credit exposures to a single counterparty, should be aggregated, taking into consideration any enforceable netting arrangements. Credit exposures should be calculated regularly and compared to credit limits. In calculating the current credit exposure for a portfolio of transactions with a counterparty, the first question is whether netting applies. If it does, the current exposure is simply the sum of positive and negative exposures on transactions in the portfolio. Though master netting agreements which cover both physical energy and derivatives positions are in the early stages of development, they are possible. More common, though, are the netting agreements for derivatives within ISDA master agreements.

Traders and end-users of derivatives should have an independent credit-risk management function that has analytical capabilities in derivatives. This would be responsible for such things as approving standards for measuring credit exposure, setting credit limits and monitoring their use, reviewing concentrations of credit risk with counterparties, and reviewing and monitoring risk-reduction arrangements, working with the legal department to check their enforceability (this may change depending on the jurisdiction of the counterparty).

The credit-risk management function should continually review the creditworthiness of counterparties and their credit limits. Traders and end-users should have a policy to use one master agreement as widely as possible with each counterparty to document existing and future derivatives transactions. Master agreements should provide for the netting of payments and close-out netting, using a full two-way payments approach.

All users of derivatives should have a clear policy on credit-risk reduction arrangements that can be useful in the management of counterparty credit risk. These should include collateral and margin arrangements, and third-party credit enhancement such as guarantees or letters of credit.

While these guidelines are by no means exhaustive, they are an attempt to capture both the spirit of what a risk-management policy should be aiming to cover and the core contents of a policy for any organization, whatever its reason for using derivatives.

# 12 Managing Financial Risk for the Environment

The energy business is already globalized and multinational, with large energy companies operating in more than 200 countries. This globalized business, coupled with the spread of information across borders through media such as the Internet and television, has significantly changed public perceptions about the environment. In effect, pollution can no longer be exported across borders as a new, globally conscious environmentalism has been created over the past decade. This is particularly true for greenhouse gas emissions, which affect the entire planet. With carbon content increasing in the atmosphere at two parts per million per year (first confirmed in the 2000/2001), the fear is that inaction will only lead to ecological disaster. Thus, the potential for web-based emissions trading is being realized, as the web is borderless and international trading platforms are global.

In the past, environmental protection in many countries followed the heavy-handed command-and-control approach that has proved to be expensive and cumbersome. Over the past decade, however, more-cost-effective market-based incentives, using tradable permits, have been gathering momentum. The initial successes to date have been the trading of chlorofluorocarbons under the Montreal Protocol of 1987 to save the ozone layer, and the U.S. emissions-trading scheme for sulfur dioxide ($SO_2$) for acid rain abatement, which began in 1995. The key to these successes in reducing air emissions has been the introduction of tradable permits combined with sanctions for non-compliance.

The private sector will take the lead on the development of emissions-trading markets since it has a vested commercial interest in reducing emissions. There is a strong belief that governments should not inhibit the growth of an emissions-trading marketplace that will motivate firms with surplus emissions rights to trade or supply those rights to the market. In effect, despite the risk of uncertainty on future rules, there are merits in moving forward early. It seems evident that industry-driven trading schemes for early action on greenhouse gas (GHG) emissions will be grandfathered in the future (that is, granted exception as a previously existing or sufficiently old condition that might otherwise be affected) as rules are more clearly defined. Thus, industry can now create its own domestic and international portfolio of emissions allowances and credits. Responsibility for compliance, however, will rest with governments.

The GHG emissions-reduction environment now offers the next commercial opportunity for commoditization, and mimics U.S. oil-market developments in the late 1970s except that this time the market maturation process will occur on a global basis. Large financial institutions are now acknowledging the need to manage the financial risk of owning generation assets (power stations) and are developing their internal emissions-trading expertise. Moreover, large oil and gas companies have already recognized these increasing risks and are beginning to create a profit-and-loss statement for managing their carbon liabilities. This is a business opportunity that is growing, and one whose corporate profile is rising each year.

Since European, Japanese and U.S.-based companies are now moving ahead to develop pilot programs, there exists a first-mover advantage in this field since waiting for regulatory approval may prove more costly in the future. Emissions rights may be traded through bilateral transaction, listing on exchanges or through brokerage houses.

In the Kyoto Protocol, it was envisioned that three international mechanisms would enable Annex I countries to reduce emissions to reach their Kyoto targets. These mechanisms — emissions trading, joint implementation (JI), and the clean-development mechanism (CDM) — were discussed in detail in earlier chapters.

All three modes are currently being used and it is thought that bilateral trade between countries will be the most effective means to trade emissions initially. The emissions unit to be traded for the six greenhouse gases is one ton of carbon dioxide ($CO_2$) equivalent. Nitrogen oxides (NOx) and methane ($CH_4$) emissions are more difficult to quantify in many countries. The U.S. has already established an OTC market for both NOx and $CO_2$ emissions. It has also completed cross-border trades with Canada.

Since trading mechanisms will be part of any long-term approach to limiting GHG emissions, the emissions market is going forward on many fronts without Kyoto approval or U.S. participation in Kyoto. It is thought that actions taken today will most likely be grandfathered into the future revised treaty. Kyoto was meant to be flexible and allow market-based solutions to trading GHG as a carbon-reduction strategy and as a means to influence the spread of energy-efficient technologies for industry. Governments also expect industry to make the largest GHG reductions and this falls heavily on electric and gas utilities, manufacturing and automakers.

## The U.S. emissions-trading experience: Ramifications for Asia

Despite the fact that many countries continue to propose emissions-trading schemes in the form of green certificates, the reality is that the U.S. is the only country that has been successful in developing such a market. This has worked well for the past eleven years and provides the model for a cap-and-trade system.

Basically, the U.S. Environmental Protection Agency (EPA) runs an emissions auction during March of each year that is supervised by the Chicago Board of Trade, a commodity futures exchange. Under Phase I, which began on January 1, 1995, the 110 highest emitting utility plants were mandated to reduce their annual $SO_2$ emissions by 3.5 million tons. This process was extended to cover NOx in 1999. Today, half of the U.S. is under the NOx trading program. The OTC forward markets for $SO_2$ trade these vintage credits through to the year 2030. Several OTC energy brokers are involved in brokering these credits including Evolution Markets, Natsource and Cantor Fitzgerald, with more than a million trades per year. Thus, the market is liquid and has created emissions credits that are a fungible financial product. It has also saved US$1 billion per year over command-and-control strategies. Under Phase II, which began on January 1, 2000, a more stringent standard calling for an additional annual reduction of five million tons of $SO_2$ was required, and the program was expanded to another 700 utility plants throughout the U.S.

Under the $SO_2$ program, utilities are given one allowance for each metric ton of $SO_2$ emitted. The utilities are given flexibility on how they meet the mandated targets, and can switch to fuels with lower sulfur content, install pollution-control equipment, or buy allowances in order to comply with the law. In order to buy allowances, other utilities must reduce their emissions below their emissions limit. These emissions allowances are fully marketable once they are allocated through an EPA auction and can be bought, sold and banked. The allowances are allocated in phases. The later phases tighten the limits on previously affected sources of pollution and are also imposed on smaller cleaner units. Compliance is assured through continuous emissions monitoring at plants and regular reports to the EPA. Under this mandatory government-regulated program, fines are imposed on companies that don't comply with the law.

The program has an allowance-trading system under which all transfers are recorded and posted on the Internet. Serial numbers allow the tracking of each allowance's trading history, and an inventory for all accounts is provided. The most interesting phenomenon from this market-based solution to pollution has been that from 1995 to 1999 the market not only met its emissions-reduction targets but was 30% under compliance. This approach has exceeded expectations by lowering emissions below the announced targets because some companies demonstrated unexpected behavior in banking rather than selling emissions credits.

## The green trading market today

The existing green trading market can be characterized as having the following characteristics: opaque prices, little trading, few participants, poor liquidity, tremendous inefficiency, and wide arbitrage opportunities. If these attributes sound familiar, they are the primary factors of all emerging markets. Having seen the emergence and maturation of oil, gas, power, weather and coal as fungible commodity trading markets, the environment is now well positioned to be the next. More uniquely, it will explode simultaneously throughout the world. Similar to developments in the oil market that took place around 1978, we are now seeing the emergence of a global carbon market as a fungible commodity trading market. Moreover, it is emerging simultaneously throughout the world — something that has never happened before.

The other unique aspect of this market is that this is a government-mandated market, despite the claims of voluntary trading in the U.S. In fact, the U.S. created the carbon template with its $SO_2$ allowance market, which has vintage credits up to the year 2030. A true carbon regime will have a span of 50 to 100 years. This is envisioned for the Kyoto Protocol after 2012 and work at the governmental level is already under way to create the longer-term market.

The environment today is coming to be framed as a corporate financial issue. Greater financial disclosure of corporate environmental risks, including climate change, has raised the environment as a corporate fiduciary responsibility. Corporate boards are increasingly concerned as shareholders question their environmental practices. Companies such as Innovest Strategic Advisors, the so-called Green Moody's, highlight these environmental financial risks and this concept is now beginning to resonate in corporate boardrooms. Moreover, it is an issue that is gaining momentum. With ratification of the Kyoto Protocol, energy markets and many private companies are moving forward with their own initiatives to comply with the treaty. Trading emissions presents a near-term viable alternative to the mechanisms available under Kyoto. So far, the greatest activity to create emissions-trading markets has been in the U.S., Canada, Japan and Europe.

There are several parallels between the development of emissions-trading schemes and the liberalization of the electric-power industry in many countries. Emissions trading and electric-power deregulation intersect since the power industry contributes to GHG emissions.

## Exchange opportunities

Since almost all environmental financial contracts for $SO_2$ or $CO_2$ are traded on the OTC markets, there is an opportunity for exchanges like NYMEX to offer OTC clearing, which would effectively make them quasi-futures contracts under government oversight and, thus, more acceptable to risk managers. NYMEX could also supplement this effort by launching environmental futures contracts such as $SO_2$, NOx, $CO_2$ and RECs. Currently, NYMEX is reviewing its trades in WTI crude oil, heating oil, gasoline, natural gas, electric power, and coal futures, which are directly linked with emissions. There is also an opportunity for the IPE in London to trade emissions in the EU.

In Japan, both the Tocom and Tokyo Stock Exchange are considering launching carbon derivatives contracts. Presently, the ground rules in Japan are in a state of flux between a cap-and-trade market and a baseline market. There is also a movement emerging to create the next trading regime beyond 2012 and the Kyoto Protocol to include developing giants such as China, India and Indonesia.

The CCX is following another route to GHG market maturation and launched a voluntary carbon exchange in the fall of 2003. This is centered on the U.S. and Canada and currently includes multinational companies such as IBM, Rolls Royce AEP and other corporations among its participants. It is the first exchange to conduct daily carbon trading in a time of changing U.S. attitudes on global warming and is a precursor to other North American exchanges entering this emerging market space.

The GHG market has been estimated at US$2.3 billion by the Council of Foreign Relations, a noted foreign-policy advisory group based in New York, and even this may be an underestimate. This market sizing attracts capital. Typically, commodity contracts trade at six to 20 times the physical underlying market. To put this in perspective, the U.S. $SO_2$ market has been estimated at US$6 billion. The energy derivatives markets, both exchange-traded futures contracts and over-the-counter swaps, have been estimated at between US$2–3 trillion. The global foreign-exchange and interest-rate swaps market is over US$120 trillion in notional value — which points to huge room for growth in the energy and emissions markets.

Exchanges may be established quickly on the Internet, following the model of the CCX. Internet-based emissions trading would allow immediate disclosure for market players and would have low operation costs. As the market matures, it is envisioned that Internet-based trading will be the platform that will enable global emissions-trading schemes and seamless cross-border carbon trading to evolve.

# Enter agriculture!

The agricultural sector is beginning to realize the market potential and financial benefits of renewable energy, not just in the form of rents from the siting of large wind towers but from self-generation, with wind and biomass. The utilization of plant and animal farm waste can produce additional cash crops to be "harvested" and commercialized for their environmental attributes. This is a particularly hot commercial topic in Asian biomass markets, where agriculture can meet an electric-power generation need. The energy and agricultural sectors in the U.S. can join forces to develop new energy supplies while reducing dependency on energy imports and creating new industries in America that can be exported throughout the world.

Together, energy and agriculture are the world's largest businesses. They are also the most deeply liquid commodity markets. Financial engineering on environmental financial products will grow cross-commodity arbitrage opportunities for energy and agricultural commodities and GHG, renewable energy and efficiency.

# Implications for project finance

Another emerging trend that may hold the key to GHG-emissions liquidity is the structured finance market; that is, "Green Finance". A shift in fuel type to greener and cleaner fuels, such as natural gas, in preference to coal or oil is becoming embedded in the fabric of new power-station project financing. Since these plants have a useful life of 30–40 years, they will bring a stream of emissions credits that can be banked or used up front. They are unlocking another avenue along which markets can evolve. This type of thinking is just beginning at investment and commercial banks in New York, London and Tokyo.

Moreover, it can be envisioned that an environmental checklist is emerging in the environmental finance arena, yet another area where financial engineering can bring about market development and liquidity. There is no time to fight past demons. Forward-thinking and globally based energy participants should embrace the inevitability that international policy on greenhouse gases is being set by both media and public perceptions. In this context, the rational response from enlightened industry participants is to develop and support market-based solutions to global pollution.

In an imperfect world, this is the reality. In order to reduce $CO_2$ emissions, emissions trading will act as the catalyst for change in the transition of world economies towards renewables and the accelerated transfer of more efficient and greener technologies.

Ironically, the global market that now seems best positioned for trading is the REC market. Renewable energy has undergone a quantum technology shift in terms of increased efficiency and lower costs, with few financial players focusing on the new factors that drive this market. The technology for wind, solar, biomass and waste-to-energy is many generations more efficient than even two to three years ago, although financial analysts have only just started to follow the sector. Once again, government mandates, called Renewal Portfolio Standards in the U.S., are driving market maturation. But in the physical market, wind and solar power are growing at 40% and 30% per annum globally, with their costs now competitive with gas and coal. Tax subsidies for waste-to-energy and biomass power generation will move the equation further. Looking at a small installed base of renewable power generation today misses the fact that the ramping-up of this technology is global. These power stations are also getting bigger, with wind turbines of 2.5 to 5.5 MW and multiple siting of 300 to 400 MW wind farms being developed. More importantly, they have created another fungible commodity market that can be traded across borders, as the credits are measured in megawatt hours. Such green power initiatives will create a highly fungible market for RECs.

## Need for price indices

Markets in environmental financial derivatives are positioned for rapid growth due to political initiatives and business opportunities, but these markets will reach their full potential only if based on reliable indices widely accepted by the trading community. To focus solely on GHG emissions misses the opportunity to capture the benefits of other energy/environmental market-based solutions to global pollution such as RECs or energy-efficiency (negawatt) trading. Therefore, in order to maximize the business opportunity for an established exchange, several environmental products for various geographic markets must be traded, using regional environmental indices as the underlying benchmarks. The composite of these financial indices will contribute to a global index as well. The need is to establish exchange-traded derivatives products for $SO_2$, nitrogen oxides, $CO_2$, RECs, negawatts, mercury and other environmental products, with the first step being the creation of several tradable indices in North America, Europe and Asia.

Because government mandates are the primary market driver for environmental financial products, the scope of activity has been limited to a small number of players. Nonetheless, the growth of emissions trading and profit opportunities are attracting a new generation of traders in the market. Commodity traders from the world's largest banks and financial institutions are responding to these opportunities by opening trading operations on both sides of the Atlantic. The inhibiting factor is the lack of a reliable index, which has, so far, muted their effort to create a liquid market. The current trading environment is handicapped by the operational complexity of having adequate allowance inventory on hand to complete a trade, so that there are still more sellers than buyers of carbon. This limits access to those with ample allowances or those who can borrow allowances. Furthermore, it takes time to transfer allowances from one party to another and the process can take weeks, limiting traders' ability to enter or exit the market with ease. An index would remove this impediment, making it possible to attract more players into the market by allowing more trade structures and by turning the environmental market into a cash-settled operation. This would have the added benefit of improving cap-and-trade policy. Because of the potential for improving regulatory policy, we expect close cooperation between government regulatory agencies and any exchange seeking to use the indices as underlying benchmarks for trading financial products.

Many countries have renewable-energy, energy-efficiency and greenhouse gas programs. Some coordination to provide consistency needs to take place, but most such programs today are, and have been, independently developed. Consistent methodologies for measuring emissions, including GHG, renewable and efficiency efforts would facilitate project investment. Consistency would facilitate the development of project templates, thereby reducing costs and gaining rapid dissemination of the learning gained from early projects. National and international markets for GHG credit trading would offer the liquidity necessary to return value to projects and, thereby, financing. To function efficiently, such markets require assurance of integrity — clear definitions, avoidance of double counting, verification and liquidity. At this point in market development, it is critical to build some consensus around the development of common metrics for the private sector and for policy-makers to analyze opportunities at the regional, national and international levels. Greenhouse gas registries managed by a third-party, non-governmental entity could serve as a model at both the state level, as in California, or at the federal level, as in most EU countries.

Today, we have a one-off market, with many companies not acting on what will ultimately benefit them financially. A few innovators are proactive, but the reality is that the environment is emerging as a financial liability of multinational corporations globally. These liabilities are the market drivers for change. The quantification of these risks will keep analysts and mathematicians busy for many years as the dynamic models have yet to be built.

## Creation of the green trading marketplace

Because of the ability to establish exchanges quickly on the Internet, it is thought that this may be a desired outcome for emissions trading. Internet-based emissions trading would allow immediate disclosure for market players and has low operation costs. The concept behind the allowances was to foster the implementation of demand-side efficiencies or use of renewable energy. These concepts are tailored to the developing $CO_2$ market and the use of the Internet as the means to implement change.

The argument today is that to do it early will probably be less costly than in the future. Using GHG-emissions allowances now is a form of insurance for industry participants. Moreover, emissions trading delivers significant environmental reductions (as reduced compliance costs) as well as promoting environmental technologies.

The global energy industry is severely affected by these new financial risks related to climate change. With growing energy demand, particularly for oil, gas, and electric power in the Asia Pacific region, market-based mechanisms for reducing carbon intensity offer a cost-effective solution to global pollution. There are several similarities between emissions-trading schemes and the liberalization of the electric-power industry in many countries. Emissions trading and electric-power deregulation intersect since the power industry contributes to GHG emissions. The green trading markets today are still embryonic, but the maturation process is starting to accelerate. Despite the apparent obstacles to creating viable green trading markets, the timing is now right as the political momentum shifts towards moving forward, with both developed and developing countries creating a regional and a global market.

There is a clear market opportunity for green trading. The market characteristics for commoditization are there and the cross-border dimension is inevitable. The essential elements for trading are also growing, the technology is available and the timing is right, even though the financial risk is real and leadership is lacking. Most importantly, the financial engineering and risk-management tools are in place, with the affected parties willing to participate. It is the most effective public–private partnership available, since government must set the rules for business to develop the market. The next few years promise to be the breakthrough time for the first financial market since oil to emerge globally.

# 13 Investment Opportunities in Emissions

Until 2005, energy hedge funds were mainly a North American phenomenon, with the vast majority being located in the New York metropolitan area. However, our continuing research into the secretive world of energy hedge funds is revealing evidence of a next wave of interest in Europe as well as an extension of the commodity-trading platform into green markets. Specifically, this involves carbon trading, renewable-energy credit trading, ethanol trading and emissions trading. The approach, as in all emerging markets with little price discovery, is to find arbitrage opportunities and a mismatch in pricing. This can be as simple as going long carbon in the hope that its value rises over time, and as sophisticated as playing the regulatory arbitrage of shorting renewable-energy credits in one state and buying long in another (some 19 U.S. states have Renewal Portfolio Standards). In the green hedge-fund market, taking on the regulatory risk takes both government policy and market knowledge to be successful. Other green venues include biofuel trading, such as ethanol, and other plays in biomass for power generation.

The more traditional hedge-fund approach has been equities. Here, one newly launched green fund (New Energy Fund LP in New York) is a pure alternative-energy play, with investments in both the U.S. and Europe. The current high and sustained fossil-fuel prices should start driving a move to alternative-energy generation globally, and in the past six months has focused much attention on the U.S. venture-capital sector on funding investment in alternative energy. Alternative energy includes not only wind and solar but also biomass, ethanol, and distributed-generation plays such as fuel cells and microturbines. One other emerging technology play is the rising interest in photovoltaic nanotechnology, which may make radical improvements in electricity generation, from the traditional 8–10% efficiency to 15% and much higher. Hedge funds that trade only long/short equities are beginning to dabble in the alternative-energy sector. As far as we know, New Energy Fund LP is the only pure alternative-energy hedge fund, although there are others that may have a portion of their portfolio in alternative energy. Some energy hedge funds intend to be involved in renewable-energy project finance on a very selected basis as well where they may fly solo or club deals.

The reason for the new flurry of activity is that the returns for all 8,100-plus hedge funds during 2004 were, at around 8%, very unimpressive. Hedge-fund investors demand more and like the energy arena now. Private investors, rather than institutions, are starting to extend their investments into emerging environmental financial markets. Some energy hedge funds were up 40–50% in 2005 and one is rumored to have been up 100% and returned money to investors in October. Other more conservative energy hedge funds are looking for 15% returns on a sustained basis. It's the more entrepreneurial funds seeking higher returns that are interested in the environmental or green trading arena.

The more developed environmental financial markets for sulfur dioxide and nitrogen oxides trading have also attracted some interest from hedge funds as well as from Wall Street in the recent past. It is not well known, but commodity powerhouse Morgan Stanley is now the largest emissions trader in the $SO_2$ markets since these are the largest and most developed in the world. Wall Street firms have told us that they will wait for more liquidity in carbon markets before jumping in but their purchase of generation assets has already given them both a carbon footprint as well as an emissions footprint. Highly successful Houston-based energy hedge fund Centaurus has been known to trade both $SO_2$ and NOx markets and is making good profits. NOx emissions traded as high as US$40,000 per ton in the Houston/Galveston markets last summer. NOx trading is being used to reduce urban ozone emissions.

The more mature $SO_2$ markets for the reduction of acid rain got a boost of adrenalin in North America last year when coal burning increased as a result of the high cost and under-supply of more environmentally friendly natural gas. With recent trades staying at the US$700 per ton level for $SO_2$ allowances, the market has now indicated that gasification technologies for coal, called IGCC, may now be economic. With a carbon-reduction regime a certainty in the U.S. despite the present stance of the Bush Administration, IGCC projects have proliferated in the past several months so that there are about 20 such projects in the pipeline. In the spring of 2004, there were none.

Hedge funds are known to trade the California RECLAIM market for $SO_2$ and NOx reductions there and are proving highly successful because of confusion over the rules and a proposed tightening of air-quality standards in Southern California.

Despite the lack of the Kyoto stamp on U.S. carbon markets, these are developing in the U.S. as well as in Europe. Trades of over one million tons took place with Gulf Coast utility Entergy in December 2004. More $CO_2$ trades are in the pipeline, with a link to carbon sequestration and enhanced oil production that uses "commodity" $CO_2$ injection. There is also increased activity and higher prices on the CCX arising from market changes in Europe.

There are about 10 carbon hedge funds being formed in the U.S. and Europe, primarily arising from the implementation of the Kyoto Protocol in February 2006 and the launch of the EU ETS the previous month. Carbon is trading at about US$2 per ton on the Chicago Climate Exchange (which is way under market value). But the green hedge funds are a little smarter than that. They are looking at carbon arbitrage plays throughout the world. Their trading strategy is basically "buy now at low prices and sell the credits in the future". In the EU, while we saw over nine million tons of carbon trade in January 2005, it should be noted that global carbon emissions per year top 24 billion tons of carbon dioxide. The beginning of a global carbon market is now emerging with all the attendant risks of emerging markets — little price discovery, low liquidity and wide arbitrage opportunities. It's the trading arbitrage mindset of the funds that is driving this change. The manager of one green hedge fund told us that an investor had asked him if he was an environmentalist. He replied that he was a trader. The investor said "Good. I'll give you the money". This is a pure trading mentality, not an altruistic value of saving the world. That's what traders do:

seek arbitrage opportunities and exploit. They have found such opportunities in the global carbon markets.

Some investors view this as an asset-diversification play into emerging markets and invest in as many as 70 different hedge funds. They are investing in green trading markets because they basically see this as a diversification play for their fund portfolios. They like opaque prices and high returns. The downside risk is that the knowledge base of fund traders is limited in these emerging commodity markets since both an industrial knowledge of trading and a knowledge of the regulatory policy of governments are required. For these are not true commodity markets but are really hybrid markets where government sets the standard and industry reduces its emissions footprint over time. In the U.S. $SO_2$ market, the federal government has set up a 35-year regime for sulfur dioxide reductions through the year 2030 and is moving to tighten standards (already the most stringent in the world) on NOx. It will also be controlling mercury using market-based trading solutions. Furthermore, every manager of a U.S. power plant, industrial facility or other stationary source of pollution knows that a carbon regime is being formulated. In fact, 28 states in the U.S. have some sort of GHG initiative under way. The funds, being pure traders, will also exploit the carbon rules between states, just as they are doing in renewable energy markets.

More recently, two more green hedge-fund plays are under way. One is to trade sugar as a surrogate for ethanol trading, as these markets are more developed. This will bring in soft-commodity giants such as Cargill and Louis Dreyfus. The other new interest that is following carbon market development is water hedge funds, which trade long-dated water rights in the Western U.S. Water is now becoming a commodity, 10 years after Enron's ill-fated foray into water trading through Azurix, but that was not a pure commodity play.

The interest in green hedge funds is great from all quarters, including Asia. Investors want returns and, since late 2005, have been focusing beyond the energy complex.

# Broader Issues for Business — Global Emissions Markets

## 14

## Moving beyond Kyoto or Kyoto II

Since European, Japanese and U.S.-based companies are now moving ahead to develop pilot programs, there exists a first-mover advantage in this field since waiting for regulatory approval may prove more costly in the future. Emissions rights may be traded through bilateral transaction, listing on exchanges or through brokerage houses.

The U.S. has already established an OTC market for both NOx and $CO_2$ emissions and it has also completed cross-border trades with Canada.

Japan has been slow to establish emissions trading although many projects have been proposed by NEDO, a semi-governmental organization under the auspices of the METI and established in 1980 with the objective of introducing alternatives to Japan's oil dependency. Later, its mission was expanded to include energy conservation and the research and development of industrial technology. This is a natural progression towards developing and implementing sustainable-development projects throughout the world. It is currently identifying and promoting potential private projects, which will reduce greenhouse gases through the introduction of energy-efficiency and alternative-energy technologies. NEDO projects are evaluated on the basis of energy savings, greenhouse gas reductions, and the effect of technology diffusion. It has proposed projects in Russia, Poland, Indonesia and Bangladesh to show the breadth of its global mission.

It has been estimated that Japan will have the highest cost of compliance in an emissions-trading market, at more than US$500 per ton of carbon. The numbers are even higher for a market without allowances and have been estimated to reach US$1,075 per ton. These are very onerous costs to industry and should accelerate the move towards the adoption of a domestic emissions-trading scheme in Japan.

Despite the fact that many countries continue to propose emissions-trading schemes in the form of green certificates, the reality is that the U.S. is the only country that has successfully developed an emissions-trading market and this has worked well for the past eleven years.

The Minneapolis-based 3M Company did not sell its $SO_2$ emissions credits, as part of its corporate philosophy to be perceived as an environmentally benign company. Other companies followed this example of corporate environmental stewardship.

Because of the ability to establish exchanges quickly on the Internet, it is thought that this may be a desired outcome for emissions trading. Internet-based emissions trading would allow immediate disclosure for market players and has low operation costs. The concept behind the allowances was to foster the implementation of demand-side efficiencies or the use of renewable energy. These concepts are tailored to the developing $CO_2$ market and the use of the Internet as a means to implement change.

The argument today is that to do it early will probably be less costly than in the future. Using GHG-emissions allowances now is a form of insurance for industry participants. Moreover, emissions trading delivers significant environmental reductions as reduced compliance costs as well as promoting environmental technologies.

Various emissions-trading schemes have similar characteristics and often intersect with deregulation of the electric-power industry which, of course, contributes to the greenhouse gas emissions. The impetus will be there to move the process forward.

The Kyoto Protocol is, unfortunately, a market failure in its present form without the participation of the U.S., which emits 25% of global greenhouse gases. Moreover, the present form of Kyoto has significantly lowered the original goals. The reduction of greenhouse gas emissions will take decades longer than the timetable outlined under Kyoto. In effect, Kyoto is a very modest effort to contain emissions. It is only a first step.

The need to create market liquidity is the primary challenge for $CO_2$ emissions trading if it is to succeed. With electric-load growth and economic activity increasing each year, there is a need to create incentives for new technologies to penetrate new markets. One obstacle to change has been the fossil-fuel subsidies in many countries. These must end since they create the wrong economic incentives. These incentives must have the flexibility to develop market-based solutions without being overly onerous.

Many private companies are moving forward with their own initiatives. They are, in effect, creating a global emissions portfolio that will develop provided that energy companies can assume the risk. The emissions-trading systems instituted internally by BP and Shell are leading the way for energy companies to reduce greenhouse gas emissions. BP has about 150 of its business units, operating in more than 100 countries, involved in a cap-and-trade scheme to reduce its greenhouse gas emissions. It began the program in January 2000. Both $CO_2$ and methane are traded in the BP system. The concept is to aggregate reductions from all business units. At the end of 2000, BP had traded 2.7 million tons of $CO_2$, at an average price of US$7.60.

In 1998 Shell pledged to reduce its GHG emissions by 10% by 2002 compared to its 1990 baseline emission levels. It achieved this target, and in 2002 its emissions were the equivalent of 94 million tons of carbon dioxide, compared to 114 million tons in 1990 for the same set of facilities. To put this into perspective, this reduction comes in the context of business change throughout the same period which would have resulted in a rise of emissions to 140 million tons had action not been taken. Shell's upstream oil and downstream refining and chemicals businesses are trading emissions. Estimates are that Shell's carbon reductions range in value from US$5 to US$40 per ton. The program is reconciled internally on a yearly basis. Both Shell and BP plan to extend their programs externally as they develop expertise and further success.

These companies and others should be encouraging companies to trade their emissions permits internally between countries as a means of accelerating technology transfer and reducing greenhouse gas emissions. In essence, we need to create global emissions-permit allocations, and have a market-based solution for global pollution. After all, the world breathes in the same atmosphere and carbon is carbon wherever it is created in the world and through whatever industrial process; it is a standardized commodity.

## Creating the global $CO_2$ emissions portfolio

The goal is a gradual reduction in emissions driven by measurable targets using market-based incentives. These can include outright purchase of emissions reductions. The aim is to encourage better technologies, better fuel choices, better results and accelerated technology transfer. Multinational companies in North America, Europe and Asia are developing emissions-reducing schemes that can be transferred to their affiliates in developing countries.

Any market needs trading liquidity in order to ensure fungibility. Currently, the $CO_2$ emissions-trading market has completed only 50 trades, including one North American/Europe carbon trade and one European/Australian trade. Other factors that influence trading are caps. The reality is that the market for greenhouse gas emissions is in its infancy and trading caps can either be adopted by government or left open-ended for the markets to decide.

There is competition to create global environmental exchanges. They need not be mutually exclusive, as today's Internet technology creates a borderless trading environment. In effect, we can have world greenhouse trade through the Internet.

Today, exchanges getting into the act include the Sydney Futures Exchange, the International Petroleum Exchange, the Paris Bourse/UNIPEDE, and the CCX. OTC brokers active in the GHG-emissions trade include Evolution Markets, Natsource, TFS, Amerex, and Cantor Fitzgerald.

## Project finance applications

But the key breakthrough for $CO_2$ trading will be the use of the project-finance mechanism to create CDM credits. In this way, a stream of emissions credits for the life of the project (say, 30 to 40 years) can be banked upfront. Investment and commercial banks can later create an environment checklist so that further streams of credits can be created. Finally, a global $CO_2$ market operated on the Internet will accelerate trading across borders and thus bring the most players to the marketplace. Green finance is thus the potential solution for global pollution and GHG-mitigation strategies through the use of financial engineering at its best.

## Environmental software

Interest in corporate environmental health and safety (EH&S) issues is at an all-time high across the globe. Pressure from shareholders and concerned citizens has increased in response to the significant environmental risks now facing corporations, while companies must also respond to increasingly rigorous regulations and standards. And nowhere are these issues more obvious than in the energy industry. More than ever, environmental risk management is becoming a board-level issue.

Today, the asset-intensive energy industry is required to monitor and report on emissions, effluents and other pollutants released into the environment, as well as ensure that appropriate work- and process-safety initiatives are defined and followed. A myriad of often-confusing regulations are already in place, requiring a variety of reports to be produced regarding emissions or safety incidents, for example. The situation is made even more complex by the fact that there are multiple agencies and levels of government with an interest in the matter.

While regulatory pressure for monitoring and reporting is already of major importance, the emergence of additional corporate concerns, such as insurance, re-insurance, public relations and the premiums now being paid by shareholders and consumers alike for environmentally friendly products, services and initiatives, may prove even more overwhelming. Increasingly, corporations are feeling the need to demonstrate compliance with regulations, even going beyond the levels required by current regulations, as a part of good corporate governance.

Additionally, emissions-credits trading has now become an accepted part of emissions management in North America, with the U.S. proposing that emissions trading be part of the international climate-change process. The EU ETS got under way in January 2005 and there are many other similar regional schemes in development or under consideration.

The growing awareness of environmental issues, increased regulations and other implications for corporations has resulted in the need for business processes that monitor compliance and for emissions-trading systems. Similarly, across the energy industry a renewed focus on asset optimization is driving the need for business processes and supporting systems that take environmental factors into account in planning.

## Managing environmental risk

Over the last several years, environmental issues and pressures have been growing and most corporations have created EH&S departments and managers to deal with them. Today, however, environmental risk management is increasingly — and rightly — being overseen by a company executive such as the CFO. There are several reasons for this elevation of the environmental issue:

- The increasing importance of socially responsible investment groups that include mutual funds, hedge funds and institutional investors that screen their investment portfolios for several social and environmental criteria. According to the Social Investment Forum of Washington, D.C., these groups now represent US$2.2 trillion-worth of assets.
- Pressure from a variety of investor and other groups to change regulations and requirements around corporate environmental disclosure is slowly gaining momentum with the SEC and other regulatory authorities.
- For North American corporations, the impact of Kyoto and subsidiary regulations and initiatives in many parts of Europe creates an additional issue: that of operating under different regulatory environments across the globe. It is easier, less confusing and more effective for the corporation to apply a single standard across its global operations rather than applying different standards in each regulatory regime.
- Existing regulations now carry mandatory jail terms for C-level executives (CEO, COO, CFO) who misreport.
- Additional auditing and insurance issues pertain to EH&S processes, and to the reporting and disclosure of environmental liabilities.

However, the most compelling reason for increased awareness and oversight of environmental risk is doubtless that this is an area of sustained historical under-investment that may now be used to both differentiate and compete more effectively in today's markets. Managing environmental risks as a component in an overall corporate-risk structure not only makes financial sense but also allows optimization of management decision-making. While corporations that manage environmental risk proactively may perform well in the eyes of shareholders, they can also hone an additional competitive edge to increase profits. As an example, consider the evolving emissions-trading environments in Europe and North America. Effective emissions monitoring allows better decisions to be made to maximize revenue generated from emissions credits or minimize exposure to the need to purchase credits.

The launch of the EU ETS in 2005 thrust energy companies and other $CO_2$ emitters into a new world of complexity. Energy companies now need to deal with carbon dioxide, and other emissions, in the context of both their operations and their financial reporting. For energy companies with generation facilities, it has a particularly significant impact on day-to-day operations, long-term planning and, potentially, on shareholder and analyst sentiment.

Carbon is now expected to become a truly global commodity market in much the same way as crude oil. Estimates vary on the potential financial value of global carbon markets from around US$100 billion in 2006 to as high as US$2.3 trillion in trades by 2012. While estimates may vary, there is consensus that there will be a significant expansion in carbon markets by 2012. According to Fusaro & Yuen, the carbon market is now at a stage in its evolution that is similar to oil markets before 1978 but that, with the emergence of cap-and-trade schemes such as the EU ETS, the market is set to build rapidly as carbon dioxide becomes a fungible commodity-trading market.

Despite the fact that the U.S. has declined to sign up for Kyoto, cap-and-trade emissions trading has been taking place there for both NOx and $SO_2$. In fact, carbon dioxide is also being traded through exchanges such as the CCX, although it is an early and immature market. The real issue with respect to the U.S.'s absence from Kyoto is that in today's global economy, U.S.-based energy companies cannot afford to simply ignore emissions and their environment. First, many have operations in Europe and elsewhere that are already subject to regimes such as the EU ETS and, secondly, their shareholders and investors are increasingly focused on social responsibility and environmental issues. U.S. energy companies are therefore as affected by Kyoto and the general environmental lobby as any other energy company in the world.

## Impact of environmental regulation

Energy companies are amongst the companies most affected by schemes such as the EU ETS by virtue of the polluting capabilities of their installations — generation facilities, refineries and plants. For example, it is estimated that the implementation of the EU ETS alone has created approximately €25 billion-worth (US$30 billion) of new assets and liabilities on the financial reports of utility companies. For such utilities, almost every detail of what they do is affected by the carbon regime now in place. The magnitude of this issue is much broader when other emissions cap-and-trade schemes are considered in the U.S. and elsewhere.

Increasingly, environmental regulation and compliance comes with real teeth. Large fines and bad publicity are just a part of the consequences paid by companies that either fail to comply or misreport. Of course, this has a broader impact upon the public perception of the company, shareholder sentiment and insurance costs, amongst other issues. In an era of socially responsible and environmentalist investors, companies will need to pay close attention to environmental issues generally and provide strategy and directions for their businesses. A significant part of this effort will be to ensure that the systems and business processes required to meet their compliance obligations are in place. In the past, this has proven somewhat difficult to perform because of the plethora of state, federal and local environmental regulations, which can be both confusing and conflicting at times. In that respect, schemes such as the EU ETS make it easier to comply since they are the result of a broader initiative.

For energy companies with generation and/or plant assets, this means reviewing business processes and support systems in areas such as plant optimization, maintenance, environmental compliance, incident reporting, health and safety, dispatch, valuation and financial performance. Plant-optimization models now also need to take into account the impact of emissions cap-and-trade schemes. For example, for an electric utility, a decision to generate may now carry an additional cost through having to acquire an additional permit, as opposed to buying power in wholesale markets and selling any unused permits. This decision is made more complex depending upon the type of generation facility, the type of fuel it uses and the emissions profile of that fuel. An emissions-trading scheme may also have the desired effect of driving generators to use cleaner generation methods such as hydropower. Indeed, the economics behind the development of such methods has also been affected by the carbon regime now in place and provides an instance of a collision between the energy and emissions markets.

The potential impact of the EU ETS and other such schemes on the future price of power and fuel now needs to be incorporated into modeling and planning as well as into the ongoing assessment of price and volume risk management and reporting. The cost of the carbon regime may well be reflected in forward power prices and, at some point in the future, have an impact on the future price of coal, natural gas and crude oil by discounting the price of cleaner fuels over those that create a larger emissions problem. Similarly, power generated using renewable or environmentally friendly facilities (green power) is already in demand and can attract a premium price.

## Compliance: Impact and software

To comply effectively with the EU ETS, energy companies need to register with the appropriate registries and report correctly. They also need to measure and manage the various emissions and effluents from each plant in an accurate and verifiable manner to ensure that they have sufficient permits to cover their emissions for any vintage and thus avoid the penalties and potential public criticism that a failure to comply might attract. Tracking and understanding their various emissions positions allows good decisions to be made regarding trading excess allowances in the market at a favorable time and price. As a financial market for emissions opens up, energy companies may also seek to engage in hedging activities to offset emissions exposure. Certainly, speculators (in the form of hedge funds and investment banks) have seen the opportunity to speculate in green financial markets.

Ultimately, the energy companies will need to ensure that their various emission positions are also reflected accurately in their overall commodity portfolio and trading books. They will need to understand, track and report those exposures in the course of normal risk reporting and they will require trading systems to support and track their emissions-trading activities as a part of their broader portfolio.

Similarly, energy companies face significant penalties for incorrect reporting to the various regulatory authorities. For example, in the U.S., in order to obtain a permit to operate certain industrial activities that pollute, companies are required to have in place an environmental management system (EMS), specific standards and processes that must be followed to ensure compliance with the various environmental regulations. Some companies are using specific information technology applications — known as Environmental Management Information Systems (EMIS) — to assist in this process.

## Environmental compliance (EMIS) software

By virtue of the scope of operations of energy companies, geographically and from a functional standpoint, the EMIS requirement has proven to be an integrated suite of business processes and software systems. Despite that, the EMIS software market is still relatively immature and most vendors offer functional components rather than a complete integrated EMIS solution. Recently, though, a small number of vendors have built sufficient components to form complete suites of solutions.

Since the EMIS software market is in the early stages of its development it is very fragmented, consisting largely of custom-built or packaged solutions with limited functionality. No one company has taken the lead in providing a complete enterprise-wide EMIS software solution. The packaged software currently available is primarily provided by environmental consultancy firms to promote their services.

While the EPA has suggested that a compliance-monitoring system is appropriate, it has not yet made it a requirement for companies to have an EMIS in place. It does require, however, that companies provide accurate information and that the information provided is personally certified by a senior operations manager (often the plant manager). While most companies with Title V permits have some system in place, these systems are often manual and non-comprehensive, resulting in a higher risk of penalties and fines.

The main purpose of an EMIS is to provide information for the management of the environmental process. It has to be able to work with whatever systems are currently in place within a plant, such as operating systems, preventive maintenance systems and continuous emissions-monitoring systems (CEMS)

There are, then, effectively two types of software required for environmental regulatory compliance and for emissions trading and plant optimization — energy-trading and risk-management software and environmental-compliance software. The two categories of software have different primary uses and have had different target markets. For environmental-compliance systems, the target market has been any entity required to monitor, manage and comply with environmental regulation and has historically been targeted at EH&S departments. For energy-trading and risk-management systems, the target has been risk managers and trading management in energy companies engaged in the business of buying and selling energy commodities. However, the emergence of emissions-trading schemes has brought significant overlap between the two categories.

While many EMIS solutions offer the ability to measure, monitor, forecast and report emissions, in reality they lack the true trading and risk-management capabilities that are needed. More importantly, they lack the ability to integrate with other energy-commodities trading, scheduling and risk-management systems. The leading vendors in this category are now building such functionality.

## Energy-trading and risk-management (ERM) software

The ERM software category has been in existence for more than 15 years but, because of the rapidly changing needs of the energy industry, there are more than 85 solutions available today. Certainly, a smaller number of key vendors have emerged — SunGard Energy, Allegro Development, KWI, New Energy Associates and OpenLink Financial, for example — but the breadth of functional coverage is so large that no single vendor can serve the needs of the entire industry. This has left plenty of room for specialist niche vendors in the market.

Generally, ERM software can capture and value deals/trades, schedule and manage the physical side of a transaction, settle trades and perform various types of risk analysis and reporting, including value-at-risk. While deal-capture/position-keeping and risk-management functions can often accommodate multiple energy commodities, the distinct and complex nature of scheduling and movement of each commodity usually requires a separate specialist system for each commodity. Integrating different systems has thus emerged as a key issue. For example, a recent UtiliPoint survey found that, on average, a North American power marketer has somewhere between six and 10 different systems in place — and that's not including systems required to support other commodities. While many of the energy-trading and risk-management vendors currently lack specific emissions-trading, tracking and risk-management functions, they have the framework and configurability to add these in relatively short order.

A further issue to consider with ERM software vendors is whether their software is targeted at the physical side of the energy business or the financial side. This is a key consideration for a utility with generation assets, for example. Many ERM vendors originated in the financial markets and lack the ability to model generation facilities correctly and to measure and manage the physical risks associated with deliverability, and the type and generation capabilities of plant. What utilities dealing with the requirements of the EU ETS and similar schemes require is a trading and risk system that was designed to cater for the physical specifics and complexity of their business.

## Overlap and competition

Plainly, as the compliance vendors add trading functionality and the ERM vendors add environmental-compliance functions, there will be considerable overlap between the two categories and confusion amongst buyers. To date, a variety of ERM software vendors claim emissions-trading and risk-management capabilities. SunGard Energy, for example, has introduced a module for its Zai*Net software to cater specifically for the EU ETS. KWI has a number of existing users currently utilizing its platform for emissions trading and forecasting in Europe. Similarly, Allegro Development, Triple Point Technologies and other vendors also claim capabilities. The leading environmental-compliance software vendors such as VisionMonitor Software, IEA and Enviance, for example, all claim emissions-monitoring, modeling and forecasting capabilities and all are eyeing emissions trading as an obvious future enhancement.

The type of system required will be a function of the breadth and type of environmental issues faced by an energy company. A total environmental solution that provides coverage for the sheer breadth of functions, from incident reporting through emissions monitoring and forecasting to trading and risk management, does not yet exist. So, for the moment, the environmental-compliance software will be the primary choice for broader compliance and reporting functions and for ensuring measurement, monitoring and forecasting capabilities.

The trading and risk-management vendors will be the natural choice primarily for the capture of emissions trades, registry interface and risk management. They will also likely be the source for asset optimization and the generation-modeling tools required to plan optimal generation and dispatch strategies. The point of initial integration between the two categories will be in providing actual emission quantities to compare against forecasts to ensure effective management of allowances, to avoid penalties and to trade unused credits.

However, the speed at which environmental business drivers are having an impact on energy companies is such that solutions are needed across all segments of the industry. Who ends up providing these solutions will emerge naturally through competition between the different vendors. With the need for new solutions will come new vendors with integrated solutions to meet the changing requirements of the industry. When consideration is given to the size of the environmental software market, this represents a much larger opportunity and market than most vendors already serve. It will be an interesting evolution.

## Development of accounting approaches to emissions credits

Another area of interest is how emissions credits are accounted for on the balance sheet. In this regard, the removal of IFRS International Accounting Standard guidelines in 2005 has created considerable confusion for the various industries affected.

The IFRIC, a committee of the International Accounting Standards Board (IASB), had previously decided that emissions allowances should be accounted for as intangible assets, in line with IAS38. Emissions were viewed as a separate contingent liability, which had the potential to create accounting problems because it is a "mixed model" that can cause volatility in a company's P&L account. This will need to be explained to investors. Similar uncertainty surrounds the determining of the fair market value of allowances. Under IAS20, allowances have to be recorded as government grants but they can be received at no cost and then traded for profit, if unused. However, some markets are still relatively illiquid, with little price discovery to allow for an accurate assessment of fair market value.

Unfortunately, at the time of writing no clear guidance is available from the accounting standard regulators on how to account for emissions rights. However, there are examples in the marketplace but these are from industry, not from the regulators.

To add further confusion, during 2005 the IASB decided to withdraw its IFRIC 3 *Emission Rights* accounting guidelines, leaving many companies unclear about acceptable accounting approaches for emissions allowances.

In the absence of definitive IFRS guidance, we are seeing a number of accounting treatments currently being considered by participants in the EU ETS. This choice is being reflected in the marketplace, where we are already seeing a number of different approaches beginning to appear in companies' financial statements.

A sample of the accounting policies that appear to have been adopted by industry participants includes the following:

| | |
|---|---|
| A multinational European energy company | Allowances recognized as intangible assets at cost (with granted allowances at zero cost). Provision recognized if the number of allowances required in a reporting period is greater than the number of allowances received. |
| A multinational European energy company | Allowances allocated from the government are included in inventory at cost once notice of allocation is received from respective governmental entities. |
| An industrial entity | Provision recognized only if a shortfall in allowances is anticipated as compared with actual emissions in a period. |
| A British integrated energy company | Provision recognized when annual emissions forecasts exceed annual grant amounts. Provision amount is based on the spot-market price of allowances at the balance sheet date. |

| | |
|---|---|
| A German integrated energy company | Purchased allowances are accounted for as intangible assets at cost, whereas allowances received free of charge are accounted for at nominal value. A provision is recognized to cover the obligation to return emissions allowances and it is measured at its probable settlement amount. |
| A continental European energy company | Follows IFRIC 3, but notes that this is subject to change when new guidance is issued. |

*Source:* Energy Markets Practice of Deloitte & Touche LLP London *for its input on these accounting approaches to emissions.* (www.deloitte.co.uk)

As accounting standards for emissions continue to develop, management of companies engaged in the risk management of emissions credits or the trading of emissions should monitor accounting news very closely.

# 15

# What the Future Holds: Opportunities for Global Market Convergence

Environmental financial risk is rising as a corporate issue throughout the world. The issues of environmental financial liabilities and the emergence of climate-change risk have made companies extremely nervous on proceeding in market development with such near-term uncertainty. This has hit the energy industry particularly hard. However, change is under way as companies are beginning to view emissions trading as a positive instrument for environmental compliance. The Fitch Ratings report, followed by the implementation of the European Union's Emissions Trading Scheme and the Kyoto Protocol, marks an acceleration of the trend towards putting climate-change risk on the balance sheets of corporations throughout the world. It is a harbinger of the shifts in thinking that are starting to permeate the global capital markets.

Cap-and-trade systems have been proven to work in reducing pollutants and in an extremely cost-effective way. What the world now needs is for structurally sound emissions and renewable-energy programs to be put in place because both the business and environment communities need certainty in order to go forward in creating markets. The end result of this process will be fungible commodities that can trade anywhere in the world. We are still a long way from that goal today. There is an opportunity to avoid a collision between separately operated and controlled emissions-trading markets around the world. More importantly, we still have an opportunity in the coming years to ensure that the emissions markets around the world are able to inter-relate and converge into one global marketplace.

Consistency and compatibility of schemes will be central to the creation of an effective global emissions-trading scheme. Changes in trading rules are disruptive to any market and could lead to sharp changes in the value of allowances. Inconsistent application of schemes could leave companies either over-investing in certain technologies, relative to future needs, or investing in remedial technologies today based on a cost-benefit analysis using output requirements which may increase or include additional pollutants over time. Bankable credits/allowances are those that are generated in the early years of an emissions-reduction period that can be used for compliance in later years. This is important for programs that have an emissions-reduction program where permissible emissions levels are reduced over time. The energy generators are provided with an incentive to reduce emissions more rapidly than required and are given more flexibility in their capital-expenditure program.

As we have seen, emissions-trading markets are not true commodity markets in that they are cap-and-trade, which means that emissions are ratcheted down over time. For the $SO_2$ markets, it has been a 35-year regimen of reductions and more stringent standards begun in 1995. For $CO_2$ and other greenhouse gas reductions, we will need a 100-year program that engages the entire world if it is going to be effective. We need to broaden the Kyoto initiative to the developing world, with longer-term targets lasting decades and we need to engage the U.S., the emitter of 25% of global greenhouse gases. The reality is that, since $CO_2$ emissions disperse in the atmosphere on a global scale, the entire world is in this together for the long haul. There is no quick technological fix as long as the world is addicted to fossil fuels. That habit is not going to change quickly as it typically takes years to implement the alternatives required to put meaningful dents into $CO_2$ emissions.

If we are going to treat $CO_2$ emissions seriously, we need a regime that will aggressively reduce global carbon intensity from both stationary and mobile sources, accelerate technology transfer, and increase energy efficiency. The technology exists today to get the job done. We have highly efficient integrated gas combined cycle (IGCC) technology now for the gasification of coal as well as other fossil fuels such as petroleum coke, wood chips and municipal solid waste. We already have affordable hybrid vehicles that reduce both tailpipe emissions and increase fuel economy. We have many energy-efficiency devices that reduce building loads from both commercial and residential buildings. And then there is the controversial GHG-free nuclear option.

The solutions exist but for many of them to become commercially viable in the near term we need governments to set the rules that can bring a financial value to emissions reductions on both national and international levels. The point is that both the $SO_2$ and NOx programs are mandated and have financial penalties for non-compliance. These real financial consequences have allowed technologies such as scrubbers and low-NOx burners to take hold, together with the acceleration of IGCC technology. Voluntary $CO_2$ programs may be useful in practicing for future global trading of such credits but hard limits will be needed to create a real market driver for change. Emissions trading is one mechanism to accomplish many of these goals. The ability to monitor and certify verifiable reductions is already in place through both third-party certification companies and geo-positioning satellites and remote sensing devices. Financial markets for the environment work. Today, companies are analyzing their risks and realize that there is a global issue that they have got to do something about now.

One of the drivers behind the GHG market is that we now have institutional shareholders forcing corporations to acknowledge the environmental risk on their books. The US$20 trillion of pension-fund monies in the Carbon Disclosure Project is a step in the right direction to put the financial pressure on companies for environmental performance.

The energy industry can be a leader of this new movement to transfer technology and wealth to the developing world through global emissions schemes. The next generation of environmentally benign, cost-effective, renewable technology, and highly efficient technology, is already here, and will get better in future years. Energy prices are now high and will remain so. The time for renewables and alternative energy should be now. The threat of disruptions to energy supplies and higher prices may lead renewable energy to the promised land which many have envisioned.

An emissions-trading program is valuable primarily because it puts a market price on the cost of emissions and thus allows companies to make an informed choice regarding compliance options. However, it should be noted that a dysfunctional trading system can result in market prices that could lead to economically sub-optimal decision-making. For an emissions-trading market to be efficient, target levels of emissions must be assigned in a consistent and coordinated fashion. With $SO_2$ in the U.S. there is one overarching regulatory body, the EPA, that allocates the allowances and monitors the compliance process. However, with carbon there will be a number of countries setting their own procedures, with varying degrees of rigor. The EU provides that sanction in Europe.

Some financial institutions such as Morgan Stanley, Goldman Sachs, Barclays Capital, Calyon Financial, ABN AMRO and others are now trading emissions, which are a natural complement to their sizable presence in the energy markets. In fact, emissions markets are traded often on the same trading department alongside energy; they have converged, as emissions is the fourth dimension and natural extension of oil, electric and natural-gas markets activities.

A few brokers, too, have found a niche in this market and include Amerex, Cantor Fitzgerald, Evolution Markets, United Power, TFS and Natsource.

Regulated futures exchanges in the U.S. and Europe have started participating in trading and clearing environmental contracts. This assists with the globalization, harmonization, and standardization of traded emissions contracts.

Exchanges such as the NYMEX and CME, which already trade energy and weather derivatives, are progressing in their $SO_2$ and NOx futures trading. The advantage of clearing trades through an exchange is that it increases price transparency, as prices are posted on a real-time basis. It also reduces counterparty risk, as the exchange steps in between the market participants.

A number of voluntary bilateral sales of GHG-reduction credits have taken place, principally under the auspices of major international and domestic corporations. However, although several schemes are already in place or under development, there is no global standard for verification of these transactions and no systematic, comprehensive and consistent recording of these reductions among registries. The implementation and use of economic tools that operate across and among registries will encourage financial and physical transactions and establish a more narrow value for GHG-reduction credits.

Current U.S. policy promotes voluntary GHG reductions, usually for carbon dioxide emissions; hence the existence of the voluntary Chicago Climate Exchange. Federal standards for mandatory reduction in GHG emissions are not being considered by the current Administration. An efficient, powerful federal registry would be very helpful in ensuring development of active bilateral and private-exchange trades in carbon dioxide reductions and allow entities to bank these reduction credits for future use or private voluntary sales, or register their current carbon footprint in order to take advantage of any early actions aimed to reduce greenhouse gases. However, this is not being actively pursued by the federal government. In response, a number of states and regions are now developing GHG registries and renewable-energy standards, but there is little uniformity with regard to many metrics, rules and protocols across the registries.

Consistent economic tools for measuring and verifying emissions reductions among the various registries would facilitate project finance and investment and the development of environmentally sound projects. Tools that allow for consistent economic recognition of these credits would facilitate development of project "templates", thereby reducing costs and gaining rapid dissemination of the learning gained from early projects. Economic tools would offer the liquidity necessary to calculate future value of GHG-reduction credits to projects and thereby assist in developmental and project financing. To function efficiently, such tools require assurance of integrity, clear definitions, avoidance of double counting, consistent verification methods, liquidity and consistent treatment of metrics.

With coordinated, interconnected conversion methods and other economic tools among state registries, it may be possible in the future to use $CO_2$-reduction credits recorded in a U.S. registry to meet the needs of Kyoto signatory nations or any other successors to Kyoto. The EU has implemented an Emissions Trading Scheme which integrates its Kyoto treaty requirements to ensure compliance with the treaty and, at the same time, allows for uniform trading of GHG credits. Similarly, consistent registries could facilitate future trading with Canada and Japan as well.

Once economic tools are developed, state mandated and/or regulated projects would qualify for future credits which could be banked now in any registry. If no internationally acceptable economic tools are developed, then these credits, even if required by state law, may never be recognized in the international community and will have a lesser financial value for U.S. companies. Not establishing a common currency and other economic tools in GHG-reduction credits across the various registries would be a further disincentive for U.S. firms and international corporations operating in the U.S. to take action now.

Climate change has opportunities and new risks for the banking and financial markets. These include hidden carbon liabilities, impaired credit quality of GHG-intensive borrowers, opportunities in financing infrastructure development, opportunities in clean-technology markets and, most importantly, opportunities to trade in the US$2–3 trillion GHG-emissions markets. Such "green revenues" are important for capital-market liquidity as well as to generate new business with the engagement of the Wall Street financial houses, whose participation is essential to facilitate market development and trading liquidity. Moreover, clients of money-center banks will also need to use market-based solutions.

While global climate change poses a significant market challenge for the U.S. energy and agricultural industries, both have incredible opportunities in the renewable-energy markets and emerging green financial markets. The U.S. is the leader in establishing liquid environmental-trading markets — sulfur dioxide since 1995 and nitrogen oxides from 1999. This experience and expertise can be applied to create jobs for Americans in the financial services, environmental technology, energy and agricultural industries.

Today, we are seeing international markets in renewable energy and greenhouse gas reductions being created simultaneously around the globe, mimicking developments in the oil market in the late 1970s. Key to these markets is a recognized certification system with broad acceptance. Well-defined national renewable and GHG certification systems will facilitate trade and return maximum value to projects. In addition to lowering cost, a common "currency" will expand project financing opportunities.

Invented in the U.S. in the early 1990s, environmental financial trading began to enter into its second phase within less than 10 years. In 2002, Global Change Associates in New York coined the term GreenTrading™ to promote the triple convergence of trading in credits associated with the reduction in greenhouse gas emissions, renewable energy and energy efficiency (negawatts) through the use of the financial markets. In this convergence, environmental financial risk is treated as a mainstream corporate financial issue. The intent of GreenTrading™ is to capture both the problem and the solution, with financial trading providing a means to ameliorate pollution. Building on the successful U.S. sulfur dioxide emissions-trading program, the long-term impact of such trading would be to reduce pollution in a cost-effective manner and accelerate the introduction of more environmentally benign technologies. It would decrease economic disruption to the capital-intensive energy industry and other industrial sources of pollution. At the same time, it would create new financial markets where "trading pollution", as it is sometimes mistakenly called, would actually create concrete and measurable emissions reductions for American business. This business model could be exported throughout the world, and it has already happened to some degree. Indeed, the generic term "green trading" has begun to be used by leading practitioners around the world.

We now see an expansion in coverage and types of players coming into the markets. For instance, the allowance system under the EU ETS covers nearly 12,000 facilities in multiple industries with varying degrees of control costs, providing the basis for a good market. Initial transactions have occurred between Shell and the Dutch utility Nuon, and between Shell and Barclays, representing the participation of energy and financial firms. Also, there was a very large trade of 10 million tons of CERs between Nuon and AgCert on Brazilian CDM credits in the 2005–2007 period. In the U.S., the CCX now has over 70 members trading GHGs on a voluntary basis and there are many other companies that have started to look seriously at self-imposed GHG caps. CCX has expanded into Europe with the ECX, linking with the electronic platform of International Petroleum Exchange, the well-established energy-futures exchange. On the level of individual corporations, we are starting to see risk managers in some major corporations handling the GHG issue, and carbon finance playing a bigger role. So, we are witnessing a market transformation.

The energy and agriculture industries — the world's leading air polluters — are the logical and likely leaders in providing environmental solutions because it is good for their business. Together, these industries constitute the world's largest businesses and, very significantly, they also have the most deeply liquid commodity markets.

Since the private sector has a vested commercial interest in emissions reduction, it will take the lead on the development of emissions-trading markets.

Cap-and-trade systems have been proven to work in reducing $SO_2$ and NOx pollutants. What we need now are structurally sound trading systems that cover green trading commodities.

As a result of the European and other U.S. efforts we can see already a very large body of work to support the development of economic tools so that credits in state and regional registries can be used in conjunction with the EU ETS and other systems alongside the Kyoto agreement in the international space. Further, these tools will take on additional significance at such time as the U.S. decides to take part in mandatory international efforts to reduce GHGs.

Energy efficiency and demand-side management programs, while effective and much applauded, have generally been isolated from the mainstream of energy planning and use. However, there are hopeful signs for their integration into sustainable energy planning and programs to address climate change. In the U.S., Pennsylvania became the first state with a clean-energy portfolio standard that includes demand-side management and some utilities have begun to seek power-supply proposals that include demand-side resources. In California, a proposed rule would require the reporting of reductions in carbon dioxide emissions associated with energy-efficiency measures.

In Italy, Britain and New South Wales (Australia), there are "white" or energy-efficiency certificate-trading schemes that are part of the overall GHG-abatement efforts. There is ongoing work to develop these approaches as well as explore their interactions/ integration with other certificate-trading schemes (for example, green or renewable certificates) and the carbon/GHG markets. Such discussions and collaborations are taking place at the national and multinational levels (among European Union countries and through the International Energy Agency's Demand-side Management Programme).

The U.S. has begun to embark on this road, with 28 states working on GHG initiatives and nearly 20 states adopting or developing renewable portfolio standards, and the beginning of load-management or demand-response programs for trading in energy efficiency at some of the independent system operators.

In summary, the world is undoubtedly at the beginning of a major economic and social transition. For the financial markets and financial players, climate change and our response to it bring many new risks but also many new opportunities. On the negative side, as mentioned earlier, new risks include these institutions' carbon liabilities — both their own and those in their portfolio — as well as potentially impaired credit quality of GHG-intensive borrowers. However, on the positive side, we can see that new or additional opportunities will open up for financing infrastructure development and clean technology as well as unprecedented opportunities to trade in the estimated $2–3 trillion GHG markets. Very importantly, these "green revenues" can enhance capital-market liquidity as well as generate economic development

In responding to the title of this book, we have seen energy markets converge with emissions, literally at the trading-desk level in banks and trading houses and in the futures markets that provide the infrastructure for the energy and emissions markets to operate side by side.

Above and beyond this convergence of emissions and energy markets, we are now starting to see a "triple convergence", as outlined in Figure 15.1. Energy efficiency generates carbon reductions. Renewable energy produces carbon reductions. Emissions footprints are now being viewed on the balance sheet.

The next five years promise to be a period of global innovation and experimentation for the maturation process of green trading markets. The technology exists to move forward and the financial markets can learn quickly how to trade the financial products needed

**Figure 15.1** Triple convergence

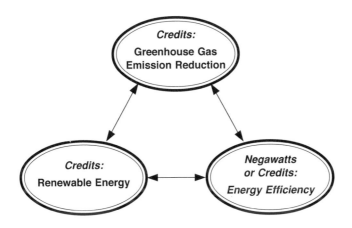

for greater price transparency, market liquidity and cost reductions. Clean and green energy is now in focus for energy hedge funds and venture capitalists. They smell money and know a good thing when they see it. Now is the time for the breakthrough in green trading. Watch this space!

# Appendix A

## Kyoto Protocol to the United Nations Framework Convention on Climate Change

The Parties to this Protocol,

Being Parties to the United Nations Framework Convention on Climate Change, hereinafter referred to as "the Convention",

In pursuit of the ultimate objective of the Convention as stated in its Article 2,

Recalling the provisions of the Convention,

Being guided by Article 3 of the Convention,

Pursuant to the Berlin Mandate adopted by decision 1/CP.1 of the Conference of the Parties to the Convention at its first session,

Have agreed as follows:

### Article 1

For the purposes of this Protocol, the definitions contained in Article 1 of the Convention shall apply. In addition:

1.  "Conference of the Parties" means the Conference of the Parties to the Convention.
2.  "Convention" means the United Nations Framework Convention on Climate Change, adopted in New York on 9 May 1992.
3.  "Intergovernmental Panel on Climate Change" means the Intergovernmental Panel on Climate Change established in 1988

jointly by the World Meteorological Organization and the United Nations Environment Programme.

4.　"Montreal Protocol" means the Montreal Protocol on Substances that Deplete the Ozone Layer, adopted in Montreal on 16 September 1987 and as subsequently adjusted and amended.

5.　"Parties present and voting" means Parties present and casting an affirmative or negative vote.

6.　"Party" means, unless the context otherwise indicates, a Party to this Protocol.

7.　"Party included in Annex I" means a Party included in Annex I to the Convention, as may be amended, or a Party which has made a notification under Article 4, paragraph 2(g), of the Convention.

## Article 2

1.　Each Party included in Annex I, in achieving its quantified emission limitation and reduction commitments under Article 3, in order to promote sustainable development, shall:

(a)　Implement and/or further elaborate policies and measures in accordance with its national circumstances, such as:

(i)　Enhancement of energy efficiency in relevant sectors of the national economy;

(ii)　Protection and enhancement of sinks and reservoirs of greenhouse gases not controlled by the Montreal Protocol, taking into account its commitments under relevant international environmental agreements; promotion of sustainable forest management practices, afforestation and reforestation;

(iii)　Promotion of sustainable forms of agriculture in light of climate change considerations;

(iv)　Research on, and promotion, development and increased use of, new and renewable forms of energy, of carbon dioxide sequestration technologies and of advanced and innovative environmentally sound technologies;

(v)　Progressive reduction or phasing out of market imperfections, fiscal incentives, tax and duty exemptions and subsidies in all greenhouse gas emitting sectors that run counter to the objective of the Convention and application of market instruments;

(vi) Encouragement of appropriate reforms in relevant sectors aimed at promoting policies and measures which limit or reduce emissions of greenhouse gases not controlled by the Montreal Protocol;

(vii) Measures to limit and/or reduce emissions of greenhouse gases not controlled by the Montreal Protocol in the transport sector;

(viii) Limitation and/or reduction of methane emissions through recovery and use in waste management, as well as in the production, transport and distribution of energy;

(b) Cooperate with other such Parties to enhance the individual and combined effectiveness of their policies and measures adopted under this Article, pursuant to Article 4, paragraph 2(e)(i), of the Convention. To this end, these Parties shall take steps to share their experience and exchange information on such policies and measures, including developing ways of improving their comparability, transparency and effectiveness. The Conference of the Parties serving as the meeting of the Parties to this Protocol shall, at its first session or as soon as practicable thereafter, consider ways to facilitate such cooperation, taking into account all relevant information.

2.    The Parties included in Annex I shall pursue limitation or reduction of emissions of greenhouse gases not controlled by the Montreal Protocol from aviation and marine bunker fuels, working through the International Civil Aviation Organization and the International Maritime Organization, respectively.

3.    The Parties included in Annex I shall strive to implement policies and measures under this Article in such a way as to minimize adverse effects, including the adverse effects of climate change, effects on international trade, and social, environmental and economic impacts on other Parties, especially developing country Parties and in particular those identified in Article 4, paragraphs 8 and 9, of the Convention, taking into account Article 3 of the Convention. The Conference of the Parties serving as the meeting of the Parties to this Protocol may take further action, as appropriate, to promote the implementation of the provisions of this paragraph.

4.    The Conference of the Parties serving as the meeting of the Parties to this Protocol, if it decides that it would be beneficial to coordinate any of the policies and measures in paragraph 1(a) above,

taking into account different national circumstances and potential effects, shall consider ways and means to elaborate the coordination of such policies and measures.

## Article 3

1.  The Parties included in Annex I shall, individually or jointly, ensure that their aggregate anthropogenic carbon dioxide equivalent emissions of the greenhouse gases listed in Annex A do not exceed their assigned amounts, calculated pursuant to their quantified emission limitation and reduction commitments inscribed in Annex B and in accordance with the provisions of this Article, with a view to reducing their overall emissions of such gases by at least 5 per cent below 1990 levels in the commitment period 2008 to 2012.

2.  Each Party included in Annex I shall, by 2005, have made demonstrable progress in achieving its commitments under this Protocol.

3.  The net changes in greenhouse gas emissions by sources and removals by sinks resulting from direct human-induced land-use change and forestry activities, limited to afforestation, reforestation and deforestation since 1990, measured as verifiable changes in carbon stocks in each commitment period, shall be used to meet the commitments under this Article of each Party included in Annex I. The greenhouse gas emissions by sources and removals by sinks associated with those activities shall be reported in a transparent and verifiable manner and reviewed in accordance with Articles 7 and 8.

4.  Prior to the first session of the Conference of the Parties serving as the meeting of the Parties to this Protocol, each Party included in Annex I shall provide, for consideration by the Subsidiary Body for Scientific and Technological Advice, data to establish its level of carbon stocks in 1990 and to enable an estimate to be made of its changes in carbon stocks in subsequent years. The Conference of the Parties serving as the meeting of the Parties to this Protocol shall, at its first session or as soon as practicable thereafter, decide upon modalities, rules and guidelines as to how, and which, additional human-induced activities related to changes in greenhouse gas emissions by sources and removals by sinks in the agricultural soils and the land-use change and forestry categories shall be added to,

or subtracted from, the assigned amounts for Parties included in Annex I, taking into account uncertainties, transparency in reporting, verifiability, the methodological work of the Intergovernmental Panel on Climate Change, the advice provided by the Subsidiary Body for Scientific and Technological Advice in accordance with Article 5 and the decisions of the Conference of the Parties. Such a decision shall apply in the second and subsequent commitment periods. A Party may choose to apply such a decision on these additional human-induced activities for its first commitment period, provided that these activities have taken place since 1990.

5.    The Parties included in Annex I undergoing the process of transition to a market economy whose base year or period was established pursuant to decision 9/CP.2 of the Conference of the Parties at its second session shall use that base year or period for the implementation of their commitments under this Article. Any other Party included in Annex I undergoing the process of transition to a market economy which has not yet submitted its first national communication under Article 12 of the Convention may also notify the Conference of the Parties serving as the meeting of the Parties to this Protocol that it intends to use an historical base year or period other than 1990 for the implementation of its commitments under this Article. The Conference of the Parties serving as the meeting of the Parties to this Protocol shall decide on the acceptance of such notification.

6.    Taking into account Article 4, paragraph 6, of the Convention, in the implementation of their commitments under this Protocol other than those under this Article, a certain degree of flexibility shall be allowed by the Conference of the Parties serving as the meeting of the Parties to this Protocol to the Parties included in Annex I undergoing the process of transition to a market economy.

7.    In the first quantified emission limitation and reduction commitment period, from 2008 to 2012, the assigned amount for each Party included in Annex I shall be equal to the percentage inscribed for it in Annex B of its aggregate anthropogenic carbon dioxide equivalent emissions of the greenhouse gases listed in Annex A in 1990, or the base year or period determined in accordance with paragraph 5 above, multiplied by five. Those Parties included in Annex I for whom land-use change and forestry constituted a net source of greenhouse gas emissions in 1990 shall include in their 1990 emissions base year or period the aggregate anthropogenic carbon dioxide equivalent emissions by sources minus removals by

sinks in 1990 from land-use change for the purposes of calculating their assigned amount.

8.   Any Party included in Annex I may use 1995 as its base year for hydrofluorocarbons, perfluorocarbons and sulphur hexafluoride, for the purposes of the calculation referred to in paragraph 7 above.

9.   Commitments for subsequent periods for Parties included in Annex I shall be established in amendments to Annex B to this Protocol, which shall be adopted in accordance with the provisions of Article 21, paragraph 7. The Conference of the Parties serving as the meeting of the Parties to this Protocol shall initiate the consideration of such commitments at least seven years before the end of the first commitment period referred to in paragraph 1 above.

10.   Any emission reduction units, or any part of an assigned amount, which a Party acquires from another Party in accordance with the provisions of Article 6 or of Article 17 shall be added to the assigned amount for the acquiring Party.

11.   Any emission reduction units, or any part of an assigned amount, which a Party transfers to another Party in accordance with the provisions of Article 6 or of Article 17 shall be subtracted from the assigned amount for the transferring Party.

12.   Any certified emission reductions which a Party acquires from another Party in accordance with the provisions of Article 12 shall be added to the assigned amount for the acquiring Party.

13.   If the emissions of a Party included in Annex I in a commitment period are less than its assigned amount under this Article, this difference shall, on request of that Party, be added to the assigned amount for that Party for subsequent commitment periods.

14.   Each Party included in Annex I shall strive to implement the commitments mentioned in paragraph 1 above in such a way as to minimize adverse social, environmental and economic impacts on developing country Parties, particularly those identified in Article 4, paragraphs 8 and 9, of the Convention. In line with relevant decisions of the Conference of the Parties on the implementation of those paragraphs, the Conference of the Parties serving as the meeting of the Parties to this Protocol shall, at its first session, consider what actions are necessary to minimize the adverse effects of climate change and/or the impacts of response measures on Parties referred to in those paragraphs. Among the issues to be considered shall be the establishment of funding, insurance and transfer of technology.

# Article 4

1.    Any Parties included in Annex I that have reached an agreement to fulfil their commitments under Article 3 jointly, shall be deemed to have met those commitments provided that their total combined aggregate anthropogenic carbon dioxide equivalent emissions of the greenhouse gases listed in Annex A do not exceed their assigned amounts calculated pursuant to their quantified emission limitation and reduction commitments inscribed in Annex B and in accordance with the provisions of Article 3. The respective emission level allocated to each of the Parties to the agreement shall be set out in that agreement.

2.    The Parties to any such agreement shall notify the secretariat of the terms of the agreement on the date of deposit of their instruments of ratification, acceptance or approval of this Protocol, or accession thereto. The secretariat shall in turn inform the Parties and signatories to the Convention of the terms of the agreement.

3.    Any such agreement shall remain in operation for the duration of the commitment period specified in Article 3, paragraph 7.

4.    If Parties acting jointly do so in the framework of, and together with, a regional economic integration organization, any alteration in the composition of the organization after adoption of this Protocol shall not affect existing commitments under this Protocol. Any alteration in the composition of the organization shall only apply for the purposes of those commitments under Article 3 that are adopted subsequent to that alteration.

5.    In the event of failure by the Parties to such an agreement to achieve their total combined level of emission reductions, each Party to that agreement shall be responsible for its own level of emissions set out in the agreement.

6.    If Parties acting jointly do so in the framework of, and together with, a regional economic integration organization which is itself a Party to this Protocol, each member State of that regional economic integration organization individually, and together with the regional economic integration organization acting in accordance with Article 24, shall, in the event of failure to achieve the total combined level of emission reductions, be responsible for its level of emissions as notified in accordance with this Article.

# Article 5

1.    Each Party included in Annex I shall have in place, no later than one year prior to the start of the first commitment period, a national system for the estimation of anthropogenic emissions by sources and removals by sinks of all greenhouse gases not controlled by the Montreal Protocol. Guidelines for such national systems, which shall incorporate the methodologies specified in paragraph 2 below, shall be decided upon by the Conference of the Parties serving as the meeting of the Parties to this Protocol at its first session.

2.    Methodologies for estimating anthropogenic emissions by sources and removals by sinks of all greenhouse gases not controlled by the Montreal Protocol shall be those accepted by the Intergovernmental Panel on Climate Change and agreed upon by the Conference of the Parties at its third session. Where such methodologies are not used, appropriate adjustments shall be applied according to methodologies agreed upon by the Conference of the Parties serving as the meeting of the Parties to this Protocol at its first session. Based on the work of, inter alia, the Intergovernmental Panel on Climate Change and advice provided by the Subsidiary Body for Scientific and Technological Advice, the Conference of the Parties serving as the meeting of the Parties to this Protocol shall regularly review and, as appropriate, revise such methodologies and adjustments, taking fully into account any relevant decisions by the Conference of the Parties. Any revision to methodologies or adjustments shall be used only for the purposes of ascertaining compliance with commitments under Article 3 in respect of any commitment period adopted subsequent to that revision.

3.    The global warming potentials used to calculate the carbon dioxide equivalence of anthropogenic emissions by sources and removals by sinks of greenhouse gases listed in Annex A shall be those accepted by the Intergovernmental Panel on Climate Change and agreed upon by the Conference of the Parties at its third session. Based on the work of, inter alia, the Intergovernmental Panel on Climate Change and advice provided by the Subsidiary Body for Scientific and Technological Advice, the Conference of the Parties serving as the meeting of the Parties to this Protocol shall regularly review and, as appropriate, revise the global warming potential of each such greenhouse gas, taking fully into account any relevant decisions by the Conference of the Parties. Any revision to a global

warming potential shall apply only to commitments under Article 3 in respect of any commitment period adopted subsequent to that revision.

## Article 6

1.   For the purpose of meeting its commitments under Article 3, any Party included in Annex I may transfer to, or acquire from, any other such Party emission reduction units resulting from projects aimed at reducing anthropogenic emissions by sources or enhancing anthropogenic removals by sinks of greenhouse gases in any sector of the economy, provided that:

(a)   Any such project has the approval of the Parties involved;

(b)   Any such project provides a reduction in emissions by sources, or an enhancement of removals by sinks, that is additional to any that would otherwise occur;

(c)   It does not acquire any emission reduction units if it is not in compliance with its obligations under Articles 5 and 7; and

(d)   The acquisition of emission reduction units shall be supplemental to domestic actions for the purposes of meeting commitments under Article 3.

2.   The Conference of the Parties serving as the meeting of the Parties to this Protocol may, at its first session or as soon as practicable thereafter, further elaborate guidelines for the implementation of this Article, including for verification and reporting.

3.   A Party included in Annex I may authorize legal entities to participate, under its responsibility, in actions leading to the generation, transfer or acquisition under this Article of emission reduction units.

4.   If a question of implementation by a Party included in Annex I of the requirements referred to in this Article is identified in accordance with the relevant provisions of Article 8, transfers and acquisitions of emission reduction units may continue to be made after the question has been identified, provided that any such units may not be used by a Party to meet its commitments under Article 3 until any issue of compliance is resolved.

# Article 7

1.   Each Party included in Annex I shall incorporate in its annual inventory of anthropogenic emissions by sources and removals by sinks of greenhouse gases not controlled by the Montreal Protocol, submitted in accordance with the relevant decisions of the Conference of the Parties, the necessary supplementary information for the purposes of ensuring compliance with Article 3, to be determined in accordance with paragraph 4 below.

2.   Each Party included in Annex I shall incorporate in its national communication, submitted under Article 12 of the Convention, the supplementary information necessary to demonstrate compliance with its commitments under this Protocol, to be determined in accordance with paragraph 4 below.

3.   Each Party included in Annex I shall submit the information required under paragraph 1 above annually, beginning with the first inventory due under the Convention for the first year of the commitment period after this Protocol has entered into force for that Party. Each such Party shall submit the information required under paragraph 2 above as part of the first national communication due under the Convention after this Protocol has entered into force for it and after the adoption of guidelines as provided for in paragraph 4 below. The frequency of subsequent submission of information required under this Article shall be determined by the Conference of the Parties serving as the meeting of the Parties to this Protocol, taking into account any timetable for the submission of national communications decided upon by the Conference of the Parties.

4.   The Conference of the Parties serving as the meeting of the Parties to this Protocol shall adopt at its first session, and review periodically thereafter, guidelines for the preparation of the information required under this Article, taking into account guidelines for the preparation of national communications by Parties included in Annex I adopted by the Conference of the Parties. The Conference of the Parties serving as the meeting of the Parties to this Protocol shall also, prior to the first commitment period, decide upon modalities for the accounting of assigned amounts.

# Article 8

1.   The information submitted under Article 7 by each Party included in Annex I shall be reviewed by expert review teams

pursuant to the relevant decisions of the Conference of the Parties and in accordance with guidelines adopted for this purpose by the Conference of the Parties serving as the meeting of the Parties to this Protocol under paragraph 4 below. The information submitted under Article 7, paragraph 1, by each Party included in Annex I shall be reviewed as part of the annual compilation and accounting of emissions inventories and assigned amounts. Additionally, the information submitted under Article 7, paragraph 2, by each Party included in Annex I shall be reviewed as part of the review of communications.

2.     Expert review teams shall be coordinated by the secretariat and shall be composed of experts selected from those nominated by Parties to the Convention and, as appropriate, by intergovernmental organizations, in accordance with guidance provided for this purpose by the Conference of the Parties.

3.     The review process shall provide a thorough and comprehensive technical assessment of all aspects of the implementation by a Party of this Protocol. The expert review teams shall prepare a report to the Conference of the Parties serving as the meeting of the Parties to this Protocol, assessing the implementation of the commitments of the Party and identifying any potential problems in, and factors influencing, the fulfilment of commitments. Such reports shall be circulated by the secretariat to all Parties to the Convention. The secretariat shall list those questions of implementation indicated in such reports for further consideration by the Conference of the Parties serving as the meeting of the Parties to this Protocol.

4.     The Conference of the Parties serving as the meeting of the Parties to this Protocol shall adopt at its first session, and review periodically thereafter, guidelines for the review of implementation of this Protocol by expert review teams taking into account the relevant decisions of the Conference of the Parties.

5.     The Conference of the Parties serving as the meeting of the Parties to this Protocol shall, with the assistance of the Subsidiary Body for Implementation and, as appropriate, the Subsidiary Body for Scientific and Technological Advice, consider:

    (a)   The information submitted by Parties under Article 7 and the reports of the expert reviews thereon conducted under this Article; and

    (b)   Those questions of implementation listed by the secretariat under paragraph 3 above, as well as any questions raised by Parties.

6.   Pursuant to its consideration of the information referred to in paragraph 5 above, the Conference of the Parties serving as the meeting of the Parties to this Protocol shall take decisions on any matter required for the implementation of this Protocol.

## Article 9

1.   The Conference of the Parties serving as the meeting of the Parties to this Protocol shall periodically review this Protocol in the light of the best available scientific information and assessments on climate change and its impacts, as well as relevant technical, social and economic information. Such reviews shall be coordinated with pertinent reviews under the Convention, in particular those required by Article 4, paragraph 2(d), and Article 7, paragraph 2(a), of the Convention. Based on these reviews, the Conference of the Parties serving as the meeting of the Parties to this Protocol shall take appropriate action.
2.   The first review shall take place at the second session of the Conference of the Parties serving as the meeting of the Parties to this Protocol. Further reviews shall take place at regular intervals and in a timely manner.

## Article 10

All Parties, taking into account their common but differentiated responsibilities and their specific national and regional development priorities, objectives and circumstances, without introducing any new commitments for Parties not included in Annex I, but reaffirming existing commitments under Article 4, paragraph 1, of the Convention, and continuing to advance the implementation of these commitments in order to achieve sustainable development, taking into account Article 4, paragraphs 3, 5 and 7, of the Convention, shall:
(a)  Formulate, where relevant and to the extent possible, cost-effective national and, where appropriate, regional programmes to improve the quality of local emission factors, activity data and/or models which reflect the socio-economic conditions of each Party for the preparation and periodic updating of national inventories of anthropogenic emissions by sources and removals by sinks of all

greenhouse gases not controlled by the Montreal Protocol, using comparable methodologies to be agreed upon by the Conference of the Parties, and consistent with the guidelines for the preparation of national communications adopted by the Conference of the Parties;
(b) Formulate, implement, publish and regularly update national and, where appropriate, regional programmes containing measures to mitigate climate change and measures to facilitate adequate adaptation to climate change:

(i) Such programmes would, inter alia, concern the energy, transport and industry sectors as well as agriculture, forestry and waste management. Furthermore, adaptation technologies and methods for improving spatial planning would improve adaptation to climate change; and

(ii) Parties included in Annex I shall submit information on action under this Protocol, including national programmes, in accordance with Article 7; and other Parties shall seek to include in their national communications, as appropriate, information on programmes which contain measures that the Party believes contribute to addressing climate change and its adverse impacts, including the abatement of increases in greenhouse gas emissions, and enhancement of and removals by sinks, capacity building and adaptation measures;

(c) Cooperate in the promotion of effective modalities for the development, application and diffusion of, and take all practicable steps to promote, facilitate and finance, as appropriate, the transfer of, or access to, environmentally sound technologies, know-how, practices and processes pertinent to climate change, in particular to developing countries, including the formulation of policies and programmes for the effective transfer of environmentally sound technologies that are publicly owned or in the public domain and the creation of an enabling environment for the private sector, to promote and enhance the transfer of, and access to, environmentally sound technologies;

(d) Cooperate in scientific and technical research and promote the maintenance and the development of systematic observation systems and development of data archives to reduce uncertainties related to the climate system, the adverse impacts of climate change and the economic and social consequences of various response strategies, and promote the development and strengthening of endogenous capacities and capabilities to participate in international and intergovernmental efforts, programmes and networks on research and systematic observation, taking into account Article 5 of the Convention;

(e)   Cooperate in and promote at the international level, and, where appropriate, using existing bodies, the development and implementation of education and training programmes, including the strengthening of national capacity building, in particular human and institutional capacities and the exchange or secondment of personnel to train experts in this field, in particular for developing countries, and facilitate at the national level public awareness of, and public access to information on, climate change. Suitable modalities should be developed to implement these activities through the relevant bodies of the Convention, taking into account Article 6 of the Convention;

(f)   Include in their national communications information on programmes and activities undertaken pursuant to this Article in accordance with relevant decisions of the Conference of the Parties; and

(g)   Give full consideration, in implementing the commitments under this Article, to Article 4, paragraph 8, of the Convention.

## Article 11

1.   In the implementation of Article 10, Parties shall take into account the provisions of Article 4, paragraphs 4, 5, 7, 8 and 9, of the Convention.

2.   In the context of the implementation of Article 4, paragraph 1, of the Convention, in accordance with the provisions of Article 4, paragraph 3, and Article 11 of the Convention, and through the entity or entities entrusted with the operation of the financial mechanism of the Convention, the developed country Parties and other developed Parties included in Annex II to the Convention shall:

(a)   Provide new and additional financial resources to meet the agreed full costs incurred by developing country Parties in advancing the implementation of existing commitments under Article 4, paragraph 1(a), of the Convention that are covered in Article 10, subparagraph (a); and

(b)   Also provide such financial resources, including for the transfer of technology, needed by the developing country

Parties to meet the agreed full incremental costs of advancing the implementation of existing commitments under Article 4, paragraph 1, of the Convention that are covered by Article 10 and that are agreed between a developing country Party and the international entity or entities referred to in Article 11 of the Convention, in accordance with that Article. The implementation of these existing commitments shall take into account the need for adequacy and predictability in the flow of funds and the importance of appropriate burden sharing among developed country Parties. The guidance to the entity or entities entrusted with the operation of the financial mechanism of the Convention in relevant decisions of the Conference of the Parties, including those agreed before the adoption of this Protocol, shall apply mutatis mutandis to the provisions of this paragraph.

3.    The developed country Parties and other developed Parties in Annex II to the Convention may also provide, and developing country Parties avail themselves of, financial resources for the implementation of Article 10, through bilateral, regional and other multilateral channels.

## Article 12

1.    A clean development mechanism is hereby defined.

2.    The purpose of the clean development mechanism shall be to assist Parties not included in Annex I in achieving sustainable development and in contributing to the ultimate objective of the Convention, and to assist Parties included in Annex I in achieving compliance with their quantified emission limitation and reduction commitments under Article 3.

3.    Under the clean development mechanism:

(a)    Parties not included in Annex I will benefit from project activities resulting in certified emission reductions; and

(b)    Parties included in Annex I may use the certified emission reductions accruing from such project activities to contribute to compliance with part of their quantified emission limitation and reduction commitments under Article 3, as determined by the Conference of the Parties serving as the meeting of the Parties to this Protocol.

4.   The clean development mechanism shall be subject to the authority and guidance of the Conference of the Parties serving as the meeting of the Parties to this Protocol and be supervised by an executive board of the clean development mechanism.

5.   Emission reductions resulting from each project activity shall be certified by operational entities to be designated by the Conference of the Parties serving as the meeting of the Parties to this Protocol, on the basis of:

  (a)   Voluntary participation approved by each Party involved;
  (b)   Real, measurable, and long-term benefits related to the mitigation of climate change; and
  (c)   Reductions in emissions that are additional to any that would occur in the absence of the certified project activity.

6.   The clean development mechanism shall assist in arranging funding of certified project activities as necessary.

7.   The Conference of the Parties serving as the meeting of the Parties to this Protocol shall, at its first session, elaborate modalities and procedures with the objective of ensuring transparency, efficiency and accountability through independent auditing and verification of project activities.

8.   The Conference of the Parties serving as the meeting of the Parties to this Protocol shall ensure that a share of the proceeds from certified project activities is used to cover administrative expenses as well as to assist developing country Parties that are particularly vulnerable to the adverse effects of climate change to meet the costs of adaptation.

9.   Participation under the clean development mechanism, including in activities mentioned in paragraph 3(a) above and in the acquisition of certified emission reductions, may involve private and/or public entities, and is to be subject to whatever guidance may be provided by the executive board of the clean development mechanism.

10.   Certified emission reductions obtained during the period from the year 2000 up to the beginning of the first commitment period can be used to assist in achieving compliance in the first commitment period.

## Article 13

1.   The Conference of the Parties, the supreme body of the Convention, shall serve as the meeting of the Parties to this Protocol.

2.    Parties to the Convention that are not Parties to this Protocol may participate as observers in the proceedings of any session of the Conference of the Parties serving as the meeting of the Parties to this Protocol. When the Conference of the Parties serves as the meeting of the Parties to this Protocol, decisions under this Protocol shall be taken only by those that are Parties to this Protocol.

3.    When the Conference of the Parties serves as the meeting of the Parties to this Protocol, any member of the Bureau of the Conference of the Parties representing a Party to the Convention but, at that time, not a Party to this Protocol, shall be replaced by an additional member to be elected by and from amongst the Parties to this Protocol.

4.    The Conference of the Parties serving as the meeting of the Parties to this Protocol shall keep under regular review the implementation of this Protocol and shall make, within its mandate, the decisions necessary to promote its effective implementation. It shall perform the functions assigned to it by this Protocol and shall:

(a)    Assess, on the basis of all information made available to it in accordance with the provisions of this Protocol, the implementation of this Protocol by the Parties, the overall effects of the measures taken pursuant to this Protocol, in particular environmental, economic and social effects as well as their cumulative impacts and the extent to which progress towards the objective of the Convention is being achieved;

(b)    Periodically examine the obligations of the Parties under this Protocol, giving due consideration to any reviews required by Article 4, paragraph 2(d), and Article 7, paragraph 2, of the Convention, in the light of the objective of the Convention, the experience gained in its implementation and the evolution of scientific and technological knowledge, and in this respect consider and adopt regular reports on the implementation of this Protocol;

(c)    Promote and facilitate the exchange of information on measures adopted by the Parties to address climate change and its effects, taking into account the differing circumstances, responsibilities and capabilities of the Parties and their respective commitments under this Protocol;

(d)    Facilitate, at the request of two or more Parties, the coordination of measures adopted by them to address climate change and its effects, taking into account the differing circumstances, responsibilities and capabilities of the Parties and their respective commitments under this Protocol;

(e) Promote and guide, in accordance with the objective of the Convention and the provisions of this Protocol, and taking fully into account the relevant decisions by the Conference of the Parties, the development and periodic refinement of comparable methodologies for the effective implementation of this Protocol, to be agreed on by the Conference of the Parties serving as the meeting of the Parties to this Protocol;

(f) Make recommendations on any matters necessary for the implementation of this Protocol;

(g) Seek to mobilize additional financial resources in accordance with Article 11, paragraph 2;

(h) Establish such subsidiary bodies as are deemed necessary for the implementation of this Protocol;

(i) Seek and utilize, where appropriate, the services and cooperation of, and information provided by, competent international organizations and intergovernmental and non-governmental bodies; and

(j) Exercise such other functions as may be required for the implementation of this Protocol, and consider any assignment resulting from a decision by the Conference of the Parties.

5.   The rules of procedure of the Conference of the Parties and financial procedures applied under the Convention shall be applied mutatis mutandis under this Protocol, except as may be otherwise decided by consensus by the Conference of the Parties serving as the meeting of the Parties to this Protocol.

6.   The first session of the Conference of the Parties serving as the meeting of the Parties to this Protocol shall be convened by the secretariat in conjunction with the first session of the Conference of the Parties that is scheduled after the date of the entry into force of this Protocol. Subsequent ordinary sessions of the Conference of the Parties serving as the meeting of the Parties to this Protocol shall be held every year and in conjunction with ordinary sessions of the Conference of the Parties, unless otherwise decided by the Conference of the Parties serving as the meeting of the Parties to this Protocol.

7.   Extraordinary sessions of the Conference of the Parties serving as the meeting of the Parties to this Protocol shall be held at such

other times as may be deemed necessary by the Conference of the Parties serving as the meeting of the Parties to this Protocol, or at the written request of any Party, provided that, within six months of the request being communicated to the Parties by the secretariat, it is supported by at least one third of the Parties.

8.     The United Nations, its specialized agencies and the International Atomic Energy Agency, as well as any State member thereof or observers thereto not party to the Convention, may be represented at sessions of the Conference of the Parties serving as the meeting of the Parties to this Protocol as observers. Any body or agency, whether national or international, governmental or non-governmental, which is qualified in matters covered by this Protocol and which has informed the secretariat of its wish to be represented at a session of the Conference of the Parties serving as the meeting of the Parties to this Protocol as an observer, may be so admitted unless at least one third of the Parties present object. The admission and participation of observers shall be subject to the rules of procedure, as referred to in paragraph 5 above.

# Article 14

1.     The secretariat established by Article 8 of the Convention shall serve as the secretariat of this Protocol.

2.     Article 8, paragraph 2, of the Convention on the functions of the secretariat, and Article 8, paragraph 3, of the Convention on arrangements made for the functioning of the secretariat, shall apply mutatis mutandis to this Protocol. The secretariat shall, in addition, exercise the functions assigned to it under this Protocol.

# Article 15

1.     The Subsidiary Body for Scientific and Technological Advice and the Subsidiary Body for Implementation established by Articles 9 and 10 of the Convention shall serve as, respectively, the Subsidiary Body for Scientific and Technological Advice and the Subsidiary Body for Implementation of this Protocol. The provisions relating to the functioning of these two bodies under the Convention shall apply mutatis mutandis to this Protocol. Sessions of the meetings of the Subsidiary Body for Scientific and Technological Advice and the

Subsidiary Body for Implementation of this Protocol shall be held in conjunction with the meetings of, respectively, the Subsidiary Body for Scientific and Technological Advice and the Subsidiary Body for Implementation of the Convention.

2.   Parties to the Convention that are not Parties to this Protocol may participate as observers in the proceedings of any session of the subsidiary bodies. When the subsidiary bodies serve as the subsidiary bodies of this Protocol, decisions under this Protocol shall be taken only by those that are Parties to this Protocol.

3.   When the subsidiary bodies established by Articles 9 and 10 of the Convention exercise their functions with regard to matters concerning this Protocol, any member of the Bureaux of those subsidiary bodies representing a Party to the Convention but, at that time, not a party to this Protocol, shall be replaced by an additional member to be elected by and from amongst the Parties to this Protocol.

# Article 16

The Conference of the Parties serving as the meeting of the Parties to this Protocol shall, as soon as practicable, consider the application to this Protocol of, and modify as appropriate, the multilateral consultative process referred to in Article 13 of the Convention, in the light of any relevant decisions that may be taken by the Conference of the Parties. Any multilateral consultative process that may be applied to this Protocol shall operate without prejudice to the procedures and mechanisms established in accordance with Article 18.

# Article 17

The Conference of the Parties shall define the relevant principles, modalities, rules and guidelines, in particular for verification, reporting and accountability for emissions trading. The Parties included in Annex B may participate in emissions trading for the purposes of fulfilling their commitments under Article 3. Any such trading shall be supplemental to domestic actions for the purpose of meeting quantified emission limitation and reduction commitments under that Article.

# Article 18

The Conference of the Parties serving as the meeting of the Parties to this Protocol shall, at its first session, approve appropriate and effective procedures and mechanisms to determine and to address cases of non-compliance with the provisions of this Protocol, including through the development of an indicative list of consequences, taking into account the cause, type, degree and frequency of non-compliance. Any procedures and mechanisms under this Article entailing binding consequences shall be adopted by means of an amendment to this Protocol.

# Article 19

The provisions of Article 14 of the Convention on settlement of disputes shall apply mutatis mutandis to this Protocol.

# Article 20

1.    Any Party may propose amendments to this Protocol.
2.    Amendments to this Protocol shall be adopted at an ordinary session of the Conference of the Parties serving as the meeting of the Parties to this Protocol. The text of any proposed amendment to this Protocol shall be communicated to the Parties by the secretariat at least six months before the meeting at which it is proposed for adoption. The secretariat shall also communicate the text of any proposed amendments to the Parties and signatories to the Convention and, for information, to the Depositary.
3.    The Parties shall make every effort to reach agreement on any proposed amendment to this Protocol by consensus. If all efforts at consensus have been exhausted, and no agreement reached, the amendment shall as a last resort be adopted by a three-fourths majority vote of the Parties present and voting at the meeting. The adopted amendment shall be communicated by the secretariat to the Depositary, who shall circulate it to all Parties for their acceptance.
4.    Instruments of acceptance in respect of an amendment shall be deposited with the Depositary. An amendment adopted in accordance with paragraph 3 above shall enter into force for those Parties having

accepted it on the ninetieth day after the date of receipt by the Depositary of an instrument of acceptance by at least three fourths of the Parties to this Protocol.

5.    The amendment shall enter into force for any other Party on the ninetieth day after the date on which that Party deposits with the Depositary its instrument of acceptance of the said amendment.

## Article 21

1.    Annexes to this Protocol shall form an integral part thereof and, unless otherwise expressly provided, a reference to this Protocol constitutes at the same time a reference to any annexes thereto. Any annexes adopted after the entry into force of this Protocol shall be restricted to lists, forms and any other material of a descriptive nature that is of a scientific, technical, procedural or administrative character.

2.    Any Party may make proposals for an annex to this Protocol and may propose amendments to annexes to this Protocol.

3.    Annexes to this Protocol and amendments to annexes to this Protocol shall be adopted at an ordinary session of the Conference of the Parties serving as the meeting of the Parties to this Protocol. The text of any proposed annex or amendment to an annex shall be communicated to the Parties by the secretariat at least six months before the meeting at which it is proposed for adoption. The secretariat shall also communicate the text of any proposed annex or amendment to an annex to the Parties and signatories to the Convention and, for information, to the Depositary.

4.    The Parties shall make every effort to reach agreement on any proposed annex or amendment to an annex by consensus. If all efforts at consensus have been exhausted, and no agreement reached, the annex or amendment to an annex shall as a last resort be adopted by a three-fourths majority vote of the Parties present and voting at the meeting. The adopted annex or amendment to an annex shall be communicated by the secretariat to the Depositary, who shall circulate it to all Parties for their acceptance.

5.    An annex, or amendment to an annex other than Annex A or B, that has been adopted in accordance with paragraphs 3 and 4 above shall enter into force for all Parties to this Protocol six months after the date of the communication by the Depositary to such Parties of the adoption of the annex or adoption of the amendment to the

annex, except for those Parties that have notified the Depositary, in writing, within that period of their non-acceptance of the annex or amendment to the annex. The annex or amendment to an annex shall enter into force for Parties which withdraw their notification of non-acceptance on the ninetieth day after the date on which withdrawal of such notification has been received by the Depositary.
6.    If the adoption of an annex or an amendment to an annex involves an amendment to this Protocol, that annex or amendment to an annex shall not enter into force until such time as the amendment to this Protocol enters into force.
7.    Amendments to Annexes A and B to this Protocol shall be adopted and enter into force in accordance with the procedure set out in Article 20, provided that any amendment to Annex B shall be adopted only with the written consent of the Party concerned.

## Article 22

1.    Each Party shall have one vote, except as provided for in paragraph 2 below.
2.    Regional economic integration organizations, in matters within their competence, shall exercise their right to vote with a number of votes equal to the number of their member States that are Parties to this Protocol. Such an organization shall not exercise its right to vote if any of its member States exercises its right, and vice versa.

## Article 23

The Secretary-General of the United Nations shall be the Depositary of this Protocol.

## Article 24

1.    This Protocol shall be open for signature and subject to ratification, acceptance or approval by States and regional economic integration organizations which are Parties to the Convention. It shall be open for signature at United Nations Headquarters in New York from 16 March 1998 to 15 March 1999. This Protocol shall be open for accession from the day after the date on which it is closed

for signature. Instruments of ratification, acceptance, approval or accession shall be deposited with the Depositary.

2.    Any regional economic integration organization which becomes a Party to this Protocol without any of its member States being a Party shall be bound by all the obligations under this Protocol. In the case of such organizations, one or more of whose member States is a Party to this Protocol, the organization and its member States shall decide on their respective responsibilities for the performance of their obligations under this Protocol. In such cases, the organization and the member States shall not be entitled to exercise rights under this Protocol concurrently.

3.    In their instruments of ratification, acceptance, approval or accession, regional economic integration organizations shall declare the extent of their competence with respect to the matters governed by this Protocol. These organizations shall also inform the Depositary, who shall in turn inform the Parties, of any substantial modification in the extent of their competence.

## Article 25

1.    This Protocol shall enter into force on the ninetieth day after the date on which not less than 55 Parties to the Convention, incorporating Parties included in Annex I which accounted in total for at least 55 per cent of the total carbon dioxide emissions for 1990 of the Parties included in Annex I, have deposited their instruments of ratification, acceptance, approval or accession.

2.    For the purposes of this Article, "the total carbon dioxide emissions for 1990 of the Parties included in Annex I" means the amount communicated on or before the date of adoption of this Protocol by the Parties included in Annex I in their first national communications submitted in accordance with Article 12 of the Convention.

3.    For each State or regional economic integration organization that ratifies, accepts or approves this Protocol or accedes thereto after the conditions set out in paragraph 1 above for entry into force have been fulfilled, this Protocol shall enter into force on the ninetieth day following the date of deposit of its instrument of ratification, acceptance, approval or accession.

4.    For the purposes of this Article, any instrument deposited by a regional economic integration organization shall not be counted as additional to those deposited by States members of the organization.

# Article 26

No reservations may be made to this Protocol.


# Article 27

1.   At any time after three years from the date on which this Protocol has entered into force for a Party, that Party may withdraw from this Protocol by giving written notification to the Depositary.
2.   Any such withdrawal shall take effect upon expiry of one year from the date of receipt by the Depositary of the notification of withdrawal, or on such later date as may be specified in the notification of withdrawal.
3.   Any Party that withdraws from the Convention shall be considered as also having withdrawn from this Protocol.


# Article 28

The original of this Protocol, of which the Arabic, Chinese, English, French, Russian and Spanish texts are equally authentic, shall be deposited with the Secretary-General of the United Nations. DONE at Kyoto this eleventh day of December one thousand nine hundred and ninety-seven. IN WITNESS WHEREOF the undersigned, being duly authorized to that effect, have affixed their signatures to this Protocol on the dates indicated.


# Annex A

Greenhouse gases
Carbon dioxide ($CO_2$)
Methane ($CH_4$)
Nitrous oxide ($N_2O$)
Hydrofluorocarbons (HFCs)
Perfluorocarbons (PFCs)
Sulphur hexafluoride (SF6)
Sectors/source categories
Energy
Fuel combustion

Energy industries
Manufacturing industries and construction
Transport
Other sectors
Other
Fugitive emissions from fuels
Solid fuels
Oil and natural gas
Other
Industrial processes
Mineral products
Chemical industry
Metal production
Other production
Production of halocarbons and sulphur hexafluoride
Consumption of halocarbons and sulphur hexafluoride
Other
Solvent and other product use
Agriculture
Enteric fermentation
Manure management
Rice cultivation
Agricultural soils
Prescribed burning of savannas
Field burning of agricultural residues
Other
Waste
Solid waste disposal on land
Wastewater handling
Waste incineration
Other

# Annex B

Party Quantified emission limitation or reduction commitment
(percentage of base year or period)
Australia 108
Austria 92
Belgium 92

Bulgaria* 92
Canada 94
Croatia* 95
Czech Republic* 92
Denmark 92
Estonia* 92
European Community 92
Finland 92
France 92
Germany 92
Greece 92
Hungary* 94
Iceland 110
Ireland 92
Italy 92
Japan 94
Latvia* 92
Liechtenstein 92
Lithuania* 92
Luxembourg 92
Monaco 92
Netherlands 92
New Zealand 100
Norway 101
Poland* 94
Portugal 92
Romania* 92
Russian Federation* 100
Slovakia* 92
Slovenia* 92
Spain 92
Sweden 92
Switzerland 92
Ukraine* 100
United Kingdom of Great Britain and Northern Ireland 92
United States of America 93

---

\* Countries that are undergoing the process of transition to a market economy.

# Appendix B

## EFET

### European Federation of Energy Traders

**Allowances Appendix**
to the
General Agreement
Concerning the Delivery and Acceptance of Electricity

# ALLOWANCES APPENDIX

dated as of _____
(the **"Allowances Appendix Effective Date"**)

Between

[_____]
(**"Party A"**)

and

[_____]
(**"Party B"**)

---

**Check the box and fill in date ONLY if you are using this Allowances Appendix to modify and supplement a previously executed General Agreement between the Parties:**

[ ]  By executing this Allowances Appendix in the signature block at the end hereof, the Parties hereby modify, supplement and amend the terms of that certain previously executed General Agreement entered into and dated as of _____, _____ to provide that the terms of this Allowances Appendix shall be incorporated therein and shall be applicable to and thereafter govern all Allowance Transactions (as defined below).

---

# ALLOWANCES APPENDIX

**Applicability of Allowances Appendix.** This Allowances Appendix to the General Agreement (inclusive of this Allowances Appendix's Annexes) modifies, supplements and amends, to the extent set forth herein, certain provisions of the General Agreement (which, pursuant to § 1.1 of the General Agreement, includes its Annexes and Election Sheet) and shall only apply to and govern all Individual Contracts entered into by the Parties for and concerning the Transfer and acceptance of Transfer of Allowances (each such Individual Contract an **"Allowance Transaction"**, and collectively, the **"Allowance Transactions"**) save as expressly provided to the contrary with respect to any Section or Sections of the General Agreement or this Allowances Appendix. Any and all future Individual Contracts between the Parties that constitute Allowance Transactions shall be automatically subject to the General Agreement, as it is modified, supplemented and amended by its Annexes, Election Sheet and this Allowances Appendix, without any further action by the Parties, unless the agreed upon terms of such Individual Contract expressly provide that it shall not be. For all other types of Individual Contracts, the General Agreement shall remain unchanged. The provisions of the General Agreement are hereby modified, supplemented and amended (except as expressly noted to the contrary herein) only in respect of such Allowance Transactions in accordance with the following:

## Part I: General Terms

**(1)    Subject of Allowances Appendix.** The EU and the Member States as well as some Non-Member States plan to establish or have established Rules under which participants may trade Allowances. The purpose of this Allowances Appendix is to modify certain provisions of the General Agreement in order that its terms facilitate the purchase, sale and Transfer of Allowances by the Parties. In addition to the provisions of the General Agreement, the provisions of this Allowances Appendix shall therefore be applicable for the purchase, sale and Transfer of Allowances between participants of

Emissions Trading Scheme(s) in both or either of Member States or Non-Member States.

**(2)    Definitions and Construction.**    Capitalized terms used but not defined in this Allowances Appendix shall have the meanings as set out in Annex 1 to this Allowances Appendix and otherwise as ascribed to them in either this Allowances Appendix or the General Agreement. In the event of any inconsistency between definitions found in this Allowances Appendix and in the General Agreement, this Allowances Appendix's definitions will prevail for purposes of all Allowance Transactions. All references to "electricity", "Network Operator", "Contract Capacity", and "Transmission" or "flows" in the General Agreement shall, in the context of Allowance Transactions, be construed as references to "**Allowances**", "**Relevant Authority**", "**Specified Vintage**", and "**Transfer(s)**" respectively. References to a Section (§) or Sections (§§) in this Allowances Appendix shall be references to a Section or Sections in the General Agreement unless otherwise stated. In the event of any inconsistency between the terms of an Allowance Transaction (whether evidenced in a Confirmation or otherwise) and the provisions of either this Allowances Appendix or the General Agreement (as amended by this Allowances Appendix), the terms of the Allowance Transaction shall prevail for the purpose of that Allowance Transaction. References to any law or statute include any amendment to, consolidation, re-enactment or replacement of such law or statute and, in the case of a Directive, its implementation under national law.

**(3)    Concluding and Confirming Allowance Transactions.**    All Allowance Transactions shall contain the information stipulated in, and if confirmed with a Confirmation shall be substantially in the form of, the sample confirmation sheet attached as Annex 2 (A) to this Allowances Appendix.

**(4)    Primary Obligations for Delivery and Acceptance of Allowances.**    For purposes of Allowance Transactions § 4 of the General Agreement is hereby amended by: (i) deletion of § 4.1 *(Delivery and Acceptance)* in its entirety and replacement with the new § 4.1 *(Delivery and Acceptance and Scheduling Obligations)* below; (ii) the following additions and deletions to the definition of "**Schedule**" found in § 4.2 *(Definition of Schedule)*; and (iii) by the addition of a new § 4.3 *(Physical Settlement Netting)* as follows:

### § 4.1   Delivery, Acceptance and Scheduling Obligations.

(a) Seller shall Schedule, sell and Transfer to Buyer, or, if applicable in accordance with the relevant provision of § 4.1(a)(i) and 4.1(a)(ii), cause to be Transferred, and Buyer shall Schedule, purchase and accept Transfer of, or, if applicable in accordance with the relevant provision of § 4.1(a)(i) and 4.1(a)(ii), cause such Transfer to be accepted, the Contract Quantity at the Delivery Point, and the Buyer shall pay to the Seller the relevant Contract Price. Unless the Parties otherwise agree, the Seller shall Transfer the Contract Quantity at the Delivery Point during a Delivery Business Day between the hours of 9:00 a.m. and 5:00 p.m. CET and any Transfer taking place at a time after 5:00 p.m. CET on a Delivery Business Day shall be deemed to have taken place at 9:00 a.m. CET on the next Delivery Business Day.

(i) For any Allowance Transaction in which no Transfer Point has been specified by the Parties, Seller shall Transfer, or cause the Transfer of, the Contract Quantity to the Delivery Point from any Trading Account in any Registry.

(ii) Parties may limit the scope of their Transfer and acceptance of Transfer obligations by designating one or more specific Delivery Points and/or Transfer Points for any Allowance Transaction:

(A) If one or more Delivery Points are specified by the Parties in respect of an Allowance Transaction, the Seller's obligations shall be limited to the obligation to Schedule, sell and Transfer to Buyer, or cause to be so Transferred, and the Buyer's obligations shall be limited to the obligation to Schedule, purchase and accept Transfer of the Contract Quantity at the Delivery Point(s) so specified.

(B) If one or more Transfer Points are specified by the Parties in respect of an Allowance Transaction, the Seller's obligations shall be limited to the obligation to Schedule, sell and Transfer to Buyer and the Buyer's obligations shall be limited to the obligation to Schedule, purchase and accept Transfer of, or cause to be accepted such Transfer of, the Contract Quantity from the Transfer Point(s) so specified.

(b) The Parties may agree in an Allowance Transaction that from an initially agreed upon list of Trading Accounts: (i) the Buyer may later select as the applicable Delivery Point(s) one or more of such Trading Accounts into which it wishes the Contract Quantity to be Transferred by the Seller on the Delivery Date (a **"Buyer's Choice Transaction"**); and/or (ii) the Seller may later select as the applicable Transfer Point(s) one or more of such Trading Accounts from which it wishes to Transfer the Contract Quantity to the Buyer on the Delivery Date (a **"Seller's Choice Transaction"**). Any such later selection shall be notified to the other Party as, and on or before any deadline, agreed upon for the giving of such notice and if such notice is not given, the Trading Accounts so specified shall be deemed to be listed in descending order of preference and the Allowance Transaction will be performed in accordance with the rules of a Cascade Transaction described in § 4.1(c) below.

(c) The Parties may also list multiple Trading Accounts in respect of an Allowance Transaction without providing for any subsequent right or obligation to give notice of the selection of one or more Trading Accounts from such list (a **"Cascade Transaction"**). The Trading Accounts so specified, unless otherwise agreed and provided, shall be listed in descending order of preference such that the Delivery Point or the Transfer Point, as applicable, for an Allowance Transaction shall be the first Trading Account so listed, unless the Party(ies) is/are, as applicable, prevented from Transferring to or Transferring from that Trading Account by an event which would be a Force Majeure if that were the only Trading Account specified by the Party affected by the event, in which case the Delivery Point that can accept Transfer of Allowances or Transfer Point from which that Party can Transfer Allowances, as applicable, shall be the next listed Trading Account, until such list of Trading Accounts has been exhausted.

(d) For the avoidance of doubt, specifying Delivery Point(s) and/or Transfer Point(s) in respect of any particular

Allowance Transaction for purposes of this § 4.1, need not preclude the Parties from designating different Trading Accounts than the Physical Settlement Netting Accounts specified for the purposes of § 4.3 *(Physical Settlement Netting)* in Part II of this Allowances Appendix.

**§ 4.2   Definition of Schedule.**   The addition at the end of the last sentence of § 4.2 *(Definition of "Schedule")* of the following words: "For the purposes of Allowance Transactions, the definition of Schedule shall include, in accordance with Applicable Rules, those actions necessary for Parties to comply with all obligations and requirements contained in the Applicable Rules, including, without limitation, the standards of the relevant Emission Trading Scheme(s) and Registry requirements in order to ensure that all their respective Trading Accounts are properly established, and that all their respective applicable requirements for effecting Transfer·from Seller to Buyer at the applicable Delivery Point are met.

**§ 4.3   Physical Settlement Netting.**

(a) If this § 4.3 is specified as applying in Part II of this Allowances Appendix; if on any date, Allowances of the same Allowance Type and Compliance Period would otherwise be Transferable in respect of two or more Allowance Transactions between the Parties and, if applicable, between designated pairs of Trading Accounts as specified as applying in Part II of this Allowances Appendix or otherwise agreed between the Parties (the **"Physical Settlement Netting Accounts"**), then, on such date, each Party's obligation to Schedule and Transfer any such Allowances will be automatically satisfied and discharged and, if the aggregate number of Allowances that would otherwise have been Transferable by one Party exceeds the aggregate number of Allowances that would otherwise have been Transferable by the other Party, replaced by an obligation upon the Party from whom the larger aggregate number of Allowances would have been Transferable to Schedule and Transfer to the other Party a number of Allowances (of the same Allowance Type and Compliance Period) equal to the excess of the larger aggregate number of Allowances over the smaller aggregate number of Allowances (the **"Net Contract Quantity"**) (such process hereinafter referred to as **"Physical Settlement Netting"**). In such circumstances the Party Transferring the Net Contract Quantity shall be the **"Net Seller"** and the Party receiving the Net Contract Quantity shall be the **"Net Buyer"**. In instances where the Net Contract Quantity for a given date and Delivery Point is zero, the Parties shall be released from any obligation to Schedule and Transfer or accept such Transfer in respect of the applicable Allowance Transactions on such date. For the avoidance of doubt and subject to this § 4.3, the Parties fully intend at the time of entering into each Individual Contract that such Individual Contract will result in the physical Transfer of Allowances.

(b)  Unless otherwise provided, if there is more than one Allowance Transaction between the Parties providing for Transfer of Allowances of the same Allowance Type and Compliance Period at the same Delivery Point on the same date, all references in the General Agreement, this Allowances Appendix and an Individual Contract to a "Seller", "Buyer", "Contract Quantity" and "Individual Contract" shall be deemed to be references to a "Net Seller", a "Net Buyer", a "Net Contract Quantity" and to all such Individual Contracts.

(c)  For the avoidance of doubt, specifying Physical Settlement Netting Accounts under this § 4.3 *(Physical Settlement Netting)* need not preclude the Parties from designating Delivery Point(s) and/or Transfer Points under § 4.1 *(Delivery, Acceptance and Scheduling Obligations)* nor is it intended to prohibit the Parties from limiting their rights and obligations in respect of any particular Allowance Transaction to Transfer and accept Transfer of Allowances in accordance with § 4.1.

**(5)  Primary Obligations for Options on Allowances.**  Except to the extent otherwise modified herein, there shall be no change to § 5 *(Primary Obligations for Options)* of the General Agreement with respect to Allowance Transactions.

**(6)      Delivery, Measurement, Transfer and Risk.**  For purposes of Allowance Transactions, § 6 of the General Agreement is hereby amended by: (i) deletion of § 6.1 *(Current/Frequency/Voltages)* and § 6.3 *(Transfer of Rights of Title)* in their entirety and replacement with the new § 6.1 *(Specified Vintage/Contract Quantity/Trading Account)* and the new § 6.3 *(No Encumbrances)* below; and (ii) the following additions and deletions to § 6.7 *(Seller and Buyer Risks)*:

**§ 6.1    Specified Vintage/Contract Quantity/Trading Account:** Allowances shall be Transferred in the Specified Vintage, Contract Quantity and at the relevant Delivery Point in accordance with the Delivery Schedule agreed in the Allowance Transaction and in accordance with the Applicable Rules, including, without limitation, the standards of the relevant Emissions Trading Scheme(s) and Registry responsible for the Delivery Point on the relevant Delivery Date.

**§ 6.3    No Encumbrances.**  In respect of each Allowances Transaction, the Seller warrants and represents to the Buyer that for each Contract Quantity it has the right to Transfer (or cause to be Transferred) to the Buyer full entitlement to the Specified Vintage(s) of Allowances at the Delivery Point free and clear of all liens, security interests, encumbrances or similar adverse claims by any person and the Seller shall indemnify and hold harmless Buyer against any such adverse claims in respect of the Delivered Quantity or any part thereof.

**§ 6.7    Seller and Buyer Risks.**  The deletion of the text of the provision and its replacement with the following: "The Buyer and Seller shall, unless otherwise expressly agreed between them, each bear all risks associated with and shall be responsible for its own respective costs in performing its obligations under § 4 *(Primary Obligations For Delivery and Acceptance of Allowances)*. Further, absent express agreement to the contrary between Buyer and Seller, all costs, fees and charges assessed or imposed by Relevant Authorities shall be the responsibility of the Party upon whom such cost, fee or charge is allocated by the Relevant Authority."

**(7)      § 7 Non-Performance Due to Force Majeure.**  For purposes of Allowance Transactions, § 7 of the General Agreement is hereby amended by deletion of § 7.1 *(Definition of Force Majeure)*, § 7.2 *(Release from Delivery and Acceptance Obligations)*, 7.3

*(Notification and Mitigation of Force Majeure)* and § 7.4 *(Effects of Force Majeure on Other Party)*, in their entirety and their replacement with a new §7.1 *(Definition of Force Majeure)*, a new § 7.2 *(Release from Delivery and Acceptance Obligations)*, a new 7.3 *(Notification and Mitigation of Force Majeure)* and a new §7.4 *(Settlement of Allowance Transaction Prevented by Force Majeure)*, as follows:

**§ 7.1 Definition of Force Majeure.** "Force Majeure" in the context of an Allowance Transaction means the occurrence of an event or circumstance beyond the control of the Party affected by Force Majeure (the **"Affected Party"**) that cannot, after using all reasonable efforts, be overcome and which makes it impossible for the Affected Party to perform its Transfer or acceptance of Transfer obligations in accordance with the terms of this Agreement and the relevant Emissions Trading Scheme. For the avoidance of doubt, but without limitation, Force Majeure shall not include an event or circumstance where there are insufficient Allowances in the relevant Trading Account(s) to effect the required Transfer whether that insufficiency is caused by the low or non-allocation of Allowances from a Member State or a Non-Member State or the failure of that Party to procure sufficient Allowances to meet its Transfer obligations.

**§ 7.2 Suspension of Delivery and Acceptance Obligations.** If a Party is fully or partly prevented due to Force Majeure from performing its obligations, as applicable, of Transfer or acceptance of Transfer, under one or more Allowance Transactions, no breach or default on the part of the Affected Party shall be deemed to have occurred and the obligations of both Parties with respect to the relevant Allowance Transaction(s) will be suspended for the period of time and to the extent that such Force Majeure prevents their performance. During the continuation of the Force Majeure, the Affected Party shall continue to use all reasonable endeavours to overcome the Force Majeure. Subject to § 7.4 *(Settlement of Allowance Transaction Prevented by Force Majeure)* below, upon the Force Majeure event being overcome or it ceasing to subsist, both Parties will, as soon as reasonably practicable thereafter (and in any event no later than the first Delivery Business Day following the cessation or Parties overcoming such Force Majeure event), resume full performance of their obligations under the Agreement in respect of the relevant Allowance Transaction(s) (including, for the avoidance of doubt, any suspended obligations).

**§ 7.3   Notification and Mitigation of Force Majeure.**   The first Party learning of the occurrence of an event of Force Majeure shall, as soon as practicable, notify the other Party of the commencement of the Force Majeure. Each Party shall then undertake in good faith to determine, and notify the other Party with, to the extent then available, a non-binding estimate of the extent and expected duration of the Force Majeure event and its impact on performance of all Allowance Transaction(s) affected by the event of Force Majeure. The Affected Party shall use all commercially reasonable efforts to mitigate the effects of the Force Majeure and shall, during the continuation of the Force Majeure, provide the other Party with reasonable updates, when and if available, of the extent and expected duration of its inability to perform.

**§7.4   Settlement of Allowance Transaction Prevented by Force Majeure.**

(a) **Termination for Force Majeure.**   Where Force Majeure continues for a period of time ending on the earlier to occur of: (a) a period of nine (9) Delivery Business Days from the date that, but for the Force Majeure, would have been the Delivery Date of the relevant Allowance Transaction(s); (b) the Reconciliation Deadline; or (c) the day which falls three (3) Delivery Business Days prior to the End of Phase Reconciliation Deadline, either Party may, by written notice to the other Party, terminate all (but not less than all) of the Allowance Transaction(s) affected by the Force Majeure.

(b) Force Majeure Termination Payment.   In the event and to the extent that an Allowance Transaction is terminated in accordance with § 7.4(a), the Parties' corresponding Transfer and acceptance of Transfer obligations under the terminated Allowance Transaction(s) shall be released and discharged. By specifying in Part II of this Allowances Appendix which of the following subparagraphs (i), (ii) or (iii) they wish to be operative, the Parties shall designate the consequences that will follow as a result of the Force Majeure event and what, if any, rights and obligations they wish to apply between them in the event of termination of an Allowance Transaction due to Force Majeure:

(i) **No Termination Payment.**   No termination payment or other financial settlement obligation shall be applicable (other than, for the avoidance of doubt, payment for any Allowances Transferred under such Allowance Transaction which were not prevented due to Force Majeure and/or payment of any damages due for non-performance of any portion of the terminated Allowance Transaction not excused due to Force Majeure (hereinafter collectively, **"Unpaid Amounts"**)) and each Party shall be permanently released and discharged of any further obligations with respect to the Allowance Transaction terminated by reason of Force Majeure.

(ii)  **Two-Way Market Quotation Termination Payment.** Each Party shall obtain five (5) midmarket quotations from Dealers for replacement Allowance Transaction(s) on the same terms as the unperformed portion(s) of the relevant Allowance Transaction(s) affected by Force Majeure (without taking into account the current credit-worthiness of the requesting Party or any Credit Support Documents or other Performance Assurance between the Parties). Each Party will then calculate the average of the quotations it obtained and the amount payable shall be equal to: (A) the sum of (i) one half of the difference between the higher amount determined by one Party ("X") and the lower amount determined by the other Party ("Y") and (ii) any Unpaid Amounts owing to X; less (B) any Unpaid Amounts owing to Y. If the resultant amount is a positive number, Y shall pay it to X; if it is a negative number, X shall pay the absolute value of such amount to Y. If the five (5) mid-market quotations cannot be obtained, all quotations will be deemed to be zero and no payment shall be due in respect of the termination of such Allowance Transaction.

(iii)  **Two-Way Loss Termination Payment.**   Each Party will determine its Loss in respect of the relevant Allowance Transaction(s) and an amount will be payable equal to one half of the difference between the Loss of the Party with the higher Loss ("X") and the Loss of the Party with the lower Loss ("Y"). If the amount payable is a positive number, Y will pay it to X; if it is a negative number, X will pay the absolute value of such amount to Y.

Payments due under this § 7.4(b) shall, unless otherwise agreed, be invoiced and made in accordance with the requirements of the Payment Cycle selected by the Parties in respect of § 13.2 *(Payment)*.

**(8)   § 8 Remedies for Failure to Deliver and Accept.** For purposes of Allowance Transactions, § 8 of the General Agreement is hereby deleted in its entirety and replaced with the following new § 8 *(Remedies for Failure to Deliver and Accept)*:

**§ 8.1   Failure to Deliver:**

(a) **One Delivery Business Day Grace Period.**  When a Seller fails to Transfer to Buyer a Contract Quantity in whole or in part on a Delivery Date as required in accordance with the terms of an Allowance Transaction, and such failure is not excused by an event of Force Majeure or the Buyer's nonperformance, the Seller may remedy such failure by Scheduling and Transferring such Contract Quantity (or undelivered portion thereof) to Buyer on the first Delivery Business Day following the Delivery Date, provided that such day is not on or after the Reconciliation Deadline following the relevant Delivery Date in respect of that Allowance, and further subject to the additional obligation of Seller to pay Buyer, as compensation for its late Transfer, interest calculated: (i) as follows for the one Delivery Business Day grace period; and (ii) as set forth in the applicable subpart of this § 8.1 for any longer period Seller fails to deliver the Allowances thereafter.

Interest for the one Delivery Business Day grace period shall accrue at the Interest Rate specified in §13.5 *(Default Interest)* for the period from (and including) the Delivery Date to (but excluding) the Delivery Business Day following the Delivery Date on the Total Contract Price of the undelivered Allowances, such Total Contract Price calculated as follows: the number of undelivered Allowances multiplied by a fraction determined by dividing the Total Contract Price by the Contract Quantity.

(b) **Buyer's Cover Costs.** In the event that the Seller fails to Transfer to Buyer all or any portion of a Contract Quantity as required by § 8.1(a) *(One Delivery Business Day Grace Period)* in accordance with the terms of an Allowance Transaction and Buyer has not agreed to a Deferred Delivery Date as provided for in § 8.1(c) *(Buyer's Right to Waive Its Cover Costs)*, Seller shall incur the obligation to pay Buyer, as compensation for its failure to Transfer, an amount (hereinafter **"Buyer's Cover Costs"**) equal to either:

(i) if no EEP or EEP Equivalent is operative or applicable to the Allowance Transaction, the sum of:

(A) the price, if any, in excess of the portion of the Total Contract Price applicable to the Allowances not Transferred to Buyer by the Seller, which the Buyer, acting in a commercially reasonable manner either did, or would have been able to, pay to purchase or otherwise acquire in an arm's length transaction from a third party or parties, a quantity of Allowances necessary to replace the Allowances not Transferred by the Seller;

(B) such reasonable additional incidental costs as Buyer incurred in attempting to make or making such replacement purchase of Allowances to the extent those costs and expenses are not recovered in § 8.1(b)(i)(A) above; and

(C) interest accrued during the one Delivery Business Day grace period as provided in §8.1(a); plus interest, at the Interest Rate specified in § 13.5 *(Default Interest)*, accrued from (and including) the Delivery Business Date following the Delivery Date, to (but excluding) the receipt by Buyer of damages for Seller's failure to deliver, such amount calculated using the following formula:

**Amount on which interest accrues**
$$= UA \times [(RP - CP)]$$

*where:*

UA means undelivered Allowances, the total number of Allowances Seller failed to deliver;

**RP** means replacement price, the price Buyer paid (or, if it could have procured replacement Allowances but did not do so, the first price which Buyer would have been able to pay) for each replacement Allowance in the UA; and

**CP** means the aggregate Contract Price that Buyer would have been required to pay to Seller for all undelivered Allowances comprising the UA had Seller not defaulted on its delivery obligation;

or

(ii) if an EEP or EEP Equivalent has been made applicable to the Allowance Transaction and has arisen, and further subject to the fulfillment of all applicable requirements imposed in § 8.3 *(Excess Emissions Penalty ("EEP") and EEP Equivalent)*, the amount calculated using the following formula:

(A) the price at which the Buyer, using reasonable endeavours and in (an) arm's length transaction(s), is or would be able to purchase, as soon as reasonably possible following the Reconciliation Deadline, replacement Allowances in the quantity of those not delivered to it by Seller (such quantity reduced, if applicable, by the number of Allowances Buyer was able to purchase prior to the Reconciliation Deadline as contemplated by § 8.1(b)(i), damages for the cost of which being recoverable pursuant to element (G) of this formula, hereinbelow) (the net resulting number of Allowances corresponding to the, as applicable, EEP or EEP Equivalent, being referred to hereinafter as the **"Undelivered EEP Amount"** or **"UEA"**);

(B) minus the price that Buyer would have been required to pay Seller for those Allowances comprising UEA, had Seller delivered those Allowances to Buyer in accordance with the terms of the Allowance Transaction;

(C) plus the amount of, as applicable, the EEP or EEP Equivalent on the UEA;

(D) plus interest accrued during the one Delivery Business Day grace period, calculated as provided in §8.1(a);

(E) plus interest, at the Interest Rate specified in § 13.5 *(Default Interest)*, accrued from (and including) the first date on which Buyer would be able to purchase, following the Reconciliation Deadline, the UEA of next Compliance Year replacement Allowances, to (but excluding) the date of Buyer's receipt of damages for Seller's failure to deliver, on the amount determined using the following formula:

**Amount on which interest accrues**
**= UEA × (REP − CP)**

*where:*

UEA  has the meaning set forth above;

REP  means the Replacement EEP Price, which shall be the (per Allowance) price of next Compliance Year Allowances calculated pursuant to § 8.1(b)(ii)(A), above; and

CP  means the per Allowance Contract Price that Buyer would have been required to pay to Seller for each undelivered Allowances comprising the UEA had Seller not defaulted on its delivery obligation;

(F) plus such reasonable additional incidental costs as Buyer incurred in, as applicable, both attempting unsuccessfully to make purchase of replacement Allowances in order to avoid the accrual of an EEP or EEP Equivalent, and in making replacement purchase(s) of next Compliance Year Allowances as described in § 8.1(b)(ii)(A), above; to the extent those costs and expenses are not recovered via § 8.1(b)(i)(A) above (which additional incidental damages, for the avoidance of doubt, may also include interest accrued at the Interest Rate specified in § 13.5 *(Default Interest)*, from (and including) the date on which an EEP or EEP Equivalent is paid, to (but excluding) the receipt by Buyer of damages for Seller's failure to deliver); and

(G) plus, if applicable, Buyer's Cover Costs incurred in replacing that portion of Allowances not Transferred to Buyer by Seller for which Buyer did not incur an EEP or EEP Equivalent (and thus not comprising the UEA)(such portion of Allowances not Transferred being hereinafter referred to as the **"Non-UEA"**), calculated in accordance with the methodology set forth in § 8.1(b)(i), which methodology shall apply equally to this § 8(b)(ii)(G);

(H) plus interest accrued on the value of the Non-UEA calculated in accordance with the methodology set forth in § 8.1(b)(i)(C), but in this context calculated on the amount of the Non-UEA, rather than the amount of the UA.

*provided, always,* that in the event that the number calculated through application of elements (A) through (H) of the formula set forth immediately above in this § 8.1(b)(ii) results in a negative number, such number shall be deemed to be zero and no damages will be owed in respect of such elements of this damages formula.

(c) **Buyer's Right to Waive Its Cover Costs.**  Buyer shall be entitled to invoice Seller for damages payable pursuant to § 8.1(b)(i) *(Buyer's Cover Costs)* in accordance with the requirements of Payment Cycle B as defined in § 13.2 *(Payment)*. However, Buyer may alternatively, but shall be under no obligation to, defer the due date on the payment of such damages for a reasonable period of time (but in no event beyond the applicable Reconciliation Deadline) if Seller has indicated to Buyer an intent to attempt to cure its Transfer default within a period of time acceptable to Buyer.

(i) At any time prior to the due date applicable to the payment of damages due to Buyer under §8.1(b), Seller may offer to Transfer to Buyer replacement Allowances to Buyer on a new Delivery Date (the **"Deferred Delivery Date"**) for those it originally failed to Transfer. Buyer may, but is not required to, agree to accept such Transfer of replacement Allowances in lieu of the damages it is entitled to recover under § 8.1(b), provided that in such case Buyer shall be entitled to invoice Seller for interest for the intervening period calculated as the sum of interest accrued during the one Delivery Business Day grace period as provided in § 8.1(a); plus interest, at the Interest Rate specified in § 13.5 *(Default Interest)*, from (and including) the first Delivery Business Day following the Delivery Date, to (but excluding) the date of actual Transfer of the previously undelivered Allowance(s), accrued on the amount calculated in accordance with the formula set forth in § 8.1(b)(i)(C).

(ii) If Buyer agrees to accept Seller's offer for Transfer of replacement Allowances on a Deferred Delivery Date as provided above in subparagraph (i), but Seller again defaults on its Transfer obligation, Buyer shall be entitled to invoice the Seller for an amount calculated in accordance with § 8.1(b) *(Buyer's Cover Costs)* save that the amount it may so invoice Seller shall account for both:

(A) interest, (1) in the event that Buyer is subsequently able to make a replacement purchase of Allowances, calculated as provided in § 8.1(b)(i)(C); or (2) in the event Buyer is unable to make a replacement purchase of Allowances before the Reconciliation Deadline for the relevant Compliance Period, calculated as provided in §8.1(b)(ii)(D); and

(B) any increase in Buyer's Cover Costs reflecting higher market prices pertaining to replacement Allowances on the Deferred Delivery Date when compared to those available in the market on the original Delivery Date.

§ 8.2   **Failure to Accept:**

(a) **One Delivery Business Day Grace Period.**   When a Buyer fails to accept Transfer of a Contract Quantity in whole or in part on a Delivery Date as required in accordance with the terms of an Allowance Transaction, and such failure is not excused by an event of Force Majeure or the Seller's nonperformance, the Seller shall afford Buyer an opportunity to remedy its failure by again attempting to Schedule and Transfer such Contract Quantity (or undelivered portion thereof) to Buyer on the first Delivery Business Day following the Delivery Date, provided that such day is not on or after the Reconciliation Deadline applicable to the Specified Vintage of the undelivered Allowance(s), and further subject to the additional obligation of Buyer to pay Seller, as compensation for its failure to accept Transfer of the Allowances, interest calculated: (i) as follows for the one Delivery Business Day grace period; and (ii) as set forth in the applicable subpart of this § 8.2 for any longer period Buyer fails to accept the Allowances thereafter.

Interest for the one Delivery Business Day grace period shall accrue at the Interest Rate specified in §13.5 *(Default Interest)* for the period from (and including) the Delivery Date to (but excluding) the Delivery Business Day following the Delivery Date on the Total Contract Price of the Allowances not accepted by Buyer, such Total Contract Price calculated as follows: the number of Allowances not accepted by Buyer multiplied by a fraction determined by dividing the Total Contract Price by the Contract Quantity.

(b) **Seller's Cover Costs.** In the event that the Buyer fails to accept Transfer of all or any portion of a Contract Quantity as required by § 8.2(a) *(One Delivery Business Day Grace Period)* in accordance with the terms of an Allowance Transaction and Seller has not agreed to a Deferred Acceptance Date as provided for in § 8.2(c) *(Seller's Right to Waive Its Cover Costs)*, Buyer shall incur the obligation to pay Seller, as compensation for its failure to accept Transfer of the Allowances, an amount (hereinafter **"Seller's Cover Costs"**) equal to the sum of:

(i) the price, if any, less than the portion of the Total Contract Price applicable to the Allowances not accepted by the Buyer, which the Seller, acting in a commercially reasonable manner either did, or would have been able to, receive, in an arm's length transaction with a third party or parties, from the resale of the Allowances not accepted by the Buyer;

(ii)   such reasonable additional incidental costs as Seller incurred in attempting to make or making such resale of the Allowances; and

(iii)   interest accrued during the one Delivery Business Day grace period as provided in § 8.1(a); plus interest, at the Interest Rate specified in § 13.5 *(Default Interest)*, accrued from (and including) the first Delivery Business Date following the Delivery Date, to (but excluding) the date of receipt by Seller of damages for Buyer's failure to accept, such amount calculated using the following formula:

**Amount on which interest accrues = ANA × CP** *where:*

ANA   means Allowances not accepted, the total number of Allowances Buyer failed to accept; and

CP   means the aggregate Contract Price that Buyer would have been required to pay to Seller for all Allowances not accepted by it.

(c)   **Seller's Right to Waive Its Cover Costs.**   Seller shall be entitled to invoice Buyer for damages payable pursuant to § 8.2(b) *(Seller's Cover Costs)* in accordance with the requirements of Payment Cycle B as defined in § 13.2 *(Payment)*. However, Seller may alternatively, but shall be under no obligation to, defer the due date on the payment of such damages for a reasonable period of time (but in no event beyond the applicable Reconciliation Deadline) if Buyer has indicated to Seller its intent to attempt to cure its acceptance default within a period of time acceptable to Seller.

(i)   At any time prior to the due date applicable to the payment of damages due to Seller under § 8.2(b), Buyer may offer to accept Transfer from Seller on a new Delivery Date (the **"Deferred Acceptance Date"**) of the Allowances it failed to accept Transfer of on the original Delivery Date. Seller may, but is not required to, agree to attempt to again Transfer such replacement Allowances to Buyer on the Deferred Acceptance Date. If it so agrees, Seller, in lieu of the damages it is entitled to recover under § 8.2(b), shall be entitled to both Transfer and receive payment of the Contract Price for the Allowances on the Deferred Acceptance Date and to further invoice Buyer for interest for the intervening period calculated as the sum of the interest accrued during the one Delivery Business Day grace period as provided in § 8.2(a) plus interest at the Interest Rate specified in § 13.5 *(Default Interest)*, from (and including) the Delivery Business Day following the Delivery Date to (but excluding) the date of actual acceptance of Transfer of the Allowance(s) previously not accepted, accrued on the amount calculated in accordance with the formula set forth in § 8.2(b)(iii).

(ii) If Seller agrees to Buyer's offer to accept Transfer of the Allowances on a Deferred Acceptance Date as provided above in subparagraph (i), but Buyer again defaults on its acceptance of Transfer obligation, Seller shall be entitled to invoice the Buyer for an amount calculated in accordance with § 8.2(b) *(Seller's Cover Costs)* save that the amount it may so invoice Buyer shall account for both:

(A) interest, calculated as provided in § 8.2(b)(iii); and

(B) any depreciation in Seller's Cover Costs reflecting lower prevailing market prices available for the resale of Allowances on the Deferred Acceptance Date when compared to those available in the market on the original Delivery Date.

## § 8.3 Excess Emissions Penalty ("EEP") and EEP Equivalent:

(a) **Applicability.** The Parties to an Allowance Transaction desiring to make EEP or EEP Equivalent inapplicable and inoperative to the calculation of Buyer's Cover Costs for such Allowance Transaction may do so either globally by specifying EEP or EEP Equivalent as not applying in Part II of this Allowances Appendix, or in the terms of the Allowance Transaction itself.

(b) **Excess Emissions Penalty.** If EEP is applicable, Buyer may invoice Seller in the amount of an EEP it incurs as the result of Seller's failure to Transfer to it Allowances when required pursuant to the terms of an Allowance Transaction.

(c) **Excess Emissions Penalty Equivalent.** If EEP Equivalent is applicable, Buyer may invoice Seller for an EEP Equivalent it incurs as the result of Seller's failure to Transfer to it Allowances when required pursuant to the terms of an Allowance Transaction.

(d) **Duty to Mitigate.** The Seller's obligation to pay the EEP or the EEP equivalent is subject always to the Buyer's overriding obligation to use commercially reasonable endeavours (including, without limitation, making use of any excess Allowances it may have available to it at the time, and/or procuring such Allowances as are available in the market) to satisfy its obligation to surrender the required number of Allowances necessary to avoid or otherwise mitigate its EEP or EEP Equivalent liability. For the avoidance of doubt, Buyers duty to mitigate its EEP or EEP Equivalent exposure is limited to management of its Allowance portfolio and shall not impose upon it any further obligation regarding its operation of any installation with an obligation to surrender Allowances to a Relevant Authority.

(e) **Evidence of Commercially Reasonable Efforts.** Upon request, Buyer shall confirm to the Seller:

(i) that it has incurred EEP or EEP Equivalent consequent upon the Seller's failure to Transfer Allowances to it;

(ii) the extent to which the requirement for the Buyer to pay the EEP or the EEP Equivalent results from the Seller's failure to make such a Transfer;

(iii) that it was unable to mitigate its EEP or EEP equivalent exposure, and shall provide Seller with evidence: (A) that the, as applicable, EEP or EEP Equivalent was incurred by it; (B) that such EEP or EEP Equivalent was incurred as a result of Seller's failure to perform its Transfer obligation; and (C) of its commercially reasonable endeavours to mitigate its exposure to such EEP or EEP Equivalent as it has invoiced to Seller; provided, however, that should Seller elect to challenge the Buyer in respect of any of the above matters, then the burden for demonstrating: (A) that such EEP or EEP Equivalent was not actually incurred by Buyer; (B) that such EEP or EEP Equivalent was not incurred by Buyer as a result of Seller's non-performance; and/or (C) the insufficiency, lack of thoroughness or unreasonableness of such endeavours shall be on the Seller and, <u>if § 22.3 *(Expert Determination)* is specified as applying in Part II of this Allowances Appendix</u> the process by which such challenge will be determined shall be in accordance with the procedures set forth in § 22.3 *(Expert Determination)*.

(f) **Later Mitigation of Recovered EEP or EEP Equivalent.** To the extent an initially assessed and recovered EEP is later reduced and/or fully or partly returned or credited to a Buyer by a Relevant Authority for any reason whatsoever, only such reduced and finally assessed EEP shall apply. EEPs recovered by a Buyer in the form of damages under this § 8 which are later reduced or returned to such Buyer shall be returned upon demand to the Seller who paid such damages, and Buyer shall provide Seller with prompt notification of any such reduction or return. Similarly, in the event a Seller has made a Buyer whole for an EEP Equivalent, and all or any portion of the underlying EEP or EEP Equivalent upon which Seller's EEP Equivalent payment was based is later returned to the Buyer by its resale customer, Buyer shall return an equivalent amount of its own EEP Equivalent payment to Seller.

**§ 8.4   Amounts Payable.**   Amounts that are due according to this § 8 shall be invoiced and paid in accordance with Payment Cycle B as defined in § 13.2 *(Payment)*.

**(9)**   Except to the extent otherwise modified herein, there shall be no change to § 9 *(Suspension of Delivery)* of the General Agreement with respect to Allowance Transactions.

**(10)   § 10 Term and Termination Rights.**   § 10 of the General Agreement is hereby amended with respect to both Individual Contracts for electricity and Individual Contracts for Allowances at any time in which the Parties have outstanding Allowance

Transactions remaining between them to be partially or fully performed by: (i) the addition in the second line of § 10.3(a) *(Termination for Material Reason)* after the words "may terminate the Agreement" of the words "or the Allowances Appendix only"; and (ii) the following amendments:

**§ 10.5  Definition of Material Reason.**  The addition at the end of the second line of § 10.5 after the words "(each a **"Material Reason"**)" of the words "save that in the event of termination pursuant to § 10.5(a) *(Non Performance)* or § 10.5(f) *(Representation or Warranty)* of the General Agreement, the Non-Defaulting Party may, at its sole discretion, elect to terminate only the Allowances Appendix and not the previously executed General Agreement, if and only when such uncured non-performance, warranty breach or misrepresentation concerns only one or more Allowance Transactions. If the Non-Defaulting Party elects to terminate only the Allowances Appendix together with all Allowance Transactions thereunder, it may do so in the manner prescribed in § 10 *(Term and Termination Rights)* and § 11 *(Calculation of Termination Amount)*, but only with respect to its Allowance Transactions and in such manner as to result in the accrual of an amount due from one party to the other party analogous to a Termination Amount but concerning only the Allowance Transaction(s) terminated (an **"Allowances Termination Amount"**)."

**§ 10.5(d)  Failure to Deliver or Accept.**  § 10.5(d) is deleted in its entirety.

**§ 10.5(e)  Force Majeure.**  § 10.5(e) is deleted in its entirety and replaced with the words: "Unless expressly agreed to the contrary by the Parties, Force Majeure's impairment of a Party's ability to perform its obligations with respect to any single Allowance Transaction shall not give rise to a Material Reason for initiating an Early Termination of either the Agreement or this Allowances Appendix and all then outstanding Allowance Transactions."

**(11)  § 11 Calculation of the Termination Amount.**  § 11 of the General Agreement is hereby amended for purposes of calculating any Allowances Termination Amount concerning one or more Allowance Transactions by the addition of the following words to § 11.2 *(Settlement Amount)* at the end of the definition of § 11.2(a)

*(Costs)*: "including, in the event that an EEP or EEP Equivalent is applicable to an Allowance Transaction, any EEP or EEP Equivalent actually assessed and not later reduced or recovered".

**(12)    § 12 Limitation of Liability.**   For the avoidance of doubt, the Parties agree that if an EEP or EEP Equivalent applies to an Allowance Transaction such EEP or EEP Equivalent shall not be considered an indirect or consequential damage of the type excluded from recovery of damages by § 12.3 *(Consequential Damage and Limitation of Liability)*, and that such maximum amount of such EEP or EEP Equivalent, being an amount identifiable by them at the time of entering into their Allowance Transaction, is neither speculative nor difficult to ascertain. The Parties further agree and acknowledge that the formulae providing for calculating the amount of EEP and EEP Equivalent in this Allowances Appendix are reasonable in light of the anticipated harm that would be incurred by a Buyer and are therefore a genuine preestimate of the nature and magnitude of such harm. Further, the payment of such damages is not viewed by either Party as a penalty or in the nature of a penalty and each Party waives the right to contest those payments as an unreasonable penalty. Except to the extent otherwise modified herein by the Parties, there shall be no further changes to § 12 *(Limitation of Liability)* of the General Agreement with respect to Allowance Transactions.

**(13)    § 13 Invoicing and Payment.**   For purposes of Allowance Transactions, § 13 of the General Agreement is hereby amended by: (i) the deletion of the last sentence in § 13.1 *(Invoice)* commencing: "Invoicing of Premiums due" and ending: "in the Individual Contracts."; (ii) the deletion of the words in the first sentence of § 13.2 *(Payment)* commencing: "On or before the later to occur of" ... up to and including the words: "following receipt of an invoice (the "**Due Date**"), a" and the addition of the words in § 13.2 as set-out below; (iii) the addition of the following new § 13.3.1 *(Cross Product Payment Netting)*; and (iv) the deletion of § 13.4 *(Invoicing and Payment of Scheduled Contract Quantities)* in its entirety and replaced with a new § 13.4 *(Physical Settlement Netting Invoicing and Payment)*, as follows :

**§ 13.2  Payment.**   Payments due in relation to Allowance Transactions shall be in accordance with either Payment Cycle A or

Payment Cycle B (each, a **"Payment Cycle"**), as specified as applying in Part II of this Allowances Appendix, as follows:

> **Payment Cycle A:** "On or before the later to occur of either (a) the twentieth (20th) day of the calendar month or if not a Business Day the immediately following Business Day or (b) the fifth (5th) Business day following receipt of an invoice (the **"Due Date"**). A"; or

> **Payment Cycle B:** "On or before the fifth (5th) Business day after the later to occur of (a) the Delivery Date or (b) following receipt of an invoice (the **"Due Date"**). A".

In the event the Parties do not designate a Payment Cycle as applying, Payment Cycle A shall apply.

**§ 13.3.1 Cross Product Payment Netting.** If the Parties have elected to make § 13.3 operative via their Election Sheet, payments in relation to Individual Contracts for electricity shall continue to be netted one against the other and payments in relation to Allowance Transactions shall also be netted one against the other, but unless so agreed and memorialized in Part II of this Allowances Appendix, payments in relation to Individual Contracts for electricity shall not be netted against payments in relation to Allowance Transactions.

**§ 13.4 Physical Settlement Netting Invoicing and Payment.** If the Parties have specified § 4.3 *(Physical Settlement Netting)* as applying in Part II of this Allowances Appendix, invoicing shall continue to be based on the Contract Quantity that would have been Transferred for an Allowance Transaction but for the provisions of § 4.3, and the invoice shall set forth the Total Contract Price on a gross basis and state the amount of VAT properly chargeable thereon as well as the net amount payable from one Party to the other Party.

**(14)  § 14 VAT and Taxes.** For purposes of Allowance Transactions, § 14 of the General Agreement is hereby amended by the deletion of § 14.1 *(VAT)*, § 14.2 *(Seller's and Buyer's Tax Obligation)* and § 14.3 *(Withholding Tax)* in their entirety and their replacement with a new § 14.1 *(VAT)* and a new § 14.2 *(Other Taxes)*, as follows:

**§ 14.1  VAT.** All amounts referred to in this Allowances Appendix are exclusive of any applicable VAT. The VAT treatment of any

Transfer under an Allowance Transaction shall be determined pursuant to the VAT law of the jurisdiction where a taxable transaction for VAT purposes is deemed to take place. If VAT is payable on any such amounts, the Buyer shall pay to the Seller an amount equal to the VAT at the rate applicable; provided, however, that such amount shall only be required to be paid once the Seller provides the Buyer with a valid VAT invoice (applicable in the jurisdiction of Transfer) in relation to that amount. Each Party shall to the extent permitted by law provide the other with any additional valid VAT invoices as required for the purposes of the Allowances Appendix.

**§ 14.2   Other Taxes.**   Subject to each Party's obligations relating to VAT, each Party shall cause all royalties, taxes, duties and other sums (including any stamp duty, other documentary taxes, climate change levy or other environmental tax or levy) legally payable by that Party arising in connection with this Allowances Appendix to be paid. In the event that the Seller is required by law to pay any tax which is properly for the account of the Buyer, the Buyer shall promptly indemnify or reimburse the Seller in respect of such tax. In the event that the Buyer is required by law to pay any tax which is properly for the account of the Seller, the Buyer may deduct the amount of any such tax from the sums due to the Seller under this Allowances Appendix and the Seller shall promptly indemnify or reimburse the Buyer in respect of any such tax not so deducted.

**(15)–(20)** Except to the extent otherwise modified herein, there shall be no change to § 15 *(Floating Prices and Fallback Procedure for Market Disruption)*, § 16 *(Guarantees and Credit Support)*, § 17 *(Performance Assurance)*, § 18 *(Provision of Financial Statements and Tangible Net Worth)*, § 19 *(Assignment)* or § 20 *(Confidentiality)* of the General Agreement with respect to Allowance Transactions.

**(21)    § 21 Representation and Warranties.**   § 21 of the General Agreement is hereby amended by the following additions and or deletions with respect only to Allowance Transactions:

**§ 21(g)**   Deletion of the word "regularly" in the first line; and

**§ 21(l)**   Deletion of § 21(l) in its entirety.

**(22)** **§ 22 Governing Law and Arbitration.** For the purposes of Allowance Transactions, § 22 of the General Agreement is hereby amended by the addition of the following words both at the end of the final sentence of § 22.1 *(Governing Law)* and the end of the first sentence of § 22.2 *(Arbitration)*: "subject to the referral to an Expert of disputes under § 8.3 *(EEP and EEP Equivalent)*"; and the addition of a new § 22(3) *(Expert Determination)*, as follows:

**§ 22.3 Expert Determination.** If specified as applying in Part II of this Allowances Appendix:

    (a) For the purposes of resolving disputes under § 8.3 *(EEP and EEP Equivalent)*, the Parties shall address payment of any disputed amounts in accordance with § 13.6 *(Disputed Amounts)* of the General Agreement. If the Parties, who shall negotiate in good faith in an attempt to resolve the dispute as speedily as possible, are unable to settle the disputed amount within a period of fourteen (14) days of the date a Party first notifies the other Party in writing of such a dispute, either Party may require this matter to be referred to an Expert for determination in accordance with this § 22.3.

    (b) If any matter under § 8.3 *(EEP and EEP Equivalent)* is referred to an Expert in accordance with this Agreement, the Expert is to be appointed by agreement between the Parties. If the Parties fail to agree upon that appointment within ten (10) Business Days of a Party notifying the other Party of its decision to refer the matter to an Expert, the General Secretary of EFET may appoint the Expert on the application of either Party.

    (c) The Expert shall act as an expert and not as an arbitrator and shall give his or her determination in writing.

    (d) Unless this § 22.3(d) is specified as not applying in Part II of this Allowances Appendix, the determination of the Expert shall, to the extent permitted by applicable law, be final, conclusive and binding upon the Parties and such determination shall be the sole and exclusive remedy of the Parties with respect to disputes arising under § 8.3

    (e) *(Evidence of Commercially Reasonable Efforts)* and both Parties agree that they will not have recourse to, if applicable under the General Agreement, either arbitration in accordance with § 22.2 *(Arbitration)* or to the courts of law of the jurisdiction specified in accordance with § 22.1 *(Governing Law)* or any other court of competent jurisdiction save that each Party shall have the right to have the Expert's determination in respect to the dispute enforced by any court of competent jurisdiction or included by such arbitrator in findings of fact and conclusions of law. For the avoidance of doubt, notwithstanding the provisions of this § 22.3(d), nothing contained herein shall limit or in any way restrict the ability of any Party to challenge the appointment of the Expert failing to satisfy the criteria set forth in the definition of Expert contained in this Allowances Appendix.

(e) The Expert shall determine the procedure to be followed by the Expert for the purpose of making a determination, but the Parties shall use their respective reasonable endeavours to ensure that the Expert makes a determination within twenty (20) Business Days of being appointed.

(f) Each of the Parties shall bear one half of the costs of the Expert unless the Expert determines otherwise.

(g) Pending determination of any dispute under this § 22.3, the Parties shall continue to the extent possible to perform their respective obligations under this Agreement.

**(23)**   Except to the extent otherwise modified herein, there shall be no change to § 23 *(Miscellaneous)* of the General Agreement with respect to Allowance Transactions.

[Balance of page intentionally left blank]

# Part II: Elections for Customization of Provisions in the Allowances Appendix:

## § 4
### Primary Obligations for Delivery and Acceptance of Allowances

§ 4.3   **Physical Settlement Netting:**

[ ]  § 4.3 shall not apply, or

[ ]  § 4.3 shall apply; and for this purpose the relevant Allowance Type(s) shall include [                    ]

and each Party's Physical Settlement Netting Accounts in their designated Registries shall be as follows:

Party A:
Account Number(s):
[                    ], in
Account Registry(ies):
[                    ]; and

Party B:
Account Number(s):
[                    ], in
Account Registry(ies)
[                    ]

## § 7
### Non-Performance Due to Force Majeure

§ 7.4(b)  **Force Majeure Termination Payment:**

[ ]  § 7.4(b)(i) **(No Termination Payment)** shall apply; or

[ ]  § 7.4(b)(ii) **(Two-Way Market Quotation Termination Payment)** shall apply; or

[ ]  § 7.4(b)(iii) **(Two-Way Loss Termination Payment)** shall apply

## § 8
## Remedies for Failure to Deliver and Accept

| | |
|---|---|
| § 8.3(a)  **EEP and EEP Equivalent** | [ ]  EEP shall <u>not</u> apply |
| | [ ]  EEP Equivalent shall <u>not</u> apply |

## § 13
## Invoicing and Payment

| | |
|---|---|
| § 13.2    **Payment:** | [ ]  Payment Cycle A shall apply, or |
| | [ ]  Payment Cycle B shall apply |
| § 13.3.1 **Cross Product Payment Netting:** | [ ]  Payments due in relation to Individual Contracts in respect of electricity shall be netted against payments due in relation to Allowance Transactions. |

## § 22
## Governing Law and Arbitration

| | |
|---|---|
| § 22.3    **Expert Determination:** | [ ]  § 22.3 shall apply, and |
| § 22.3(d) | [ ]  § 22.3(d) shall not apply; or |
| | [ ]  § 22.3 shall not apply |

# Annex 1
## to the
## Allowances Appendix

### Defined Terms

**"Delivery Business Day"**   The relevant jurisdiction for the purposes of the definition of Delivery Business Day that each Party specifies as applying to it shall be as follows:

Party A:

_____; and

Party B:

_____


## ADDITIONAL PROVISIONS APPLICABLE ONLY TO ALLOWANCE TRANSACTIONS:

[                                                    ]

**This page need ONLY be executed by Parties that checked and completed the box on the first page hereof. Those appending this Allowance s Appendix to a General Agreement at the time of its execution need only append it to the General Agreement.**

IN WITNESS whereof this Allowances Appendix has been duly executed by the authorized representatives of each Party on the respective dates set out below with effect from the Allowances Appendix Effective Date.

**"Party A"**                                    **"Party B"**


_____            _____

[Name of Party]                              [Name of Party]


_____            _____

[Name of Signatory/ies]                 [Name of Signatory/ies]


_____            _____

[Title of Signatory/ies]                   [Title of Signatory/ies]

# EFET

# European Federation of Energy Traders

### ANNEX I
### to the
### ALLOWANCES APPENDIX

**Defined Terms**

Terms used in this Allowances Appendix shall have the following meanings:

**"Allowance"** means an allowance to emit one tonne of carbon dioxide ($CO_2$) or equivalent during a specified period valid for the purposes of meeting the requirements of applicable law and the relevant Emissions Trading Scheme applicable to the Buyer and the Delivery Point on the Delivery Date.

**"Allowances Appendix"** means this Allowances Appendix to the General Agreement (inclusive of its Annexes).

**"Allowance Type"** means a specific type of Allowance as defined by the Applicable Rules that the Parties have specified as applying in Part II of this Allowances Appendix or in an Individual Contract which may be used for determining compliance with emissions limitation commitments pursuant to and in accordance with the relevant Emissions Trading Scheme.

**"Applicable Rule(s)"** means that subset of the Rules which govern, relate to or otherwise concern the valid Transfer of Allowances to Buyer's Trading Account in satisfaction of Seller's obligation under an Allowance Transaction and, when applicable in context, which govern an entity's emission-related obligations to its Relevant Authority.

**"Allowances Termination Amount"** shall have the meaning given in § 10.5 of this Allowances Appendix.

**"Allowance Transaction"** shall have the meaning given in the first paragraph of this Allowances Appendix.

**"Buyer's Choice Transaction"** shall have the meaning given in § 4.1(b) of this Allowances Appendix.

**"Cascade Transaction"** shall have the meaning given in § 4.1(c) of this Allowances Appendix.

**"Compliance Period"** means that period of time in which an Allowance is valid for purposes of fulfilling the requirements of an entity subject to the jurisdiction and requirements of the Relevant Authority pursuant to its Applicable Rules.

**"Compliance Year"** means that period of time between each Reconciliation Deadline (if more than one) in a Compliance Period.

**"Contract Price"** means, in respect of an Allowance Transaction for a particular Specified Vintage, the amount agreed to be the purchase price for that Contract Quantity, excluding applicable taxes.

**"Contract Quantity"** means, in respect of an Allowance Transaction, the number of Allowances of one or more Specified Vintages as agreed to be bought and sold between the Parties.

**"Delivery Business Day"** means, in respect of an Allowance Transaction, and for the purposes of this Allowances Appendix only, any day which is not a Saturday or Sunday, on which commercial banks are open for general business at the places where each party specifies as applying to it in Part II of this Allowances Appendix. In the event that a Party does not so specify a place in Part II of this Allowances Appendix, then (that/those) place(s) shall be deemed to be the Seller and the Buyer's addresses, as applicable, specified in § 23.2 **(Notices, Invoices and Payments)** of the General Agreement or, if no such addresses have been specified in § 23.2, at the place(s) where (that/those) Party(ies) (has/have) (its/their) registered office.

**"Delivered Quantity"** means, in respect of an Allowance Transaction, the number of Allowances of a Specified Vintage of a Contract Quantity Transferred by the Buyer and accepted by the Seller at the Delivery Point.

**"Delivery Date"** means, in respect of an Allowance Transaction, the day agreed between the Parties on which the relevant Transfer from

Seller to Buyer is to take place at the Delivery Point. If the Delivery Date is not a Delivery Business Day, it shall be deemed to be the first Delivery Business Day following the agreed day.

**"Delivery Point"** means, in respect of an Allowance Transaction, the Buyer's Trading Account(s) that it has nominated in one or more Registry(ies) or such other Trading Account(s) as the Parties may agree in an Allowance Transaction.

**"Delivery Schedule"** means, in respect of an Allowance Transaction, the Schedule of Delivery Dates for the Transfer of (each) Contract Quantity(ies) as the Buyer and Seller may agree in an Allowance Transaction.

**"Directive"** means any EU directive or directives which govern the purchase, sale and Transfer of Allowances.

**"Directive 2003/87/EC"** means the Directive of the European Parliament and of the Council of 13 October 2003 establishing a scheme for greenhouse gas emissions allowance trading and amending Council Directive 96/61/EC.

**"End of Phase Reconciliation Deadline"** means, in respect of an Allowance Transaction, the final Reconciliation Deadline determined in accordance with Applicable Rules for the surrender of Allowances in respect of a Compliance Period for a Specified Vintage.

**"Emissions Trading Scheme(s)"** means the scheme(s) to effect the Transfer of Allowances between participants in both or either of Member or Non-Member States as implemented by and including its Applicable Rules.

**"EU"** means the European Community as it exists from time to time.

**"Excess Emissions Penalty"** or **"EEP"** means a financial payment required to be made to a Relevant Authority pursuant to and in accordance with Article 16(3) or Article 16(4) of Directive 2003/87/ EC (which, for the avoidance of doubt, shall not include any costs relating to or arising from the obligation to purchase and/or surrender Allowances in the following Compliance Year), or its equivalent under any other Emissions Trading Scheme.

**"Excess Emissions Penalty Equivalent"** or **"EEP Equivalent"** means an amount which the Buyer must pay to a third party in respect of any amount payable by that third party which arose as a result of the Buyer's failure to Transfer the required Allowances to that third party and which in turn was a consequence of the Seller's failure to Transfer the Contract Quantity to the Buyer under this Agreement (which, for the avoidance of doubt, shall not include any costs relating to the obligation to purchase and/or surrender Allowances in the following Compliance Year).

**"Expert"** means a person qualified by education, experience and/or training with the applicable Emissions Trading Schemes, Applicable Rules and Allowance Transactions who is able to review and understand the contents of a Party's emission allowance trading portfolio and who neither is nor has been directly or indirectly under the employ of, affiliated with, or under the influence of either of the Parties or otherwise has any conflicting interest or duty.

**"Loss"** means an amount that each Party reasonably determines in good faith to be its total losses and costs (or gain, in which case it shall be expressed as a negative number) in connection with the termination of the applicable Allowance Transaction(s), or any unperformed portions thereof, including, if applicable, any EEP or EEP Equivalent, any loss of bargain, cost of funding (based on the actual costs of such Party whether or not greater than market costs) or, without duplication, loss or cost incurred as a result of its terminating, liquidating, obtaining or re-establishing any related trading position (or any gain resulting from any of them). Loss shall not include legal fees or similar out-of-pocket expenses. Each Party may (but need not) determine its Loss by reference to quotations of average relevant rates or prices from two or more leading Dealers.

**"Member State"** means any one of the signatories to the EU from time to time.

**"Non-Member State"** means any state that is not a Member State.

**"Participating Agreement"** means any agreement, rule, procedure, instrument or other law or regulation which governs a Non-Member States' participation in and the Transfer of Allowances to the Emissions Trading Scheme(s) of a Member State or another Non-Member State, as applicable.

**"Payment Cycle"** means either Payment Cycle A or Payment Cycle B as defined in § 13.2 *(Payment)*.

**"Physical Settlement Netting Accounts"** shall have the meaning given in § 4.3(a) of this Allowances Appendix.

**"Reconciliation Deadline"** means, in respect of an Allowance Transaction, 30 April in any calendar year in relation to the immediately preceding calendar year, or as otherwise specified in the relevant Emissions Trading Scheme.

**"Registry"** means the registry established by each Member or Non-Member State, in accordance with Applicable Rules, in order to ensure the accurate accounting of the issue, holding, Transfer, surrender, cancellation and replacement of Allowances.

**"Relevant Authority"** means the body established by each Member State or Non-Member State from time to time to administer the relevant Emissions Trading Scheme(s) and emissions compliance responsibilities in its jurisdiction.

**"Rules"** mean the Directive, Emissions Trading Scheme(s), Participating Agreement and all other applicable guidance, regulations, rules and procedures (whether made at the direction of a government, governmental body, regulator, competent authority or otherwise) as modified, amended and/or supplemented from time to time relating to the trade of Allowances as contemplated by this Allowances Appendix.

**"Seller's Choice Transaction"** shall have the meaning given in § 4.1(b) of this Allowances Appendix.

**"Specified Vintage"** means, in respect of an Allowance Transaction and a Contract Quantity, the Compliance Period for which an Allowance is allocated in accordance with the relevant Emissions Trading Scheme(s), as agreed between the Parties at the time of entering into an Allowance Transaction.

**"Total Contract Price"** means the aggregate price to be paid for all Allowances required to be Transferred on a Delivery Date under an Allowance Transaction.

**"Trading Account"** means the form of record maintained by and in the relevant Registry to record the allocation (if applicable), Transfer and holding of Allowances.

**"Transfer"** means (whether used as a verb or a noun) the movement of Allowances from one Trading Account to another under and in accordance with and for the purposes of the relevant Emissions Trading Scheme(s) (or, such similar or analogous procedure or mechanism as, in effect on the Delivery Date, evidences the delivery and acceptance of the Allowance(s) and the vesting in, or for the benefit of, Buyer, the economic benefits of such Allowance(s)), and **Transferable**, **Transferring** and **Transferred** are to be construed accordingly.

**"Transfer Point"** means, in respect of an Allowance Transaction, the Seller's Trading Account(s) that it has nominated in one or more Registry(ies) or such other Trading Account(s) as the Parties may agree in an Allowance Transaction.

**"Undelivered EEP Amount"** or **"UEA"** shall have the meaning given in § 8.1(b)(ii)(A).

**"Unpaid Amounts"** shall have the meaning given in § 7.4(b)(i).

**"Value Added Tax"** or **"VAT"** means any value added tax or any tax analogous thereto but excluding any statutory late payment of interest or penalties.

# EFET

## European Federation of Energy Traders

### ANNEX II (A)
### to the
### ALLOWANCES APPENDIX

CONFIRMATION OF ALLOWANCE TRANSACTION
(Fixed Price)

between

_____ as Seller

and

_____ as Buyer.

concluded on: __/__/____, __.__ hours (**Trade Date**)

**Delivery Schedule** (Delivery Date to each Delivery Point for each Contract Quantity and Specified Vintage)

| Transfer Point(s) Trading Account and Registry of Seller | Delivery Point(s) Trading Account and Registry of the Buyer | Specified Vintage | Contract Quantity | Allowance Type | Delivery Date | Price per Allowance | Total Contract Price / Specified Vintage |
|---|---|---|---|---|---|---|---|
|  |  |  |  |  |  |  |  |
|  |  |  |  |  |  |  |  |
|  |  |  |  |  |  |  |  |

**Total Contract Quantity:**      **Total Contract Price:**

Name of Broker (if applicable):

Special Conditions & Terms:

For this specific Allowances Transaction:

[ ] EEP shall not apply.      [ ] EEP Equivalent shall not apply.

[ ] EEP shall apply.[1]      [ ] EEP Equivalent shall apply.[1]

[1] Parties need only check the box to apply EEP and/or EEP Equivalent if they have specifically opted-out of either EEP and/or EEP Equivalent in § 8.3(a) (*EEP and EEP Equivalent*) of the EFET Allowances Appendix agreed between them.

Other:

Physical Settlement Netting Accounts:

Party A:  Account Number(s):   [                              ], in

Account Registry(ies): [                              ]; and

Party B:  Account Number(s):   [                              ], in

Account Registry(ies): [                              ]

[ ]   Buyer's Choice Transaction

Notification Deadline: _____

[ ]   Seller's Choice Transaction

Notification Deadline: _____

[ ]   Cascade Transaction

This Confirmation confirms the Allowance Transaction entered into pursuant to the EFET General Agreement Concerning the Delivery and Acceptance of Electricity between the Parties (General Agreement) as modified, supplemented and amended by the Allowances Appendix between the Parties (Allowances Appendix) and forms part of that General Agreement. In case of any inconsistencies between the terms of this Confirmation and the Allowance Transaction, please contact us immediately.

Date: _____     Signature: _____

Name:      _____

Title:      _____

# Appendix C

## IETA

## EMISSIONS TRADING MASTER AGREEMENT FOR THE EU SCHEME©

## Version 2.1    2005

This draft Agreement has been developed by the International Emissions Trading Association (IETA) to facilitate trading under the EU emissions trading scheme. IETA encourages the use of this document by all interested parties.

# Foreword

The International Emissions Trading Association (IETA) is a non profit organization created in June 1999 to establish a functional international framework for trading greenhouse gas emissions reductions. Our 103 international members include leading multinational companies from across the carbon trading cycle: emitters, solution providers, brokers, insurers, verifiers and law firms.

IETA works for the development of an active, global greenhouse gas market, consistent across national boundaries. In doing so IETA focuses on the creation of systems and instruments that will ensure effective business participation.

This version 2.1 of the Emissions Trading Master Agreement for the EU Scheme, dated 13 June 2005, reflects further market development, input from market players and a considerable effort in cooperating with the International Swaps and Derivatives Association (ISDA) and the European Federation of Energy Traders (EFET) to harmonise provisions between all master agreements used by participants in this market. We feel that the current version addresses many of the issues raised and will help increase liquidity in this rapidly developing market.

Andrei Marcu
President & CEO, IETA

## Questions or comments?

For general comments regarding this document and questions concerning the work of IETA please contact Martina Priebe, IETA at +41 22 839 3101 or priebe@ieta.org.

# EMISSIONS TRADING MASTER AGREEMENT FOR THE EU SCHEME©

## v. 2.1    2005

DATED: [•]

BETWEEN

[•]

AND

[•]

# Table of Contents

# EMISSIONS TRADING MASTER AGREEMENT FOR THE EU SCHEME

## Dated _____

**Between**

> [Entity name] a [corporation, limited partnership, etc.] existing under the laws of [•] (Registered No: [•]) whose [registered/principal/operational] office is at [•] ("**Party A**");

> and

> [Entity name] a [corporation, limited partnership, etc.] existing under the laws of [•] (Registered No: [•]) whose [registered/principal/operational office is at [•] ("**Party B**").

**Recitals**

A.   The EU and the Member States, in accordance with the Directive, as well as some non-Member States, have established a scheme under which participants may buy and sell allowances for greenhouse gas emissions.

B.   The Parties have entered into or expect to enter into one or more Transactions that are or will be governed by the terms and conditions of this Emissions Trading Master Agreement for the EU Scheme (this "**Agreement**").

C.   Each Transaction relates or will relate to a trade of Allowances through the effecting of Transfers.

D.   The Parties intend that each Transaction provides for a trade of Allowances in accordance with the Scheme.

In consideration of the mutual undertakings in this Agreement and for other good and valuable consideration, the receipt and sufficiency of which the Parties acknowledge, **the Parties agree as follows**.

**1        Interpretation and Construction**

1.1      **Definitions**. Capitalized terms not defined in the body of this Agreement have the meanings assigned to them in Schedule 1.

1.2      **Single Agreement**. All Transactions are entered into in reliance on the fact that this Agreement (including, for the avoidance of doubt, all of its Schedules), all Confirmations and all Transactions form a single agreement between the Parties, and the Parties acknowledge and agree that they would not otherwise enter into any Transactions.

1.3      **Interpretation**. The following interpretive provisions apply to this Agreement.

(a)   Reference to any law or statute includes any amendment to, consolidation, re-enactment or replacement of such law or statute.

(b)   Any reference to a "clause" or "schedule" is a reference to a clause or schedule of this Agreement.

(c)   Words in the singular are to be interpreted as including the plural, and vice versa, to the extent the context permits or requires.

(d)   The terms "including" and "in particular" are used for illustration or emphasis only and not to limit the generality of any preceding words, whether or not non-limiting language (such as "without limitation", "but not limited to" and similar expressions) is used with reference to them.

(e)   If there is any conflict between the provisions of Schedule 2 and any other provisions of this Agreement, the terms of Schedule 2 shall prevail. If, in relation to any Transaction, there is any conflict between the provisions of the relevant Confirmation and any other provisions of this Agreement (including Schedule 2), the terms of such Confirmation shall prevail for the purpose of the relevant Transaction.

(f)   Any reference to "time" is to Central European Time.

(g)   Unless otherwise specified, where anything is to be done under this Agreement:

(i)   by or not later than a Banking Day or Delivery Banking Day, or any period is to run to a Banking Day or Delivery Banking Day, such thing may be done by or such period is to run to 17:00 hours on that Banking Day or Delivery Banking Day (as the case may be);

(ii) from or not earlier than a Banking Day or Delivery Banking Day, or any period is to run from a Banking Day or Delivery Banking Day, such thing may be done or such period is to run from 09:00 hours on that Banking Day or Delivery Banking Day (as the case may be);

(iii) on a Banking Day or Delivery Banking Day, it is to be treated as having been done on the next following Banking Day or Delivery Banking Day if it is done after 17:00 hours on that Banking Day or Delivery Banking Day (as the case may be);

(iv) by or not later than a day or any period is to run to a day, such thing may be done or such period is to run up to the end of that day; and

(v) from or not earlier than a day or any period is to run from a day, such thing may be done or such period is to run from the start of that day.

| 2 | **Confirmation Procedure** |
|---|---|
| 2.1 | **Agreement of a Transaction.** The Parties intend that they shall be legally bound by the terms of each Transaction from the moment they agree to those terms (whether orally or otherwise). |
| 2.2 | **Exchange of Confirmations.** |

(a) Unless otherwise agreed, the Seller shall send to the Buyer by facsimile (or such other means, if any, specified in Schedule 2) a Confirmation materially in the form set out in Schedule 3 recording the details of the Transaction within three Banking Days of a Transaction having been entered into.

(b) If the Buyer is satisfied that the Confirmation accurately reflects the terms of the Transaction, the Buyer shall countersign and return the Confirmation to the Seller by facsimile (or such other means, if any, specified in Schedule 2) within three Banking Days of receipt of the Confirmation from the Seller.

(c) If the Buyer is not satisfied that the Confirmation accurately reflects the terms of the Transaction, the Buyer shall inform the Seller of any inaccuracies within three

Banking Days of receipt of the Confirmation. If the Seller agrees that the Confirmation is inaccurate, the Seller shall issue a new Confirmation, and the provisions of clauses 2.2(a) and 2.2(b) will apply with all necessary changes.

(d) If the Buyer has not received a Confirmation from the Seller within three Banking Days of a Transaction having been entered into, the Buyer shall send to the Seller a Confirmation. Clauses 2.2(b) and 2.2(c) shall apply in relation to any such Confirmation by replacing all references to "Buyer" with "Seller" and all references to "Seller" with "Buyer".

(e) Failure by either Party to send or return a Confirmation does not (i) affect the validity or enforceability of any Transaction, or (ii) constitute a material breach of this Agreement under clause 12.2(c).

2.3    **Evidence of a Transaction**. The Parties consent to the recording of all telephone conversations between the Parties relating in whole or part to this Agreement. Each Party agrees to notify its employees of that consent and obtain their consent to that recording if required by law. Any resulting recordings and other evidence may be introduced to prove a Transaction between the Parties and to establish any matters pertinent to a Transaction. The priority of evidence of the terms of a Transaction contained in recordings made under this clause 2.3 is as specified in Schedule 2.

3      **General Obligations, Representations and Warranties**
3.1    **Representations and Warranties**. Each Party represents and warrants to the other Party (which representations and warranties shall be deemed to be repeated by each Party on each date on which a Transaction is entered into) that:

(a) **Status**. It is duly organised and validly existing under the laws of the jurisdiction of its organisation or incorporation (and, if relevant under those laws, in good standing).

(b) **Power**. It has the power:
   (i)   to execute this Agreement and any other documentation relating to this Agreement to which it is a party;
   (ii)  to deliver this Agreement and any other documentation relating to this Agreement that it is required by this Agreement to deliver; and

(iii) to perform its obligations under this Agreement and any obligations it has under any Credit Support Document to which it is a party,

and has taken, or obtained, as the case may be, all approvals, consents, resolutions or other actions that are legally required in the relevant jurisdiction(s) to authorise such execution, delivery and performance.

(c) **No Violation or Conflict**. The execution, delivery and performance referred to in clause 3.1(b) do not violate or conflict with any law or statute applicable to it, including without limitation any provision of its constitutional documents, any order or judgment of any court or other agency of government applicable to it or any of its assets, or any contractual restriction binding on or affecting it or any of its assets.

(d) **Required Authorisations**. All Required Authorisations have been obtained and are in full force and effect, and all conditions of any Required Authorisations have been complied with.

(e) **Obligations Binding**. Its obligations under this Agreement and any Credit Support Document to which it is a party constitute its legal, valid and binding obligations, enforceable in accordance with their respective terms subject to applicable bankruptcy, reorganisation, insolvency, moratorium or similar laws affecting creditors' rights generally and to equitable principles of general application.

(f) **No Event of Default**. No Event of Default, or event that with notice or lapse of time or both would constitute an Event of Default, has occurred with respect to it and no such event would occur as a result of its entering into or performing its obligations under this Agreement or any Credit Support Document to which it is a party.

(g) **No Litigation**. No litigation, arbitration or administrative suit or proceeding at law or in equity or before any court, tribunal, governmental body, agency, official or arbitrator is pending or, so far as it is aware, threatened against it or, if applicable, any Credit Support Provider that would, if adversely determined, result in a material adverse change in its financial condition or its ability to perform its obligations under this Agreement or any Credit Support Document to which it is a party, or that is likely to affect the legality, validity or enforceability against it of this Agreement or that Credit Support Document or its ability to perform its obligations under this Agreement or that Credit Support Document.

(h) **No Reliance**. It is not relying upon any representations of the other Party other than those expressly set out in this Agreement or any Credit Support Document to which it is a party.

(i) **Principal**. Unless otherwise specified in Schedule 2, it has negotiated, entered into and executed this Agreement and any Credit Support Document to which it is a party as principal (and not as agent or in any other capacity, fiduciary or otherwise).

(j) **Risk Assumption**. It has entered into this Agreement and any Credit Support Document to which it is a party after a full opportunity to review their terms and conditions, has a full understanding of those terms and conditions and of their risks, and is capable of assuming those risks.

(k) **No Advice**. The other Party is not acting as a fiduciary or an advisor for it, nor has the other Party given to it any advice, representation, assurance or guarantee as to the expected performance, benefit or result of this Agreement.

(l) **Accurate Information**. All applicable information (other than, for the avoidance of doubt, information provided according to clause 3.3 (*Provision of Annual Accounts*) that is furnished in writing by or on behalf of it to the other Party and is identified as being subject to or connected to this Agreement is, as of the date it is furnished to the other Party, true, accurate and complete in every material respect.

(m) **No Encumbrances**. It shall, if the Seller, deliver to the Buyer the Compliance Period Traded Allowances free and clear of all liens, security interests, claims and encumbrances or any interest in or to them by any person.

3.2 **The Scheme**. Without prejudice to clause 4.2 (*Sufficient Allowances*), each Party shall:

(a) ensure that it has one or more Holding Accounts validly registered in a Registry; and

(b) conduct its affairs so as not to give the Relevant Authority cause to:

    (i)   refuse, reject or cancel any Transfer (whether in whole or in part) requested to be made pursuant to this Agreement; or

    (ii)  suspend or restrict either Party's right to request or effect any Transfer (including, without limitation, suspension or cancellation of any relevant Holding Account).

3.3    **Provision of Annual Accounts.** If requested in writing by a Party, the other Party shall deliver for its last completed fiscal year within 120 days following the end of that fiscal year a copy of such Party's (or for such period that such Party's obligations are supported by a Credit Support Provider, its Credit Support Provider's) annual report containing audited consolidated financial statements for such fiscal year if those are not freely available on the Internet on the homepage for such Party or its Credit Support Provider (as the case may be), together with the annual report made to shareholders, debt holders or other stakeholders. In all cases the financial statements referred to in this clause 3.3 are to be prepared in accordance with generally accepted accounting principles in the relevant jurisdiction.

**4**    **Allowance Transfers**

**4.1**    **Primary Obligation.**

    (a)  In relation to a Transaction, the Seller agrees to sell and transfer and the Buyer agrees to purchase and accept the Compliance Period Traded Allowances subject to and in accordance with the terms and conditions of this Agreement and the Scheme Rules.

    (b)  A Transaction may relate to one or more Specified Compliance Periods and, accordingly, may specify a CPTA Quantity and a Delivery Date for one or more Specified Compliance Periods. References in this Agreement to a part of a Transaction are to each individual CPTA Quantity where the Transaction relates to more than one Specified Compliance Period.

    (c)  The Seller agrees to Transfer (or procure the Transfer of) the Compliance Period Traded Allowances from any Holding Account in any Registry to the Delivery Point; provided, however, that if one or more Seller's Holding Accounts are specified in Schedule 2 (or, if different, in the Confirmation for the relevant Transaction), the Buyer agrees that the Seller's obligation to Transfer Allowances under this Agreement shall be limited to an obligation to Transfer the Compliance Period Traded Allowances for the relevant Transaction from such Seller's Holding Account(s) to the Delivery Point.

(d)  A Transfer (or part of a Transfer) shall be considered to be completed for the purposes of this Agreement when the relevant Compliance Period Traded Allowances are received at the Delivery Point, whereupon risk of loss related to the Compliance Period Traded Allowances or any portion of them transfers from the Seller to the Buyer.

**4.2**   **Sufficient Allowances.** In relation to a Transaction and a CPTA Quantity, the Seller shall, subject to clause 9 (*Force Majeure*), ensure that there are sufficient transferable Allowances in the Holding Account from which the Transfer is to be effected to ensure that the Transfer Request will be accepted under the Scheme at the time at which it is to be accepted in accordance with this Agreement.

**5**     **Effecting Transfers**

**5.1**   For the purposes of clause 4.1(a), the Seller shall make a Transfer Request in order to ensure that the relevant Compliance Period Traded Allowances are transferred to the relevant Delivery Point by the relevant Delivery Date and shall notify the Buyer that the Transfer Request has been submitted to the Registry.

**5.2**   The Seller shall ensure that each Transfer Request accurately reflects all the relevant details of Transfers constituting the Transaction (or relevant part of it, as the case may be) and complies with the information requirements under the Scheme such that each Transfer Request can be accepted for the purposes of the Scheme.

**5.3**   Without prejudice to clauses 5.1 and 5.2, the Parties agree to co-operate with each other in relation to each Transaction and to do such things as are necessary in accordance with and as required by the Scheme in order to Transfer the relevant Compliance Period Traded Allowances to the relevant Delivery Point by the relevant Delivery Date (and to refrain from doing such things as impede or would reasonably be expected to impede such Transfer).

5.4     Each Party shall ensure that it has and maintains such communication links and complies with such other conditions and requirements as are necessary in order to make Transfer Requests and effect Transfers in accordance with the Scheme.

**6       Transfer Failure**
**6.1     Failure to Transfer**
**6.1.1   Where in accordance with Schedule 2 or the Confirmation for the relevant Transaction Excess Emissions Penalty does not apply.**
Except to the extent:
(a)  caused by the Buyer's non-performance under this Agreement; or
(b)  that the Seller is relieved from complying with a relevant obligation under clause 9 (*Force Majeure*); or
(c)  that the Seller is relieved from complying with a relevant obligation under clause 12.6 (*Illegality*),
if the Seller fails to make a Transfer to the Delivery Point on or before the Delivery Date for any reason or makes a Transfer Request in respect of a Holding Account other than the Delivery Point (in either case in breach of clause 4 (*Allowance Transfers*) or 5 (*Effecting Transfers*) or both of them), then the Buyer may, by notice to the Seller (which, notwithstanding clause 14.5 (*Notices*), shall be effective on the date of receipt (or if such day is not a Delivery Banking Day, on the next Delivery Banking Day)), require the Seller to remedy such failure and:
(x)  if such failure is remedied by the Seller within one (1) Delivery Banking Day after receipt of such notice (the "**Final Delivery Date**"), then (I) the Buyer shall pay to the Seller the Contract Amount and (II) the Seller shall pay to the Buyer interest on an amount equal to the Contract Price multiplied by the number of Compliance Period Traded Allowances not Transferred to the Delivery Point by the Delivery Date for the period from (and including) the Delivery Date to (but excluding) the actual date of Transfer to the Buyer at the rate specified in clause 8.5(a); but
(y)  if such failure is not remedied by the Seller on or before the Final Delivery Date, the Buyer may, by written notice to the Seller, terminate that Transaction. In such a case,

the Seller shall pay to the Buyer the Buyer's Replacement Cost on or before the third Banking Day following receipt of such written notice of termination from the Buyer,

in either case adjusted to take into account any amount previously paid by the Buyer to the Seller in respect of that Transaction.

6.1.2    **Where in accordance with Schedule 2 or the Confirmation for the relevant Transaction Excess Emissions Penalty does apply.**

6.1.2.1  Except to the extent:

(a) caused by the Buyer's non-performance under this Agreement; or

(b) that the Seller is relieved from complying with a relevant obligation under clause 9 (*Force Majeure*); or

(c) that the Seller is relieved from complying with a relevant obligation under clause 12.6 (*Illegality*),

if the Seller fails to make a Transfer to the Delivery Point on or before the Delivery Date for any reason or makes a Transfer Request in respect of a Holding Account other than the Delivery Point (in either case in breach of clause 4 (*Allowance Transfers*) or 5 (*Effecting Transfers*) or both of them), then the Buyer may, by notice to the Seller (which, notwithstanding clause 14.5 (*Notices*), shall be effective on the date of receipt (or if such day is not a Delivery Banking Day, on the next Delivery Banking Day)), require the Seller to remedy such failure and:

(x) if such failure is remedied on or before the Final Delivery Date, then (I) the Buyer shall pay to the Seller the Contract Amount and (II) the Seller shall pay to the Buyer interest on an amount equal to the Contract Price multiplied by the number of Compliance Period Traded Allowances not Transferred to the Delivery Point by the Delivery Date for the period from (and including) the Delivery Date to (but excluding) the actual date of Transfer to the Buyer at the rate specified in clause 8.5(a); but

(y) if such failure is not remedied by the Seller on or before the Final Delivery Date, the Buyer may, by written notice to the Seller, terminate that Transaction. In such a case, the Seller shall pay to the Buyer the Buyer's Replacement Cost on or before the third Banking Day following the day on which the Buyer is able to effect a Buy-In (which may be a Buy-In, on any such date, of less than the entire number of Undelivered Allowances) if and to the extent that paragraph (b)(i)(A) or (b)(i)(B)(1) of Buyer's Replacement Cost applies, or on the third Banking Day following the day on which the Buyer is or would be able to effect a purchase of Allowances in accordance with paragraph (b)(i)(B)(2) of Buyer's Replacement Cost, if and to the extent that paragraph applies, in either case adjusted to take into account any amount previously paid by the Buyer to the Seller in respect of that Transaction.

6.1.2.2 Subject to clause 6.1.2.3, if as a result of the Seller's failure to make a Transfer (in whole or in part) the Buyer becomes liable to pay any EEP Amount, then the Buyer shall provide to the Seller, upon its reasonable request, evidence to the reasonable satisfaction of the Seller:

(a) that the Buyer has incurred an EEP Amount consequent on the Seller's failure to make a Transfer (in whole or in part);

(b) the extent to which the requirement for the Buyer to pay any EEP Amount results from the Seller's failure to make such Transfer; and

(c) that the Buyer could not have used Allowances to which it had title in any Holding Account(s) in any Registry in order to avoid or reduce its liability to pay any EEP Amount which it claims from the Seller as part of the Buyer's Replacement Cost.

6.1.2.3 The Seller's obligation to pay any EEP Amount under this clause 6.1.2 is subject always to the Buyer's overriding obligation to use its reasonable endeavours to avoid becoming liable for such EEP Amount or, when liable, to mitigate the payment obligation in relation to such EEP Amount and to allocate any such EEP Amount pro rata between all counterparties of the Buyer that have failed to make any Transfer; provided, however, that where the Buyer confirms that it has been unable to avoid becoming liable for any EEP Amount, it shall be for the Seller to show that it has been as a result of the Buyer failing to use its reasonable endeavours to do so.

6.1.2.4 The Seller shall pay such determined EEP Amount to the Buyer within two (2) Banking Days against the Buyer's VAT invoice in respect thereof.

6.1.2.5  In the event recovery of the EEP Amount component of any Buyer's Replacement Costs payable under this clause 6.1.2 is prohibited by any court or system of law, and such EEP Amount would be recoverable under such system of law or within such court in the form of an indemnification obligation, the Seller agrees to indemnify and make the Buyer whole for the amount of such EEP Amount that would otherwise have been due pursuant to this clause 6.1.2.

6.2      **Failure to Accept**

Except to the extent:

(a)  caused by the Seller's non-performance under this Agreement; or

(b)  that the Buyer is relieved from complying with a relevant obligation under clause 9 (*Force Majeure*); or

(c)  that the Buyer is relieved from complying with a relevant obligation under clause 12.6 (*Illegality*),

if the Buyer fails to accept a Transfer to the Delivery Point by the Delivery Date for any reason or specifies an incorrect Holding Account other than the Delivery Point (in either case in breach of clause 4 (*Allowance Transfers*) or 5 (*Effecting Transfers*) or both of them), then the Seller may, by notice to the Buyer (which, notwithstanding clause 14.5 (*Notices*), shall be effective on the date of receipt (or if such day is not a Delivery Banking Day, on the next Delivery Banking Day)), require the Buyer to remedy such failure and:

(x)  if such failure is remedied by the Buyer on or before the Final Delivery Date, the Buyer shall pay to the Seller interest on an amount equal to the Contract Price multiplied by the number of Compliance Period Traded Allowances not Transferred to the Delivery Point by the Delivery Date for the period from (and including) the Delivery Date to (but excluding) the actual date of Transfer to the Buyer at the rate specified in clause 8.5(a); but

(y)  if such failure is not remedied by the Buyer on or before the Final Delivery Date, the Seller may, by written notice to the Buyer, terminate that Transaction. In such a case, the Buyer shall pay to the Seller the Seller's Replacement Cost on or before the third Banking Day following receipt of such written notice of termination from the Seller, in either case adjusted to take into account any amount previously paid by the Buyer to the Seller in respect of that Transaction.

7    Value Added Taxes
7.1  **Value Added Taxes**. All amounts referred to in this Agreement are exclusive of any applicable VAT chargeable on the supply or supplies for which such amounts form the whole or part of the consideration for VAT purposes. The VAT treatment of any Transfer under a Transaction shall be determined pursuant to the VAT law of the jurisdiction where a taxable transaction for VAT purposes is deemed to take place. If VAT is properly chargeable on any such supply or supplies, the Buyer shall pay to the Seller an amount equal to the VAT, if any, chargeable in the Seller's jurisdiction; provided, however, that (i) such amount shall only be required to be paid once the Seller provides the Buyer with a valid VAT invoice in relation to that amount and (ii) the Buyer shall be under no obligation to make any payment to the Seller in respect of VAT which the Buyer must self-assess under the reverse charge rule or any similar system in the Buyer's jurisdiction. Each Party shall to the extent permitted by law provide the other with any additional valid VAT invoices as required for the purposes of this Agreement and, to the extent required by law, shall correctly account for any VAT properly due in its jurisdiction.
7.2  **Other Taxes**. Subject to each Party's obligations relating to Value Added Taxes, each Party shall cause all royalties, taxes, duties and other sums (including any stamp duty, other documentary taxes, climate change levy or other environmental tax or levy) legally payable by that Party arising in connection with this Agreement to be paid. In the event that the Seller is required by law to pay any tax which is properly for the account of the Buyer, the Buyer shall promptly indemnify or reimburse the Seller in respect of such tax. In the event that the Buyer is required by law to pay any tax which is properly for the account of the Seller, the Buyer may deduct the amount of any such tax from the sums due to the Seller under this Agreement and the Seller shall promptly indemnify or reimburse the Buyer in respect of any such tax not so deducted.

7.3    **Minimisation of Taxes.** Both Parties shall use reasonable efforts to administer this Agreement and to implement its provisions in accordance with the intent to minimise, where reasonable and possible, the accrual of tax payment obligations.

**8      Billing and Payment**

8.1    **Payment Due Date.** Payment for each Transaction shall be due on the date specified in item 8.1 of Schedule 2 (the **"Payment Due Date"**).

8.2    **Statement.**

(a)   Subject to clause 8.2(b), as soon as practicable after the Delivery Date for each Transaction, the Seller shall send to the Buyer a written statement (the **"Statement"**) showing for such Transaction (or the relevant part of it, as the case may be):

(i)     the CPTA Quantity;

(ii)    the Contract Price;

(iii)   the Contract Amount;

(iv)    the number of Delivered Allowances and the dates of such deliveries;

(v)     the number of Physically Netted Allowances and full details of the Transaction(s) against which such Allowances were netted;

(vi)    any amount owing from one Party to the other, including any amount owing by reason of clause 6 (*Transfer Failure*), 8.4 (*Disputed Payments*) or 12 (*Termination*), stating any part of that amount or any other amount that has already been paid or set off under clause 8.6 (*Payment Netting*);

(vii)   the net amount payable from one Party to the other after taking into account all the matters set out above (the **"Statement Amount"**); and

(viii)  VAT on the Contract Amount and any other applicable amount payable under clause 7 (*Value Added Taxes*).

Each Party shall provide to the other Party such further information as may reasonably be requested by the other Party to substantiate the information contained in any Statement issued pursuant to this clause 8.2.

(b)   For the avoidance of doubt, where a Monthly Billing Cycle is adopted by the Parties, only one consolidated

Statement needs to be issued for each calendar month as soon as practicable after the end of that month. Each consolidated Statement will specify (i) each of the above points on a transaction-by-transaction basis and (ii) aggregate totals for each of the above points for the entire month.

(c) Where, in respect of a Transaction (or a part of it, as the case may be), the Delivered Allowance Volume exceeds the relevant CPTA Quantity, as long as the Buyer has taken all steps reasonably within its power to Transfer the excess number of Allowances back to the Seller's Holding Account, the Contract Amount is to be determined by reference to the CPTA Quantity rather than to the Delivered Allowance Volume.

8.3    **Payment Mechanics**.

(a) On the Payment Due Date, the Buyer or the Seller, as the case may be, shall pay to the other Party the Statement Amount.

(b) Payment shall be made in Euros by direct bank transfer or equivalent transfer of immediately available funds to the credit of the account specified by the Party to whom such payment is due.

8.4    **Disputed Payments**.

(a) If a Party disputes in good faith any sum shown in the Statement payable in respect of an EEP Amount under clause 6.1.2.2, or of which it is notified in accordance with clause 8.9 (*No Accurate Information Available*), as being payable by that Party, it shall give notice to the other Party of the amount in dispute and the reasons for the dispute and shall pay:

(i) if this clause 8.4(a)(i) is specified as applying in Schedule 2, the full amount invoiced by no later than the Payment Due Date; or

(ii) if this clause 8.4(a)(ii) is specified as applying in Schedule 2, the undisputed amount invoiced by no later than the Payment Due Date.

(b) The Parties shall seek to settle the disputed amount as soon as reasonably possible. If they are unable to do so within a period of fourteen (14) days of the date a Party first notifies the other Party of such a dispute, either Party may, if so specified in Schedule 2, require this matter to be referred to an Expert for determination in accordance with clause 14.9 (*Expert Determination*).

(c) Any adjustment payment required to be made in accordance with the resolution of a dispute shall be made, with interest payable in accordance with clause 8.5 (*Interest*), within three Banking Days of that resolution.

(d) All Statements are conclusively presumed final and accurate unless objected to in writing, with adequate explanation and documentation, within two years after the month the Statement was received, or should have been received, by the Buyer.

8.5    **Interest**.

(a) If a Party fails to pay to the other Party any amount due by the Payment Due Date as set out in this Agreement (or otherwise determined by any dispute resolution process), interest shall be payable on that amount at an annual rate equal to EURIBOR applicable from time to time plus three per cent (3%) compounded monthly from and including the Payment Due Date to but excluding the date payment is made.

(b) If, following the resolution of a dispute or otherwise to correct any mistaken overpayment or underpayment made in good faith, one Party is required to pay an amount to the other Party, interest shall be payable on that amount at an annual rate equal to EURIBOR applicable from time to time plus one per cent (1%) compounded monthly from the date when the amount would have been paid or not paid (as applicable) if the dispute, overpayment or underpayment had not occurred to but excluding the date payment is made.

(c) If the rate in clause 8.5(a) or 8.5(b) ceases temporarily or permanently to be published then the Party owed money may substitute a rate published by a European clearing bank that it considers in good faith to be the equivalent of that rate.

8.6    **Payment Netting**. If on any date Statement Amounts would otherwise be payable by each Party to the other, whether under one or more Transactions, then, on that date, each Party's obligation to make payment of any such amount will be automatically satisfied and discharged and, if the aggregate of the Statement Amounts that would otherwise have been payable by one Party exceeds the aggregate of the Statement Amounts that would otherwise have been payable by the other Party, replaced by an obligation upon the Party by whom the larger aggregate of the Statement Amounts would have been payable to pay to the other Party the excess of the larger aggregate of the Statement Amounts over the smaller aggregate of the Statement Amounts.

8.7 **Physical Netting of Deliveries.** Unless otherwise specified in Schedule 2, if on any date Allowances of the same Allowance Type and Compliance Period would otherwise be deliverable by the Parties in respect of two or more Transactions which provide for intra-registry delivery or delivery between a Registry Pair, then on such date each Party's obligation to make delivery of any such Allowances will be automatically satisfied and discharged and, if the aggregate number of Allowances that would otherwise have been deliverable by one Party exceeds the aggregate number of Allowances that would otherwise have been deliverable by the other Party, replaced by an obligation upon the Party from whom the larger aggregate number of Allowances would have been deliverable to deliver to the other Party a number of Allowances (of the same Allowance Type and Compliance Period) equal to the excess of the larger aggregate number of Allowances over the smaller aggregate number of Allowances.

8.8 **Failure to Issue Statement.** If the Seller fails to issue a Statement in accordance with clause 8.2 (*Statement*) or 8.3 (*Payment Mechanics*), then the Buyer may issue that Statement to the Seller and, once issued, that Statement shall be treated as a Statement issued by the Seller for the purposes of this Agreement. Failure to issue a Statement does not affect the rights and obligations of the Parties under this Agreement and is not a breach of a material obligation of this Agreement under clause 12.2(c).

8.9 **No Accurate Information Available.** If any information required to prepare a Statement is not available at the time the Statement in question is prepared, then a Party may prepare the Statement in question based on its reasonable estimate of that information. If there is any change to the information used to prepare the Statement in question after it has been received or information that was estimated in order to prepare it becomes available, then, within two years of the date the relevant Statement was received, either Party may, by notice to the other, require an adjustment payment to be made to reflect the changed or newly available information. The adjustment payment is to be made within three (3) Banking Days of receipt of the notice together with interest calculated in accordance with clause 8.5(b).

9      **Force Majeure**

9.1    **Force Majeure**. Upon the occurrence of a Force Majeure, either Party may notify the other Party in writing of the commencement of the Force Majeure. Where the notification is from the Party affected by the Force Majeure (the "**FM Affected Party**"), to the extent available to such Party, it should also provide details of the Force Majeure and a non-binding estimate of the extent and the expected duration of its inability to perform its obligations due to the Force Majeure.

The obligations of both Parties under this Agreement with respect to the Transaction(s) affected by the Force Majeure (the "**FM Affected Transactions**") will be suspended for the duration of the Force Majeure. During the continuation of the Force Majeure, the FM Affected Party shall use all reasonable endeavours to overcome the Force Majeure. Upon the Force Majeure being overcome or it ceasing to subsist, both Parties will, as soon as reasonably practicable thereafter, resume full performance of their obligations under this Agreement with respect to the FM Affected Transactions (including, for the avoidance of doubt, any suspended obligations).

Where a Force Majeure (a) continues for a period of nine (9) Delivery Banking Days or (b) continues up until three (3) Delivery Banking Days prior to any End of Phase Reconciliation Deadline (if sooner), either Party may, by written notice to the other Party, terminate all (but not less than all) FM Affected Transactions.

9.2    **Force Majeure Termination Payment**. If an FM Affected Transaction is terminated in accordance with clause 9.1 (*Force Majeure*), the Parties' corresponding delivery and acceptance obligations shall be released and discharged and the Force Majeure termination payment to be made between the Parties (if any) shall be calculated in accordance with paragraph (a), (b) or (c) below, as selected by the Parties in Schedule 2.

(a) **No Termination Payment.** No Force Majeure termination payment shall be made between Parties; provided, however, that the obligation to pay any Unpaid Amounts shall survive the termination of the FM Affected Transaction.

(b) **Two-way Market Quotation Termination Payment.** Both Parties shall go into the market and obtain five (5) mid-market quotations from third party dealers for a replacement Transaction for the same amount of Compliance Period Traded Allowances having the same EEP Status (without taking into account the current credit-worthiness of the requesting Party or any existing Credit Support Document). Each Party will then calculate the average of the quotations it obtained and the amount payable shall be equal to (A) the sum of (I) one-half of the difference between the higher amount so determined (by party "X") and the lower amount so determined (by party "Y") and (II) any Unpaid Amounts owing to X less (B) any Unpaid Amounts owing to Y. If the resultant amount is a positive number, Y shall pay it to X; if it is a negative number, X shall pay the absolute value of such amount to Y. If five (5) mid-market quotations cannot be obtained, all quotations will be deemed to be zero.

(c) **Two-way Loss Termination Payment.** Each Party will determine its Loss in respect of the FM Affected Transaction and an amount will be payable equal to one half of the difference between the Loss of the Party with the higher Loss ("X") and the Loss of the Party with the lower Loss ("Y"). If the amount payable is a positive number, Y will pay it to X; if it is a negative number, X will pay the absolute value of such amount to Y.

9.3　　Where an event or circumstance that would otherwise constitute or give rise to an Event of Default also constitutes Force Majeure, it is to be treated as Force Majeure and not as an Event of Default.

**10　　Confidentiality**

10.1　The Parties shall treat the terms of this Agreement and all information provided under or in connection with it, including the financial statements provided under clause 3.3 (*Provision of Annual Accounts*) (collectively, "**Confidential Information**") as confidential and may not either disclose Confidential Information or use it other than for *bona fide* purposes connected with this Agreement without the prior written consent of the other Party, except that consent is not required for disclosure to:

(a)  directors, employees or Affiliates of a Party, as long as they in turn are required by that Party to treat the Confidential Information as confidential in favour of the other Party on terms substantially the same as those set out in this clause 10;

(b)  persons professionally engaged by a Party, as long as they in turn are required by that Party to treat the Confidential Information as confidential in favour of the other Party on terms substantially the same as those set out in this clause 10;

(c)  the extent required by any government department or agency or regulatory authority having jurisdiction over that Party (including the Relevant Authority);

(d)  any bank, other financial institution or rating agency to the extent required in relation to the financing of a Party's business activities, as long as the bank or other financial institution or rating agency, as the case may be, is required by that Party to treat the Confidential Information as confidential in favour of the other Party on terms substantially the same as those set out in this clause 10;

(e)  the extent required by any applicable laws, judicial process or the rules and regulations of any regulated market or recognised stock exchange;

(f)  any intending assignee of the rights and interests of a Party under this Agreement or under a Transaction or to a person intending to acquire an interest in a Party or that Party's Affiliate holding company as long as the intending assignee or acquirer in turn is required by that Party to treat the Confidential Information as confidential in favour of the other Party on terms substantially the same as those set out in this clause 10;

(g)  the extent that the Confidential Information is in or lawfully comes into the public domain other than by breach of this clause 10; or

(h) price reporting agencies for the calculation of an index as long as the identity of the other party is not revealed. It must also be a precondition of the disclosure agreement between a party and the price reporting agency that only the price is released by the price reporting agency and not the identity of either party.

**11 Assignment**

11.1 **Prohibition of Assignment.** Subject to clause 11.2 (*Assignment of Termination Payments*), neither Party may assign or transfer to any person any of its rights or obligations in respect of this Agreement without the written consent of the other Party (which consent shall not be unreasonably withheld or delayed). For these purposes, it shall be unreasonable to withhold consent to an assignment or transfer of all, but not part only, of a Party's rights and obligations in the case of an assignee or transferee that (a) is demonstrably capable of fulfilling the obligations of the assignor or transferor under this Agreement; (b) has a financial standing no worse than that of the assignor or transferor at the date such person becomes a party to this Agreement and as of the date it entered into the relevant Transactions; (c) is demonstrably capable of continuing to provide security and / or performance assurance at least equal to that provided (or required to be provided) by the assignor or transferor; and (d) has its registered office in a same jurisdiction as that of the assignor or transferor.

11.2 **Assignment of Termination Payments.** A Party may assign all or any part of its interest in any Termination Payment payable to it under Clause 12.5 (*Termination Payments*).

**12 Termination**

12.1 **Termination Rights.** If, at any time, an Event of Default (as defined below) has occurred and is continuing, the Non-Defaulting Party may designate a day as an early termination date (the **"Early Termination Date"**) in respect of all outstanding Transactions between the Parties by giving not more than twenty days' notice to the Defaulting Party. This notice must specify the relevant Event of Default. The Early Termination Date may not be earlier than the day the notice is effective. If, however, "Automatic Early Termination" is specified in Schedule 2 as applying to a Party then an Early Termination Date in respect of all outstanding Transactions will occur immediately upon the occurrence with respect to such Party or its Credit Support Provider of an Event of Default specified in clause 12.2(d)(i), (iii), (v), (vi), (vii), or to the extent analogous thereto, (viii), and as of the time immediately preceding the institution of the relevant proceeding or the presentation of the relevant petition upon the occurrence with respect to such Party or its Credit Support Provider of an Event of Default specified in clause 12.2(d)(iv) or, to the extent analogous to it, (viii).

12.2    **Events of Default.** Subject to clause 12.7 (*Event of Default, Illegality and Force Majeure*), an "**Event of Default**" means the occurrence at any time with respect to a Party or, if applicable, any Credit Support Provider of that Party (the "**Defaulting Party**") of any of the following events:

(a)    **Non-payment.** The Party fails to pay any amount when due under this Agreement, and that failure is not remedied on or before the third Banking Day after the Non-Defaulting Party gives the Defaulting Party notice of that failure.

(b)    **Representation or Warranty.** Any representation or warranty made, or deemed to have been made, by the Party or any Credit Support Provider of that Party in this Agreement or any Credit Support Document proves to have been false or materially misleading at the time it was made or was deemed to have been made.

(c)    **Material Obligations.** The Party fails to perform a material obligation under this Agreement (other than an obligation referred to in clauses 12.2(a) and 12.2(b)) and that failure is not remedied within five Banking Days of the Non-Defaulting Party giving the Defaulting Party notice of that failure.

(d)    **Insolvency.** The Party or any Credit Support Provider of the Party:

(i)    is dissolved (other than pursuant to a consolidation, amalgamation or merger);

(ii)   becomes insolvent or is unable to pay its debts generally as they fall due, fails generally to pay, or admits in writing its inability generally to pay its debts as they become due;

(iii)    makes a general assignment, arrangement, composition or other arrangement with or for the benefit of its creditors;

(iv)    institutes or has instituted against it a proceeding seeking a judgment of insolvency or bankruptcy or any other relief under any bankruptcy or insolvency law or other similar law affecting creditors' rights, or a petition is presented for its winding-up or liquidation, and, in the case of any such proceeding or petition instituted or presented against it, that proceeding or petition (A) results in a judgment of insolvency or bankruptcy or the entry of an order for relief or the making of an order for its winding-up or liquidation or (B) is not withdrawn, dismissed, discharged, stayed or restrained in each case within thirty days of the institution or presentation of that proceeding or petition;

(v)    has a resolution passed for its winding-up, official management or liquidation (other than pursuant to a consolidation, amalgamation or merger);

(vi)    seeks or becomes subject to the appointment of an administrator, provisional liquidator, conservator, receiver, trustee, custodian or other similar official for it or for all or substantially all its assets;

(vii)    has a secured party take possession of all or substantially all its assets or has a distress, execution, attachment, sequestration or other legal process levied, enforced or sued on or against all or substantially all its assets and that secured party maintains possession, or that process is not withdrawn, dismissed, discharged, stayed or restrained, in each case within fifteen days of that event;

(viii)    causes or is subject to any event with respect to it that, under the applicable laws of any jurisdiction, has an analogous effect to any of the events specified in sub-paragraphs (i) to (vii) (inclusive) of this clause 12.2(d); or

(ix)    takes any action in furtherance of, or indicating its consent to, approval of, or acquiescence in, any of the acts referred to in this clause 12.2(d).

(e) **Credit Support.**
(i) The Party or any Credit Support Provider or Performance Assurance Provider of the Party fails to comply with or perform any agreement or obligation to be complied with or performed by it in accordance with any Credit Support Document or Performance Assurance if that failure is not remedied within three Banking Days of notification;

(ii) any Credit Support Document or Performance Assurance expires or terminates, is due to expire or terminate within thirty days or such other period as is specified in Schedule 2, or fails or ceases to be in full force and effect for the purpose of this Agreement (in each case other than in accordance with its terms) prior to the satisfaction of all obligations of the Party under each Transaction to which that Credit Support Document or Performance Assurance (as the case may be) relates without the written consent of the other Party and such expiration or termination is not remedied within three Banking Days of notification; or

(iii) the Party or any Credit Support Provider or Performance Assurance Provider of that Party disaffirms, disclaims, repudiates or rejects, in whole or in part, or challenges the validity of, that Credit Support Document or Performance Assurance or otherwise fails to comply with or perform its obligations under or in respect of a Credit Support Document and that failure is continuing after any applicable grace or cure period.

(f) **Cross Default.** Unless cross default is specified not to apply to the Party in Schedule 2, there occurs or exists:
(i) a default, event of default or other similar condition or event (however described) in respect of the Party or any Credit Support Provider of the Party under one or more agreements or instruments relating to Indebtedness of any of them (individually or collectively) in an aggregate amount of not less than the Cross Default Threshold that has resulted in that Indebtedness becoming due and payable under those agreements or instruments before it would otherwise have been due and payable; or

(ii)   a default by that Party or that Credit Support Provider (individually or collectively) in making one or more payments on the due date for those purposes under those agreements or instruments in an aggregate amount of not less than the Cross Default Threshold (after giving effect to any applicable notice requirement or grace period).

(g) **Default under Specified Transaction**. The Party or any Credit Support Provider of the Party:

   (i)   defaults under a Specified Transaction and, after giving effect to any applicable notice requirement or grace period, there occurs a liquidation of, an acceleration of obligations under, or an early termination of, that Specified Transaction;

   (ii)   defaults (A) in making any payment due on the last date for that payment under the Specified Transaction, or (B) in making any payment on early termination of a Specified Transaction, after giving effect to any applicable notice requirement or grace period or, in each case where there is no applicable notice requirement or grace period, where that default continues for at least three Banking Days; or

   (iii)   disaffirms, disclaims, repudiates or rejects, in whole or in part, a Specified Transaction (or that action is taken by any Entity appointed or empowered to act on its behalf).

(h) **Material Adverse Change**. The Party fails, within three Banking Days of receipt of the notice referred to below, to provide the other Party (the "**Requesting Party**") with, or increase the amount of, a Performance Assurance when the Requesting Party believes in good faith that a Material Adverse Change has occurred or its exposure in respect of such Party under a continuing Material Adverse Change has increased and the Requesting Party serves written notice on that Party. For the purposes of this Event of Default, a "**Material Adverse Change**" has occurred if any one or more of the following events has occurred and is continuing:

   (i)   **Credit Rating**. If the Credit Rating (where available) of an Entity listed in paragraph (A), (B) or (C) below, each such Entity being a "**Relevant Entity**", is withdrawn or downgraded below the ratings specified in Schedule 2:

(A) the Party in question (unless all that Party's financial obligations under this Agreement are fully guaranteed or assured under a Credit Support Document or there is a Control and Profit Transfer Agreement in place in respect of that Party); or

(B) that Party's Credit Support Provider (other than a bank); or

(C) that Party's Controlling Party.

(ii) **Credit Rating of a Credit Support Provider that is a bank.** If the Credit Rating of a bank serving as the Party's Credit Support Provider is withdrawn or downgraded below Standard & Poor's Rating Group "A-" or Moody's Investor's Service Inc. or Fitch Ratings Ltd. equivalent rating.

(iii) **Failure of a Control and Profit Transfer Agreement.** If any Control and Profit Transfer Agreement entered into by any Controlling Party of the Party expires (and is not renewed) or terminates in whole or in part or ceases to be in full force and effect for the purpose of this Agreement (in any case other than in accordance with its terms) prior to the satisfaction of all obligations of the Party under each Transaction.

(iv) **Impaired Ability to Perform.** If in the reasonable and good faith opinion of the Requesting Party, the ability of the Relevant Entity to perform its obligations under this Agreement, any Credit Support Document or any Control and Profit Transfer Agreement, as the case may be, is materially impaired.

(v) **Credit Event upon Merger.** If the Party or its Credit Support Provider or Controlling Party undergoes a change of control, consolidates or amalgamates with, or merges with or into, or transfers all or substantially all its assets to, or reorganises, incorporates, reincorporates or reconstitutes into or as another Entity, or another Entity transfers all or substantially all its assets to, or reorganises, incorporates, reincorporates or reconstitutes into or as such Party or its Credit Support Provider or Controlling Party and:

(A) the creditworthiness of such Party, its Credit Support Provider or Controlling Party or the resulting surviving transferee or successor Entity is, in the reasonable and good faith opinion of the Requesting Party, materially weaker than that of the Party or such Credit Support Provider or Controlling Party, as the case may be, immediately prior to such action;

(B) the resulting surviving transferee or successor Entity fails to assume all the obligations of that Party or such Credit Support Provider or Controlling Party under this Agreement or any Credit Support Document to which it or its predecessor was a party either by operation of law or pursuant to an agreement reasonably satisfactory to the Requesting Party; or

(C) the benefits of any Credit Support Document cease or fail to extend (without the consent of the Requesting Party) to the performance by such resulting surviving transferee or successor Entity of its obligations under this Agreement.

(vi) **Decline in Tangible Net Worth.** If the Tangible Net Worth of any Relevant Entity falls below the amount specified in Schedule 2.

(vii) **Financial Covenants.** If a Party does not have a Credit Rating, any Relevant Entity fails to fulfil any of the following requirements as determined by reference to the most recent relevant financial statements:

(A) the ratio of (1) earnings before interest and taxes to (2) the sum of all interest and any amounts in the nature of interest charged to expense relating to Total Debt is for the Party or its Credit Support Provider in any fiscal year greater than the ratio specified in Schedule 2,

(B) the ratio of (1) the amount of cash generated or employed by the Party or its Credit Support Provider in its operating activities to (2) Total Debt of the Party or its Credit Support Provider in any fiscal year is greater than the ratio specified in Schedule 2, and

(C) the ratio of (1) Total Debt to (2) the sum of Total Debt and all paid up shareholder cash contributions to the share capital account or any other capital account of the Party or its Credit Support Provider ascribed for such purposes is less than the ratio specified in Schedule 2.

12.3    **Suspension.** Notwithstanding any other provision of this Agreement, after the occurrence of either an Event of Default or an event that, with the giving of notice or the passage of time or both, would constitute an Event of Default with respect to a Party, the other Party may, in addition to any other remedies that it may have and subject to clause 13 (*Liabilities*), for the period that the relevant event subsists or, if shorter, thirty days, do any one or more of the following:

(a) withhold or suspend payments under this Agreement; or

(b) suspend its compliance with clauses 4 (*Allowance Transfers*) and 5 (*Effecting Transfers*) or both of them.

12.4    **Early Termination Date.** If notice designating an Early Termination Date is given under clause 12.1 (*Termination Rights*), the Early Termination Date occurs on the date so designated even if the circumstances giving rise to the Event of Default are no longer continuing. Upon the effective designation of an Early Termination Date: (a) no further payments or compliance with clauses 4 (*Allowance Transfers*) or 5 (*Effecting Transfers*) or both of them is required in respect of any Transaction, and (b) the amount, if any, payable in respect of an Early Termination Date is to be determined pursuant to clause 12.5 (*Termination Payments*).

12.5    **Termination Payments.**

(a) On, or as soon as reasonably practicable after, the Early Termination Date, the Non-Defaulting Party shall in good faith calculate the termination payment (the **"Termination Payment"**), which is the Loss for all Transactions (expressed in Euros) unless the Market Amount (expressed in Euros) is specified as the termination payment method in Schedule 2 (in which case it is the Market Amount).

(b) The Non-Defaulting Party shall notify the Defaulting Party of the Termination Payment including detailed support for the Termination Payment calculation.

(c) A Party is not required to enter into replacement transactions in order to determine the Termination Payment.

(d) If the Termination Payment is a positive number, the Defaulting Party shall pay the Termination Payment to the Non-Defaulting Party within three Banking Days of invoice or notification of the Termination Payment amount (the "**Termination Payment Date**"), which amount bears interest in accordance with clause 8.5 (*Interest*).

(e) If the Termination Payment is a negative number, the Non-Defaulting Party shall pay an amount equal to the absolute value of the Termination Payment to the Defaulting Party within thirty Banking Days of the Termination Payment Date, which amount bears interest in accordance with clause 8.5 (*Interest*).

(f) The Non-Defaulting Party may, at its option, set off the Termination Payment against any other amounts owing (whether or not matured, contingent or invoiced) between the Parties under this Agreement or under any other agreements, instruments or undertakings between the Parties. The right of set-off is without prejudice and in addition to any other right of set-off, combination of accounts, lien, charge or other right to which any Party is at any time otherwise entitled (whether by operation of law, by contract or otherwise). If an amount is unascertained, the Non-Defaulting Party may reasonably estimate the amount to be set off. The Parties shall make any adjustment payment required within three Banking Days of the amount becoming ascertained.

(g) Disputed amounts under this clause 12.5 are to be paid by the Defaulting Party subject to refund with interest calculated in accordance with clause 8.5(b) if the dispute is resolved in favour of the Defaulting Party.

12.6 **Illegality.** If, due to the adoption of, or any change in, any applicable law after the date on which a Transaction is entered into, or due to the promulgation of, or any change in, the interpretation by any court, tribunal or regulatory authority

346 Energy and Emissions Markets

with competent jurisdiction of any applicable law after that date, it becomes unlawful (other than as a result of a breach by the relevant party of clause 3.2 (*The Scheme*)) for a Party (the "**Affected Party**"):

(a) to perform any absolute or contingent obligation to make a payment or delivery or to receive a payment or delivery in respect of that Transaction or to comply with any other material provision of this Agreement relating to that Transaction; or

(b) to perform, or for any Credit Support Provider of that Party to perform, any contingent or other obligation that the Party (or that Credit Support Provider) has under any Credit Support Document relating to that Transaction (in either case, an "**Illegality**"),

then, unless the Parties otherwise agree in writing, either Party may elect to terminate that Transaction in accordance with clauses 12.1 (*Termination Rights*), 12.4 (*Early Termination Date*) and 12.5 (*Termination Payments*), except that, for the purposes of clause 12.1 (*Termination Rights*), either Party may designate an Early Termination Date and, for the purposes of clause 12.5 (*Termination Payments*), (i) the Termination Payment shall be calculated on the basis of Loss and (ii) references to the Defaulting Party are to be read as references to the Affected Party, references to the Non-Defaulting Party are to be read as references to the Party that is not the Affected Party, and references to "all Transactions" are to be read as references to only those Transactions affected by the Illegality ("**Illegality Affected Transactions**"). However, if both Parties are Affected Parties, each Party will determine its Loss in respect of the affected Transaction and an amount will be payable equal to one half of the difference between the Loss of the Party with the higher Loss and the Loss of the Party with the lower Loss. Such amount will be payable by the Party with the lower Loss to the Party with the higher Loss.

12.7 **Event of Default, Illegality and Force Majeure**. If an event or circumstance that would otherwise constitute or give rise to an Event of Default also constitutes an Illegality it is to be treated as an Illegality and does not constitute an Event of Default. If an event or circumstance that would otherwise constitute or give rise to Force Majeure also constitutes an

Illegality, it is to be treated as an Illegality and does not constitute Force Majeure.

12.8 **Change in Taxes**. If change in taxes is specified as applying in Schedule 2 and, due to any action taken by a taxing authority or brought in a court of competent jurisdiction on or after the date on which a Transaction is entered into (regardless of whether that action is taken or brought with respect to a Party) or to a Change in Tax Law, a Party (the "**Affected Tax Party**") will, or there is a substantial likelihood that it will, on the next Due Date either:

(a) be required to pay an amount in respect of a Relevant Tax; or

(b) receive a payment from which an amount is required to be deducted or withheld for or on account of a Relevant Tax and no additional amount is required to be paid in respect of that Relevant Tax,

other, in either case, than in respect of interest payable under this Agreement (a "**Relevant Change in Tax**"), then the Affected Tax Party may give a notice electing to terminate, liquidate and accelerate any uncompleted portions of that Transaction in accordance with clauses 12.1 (*Termination Rights*), 12.4 (*Early Termination Date*) and 12.5 (*Termination Payments*), except that, for the purposes of clause 12.1 (*Termination Rights*), either Party may designate an Early Termination Date and, for the purposes of clause 12.4 (*Early Termination Date*) and 12.5 (*Termination Payments*), references to the Defaulting Party are to be read as references to the Affected Tax Party, references to the Non-Defaulting Party are to be read as references to the Party that is not the Affected Tax Party, references to "all Transactions" are to be read as references to only those Transactions affected by the Relevant Change in Tax, and the notice given by the Affected Tax Party electing to terminate, liquidate and accelerate any uncompleted portions of the Transaction is deemed to be the notice to terminate, liquidate and accelerate to be given by the Non-Defaulting Party for the purposes of clause 12.1 (*Termination Rights*). However, if both Parties are Affected Tax Parties, each Party shall determine the Termination Payment in respect of the terminated Transactions and the amount payable is the average of the two Termination Payments.

**13      Liabilities**

13.1    **No Consequential Loss**. Except to the extent included in any payment made in accordance with clause 6.1 (*Failure to Transfer*), 9.2 (*Force Majeure Termination Payment*), 12.5 (*Termination Payments*) or 12.6 (*Illegality*), neither Party is liable to the other, whether in contract, tort (including negligence and breach of duty) or otherwise at law, for any business interruption or loss of use, profits, contracts, production, or revenue or for any consequential or indirect loss or damage of any kind however arising.

13.2    **Breach of Warranty**. Neither Party shall be liable in respect of any breach of warranty under clause 3 (*General Obligations, Representations and Warranties*) in relation to any Allowance for any greater sum than it would be liable for under clause 12 (*Termination*) in relation to such Allowance for any breach of clause 4 (*Allowance Transfers*) or 5 (*Effecting Transfers*).

13.3    **Unlimited Liability**. Notwithstanding anything to the contrary contained in this Agreement, the liability of a Party to the other Party for:
(a) death or personal injury resulting from negligence of the Party liable, its employees, agents and contractors; or
(b) fraud or fraudulent misrepresentation
is unlimited save that nothing in this clause 13.3 confers a right or remedy upon the other Party to which that Party would not otherwise have been entitled.

13.4    **Reasonable Pre-estimate and Maximum Liability**. Each Party acknowledges that the payment obligations in clauses 6 (*Transfer Failure*), 9 (*Force Majeure*) and 12 (*Termination*) are reasonable in the light of the anticipated harm and the difficulty of estimation or calculation of actual damages. Each Party waives the right to contest those payments as an unreasonable penalty. Each Party further acknowledges that the payment obligation in clause°12 (*Termination*) shall constitute the maximum liability in the event of termination of this Agreement.

13.5    **Sole Remedy**. The rights to suspend, take action, terminate, liquidate and accelerate and to be paid a Termination Payment under clause 12 (*Termination*) are in full and final satisfaction of the rights of the Non-Defaulting Party if an Event of Default occurs in respect of the Defaulting Party.

**14      Miscellaneous**

14.1    **Waiver.** No waiver by either Party of any breach by the other of this Agreement operates unless expressly made in writing, and any such waiver is not to be construed as a waiver of any other breach.

14.2    **Variation.** No variation to the provisions of this Agreement is valid unless it is in writing and signed by each Party.

14.3    **Entire Agreement.** The Agreement constitutes the entire agreement and understanding of the Parties with respect to its subject matter and supersedes and extinguishes any representations previously given or made with respect to its subject matter other than those given or made in this Agreement, but nothing in this clause 14.3 limits or excludes any liability for fraud in relation to those representations.

14.4    **Severability.** If any provision or part of a provision of this Agreement is found by a court, arbitrator or other authority of competent jurisdiction to be void or unenforceable, that provision or part of a provision is to be deemed deleted from this Agreement and the remaining provisions to continue in full force and effect. The Parties shall in this event seek to agree upon a valid and enforceable provision or part of a provision to replace the provision or part of a provision found to be void and unenforceable.

14.5    **Notices.** Any notice or other written communication to be given or made in respect of this Agreement by one Party to the other is to be given or made in writing to the other at the address or contact number that the other Party gives to the notifying party from time to time or, if no address or contact number has been so given, at the other Party's registered office. A written notice is deemed to have been received:

(a)  if delivered by hand, on the Banking Day of delivery or on the first Banking Day after the date of delivery if delivered on a day other than a Banking Day;

(b)  if sent by registered mail, on the second Banking Day after the date of posting or, if sent from one country to another, on the fifth Banking Day after the date of posting; or

(c)  if sent by facsimile transmission and a valid transmission report confirming good receipt is generated, on the day of transmission if transmitted before 17:00 hours on a Banking Day or otherwise at 09:00 hours on the first Banking Day after transmission.

14.6    **Third Party Rights**. Subject to the rights that may accrue to any successor or permitted assignees of the Parties, no provision of this Agreement is be construed as creating any rights enforceable by a third party, and all third party rights implied by law are, to the extent permissible by law, excluded from this Agreement.

14.7    **Applicable Law**. The Agreement is governed by and is to be construed in accordance with English law, unless otherwise specified in Schedule 2. Subject to the express referral of any matter to the Expert under this Agreement and subject to clause 14.8 (*Arbitration*) (if it applies), the Parties submit to the non-exclusive jurisdiction of the English courts, unless otherwise specified in Schedule 2, for the purposes of any dispute under or in connection with this Agreement.

14.8    **Arbitration**. If this clause 14.8 is specified as applying in Schedule 2, save for those disputes that are expressed under this Agreement to be subject to expert determination in accordance with clause 14.9 (*Expert Determination*), the Parties agree that any difference or dispute arising under, out of or in connection with this Agreement that the Parties are unable to settle between themselves is to be resolved by arbitration in accordance with the rules of arbitration, the number of arbitrators and at the place specified in Schedule 2. The language of arbitration is English. The appointing authority is the Secretary-General of the Permanent Court of Arbitration unless the rules chosen in Schedule 2 specify otherwise. Unless indicated otherwise in Schedule 2, the number of arbitrators is one.

14.9    **Expert Determination**.

(a) If any matter is referred to an independent expert (the "**Expert**") in accordance with this Agreement, the Expert is to be appointed by agreement between the Parties. If the Parties fail to agree upon that appointment within ten Banking Days of a Party notifying the other Party of its decision to refer the matter to an Expert, the President of the International Emissions Trading Association may appoint the Expert on the application of either Party.

(b) In the absence of the Parties agreeing to any amendments to this Agreement, if that failure to agree is referable to the Expert, the Expert is empowered to make amendments binding on the Parties consistent with any relevant requirements, purposes or restrictions concerning those amendments expressly provided for in this Agreement. The Parties agree that it is their intention that in the absence of their ability to agree to any required amendments to this Agreement, this Agreement should continue and not come to an end or be deemed to be void or voidable in accordance with the doctrine of frustration or any other legal theory. Accordingly, if the Expert is unable to decide upon any amendments based on the express or implied intentions of the Parties, the Expert is entitled to have regard to the way in which similar issues or amendments are addressed or are proposed to be addressed by other participants trading Allowances and to substitute the Expert's own view of what is reasonable in all the circumstances.

(c) The Expert shall act as an expert and not as an arbitrator and shall give his or her determination in writing.

(d) The determination of the Expert shall be final, conclusive and binding upon the Parties unless a Party notifies the other Party that it disputes the Expert's determination within twenty one days of receipt of that determination, in which case the dispute is to be referred either to the courts of law of the jurisdiction specified in accordance with Clause 14.7 (*Applicable Law*) or, if Clause 14.8 (*Arbitration*) applies, to arbitration in accordance with Clause 14.8 (*Arbitration*).

(e) The Expert shall determine the procedure to be followed by the Expert for the purpose of making a determination, but the Parties shall use their respective reasonable endeavours to ensure that he or she makes his or her determination within twenty Banking Days of being appointed.

(f) Each of the Parties shall bear one half of the costs of the Expert unless the Expert determines otherwise.

(g) Pending the determination of any amendments to this Agreement by the Parties or the Expert, the Parties shall continue to the extent possible to perform their obligations under this Agreement.

14.10 **Party Preparing this Agreement**. The Party (the "**Relevant Party**") who has prepared copies of this Agreement for execution (as indicated in paragraph 14.10 of Schedule 2) warrants and undertakes to the other Party that no changes have been made to the standard form Emissions Trading Master Agreement For The EU Scheme (Version 2.1 2005) posted by the International Emission Trading Association on its website on 13 June 2005, except (i) the elections as set out in Part 1 of Schedule 2 and (ii) any revisions specifically agreed in Part 2 of Schedule 2.

**IN WITNESS WHEREOF** the Parties have duly executed and delivered this Agreement on the respective dates set out below with effect from the date set out on the first page of this document.

**[Company name]**                    **[Company name]**

By: _____            By: _____

Name: [•]                        Name: [•]

Title: [•]                       Title: [•]

Date: [•]                        Date: [•]

# SCHEDULE 1

# DEFINITIONS

The following words or phrases, where they appear in this Agreement, have the following respective meanings:

**"Affected Party"** has the meaning given to it in clause 12.6 (*Illegality*).

**"Affected Tax Party"** has the meaning given to it in clause 12.8 (*Change in Taxes*).

**"Affiliate"** means, with respect to any Entity, any other Entity that directly or indirectly through one or more intermediaries controls or is controlled by or is under common control with the Entity. The terms "controls", "controlled by" and "under common control with" mean the possession, directly or indirectly through one or more intermediaries, of more than 50% of the outstanding voting stock of, or the power to direct or cause the direction of the management policies of, any Entity, whether through ownership of stock, as a general partner or trustee, by contract or otherwise.

**"Agreement"** has the meaning given to it in Recital B.

**"Allowance"** means any one or more of an EU Allowance, a CER and an Alternative Allowance.

**"Allowance Type"** means EU Allowance, CER or Alternative Allowance.

**"Alternative Allowance"** means a unit of account, representing a right to emit 1 tonne of carbon dioxide equivalent, either issued by a Member State in return for a similar unit from an emissions trading scheme in a non-Member State pursuant to Article 25 of the Directive or an allowance from an emissions trading scheme in a non-Member State recognised by the EU Commission pursuant to the Directive, that may be used for determining compliance with emissions limitation commitments as prescribed by the Scheme Rules.

**"Banking Day"** means any day (other than a Saturday or Sunday) on which commercial banks are open for general business in the jurisdiction(s) of both the Buyer and the Seller specified in Schedule 2.

**"Buy-In"** means the purchase of Allowances by the Buyer in accordance with the procedures described in Buyer's Replacement Cost.

**"Buy-In Period"** has the meaning given to it in paragraph (b)(i)(A) of the definition of Buyer's Replacement Cost.

**"Buyer"** means the Party agreed as such by the Parties for the purposes of a Transaction.

**"Buyer's Delivery Banking Day Location"** means, in relation to a Transaction, the place specified as such in the Confirmation for the relevant Transaction, or, if a place is not so specified: (i) the place specified as such in Schedule 2; or (ii) if no such place is specified, the place in which the Buyer's address for the purposes of receiving notices connected with the relevant Transaction is located; or (iii) if no such address is given, the place in which the Buyer has its registered office.

**"Buyer's Replacement Cost"** means, in respect of a failure to Transfer a number of Allowances of a particular Allowance Type and Compliance Period pursuant to clause 6.1 (*Failure to Transfer*) (being the **"Undelivered Allowances"**):

(a)  for the purposes of clause 6.1.1, (A) the positive difference, if any, between (i) the price the Buyer, acting in a commercially reasonable manner, does or would pay in an arm's length transaction for an equivalent quantity of Compliance Period of Allowances to replace the Default Quantity, and (ii) the Contract Price multiplied by the Default Quantity, plus (B) interest for the period from (and including) the Delivery Date to (but excluding) the date of termination calculated on an amount equal to the product of the Default Quantity and an amount equal to the excess, if any, of the price determined pursuant to paragraph (A)(i) above over the Contract Price at the rate specified in clause 8.5(a), plus (C) the amount of such reasonable costs and expenses which the Buyer incurs in respect of the Default Quantity (including, without limitation, broker fees, commissions and legal fees, but not including, for the avoidance of doubt, the amount, if any, payable in respect of Excess Emissions Penalty); or

(b)  for the purposes of clause 6.1.2, an amount (if positive) equal to the sum of:

(i) either:

(A) if in one or more arm's length transactions the Buyer is able, using its reasonable endeavours, to purchase a number of Allowances of the same Allowance Type and Compliance Period as the Undelivered Allowances (**"Replacement Allowances"**), to be delivered during the period from (but excluding) the Final Delivery Date to (and including) the Reconciliation Deadline on or immediately following the Delivery Date (the **"Buy-In Period"**), which in respect of each such individual purchase of Allowances, when aggregated with other such purchases, amounts to a purchase of a number of Allowances equal to the number of Undelivered Allowances:

  (1) the price (per Allowance) at which the Buyer is able to purchase the relevant number of Replacement Allowances; less

  (2) the Contract Price agreed by the Parties in respect of the Undelivered Allowances; multiplied by

  (3) the number of Replacement Allowances which the Buyer is able to purchase at the price indicated in (1); plus

  (4) interest for the period from (and including) the Delivery Date to (but excluding) the date of termination calculated on an amount equal to the product of the number of Undelivered Allowances and an amount equal to the excess, if any, of the price determined pursuant to (1) over the Contract Price agreed between the Parties in respect of the Undelivered Allowances at the rate specified in clause 8.5(a); or

(B) if in one or more arm's length transactions the Buyer, using its reasonable endeavours, is unable to purchase a number of Replacement Allowances equivalent to the Undelivered Allowances to be delivered during the Buy-In Period:

  (1) in respect of the number of Replacement Allowances for which the Buyer is able to effect a Buy-In during the Buy-In Period, an amount for such Allowances calculated in accordance with paragraph (A) above; and

(2) in respect of the number of Replacement Allowances equal to the number of Undelivered Allowances minus the number of Replacement Allowances referred to in (B)(1) above (the **"Shortfall"**), the sum of:

(I) the price (per Allowance) at which the Buyer, using its reasonable endeavours and in an arm's length transaction, is or would be able to purchase as soon as reasonably possible after the Reconciliation Deadline a number of Replacement Allowances equal to the Shortfall; less

(II) the Contract Price agreed by the Parties in respect of the Undelivered Allowances; plus

(III) the EEP Amount; multiplied by

(IV) the Shortfall; plus

(V) interest for the period from (and including) the Delivery Date to (but excluding) the date the Buyer is or would be able to purchase Replacement Allowances in accordance with paragraph (B)(2)(I) above on an amount equal to the product of the Shortfall and an amount equal to the excess, if any, of the price determined pursuant to paragraph (B)(2)(I) above over the Contract Price agreed between the Parties in respect of the Undelivered Allowances at the rate specified in clause 8.5(a); and

(ii) such reasonable costs and expenses which the Buyer incurs as a result of the Seller's failure to deliver the Shortfall (including, without limitation, broker fees, commissions and legal fees) to the extent that those costs and expenses are not reflected in paragraphs (i)(A) or (i)(B) above.

Where the Buyer confirms that it has been unable to purchase Replacement Allowances during the Buy-In Period, it shall be for the Seller to show that it has been as a result of the Buyer failing to use its reasonable endeavours to do so.

**"Certified Emissions Reduction"** or **"CER"** means a unit of account on a Government or Intergovernmental registry representing 1 tonne of carbon dioxide equivalent issued by the CDM Executive Board in accordance with Decision 17 (17/CP.7) of the Conference of the Parties to the UNFCCC.

**"Central European Time"** or **"CET"** means Central European Time and shall include Central European Winter Time and Central European Summer Time, as applicable.

**"Change in Tax Law"** means the enactment, promulgation, execution or ratification of, or any change in or amendment to, any law (or in the application or official interpretation of any law) affecting the tax treatment accorded the Transfer of Allowances that occurs on or after the date on which the relevant Transaction is entered into.

**"Compliance Period"** means the three-year period referred to in Article 11(1) of the Directive or, as the case may be, the relevant subsequent five-year period referred to in Article 11(2) of the Directive, as agreed between the Parties at the time of entering into the Transaction.

**"Compliance Period Traded Allowance"** means, in relation to a Transaction, an Allowance that the Seller agrees to transfer to the Buyer and the Buyer agrees to accept from the Seller that is of the Specified Compliance Period.

**"Confidential Information"** has the meaning given to it in clause 10 (*Confidentiality*).

**"Confirmation"** means a confirmation substantially in the form set out in Schedule 3 completed with details agreed between the Parties relating to an individual Transaction.

**"Contract Amount"** means, for each Transaction, the amount (expressed in Euros unless otherwise agreed) calculated by multiplying the Contract Price by the CPTA Quantity for that Transaction.

**"Contract Value"** means, for any Undelivered Allowances, the amount (expressed in Euros unless otherwise agreed) calculated by multiplying the Contract Price by the number of Undelivered Allowances.

**"Contract Price"** means, for a particular CPTA Quantity, Specified Compliance Period and Transaction, the amount agreed to be the contract price for that CPTA Quantity (expressed in Euros per Allowance unless otherwise agreed), excluding applicable taxes.

**"Control and Profit Transfer Agreement"** means, unless otherwise specified in Schedule 2, an agreement in form and substance satisfactory to one of the Parties executed by the other Party's Controlling Party with respect to the maintenance of control of that other Party by the Controlling Party and of the capitalization, the creditworthiness and the ability to perform obligations under this Agreement of the other Party.

**"Controlling Party"** means, where "Controlling Party" is specified in Schedule 2 as applying to a Party, the Entity named as the Controlling Party with respect to that Party (being the Entity who is a party to a Control and Profit Transfer Agreement with that Party and where that Party is, in relation to such Entity, its subsidiary over which such Entity has control).

**"CPTA Quantity"** means, in relation to a Transaction and a Specified Compliance Period, the number of Compliance Period Traded Allowances that the Parties have agreed to buy and sell for that Transaction and that Specified Compliance Period.

**"Credit Rating"** means in respect of an Entity any of the following: (i) the long-term unsecured, unsubordinated (unsupported by third party credit enhancement) public debt rating; (ii) the debt issuer's credit rating; or (iii) the corporate credit rating given to that person, in each of cases (i) to (iii) by Standard & Poor's Rating Group (a division of McGraw-Hill Inc.) or Moody's Investor Services Inc. or Fitch Ratings Ltd. equivalent.

**"Credit Support Document"** means, for a Party, any agreement or instrument that is specified as such in Schedule 2 in relation to that Party.

**"Credit Support Provider"** has the meaning given to it in Schedule 2.

**"Cross Default Threshold"** means, for a Party, the amount set out in Schedule 2.

**"Default Quantity"** means, in respect of a Transaction, the quantity equal to the difference between (a) the CPTA Quantity and (b) the quantity of Compliance Period Traded Allowances duly and timely delivered.

**"Defaulting Party"** has the meaning given to it in clause 12.2 (*Events of Default*).

"**Delivered Allowance Volume**" means the aggregate number of Delivered Allowances and Physically Netted Allowances.

"**Delivered Allowances**" means Compliance Period Traded Allowances actually delivered by (or at the request of) the Seller to the Delivery Point.

"**Delivery Banking Day**" means, in relation to a Transaction, any day (other than a Saturday or Sunday) on which commercial banks are open for general business in both the Seller's Delivery Banking Day Location and the Buyer's Delivery Banking Day Location.

"**Delivery Date**" means, in relation to a Transaction, the Delivery Banking Day agreed between the Parties as the delivery date (that is to say, the date by which the relevant Transfer is to be completed) at the time of entering into the Transaction, but can in no event be a date prior to either the allocation of Allowances under the Scheme or the establishment of registries capable of recognizing and tracking Transfers.

"**Delivery Point**" means the Buyer's Holding Account(s) specified in Schedule 2 or such other account(s) as the Buyer may specify in a Confirmation. If multiple Buyer's Holding Accounts are specified in Schedule 2 or in the Confirmation for any Transaction, the Delivery Point shall be the first Holding Account so listed, unless due to the operation of clause 9.1 (*Force Majeure*) or clause 12.6 (*Illegality*) it is not possible to accept delivery of the Compliance Period Traded Allowances into that Holding Account, in which case the Delivery Point shall be the next listed Holding Account that can accept delivery of the Compliance Period Traded Allowances.

"**Directive**" means Directive 2003/87/EC of the European Parliament and of the Council of 13°October 2003 establishing a scheme for greenhouse gas emissions allowance trading and amending Council Directive 96/61/EC, as amended from time to time.

"**EEP Amount**" means an amount (expressed as an amount per Allowance) that the Buyer determines, acting in good faith and using commercially reasonable procedures, to be its total losses and costs which result from the Seller's failure to deliver the Shortfall to the extent that those losses and costs are not reflected elsewhere in the definition of Buyer's Replacement Cost and to the extent that they relate to:

(a)   if this sub-paragraph (a) is specified in Schedule 2 as applying, any Excess Emissions Penalty which the Buyer must pay to a Relevant Authority in accordance with the terms of the Scheme; or

(b)   if this sub-paragraph (b) is specified in Schedule 2 as applying, any amount which the Buyer must pay to a third party in respect of any such penalty payable to any other party (including a Relevant Authority) by that third party as a result of the Seller's failure to deliver the Shortfall.

"**EEP Status**" means whether or not the Parties have elected in Schedule 2 or the Confirmation for the relevant Transaction that Excess Emissions Penalty applies to the relevant Compliance Period Traded Allowances.

"**End of Phase Reconciliation Deadline**" means the final Reconciliation Deadline in any period referred to in Article 11(1) or (2) of the Directive.

"**Entity**" means an individual, government or state or division of it, government or state agency, corporation, partnership or such other entity as the context may require.

"**EU**" means the European Union as it exists from time to time.

"**EU Allowance**" means an "allowance" as defined in the Directive.

"**EURIBOR**" means, in relation to an amount owed under this Agreement on which interest is to accrue in Euros:

(a)   the interest rate for Euro deposits for a period of one month that appears on Reuters Page EURIBOR01 (or such other screen display or service as may replace it for the purpose of displaying the interest rates for Euro deposits offered in the euro-zone) as at 11.00 a.m. on the Due Date, and where the amount or any part of it remains overdue one month after the Due Date such interest rate as appears on such page for such deposits as at such time as at the day one month after the Due Date and thereafter as at monthly intervals until the amount is no longer overdue; or

(b)   if no such interest rate appears on Reuters (or such replacement), the arithmetic mean (rounded upwards to 3 decimal places) of the rates per annum at which each of not less than two major banks in the Euro-zone interbank market quoted that they were offering Euro deposits in an amount comparable with that overdue amount to major banks in the Euro-zone interbank market for a period of one month as at 11.00°a.m. on the Due Date or as at the day one month after the Due Date or as at monthly intervals thereafter as the case may be.

**"Euro"** means the lawful currency of the member states of the European Union that adopt the single currency in accordance with the Treaty establishing the European Community, as amended by the Treaty on European Union.

**"Event of Default"** has the meaning given to it in clause 12.2 (*Events of Default*).

**"Excess Emissions Penalty"** has the meaning given to it in the Directive.

**"Expert"** has the meaning given to it in clause 14.9(a).

**"Final Delivery Date"** has the meaning given to it in clause 6.1.1.

**"FM Affected Party"** has the meaning given to it in clause 9.1 (*Force Majeure*).

**"FM Affected Transaction"** has the meaning given to it in clause 9.1 (*Force Majeure*).

**"FM Termination Date"** means any date on which an FM Affected Transaction is terminated in accordance with clause 9.1 (*Force Majeure*).

**"Force Majeure"** means the occurrence of any event or circumstance, beyond the control of the FM Affected Party, that could not, after using all reasonable efforts, be overcome and which makes it impossible for the FM Affected Party to either (i) deliver the Compliance Period Traded Allowances from any Holding Account in any Registry (or if one or more Seller's Holding Accounts are specified in Schedule 2 (or, if different, in the Confirmation for the relevant Transaction), from such Seller's Holding Account(s)) or (ii) accept the Compliance Period Traded Allowances into the Buyer's Holding Account(s) specified in Schedule 2 (or, if different, in the Confirmation for the relevant Transaction), in accordance with the Scheme. The inability of a Party to perform a relevant delivery or acceptance obligation as a result of it having insufficient Compliance

Period Traded Allowances in the relevant Holding Account (whether caused by the low or non-allocation of Allowances from a Member State or Non-Member State or the failure of that Party to procure sufficient allowances to meet its delivery obligations) shall not constitute a Force Majeure; provided, however, that this is not an exhaustive list of events which will not constitute a Force Majeure and is provided for the avoidance of doubt only.

"**Holding Account**" means any digital record of a Party or Person in any relevant Registry that will be used to record the issue (if applicable), holding, transfer, acquisition, surrender, cancellation, and replacement of Allowances.

"**Illegality**" has the meaning given to it in clause 12.6 (*Illegality*).

"**Illegality Affected Transactions**" has the meaning given to it in clause 12.6 (*Illegality*).

"**Indebtedness**" means any obligation (whether present or future, contingent or otherwise, as principal or surety or otherwise) in respect of borrowed money.

"**Installation**" has the meaning given to it in the Directive.

"**Letter of Credit**" means an irrevocable standby letter of credit payable on demand in a form and substance satisfactory to the Requesting Party and issued or confirmed by a financial institution whose credit rating is at least Standard & Poor's Rating Group "A-", Moody's Investor's Service Inc. equivalent, or Fitch Ratings Ltd. equivalent.

"**Loss**" means:

(a)  for the purposes of clause 9.2(c), an amount that each Party reasonably determines in good faith to be its total losses and costs (or gain, in which case expressed as a negative number) in connection with the termination of the FM Affected Transaction(s) or any uncompleted portions of them, including any EEP Amount (if applicable, in which case clauses 6.1.2.2 through 6.1.2.4 shall apply equally to the determination of such amount), any loss of bargain, cost of funding (based on the actual costs of such Party whether or not greater than market costs) or, without duplication, loss or cost incurred as a result of its terminating, liquidating, obtaining or re-establishing any related trading position (or any gain resulting from any of them). Loss does not include legal fees or out-of-pocket expenses. Each Party may (but need not) determine its Loss by reference to quotations of average relevant rates or prices from two or more leading brokers in the Allowances trading market who are independent of the Parties; or

(b) for the purposes of clause 12.5 (*Termination Payments*), an amount that the Non-Defaulting Party reasonably determines in good faith to be its total losses and costs (or gain, in which case expressed as a negative number) in connection with the termination of the Transactions or any uncompleted portions of them, including any EEP Amount (if applicable, in which case clauses 6.1.2.2 through 6.1.2.4 shall apply equally to the determination of such amount), any loss of bargain, cost of funding (based on the actual costs of the Non-Defaulting Party whether or not greater than market costs) or, at the election of the Non-Defaulting Party but without duplication, loss or cost incurred as a result of its terminating, liquidating, obtaining or re-establishing any related trading position (or any gain resulting from any of them). Loss includes losses and costs (or gains) in respect of any payment required to have been made and not made or non-compliance with clause 4 (*Allowance Transfers*) or 5 (*Effecting Transfers*) (whether or not as a result of the suspension of the obligation to pay or comply with those clauses under clause 12.3 (*Suspension*) or 12.4 (*Early Termination Date*)) on or before the Early Termination Date. Loss does not include the Non-Defaulting Party's legal fees or out-of-pocket expenses. The Non-Defaulting Party may (but need not) determine its Loss by reference to quotations of average relevant rates or prices from two or more leading brokers in the Allowances trading market who are independent of the Parties; or

(c) for the purposes of clause 12.6 (*Illegality*):

(i) if there is only one Affected Party, as per the definition for the purposes of clause 12.5 (*Termination Payments*) as set forth above; or

(ii) if both Parties are Affected Parties, an amount that each Party reasonably determines in good faith to be its total losses and costs (or gain, in which case expressed as a negative number) in connection with the termination of the Illegality Affected Transaction(s) or any uncompleted portions of them, including any EEP Amount (if applicable, in which case clauses 6.1.2.2 through 6.1.2.4 shall apply equally to the determination of such amount), any loss of bargain, cost of funding (based on the actual costs of such Party whether or not greater than market costs) or, without duplication, loss or cost incurred as a result of its terminating, liquidating, obtaining or re-establishing any related trading position (or any gain resulting from any of them). Loss does not include legal fees or out-of-pocket expenses. Each Party may (but need not) determine its Loss by reference to quotations of average relevant rates or prices from two or more leading brokers in the Allowances trading market who are independent of the Parties.

"**Market Amount**" means the sum (whether positive or negative) of (i) the Market Quotation for the Transactions if a Market Quotation is determined and (ii) losses and costs (or gains) in respect of any payment required to have been made and not made or non-compliance with clause 4 (*Allowance Transfers*) or 5 (*Effecting Transfers*) on or before the Early Termination Date or as a result of suspension under clause 12.3 (*Suspension*); or, for the purposes of clause 12.5 (*Termination Payments*), the Non-Defaulting Party's Loss (whether positive or negative) for the Transactions if a Market Quotation cannot be determined or would not (in the reasonable belief of the Non-Defaulting Party) produce a commercially reasonable result.

"**Market Quotation**" means, with respect to the Non-Defaulting Party, an amount determined on the basis of the average of quotations from Reference Market Makers. Each quotation will be for an amount, if any, that would be paid to the Non-Defaulting Party (expressed as a negative number) or by the Non-Defaulting Party (expressed as a positive number) in consideration of an agreement between the Non-Defaulting Party and the quoting Reference Market Maker to enter into Replacement Transactions for the same amount of Compliance Period Traded Allowances having the same EEP Status. The quotation shall (i) take into account any existing Credit Support Document with respect to the obligations of the Non-Defaulting Party but (ii) disregard any losses, costs (or gains) in respect of any payment required to have been made and not made or non-compliance with clause 4 (*Allowance Transfers*) or 5 (*Effecting Transfers*) on or before the Early Termination Date.

"**Marrakech Accords**" means the decisions taken by the Conference of the Parties at its seventh meeting as contained in the UNFCCC documents FCCC/CP/2001/13 and FCCC/CP/2001/13/Add.1 – Add.4.

**"Master Agreement"** has the meaning ascribed to it in Recital B.

**"Material Adverse Change"** has the meaning given to it in clause 12.2(h).

**"Member State"** means any one of the signatories to the European Community from time to time – currently Belgium, Cyprus, Czech Republic, Denmark, Estonia, Germany, Greece, Hungary, Latvia, Lithuania, Malta, Poland, Slovakia, Slovenia, Spain, France, Luxembourg, the Netherlands, Austria, Portugal, Ireland, Italy, Finland, Sweden and the United Kingdom.

**"Monthly Billing Cycle"** means that payments fall due in accordance with the first elective in item 8.1 of Schedule 2.

**"Non-Defaulting Party"** means the Party that is not the Defaulting Party.

**"Party"** means one or other of the parties to this Agreement and "Parties" is to be construed accordingly.

**"Payment Due Date"** has the meaning given to it in clause 8.1 (*Payment Due Date*).

**"Performance Assurance"** means a Letter of Credit, cash or other security in form and amount reasonably satisfactory to the Requesting Party.

**"Performance Assurance Provider"** means, as the context requires, any Entity that provides Performance Assurance on behalf of one of the Parties.

**"Physically Netted Allowances"** means those Compliance Period Traded Allowances which were not actually delivered to the Delivery Point as a result of the operation of clause 8.7 (*Physical Netting of Deliveries*).

**"Reconciliation Deadline"** means 30 April of any calendar year in relation to the immediately preceding calendar year, or as otherwise specified in the Scheme Rules.

**"Reference Market Maker"** means three leading traders in the Allowances trading market selected by the Non-Defaulting Party in good faith which satisfy all the criteria that the Non-Defaulting Party applies generally at the time in deciding whether to offer or to make an extension of credit and which are independent of the Parties.

**"Registry"** means the registry established by each Member State or non-Member State pursuant to of the Directive, in order to ensure the accurate accounting of the issue, holding, transfer, acquisition, surrender, cancellation, and replacement of Allowances.

**"Registry Pair"** means a pair of Registries identified by the Parties in Schedule 2 or in a Confirmation with respect to which physical netting of deliveries pursuant to clause 8.7 (*Physical Netting of Deliveries*) may be affected.

**"Relevant Authority"** means the body established by a Member State or non-Member State from time to time to administer the Scheme in its jurisdiction.

**"Relevant Change in Tax"** has the meaning given to it in clause 12.8 (*Change in Taxes*).

**"Relevant Entity"** has the meaning given to it in clause 12.2(h)(i).

**"Relevant Party"** has the meaning given to it in clause 14.10 (*Party Preparing this Agreement*).

**"Relevant Tax"** means any present or future tax, levy, impost, duty, charge, assessment or fee of any nature (including interest or penalties) that is imposed by any government or other taxing authority directly in respect of any payment or transfer request under this Agreement other than stamp, registration, documentation or similar tax. Relevant Tax does not include, without limitation, income tax, taxes on emissions or the activities giving rise to emissions (as the term "emissions" is defined in the Scheme) or taxes imposed generally on a Party's business.

**"Replacement Allowances"** has the meaning given to it in paragraph (b)(i)(A) of the definition of Buyer's Replacement Cost.

**"Replacement Transactions"** means transactions that would have the effect of preserving for the Non-Defaulting Party the economic equivalent of any payment or compliance with clause 4 (*Allowance Transfers*) or 5 (*Effecting Transfers*) (whether the underlying obligation was absolute or contingent) that would, but for the occurrence of the relevant Early Termination Date, have been required after that date.

**"Required Authorisations"** means all governmental and other licences, authorisations, permits, consents, contracts and other approvals (if any) that are required to enable the Party to fulfil any of its obligations under this Agreement.

**"Schedule"** means a schedule to this Agreement.

**"Scheme"** means the scheme of transferring Allowances between either or both of (a) persons within the EU and (b) persons in third countries, in either case as recognized in accordance with, and subject to, the procedure of the Directive established in, and as implemented by the national laws of, each Member State and certain non-Member States.

**"Scheme Rules"** means the rules and regulations of participation in, and operation of, the Scheme as applicable in a Member State and certain non-Member States as amended from time to time.

**"Seller"** means the Party agreed as such by the Parties for the purposes of a Transaction.

**"Seller's Delivery Banking Day Location"** means, in relation to a Transaction, the place specified as such in the Confirmation for the relevant Transaction, or, if a place is not so specified: (i) the place specified as such in Schedule 2; or (ii) if no such place is specified, the place in which the Seller's address for the purposes of receiving notices connected with the relevant Transaction is located; or (iii) if no such address is given, the place in which the Seller has its registered office.

**"Seller's Holding Account"** means those Holding Account(s) specified in Schedule 2 or such other account(s) as the Seller may specify in a Confirmation. If multiple Seller's Holding Accounts are specified in Schedule 2 or in the Confirmation for any Transaction, the Seller shall Transfer the Compliance Period Traded Allowances from the first Holding Account so listed, unless due to the operation of clause 9.1 (*Force Majeure*) or clause 12.6 (*Illegality*) it is not possible to Transfer such Compliance Period Traded Allowances from that Holding Account, in which case the Seller Transfer the Compliance Period Traded Allowances from the next listed Holding Account that such Compliance Period Traded Allowances can be Transferred from.

"**Seller's Replacement Cost**" means (A) the positive difference if any between (i) the Contract Price multiplied by the Default Quantity, and (ii) the price the Seller, acting in a commercially reasonable manner, does or would receive in an arm's length transaction for an equivalent quantity and Compliance Period of Allowances to replace the Default Quantity, plus (B) interest for the period from (and including) the Delivery Date to (but excluding) the date of termination calculated on an amount equal to the product of the Default Quantity and an amount equal to the excess, if any, of the price determined pursuant to paragraph (A)(i) above over the Contract Price at the rate specified in clause 8.5(a), plus (C) the amount of such reasonable costs and expenses which the Seller incurs in respect of the Default Quantity (including, without limitation, broker fees, commissions and legal fees).

"**Shortfall**" has the meaning given to it in paragraph (b)(i)(B)(2) of the definition of Buyer's Replacement Cost.

"**Specified Compliance Period**" means, in relation to a Transaction and a CPTA Quantity, the relevant Compliance Period of issue of Allowances.

"**Specified Transaction**" means any transaction (including an agreement with respect to the transaction) existing at the date of this Agreement or after that date entered into between one Party (or any Credit Support Provider of that Party) and the other Party (or any Credit Support Provider of that other Party) that is a commodity forward or future, commodity option, commodity swap or other commodity transaction, including any contract for differences or transaction, or any other similar transaction except that, where so specified in Schedule 2 in relation to a Party, "Specified Transaction" includes any of the above only to the extent that they relate to the commodity or commodities so specified in relation to that Party.

"**Statement**" has the meaning given to it in clause 8.2(a).

"**Statement Amount**" means, for a Statement, the aggregate amount payable as shown in that Statement.

"**Suspension Period**" has the meaning given to it in clause 9.1 (*Force Majeure*).

"**Tangible Net Worth**" means the sum of all paid up shareholder contributions to the share capital account or any other capital account ascribed for such purposes and any accumulated earnings less any accumulated retained losses and intangible assets including, but not limited to, goodwill.

**"Termination Payment"** has the meaning given to it in clause 12.5(a).

**"Termination Payment Date"** has the meaning given to it in clause 12.5(d).

**"Total Debt"** means, for a specified period, the sum of financial indebtedness for borrowed money (which includes debts payable to Affiliates as well as debt instruments to financial institutions).

**"Transaction"** means an oral or written agreement between the Parties to undertake one or more Transfers, subject to the terms of this Agreement.

**"Transfer"** means (whether used as a verb or a noun) the transfer of Allowances from one Holding Account to another under and in accordance with and for the purposes of the Scheme, and **"Transferred"** is to be construed accordingly.

**"Transfer Request"** means a request made in accordance with the Scheme to effect a Transfer.

**"Transferred Allowance"** means a Compliance Period Traded Allowance that has been Transferred.

**"UNFCCC"** means the United Nations Framework Convention on Climate Change adopted in New York on May 9, 1992.

**"Undelivered Allowances"** has the meaning given to it in the definition of Buyer's Replacement Cost.

**"Unpaid Amounts"** owing to any Party means any amount that became payable to that Party prior to the first day of the Suspension Period which remains unpaid.

**"Value Added Tax"** or **"VAT"** means (a) any value added tax imposed by any Member State or non-Member State, or (b) any replacement or other tax levied by reference to value added to a transaction.

## SCHEDULE 2

## AGREEMENT INFORMATION (ELECTIONS)

## PART 1 — ELECTIONS

2.2(a)  **Confirmations.** Confirmations shall be delivered by:

[ ]  Facsimile, *or*

[ ]  _____ .

2.3  **Evidence of a Transaction.** Evidence of the terms of a Transaction contained in recordings:

[ ]  prevails over (a) other oral or written evidence, and (b) the terms contained in any disputed Confirmation, *or*

[ ]  is subject to the terms of any signed and delivered Confirmation regarding that Transaction.

3.1(i)  **Principal/Agent.** Each party is acting as principal under this Agreement unless otherwise specified here:

[ ]  Party A is acting as the agent of_____ .

[ ]  Party B is acting as the agent of _____ .

4.1(c)  **Seller's Holding Account(s).** The Seller's Holding Account(s) for each Party are:

Party A: _____ .

Party B: _____ .

6.1  **Excess Emissions Penalty.** Excess Emissions Penalty does not apply unless otherwise specified here:

[ ]  Excess Emissions Penalty applies.

If Excess Emissions Penalty applies, sub-paragraphs (a) and (b) of the definition of EEP Amount shall apply unless otherwise specified here:

[ ]  sub-paragraph (b) of the definition of EEP Amount does not apply.

8.1   **Payment Due Date.** The Payment Due Date shall be:

[  ]   the later of (i) the twentieth ($20^{th}$) day of the month following the month in which the relevant Delivery Date occurred (or if such day is not a Banking Day, the immediately following Banking Day) and (ii) the fifth ($5^{th}$) Banking Day after the date on which the Statement is delivered to the Buyer in accordance with clause 8.2 (*Statement*); *or*

[  ]   the fifth ($5^{th}$) Banking Day after the later of (i) the Delivery Date and (ii) the date on which the Statement is delivered to the Buyer in accordance with clause 8.2 (*Statement*).

8.4(a)   **Disputed Payments.** For the purposes of clause 8.4(a):

[  ]   sub-paragraph (i) applies, *or*

[  ]   sub-paragraph (ii) applies.

8.4(b)   **Disputed Payments.** Reference of disputed amounts to Expert for determination in accordance with clause 14.9 (*Expert Determination*):

[  ]   applies, *or*

[  ]   does not apply.

8.7   **Physical Netting of Deliveries.** Physical netting of deliveries under clause 8.7 (*Physical Netting of Deliveries*) applies unless otherwise specified here:

[  ]   does not apply.

If physical netting of deliveries under clause 8.7 (*Physical Netting of Deliveries*) applies, the relevant Registry(ies) applicable to:

Party A is (are): _____ ; and

Party B is (are): _____ .

9.2   **Force Majeure Termination Payment.** If no Seller's Holding Account is specified for the Party acting as Seller in the FM Affected Transaction, sub-paragraph (a) of clause 9.2 (*Force Majeure Termination Payment*) applies unless otherwise specified here:

[  ]  sub-paragraph (b) of clause 9.2 (*Force Majeure Termination Payment*) applies, *or*

[  ]  sub-paragraph (c) of clause 9.2 (*Force Majeure Termination Payment*) applies.

If one or more Seller's Holding Account(s) are specified for the Party acting as Seller in the FM Affected Transaction, sub-paragraph (c) of clause 9.2 (*Force Majeure Termination Payment*) applies unless otherwise specified here:

[  ]  sub-paragraph (a) of clause 9.2 (*Force Majeure Termination Payment*) applies, *or*

[  ]  sub-paragraph (b) of clause 9.2 (*Force Majeure Termination Payment*) applies.

12.1    **Automatic Early Termination**. Automatic Early Termination:

[  ]  applies to Party A, *or*

[  ]  does not apply to Party A; and

[  ]  applies to Party B, *or*

[  ]  does not apply to Party B.

12.2(e)(ii)    **Credit Support**. The expiry period applicable to any Credit Support Document or Performance Assurance is:

[  ]  30 days, *or*

[  ]  _____ .

12.2(f)    **Cross Default**. Cross Default:

[  ]  applies to Party A, *or*

[  ]  does not apply to Party A; and

[  ]  applies to Party B, *or*

[  ]  does not apply to Party B.

If Cross Default applies, the Cross Default Threshold applicable to:

Party A is € _____ (or its equivalent in any other currency), and

Party B is € _____ (or its equivalent in any other currency).

12.2(h)(i) **Credit Rating Threshold**. The minimum Credit Rating applicable to:

Party A is _____, and

Party B is _____.

12.2(h)(vi) **Tangible Net Worth**. The amount applicable to:

Party A is € _____ (or its equivalent in any other currency), and

Party B is € _____ (or its equivalent in any other currency).

12.2(h)(vii) **Financial Covenants**. The ratios for each subclause of 12.2(h)(vii) for each Party are as follows:

| Party A | Party B |
|---|---|
| (A): _____ | (A): _____ |
| (B): _____ | (B): _____ |
| (C): _____ | (C): _____. |

12.5 **Termination Payment Method**. The applicable termination payment method shall be Loss, unless otherwise specified here:

[ ] the applicable termination payment method shall be Market Amount.

12.8 **Change in Taxes**. Clause 12.8 (*Changes in Taxes*):

[ ] applies to Party A, *or*

[ ] does not apply to Party A; and

[ ] applies to Party B, *or*

[ ] does not apply to Party B.

14.7 **Applicable Law**. The Agreement is governed by and is to be construed in accordance with English law unless otherwise specified here:

[ ] _____ .

The Parties submit to the non-exclusive jurisdiction of the English courts unless otherwise specified here:

[   ] _____ .

14.8    **Arbitration**. Clause 14.8 (*Arbitration*):

[   ]  applies, *or*

[   ]  does not apply.

If Clause 14.8 (*Arbitration*) applies, the number of arbitrators shall be:

_____,

the place of arbitration shall be:

_____, and

the applicable rules of arbitration shall be:

[   ]  The International Chamber of Commerce Arbitration Rules, as in effect:

[   ]  on the date of this Agreement, *or*

[   ]  at the time of commencement of arbitration; *or*

[   ]  The Permanent Court of Arbitration "Optional Rules for Arbitration of Disputes Relating to Natural Resources and/or the Environment", as in effect:

[   ]  on the date of this Agreement, *or*

[   ]  at the time of commencement of arbitration; *or*

[   ]  The "United Nations Commission on International Trade Law (UNCITRAL) Arbitration Rules", as in effect:

[   ]  on the date of this Agreement, *or*

[   ]  at the time of commencement of arbitration; or

[   ]  Other: _____,
       as in effect:

[   ]  on the date of this Agreement, *or*

[   ]  at the time of commencement of arbitration.

14.10     **Party Preparing this Agreement**. The Party preparing this Agreement is:

[ ]   Party A, *or*

[ ]   Party B.

Schedule 1 **Banking Day**. The relevant jurisdiction(s) for the purposes of the definition of Banking Day are the jurisdiction(s) where the registered offices of the Parties are located, unless otherwise specified here:

[ ]   Party A:

    [ ]   the principal financial centre in the country of each Holding Account specified in this Schedule or the relevant Confirmation, *or*

    [ ]   the jurisdiction(s) of incorporation of the Parties, *or*

    [ ]   _____.

[ ]   Party B:

    [ ]   the principal financial centre in the country of each Holding Account specified in this Schedule or the relevant Confirmation, *or*

    [ ]   the jurisdiction(s) of incorporation of the Parties, *or*

    [ ]   _____.

Schedule 1 **Buyer's Delivery Banking Day Location**. The Buyer's Delivery Banking Day Location applicable to:

Party A is: _____, and

Party B is: _____.

Schedule 1 **Control and Profit Transfer Agreement**. Control and Profit Transfer Agreement has the meaning given to it in Schedule 1 unless otherwise specified here:

[ ]   As it applies to Party A: _____.

[ ]   As it applies to Party B: _____.

Schedule 1 **Controlling Party.** Controlling Party:

> [ ] applies to Party A, *or*
>
> [ ] does not apply to Party A; and
>
> [ ] applies to Party B, *or*
>
> [ ] does not apply to Party B.

Schedule 1 **Credit Support Document.** The Credit Support Document(s) applicable to:

> Party A is (are): _____ ; and
>
> Party B is (are): _____ .

Schedule 1 **Credit Support Provider.** The Credit Support Provider applicable to:

> Party A is: _____ ; and
>
> Party B is: _____ .

Schedule 1 **Delivery Point.** The Buyer's Holding Account(s) for each Party are:

> Party A: _____ .
>
> Party B: _____ .

Schedule 1 **Seller's Delivery Banking Day Location.** The Seller's Delivery Banking Day Location applicable to:

> Party A is: _____ ; and
>
> Party B is: _____ .

Schedule 1 **Specified Transaction.** The definition of "Specified Transaction" is limited to the following commodities: [*If no election is made, "Specified Transaction" covers all commodity trading.*]

> As it applies to Party A: _____ .
>
> As it applies to Party B: _____ .

Bank details:

Party A: _____

_____

_____

_____

_____

Party B: _____

_____

_____

_____

_____

# PART 2 — OTHER PROVISIONS

# SCHEDULE 3

# FORM OF CONFIRMATION

This Confirmation evidences the terms of the binding agreement between the Seller and the Buyer named below regarding the Transaction described in this Confirmation. This Confirmation is subject to, supplements and forms part of the Emissions Trading Master Agreement for the EU Scheme (the "Master Agreement") entered into between the Seller and the Buyer and dated [•].

| | |
|---|---|
| Seller and contact person: | |
| Buyer and contact person: | |
| Buyer's Holding Account(s): | As specified in Schedule 2 of the Master Agreement, or if different, as follows: |
| Seller's Holding Account(s): | As specified in Schedule 2 of the Master Agreement, or if different, as follows: |
| Buyer's Delivery Banking Day Location: | As specified in Schedule 2 of the Master Agreement, or if different, as follows: |
| Seller's Delivery Banking Day Location: | As specified in Schedule 2 of the Master Agreement, or if different, as follows: |
| Date and Time Transaction Agreed: | |
| Allowance Type (EU Allowance / Alternative Allowance / CER): | |
| Specified Compliance Period(s): | |
| CPTA Quantity (for each Specified Compliance Period) (expressed in number of Allowances): | |

| | |
|---|---|
| Delivery Date (for each CPTA Quantity): | |
| Contract Price(s) (€ / Allowance) for each Specified Compliance Period: | |
| Total amount: | |
| Payment Date: | |
| Name of Broker (if applicable): | |
| Bank details: | As specified in Schedule 2 of the Master Agreement, or if different, as follows: Seller: Buyer: |
| Netting of physical delivery obligations: | As specified in Schedule 2 of the Master Agreement, or if different, as follows: |
| Special Conditions: | |

Additional Terms:

1. **Definitions.** Capitalized terms not defined in this Confirmation have the meaning given to them in the Master Agreement.
2. **Counterparts.** This Confirmation may be executed and delivered in counterparts with the same effect as if both Parties had executed and delivered the same copy, and when each Party has signed and delivered a counterpart, all counterparts together constitute one agreement that evidences a binding supplement to the Master Agreement. Delivery of a copy of this Confirmation by facsimile is good and sufficient delivery.
3. **Authority.** Each Party executing this Confirmation represents that the execution, delivery and performance of this Confirmation have been duly authorized by all necessary action and that the person executing this Confirmation has the authority to execute and deliver it on behalf of such Party.
4. **Relationship Between the Parties.** Each Party represents to the other that:

(a) **Non-Reliance.** □Ñ is acting for its own account, and it has made its own independent decisions to enter into the Transaction and as to whether the Transaction is appropriate or proper for it based upon its own judgement and upon advice from such advisers as it has deemed necessary. It is not relying on any communication (written or oral) of the other Party as investment advice or as a recommendation to enter into the Transaction; it being understood that information and explanations related to the terms and conditions of the Transaction are not to be considered investment advice or a recommendation to enter into the Transaction. No communication (written or oral) received from the other Party is to be deemed to be an assurance or guarantee as to the expected results of the Transaction.

(b) **Assessment and Understanding.** It is capable of assessing the merits of and understanding (on its own behalf or through independent professional advice), and understands and accepts, the terms, conditions and risks of the Transaction. It is also capable of assuming, and assumes, the risks of the Transaction.

(c) **Status of Parties.** The other party is not acting as a fiduciary for or an adviser to it in respect of the Transaction.

If this Confirmation correctly sets out the terms of our agreement, please sign and return a copy of this Confirmation within 3 Banking Days from receipt of this Confirmation. If you believe that this Confirmation does not correctly set out the terms of our agreement, send a response within 3 Banking Days from receipt of this Confirmation that sets out in detail the alleged inaccuracy.

If your response contains additional or different terms from those set out in this Confirmation or this Agreement, they only become part of the Transaction if we expressly agree to them in a supplemental written confirmation.

Dated: _____     Dated: _____

Signed: _____     Signed: _____

Name:                                Name:

Title:                               Title:

Duly authorised on behalf of         Duly authorised on behalf of
the Seller                           the Buyer

# Appendix D

## ISDA

**(Multicurrency — Cross Border)**

# ISDA®

International Swap Dealers Association, Inc.

# MASTER AGREEMENT

dated as of ......................................

.................................................. and ......................................................

have entered and/or anticipate entering into one or more transactions (each a "Transaction") that are or will be governed by this Master Agreement, which includes the schedule (the "Schedule"), and the documents and other confirming evidence (each a "Confirmation") exchanged between the parties confirming those Transactions.

Accordingly, the parties agree as follows: —

## 1.    Interpretation

(a)    *Definitions.* The terms defined in Section 14 and in the Schedule will have the meanings therein specified for the purpose of this Master Agreement.

(b)   *Inconsistency.* In the event of any inconsistency between the provisions of the Schedule and the other provisions of this Master Agreement, the Schedule will prevail. In the event of any inconsistency between the provisions of any Confirmation and this Master Agreement (including the Schedule), such Confirmation will prevail for the purpose of the relevant Transaction.

(c)   *Single Agreement.* All Transactions are entered into in reliance on the fact that this Master Agreement and all Confirmations form a single agreement between the parties (collectively referred to as this "Agreement"), and the parties would not otherwise enter into any Transactions.

## 2.   Obligations

(a)   *General Conditions.*

(i)   Each party will make each payment or delivery specified in each Confirmation to be made by it, subject to the other provisions of this Agreement.

(ii)   Payments under this Agreement will be made on the due date for value on that date in the place of the account specified in the relevant Confirmation or otherwise pursuant to this Agreement, in freely transferable funds and in the manner customary for payments in the required currency. Where settlement is by delivery (that is, other than by payment), such delivery will be made for receipt on the due date in the manner customary for the relevant obligation unless otherwise specified in the relevant Confirmation or elsewhere in this Agreement.

(iii)   Each obligation of each party under Section 2(a)(i) is subject to (1) the condition precedent that no Event of Default or Potential Event of Default with respect to the other party has occurred and is continuing, (2) the condition precedent that no Early Termination Date in respect of the relevant Transaction has occurred or been effectively designated and (3) each other applicable condition precedent specified in this Agreement.

(b)   *Change of Account.* Either party may change its account for receiving a payment or delivery by giving notice to the other party at least five Local Business Days prior to the scheduled date for the payment or delivery to which such change applies unless such other party gives timely notice of a reasonable objection to such change.

(c)   *Netting.* If on any date amounts would otherwise be payable: —

(i)   in the same currency; and

(ii)   in respect of the same Transaction,

by each party to the other, then, on such date, each party's obligation to make payment of any such amount will be automatically satisfied and discharged and, if the aggregate amount that would otherwise have been payable by one party exceeds the aggregate amount that would otherwise have been payable by the other party, replaced by an obligation upon the party by whom the larger aggregate amount would have been payable to pay to the other party the excess of the larger aggregate amount over the smaller aggregate amount.

The parties may elect in respect of two or more Transactions that a net amount will be determined in respect of all amounts payable on the same date in the same currency in respect of such Transactions, regardless of whether such amounts are payable in respect of the same Transaction. The election may be made in the Schedule or a Confirmation by specifying that subparagraph (ii) above will not apply to the Transactions identified as being subject to the election, together with the starting date (in which case subparagraph (ii) above will not, or will cease to, apply to such Transactions from such date). This election may be made separately for different groups of Transactions and will apply separately to each pairing of Offices through which the parties make and receive payments or deliveries.

(d)   *Deduction or Withholding for Tax.*

(i)   *Gross-Up.* All payments under this Agreement will be made without any deduction or withholding for or on account of any Tax unless such deduction or withholding is required by any applicable law, as modified by the practice of any relevant governmental revenue authority, then in effect. If a party is so required to deduct or withhold, then that party ("X") will: —

(1)   promptly notify the other party ("Y") of such requirement;

386 Energy and Emissions Markets

(2)  pay to the relevant authorities the full amount required to be deducted or withheld (including the full amount required to be deducted or withheld from any additional amount paid by X to Y under this Section 2(d)) promptly upon the earlier of determining that such deduction or withholding is required or receiving notice that such amount has been assessed against Y;

(3)  promptly forward to Y an official receipt (or a certified copy), or other documentation reasonably acceptable to Y, evidencing such payment to such authorities; and

(4)  if such Tax is an Indemnifiable Tax, pay to Y, in addition to the payment to which Y is otherwise entitled under this Agreement, such additional amount as is necessary to ensure that the net amount actually received by Y (free and clear of Indemnifiable Taxes, whether assessed against X or Y) will equal the full amount Y would have received had no such deduction or withholding been required. However, X will not be required to pay any additional amount to Y to the extent that it would not be required to be paid but for: —

(A)  the failure by Y to comply with or perform any agreement contained in Section 4(a)(i), 4(a)(iii) or 4(d); or

(B)  the failure of a representation made by Y pursuant to Section 3(f) to be accurate and true unless such failure would not have occurred but for (I) any action taken by a taxing authority, or brought in a court of competent jurisdiction, on or after the date on which a Transaction is entered into (regardless of whether such action is taken or brought with respect to a party to this Agreement) or (II) a Change in Tax Law.

(ii)  *Liability.* If: —

(1)  X is required by any applicable law, as modified by the practice of any relevant governmental revenue authority, to make any deduction or withholding in respect of which X would not be required to pay an additional amount to Y under Section 2(d)(i)(4);

(2)   X does not so deduct or withhold; and

(3)   a liability resulting from such Tax is assessed directly against X,

then, except to the extent Y has satisfied or then satisfies the liability resulting from such Tax, Y will promptly pay to X the amount of such liability (including any related liability for interest, but including any related liability for penalties only if Y has failed to comply with or perform any agreement contained in Section 4(a)(i), 4(a)(iii) or 4(d)).

(e)   *Default Interest; Other Amounts.* Prior to the occurrence or effective designation of an Early Termination Date in respect of the relevant Transaction, a party that defaults in the performance of any payment obligation will, to the extent permitted by law and subject to Section 6(c), be required to pay interest (before as well as after judgment) on the overdue amount to the other party on demand in the same currency as such overdue amount, for the period from (and including) the original due date for payment to (but excluding) the date of actual payment, at the Default Rate. Such interest will be calculated on the basis of daily compounding and the actual number of days elapsed. If, prior to the occurrence or effective designation of an Early Termination Date in respect of the relevant Transaction, a party defaults in the performance of any obligation required to be settled by delivery, it will compensate the other party on demand if and to the extent provided for in the relevant Confirmation or elsewhere in this Agreement.

## 3.   Representations

Each party represents to the other party (which representations will be deemed to be repeated by each party on each date on which a Transaction is entered into and, in the case of the representations in Section 3(f), at all times until the termination of this Agreement) that:—

(a)   *Basic Representations.*

(i)   *Status.* It is duly organised and validly existing under the laws of the jurisdiction of its organisation or incorporation and, if relevant under such laws, in good standing;

(ii)   *Powers.* It has the power to execute this Agreement and any other documentation relating to this Agreement to which it is a party, to deliver this Agreement and any other documentation relating to this Agreement that it is required by this Agreement to deliver and to perform its obligations under this Agreement and any obligations it has under any Credit Support Document to which it is a party and has taken all necessary action to authorise such execution, delivery and performance;

(iii)   *No Violation or Conflict.* Such execution, delivery and performance do not violate or conflict with any law applicable to it, any provision of its constitutional documents, any order or judgment of any court or other agency of government applicable to it or any of its assets or any contractual restriction binding on or affecting it or any of its assets;

(iv)   *Consents.* All governmental and other consents that are required to have been obtained by it with respect to this Agreement or any Credit Support Document to which it is a party have been obtained and are in full force and effect and all conditions of any such consents have been complied with; and

(v)   *Obligations Binding.* Its obligations under this Agreement and any Credit Support Document to which it is a party constitute its legal, valid and binding obligations, enforceable in accordance with their respective terms (subject to applicable bankruptcy, reorganisation, insolvency, moratorium or similar laws affecting creditors' rights generally and subject, as to enforceability, to equitable principles of general application (regardless of whether enforcement is sought in a proceeding in equity or at law)).

(b)   *Absence of Certain Events.* No Event of Default or Potential Event of Default or, to its knowledge, Termination Event with respect to it has occurred and is continuing and no such event or circumstance would occur as a result of its entering into or performing its obligations under this Agreement or any Credit Support Document to which it is a party.

(c)   *Absence of Litigation.* There is not pending or, to its knowledge, threatened against it or any of its Affiliates any action, suit or proceeding at law or in equity or before any court, tribunal, governmental body, agency or official or any arbitrator that is likely to affect the legality, validity or enforceability against it of this Agreement or any Credit Support Document to which it is a party or its ability to perform its obligations under this Agreement or such Credit Support Document.

(d)   *Accuracy of Specified Information.* All applicable information that is furnished in writing by or on behalf of it to the other party and is identified for the purpose of this Section 3(d) in the Schedule is, as of the date of the information, true, accurate and complete in every material respect.

(e)   *Payer Tax Representation.* Each representation specified in the Schedule as being made by it for the purpose of this Section 3(e) is accurate and true.

(f)   *Payee Tax Representations.* Each representation specified in the Schedule as being made by it for the purpose of this Section 3(f) is accurate and true.

## 4.   Agreements

Each party agrees with the other that, so long as either party has or may have any obligation under this Agreement or under any Credit Support Document to which it is a party: —

(a)   *Furnish Specified Information.* It will deliver to the other party or, in certain cases under subparagraph (iii) below, to such government or taxing authority as the other party reasonably directs: —

(i)   any forms, documents or certificates relating to taxation specified in the Schedule or any Confirmation;

(ii)   any other documents specified in the Schedule or any Confirmation; and

(iii)   upon reasonable demand by such other party, any form or document that may be required or reasonably requested in writing in order to allow such other party or its Credit Support Provider to make a payment under this Agreement or any applicable Credit Support Document without any deduction or withholding for or on account of any Tax or with such deduction or withholding at a reduced rate (so long as the completion, execution or submission of such form or document would not materially prejudice the legal or commercial position of the party in receipt of such demand), with any such form or document to be accurate and completed in a manner reasonably satisfactory to such other party and to be executed and to be delivered with any reasonably required certification,

in each case by the date specified in the Schedule or such Confirmation or, if none is specified, as soon as reasonably practicable.

(b)  *Maintain Authorisations.* It will use all reasonable efforts to maintain in full force and effect all consents of any governmental or other authority that are required to be obtained by it with respect to this Agreement or any Credit Support Document to which it is a party and will use all reasonable efforts to obtain any that may become necessary in the future.

(c)  *Comply with Laws.* It will comply in all material respects with all applicable laws and orders to which it may be subject if failure so to comply would materially impair its ability to perform its obligations under this Agreement or any Credit Support Document to which it is a party.

(d)  *Tax Agreement.* It will give notice of any failure of a representation made by it under Section 3(f) to be accurate and true promptly upon learning of such failure.

(e)  *Payment of Stamp Tax.* Subject to Section 11, it will pay any Stamp Tax levied or imposed upon it or in respect of its execution or performance of this Agreement by a jurisdiction in which it is incorporated, organised, managed and controlled, or considered to have its seat, or in which a branch or office through which it is acting for the purpose of this Agreement is located ("Stamp Tax Jurisdiction") and will indemnify the other party against any Stamp Tax levied or imposed upon the other party or in respect of the other party's execution or performance of this Agreement by any such Stamp Tax Jurisdiction which is not also a Stamp Tax Jurisdiction with respect to the other party.

**5.   Events of Default and Termination Events**

(a)  *Events of Default.* The occurrence at any time with respect to a party or, if applicable, any Credit Support Provider of such party or any Specified Entity of such party of any of the following events constitutes an event of default (an "Event of Default") with respect to such party: —

(i)  ***Failure to Pay or Deliver.*** Failure by the party to make, when due, any payment under this Agreement or delivery under Section 2(a)(i) or 2(e) required to be made by it if such failure is not remedied on or before the third Local Business Day after notice of such failure is given to the party;

(ii)  ***Breach of Agreement.*** Failure by the party to comply with or perform any agreement or obligation (other than an obligation to make any payment under this Agreement or delivery under Section 2(a)(i) or 2(e) or to give notice of a Termination Event or any agreement or obligation under Section 4(a)(i), 4(a)(iii) or 4(d)) to be complied with or performed by the party in accordance with this Agreement if such failure is not remedied on or before the thirtieth day after notice of such failure is given to the party;

(iii)  ***Credit Support Default.***

(1)  Failure by the party or any Credit Support Provider of such party to comply with or perform any agreement or obligation to be complied with or performed by it in accordance with any Credit Support Document if such failure is continuing after any applicable grace period has elapsed;

(2)  the expiration or termination of such Credit Support Document or the failing or ceasing of such Credit Support Document to be in full force and effect for the purpose of this Agreement (in either case other than in accordance with its terms) prior to the satisfaction of all obligations of such party under each Transaction to which such Credit Support Document relates without the written consent of the other party; or

(3)  the party or such Credit Support Provider disaffirms, disclaims, repudiates or rejects, in whole or in part, or challenges the validity of, such Credit Support Document;

(iv)  ***Misrepresentation.*** A representation (other than a representation under Section 3(e) or (f)) made or repeated or deemed to have been made or repeated by the party or any Credit Support Provider of such party in this Agreement or any Credit Support Document proves to have been incorrect or misleading in any material respect when made or repeated or deemed to have been made or repeated;

(v)    ***Default under Specified Transaction.*** The party, any Credit Support Provider of such party or any applicable Specified Entity of such party (1) defaults under a Specified Transaction and, after giving effect to any applicable notice requirement or grace period, there occurs a liquidation of, an acceleration of obligations under, or an early termination of, that Specified Transaction, (2) defaults, after giving effect to any applicable notice requirement or grace period, in making any payment or delivery due on the last payment, delivery or exchange date of, or any payment on early termination of, a Specified Transaction (or such default continues for at least three Local Business Days if there is no applicable notice requirement or grace period) or (3) disaffirms, disclaims, repudiates or rejects, in whole or in part, a Specified Transaction (or such action is taken by any person or entity appointed or empowered to operate it or act on its behalf);

(vi)    ***Cross Default.*** If "Cross Default" is specified in the Schedule as applying to the party, the occurrence or existence of (1) a default, event of default or other similar condition or event (however described) in respect of such party, any Credit Support Provider of such party or any applicable Specified Entity of such party under one or more agreements or instruments relating to Specified Indebtedness of any of them (individually or collectively) in an aggregate amount of not less than the applicable Threshold Amount (as specified in the Schedule) which has resulted in such Specified Indebtedness becoming, or becoming capable at such time of being declared, due and payable under such agreements or instruments, before it would otherwise have been due and payable or (2) a default by such party, such Credit Support Provider or such Specified Entity (individually or collectively) in making one or more payments on the due date thereof in an aggregate amount of not less than the applicable Threshold Amount under such agreements or instruments (after giving effect to any applicable notice requirement or grace period);

(vii)    ***Bankruptcy.*** The party, any Credit Support Provider of such party or any applicable Specified Entity of such party: —

(1)    is dissolved (other than pursuant to a consolidation, amalgamation or merger); (2) becomes insolvent or is unable to pay its debts or fails or admits in writing its

inability generally to pay its debts as they become due; (3) makes a general assignment, arrangement or composition with or for the benefit of its creditors; (4) institutes or has instituted against it a proceeding seeking a judgment of insolvency or bankruptcy or any other relief under any bankruptcy or insolvency law or other similar law affecting creditors' rights, or a petition is presented for its winding-up or liquidation, and, in the case of any such proceeding or petition instituted or presented against it, such proceeding or petition (A) results in a judgment of insolvency or bankruptcy or the entry of an order for relief or the making of an order for its winding-up or liquidation or (B) is not dismissed, discharged, stayed or restrained in each case within 30 days of the institution or presentation thereof; (5) has a resolution passed for its winding-up, official management or liquidation (other than pursuant to a consolidation, amalgamation or merger); (6) seeks or becomes subject to the appointment of an administrator, provisional liquidator, conservator, receiver, trustee, custodian or other similar official for it or for all or substantially all its assets; (7) has a secured party take possession of all or substantially all its assets or has a distress, execution, attachment, sequestration or other legal process levied, enforced or sued on or against all or substantially all its assets and such secured party maintains possession, or any such process is not dismissed, discharged, stayed or restrained, in each case within 30 days thereafter; (8) causes or is subject to any event with respect to it which, under the applicable laws of any jurisdiction, has an analogous effect to any of the events specified in clauses (1) to (7) (inclusive); or (9) takes any action in furtherance of, or indicating its consent to, approval of, or acquiescence in, any of the foregoing acts; or

(viii) **Merger Without Assumption.** The party or any Credit Support Provider of such party consolidates or amalgamates with, or merges with or into, or transfers all or substantially all its assets to, another entity and, at the time of such consolidation, amalgamation, merger or transfer: —

(1)  the resulting, surviving or transferee entity fails to assume all the obligations of such party or such Credit

Support Provider under this Agreement or any Credit Support Document to which it or its predecessor was a party by operation of law or pursuant to an agreement reasonably satisfactory to the other party to this Agreement; or

(2)   the benefits of any Credit Support Document fail to extend (without the consent of the other party) to the performance by such resulting, surviving or transferee entity of its obligations under this Agreement.

(b)   *Termination Events.* The occurrence at any time with respect to a party or, if applicable, any Credit Support Provider of such party or any Specified Entity of such party of any event specified below constitutes an Illegality if the event is specified in (i) below, a Tax Event if the event is specified in (ii) below or a Tax Event Upon Merger if the event is specified in (iii) below, and, if specified to be applicable, a Credit Event Upon Merger if the event is specified pursuant to (iv) below or an Additional Termination Event if the event is specified pursuant to (v) below: —

(i)   *Illegality.* Due to the adoption of, or any change in, any applicable law after the date on which a Transaction is entered into, or due to the promulgation of, or any change in, the interpretation by any court, tribunal or regulatory authority with competent jurisdiction of any applicable law after such date, it becomes unlawful (other than as a result of a breach by the party of Section 4(b)) for such party (which will be the Affected Party): —

(1)   to perform any absolute or contingent obligation to make a payment or delivery or to receive a payment or delivery in respect of such Transaction or to comply with any other material provision of this Agreement relating to such Transaction; or

(2)   to perform, or for any Credit Support Provider of such party to perform, any contingent or other obligation which the party (or such Credit Support Provider) has under any Credit Support Document relating to such Transaction;

(ii)   *Tax Event.* Due to (x) any action taken by a taxing authority, or brought in a court of competent jurisdiction, on or after the date on which a Transaction is entered into (regardless of whether such action is taken or brought with respect to a party to this Agreement) or (y) a Change in Tax Law, the party (which will be the Affected Party) will, or there is a substantial likelihood that it will, on the next succeeding Scheduled Payment Date (1) be required to pay to the other party an additional amount in respect of an Indemnifiable Tax under Section 2(d)(i)(4) (except in respect of interest under Section 2(e), 6(d)(ii) or 6(e)) or (2) receive a payment from which an amount is required to be deducted or withheld for or on account of a Tax (except in respect of interest under Section 2(e), 6(d)(ii) or 6(e)) and no additional amount is required to be paid in respect of such Tax under Section 2(d)(i)(4) (other than by reason of Section 2(d)(i)(4)(A) or (B));

(iii)   *Tax Event Upon Merger.* The party (the "Burdened Party") on the next succeeding Scheduled Payment Date will either (1) be required to pay an additional amount in respect of an Indemnifiable Tax under Section 2(d)(i)(4) (except in respect of interest under Section 2(e), 6(d)(ii) or 6(e)) or (2) receive a payment from which an amount has been deducted or withheld for or on account of any Indemnifiable Tax in respect of which the other party is not required to pay an additional amount (other than by reason of Section 2(d)(i)(4)(A) or (B)), in either case as a result of a party consolidating or amalgamating with, or merging with or into, or transferring all or substantially all its assets to, another entity (which will be the Affected Party) where such action does not constitute an event described in Section 5(a)(viii);

(iv)   *Credit Event Upon Merger.* If "Credit Event Upon Merger" is specified in the Schedule as applying to the party, such party ("X"), any Credit Support Provider of X or any applicable Specified Entity of X consolidates or amalgamates with, or merges with or into, or transfers all or substantially all its assets to, another entity and such action does not constitute an event described in Section 5(a)(viii) but the creditworthiness of the resulting, surviving or transferee entity is materially weaker than that of X, such Credit Support Provider or such Specified Entity, as the case may be, immediately prior to such action (and, in such event, X or its successor or transferee, as appropriate, will be the Affected Party); or

(v)   *Additional Termination Event.* If any "Additional Termination Event" is specified in the Schedule or any Confirmation as applying, the occurrence of such event (and, in such event, the Affected Party or Affected Parties shall be as specified for such Additional Termination Event in the Schedule or such Confirmation).

(c)   *Event of Default and Illegality.* If an event or circumstance which would otherwise constitute or give rise to an Event of Default also constitutes an Illegality, it will be treated as an Illegality and will not constitute an Event of Default.

## 6.   Early Termination

(a)   *Right to Terminate Following Event of Default.* If at any time an Event of Default with respect to a party (the "Defaulting Party") has occurred and is then continuing, the other party (the "Non-defaulting Party") may, by not more than 20 days notice to the Defaulting Party specifying the relevant Event of Default, designate a day not earlier than the day such notice is effective as an Early Termination Date in respect of all outstanding Transactions. If, however, "Automatic Early Termination" is specified in the Schedule as applying to a party, then an Early Termination Date in respect of all outstanding Transactions will occur immediately upon the occurrence with respect to such party of an Event of Default specified in Section 5(a)(vii)(1), (3), (5), (6) or, to the extent analogous thereto, (8), and as of the time immediately preceding the institution of the relevant proceeding or the presentation of the relevant petition upon the occurrence with respect to such party of an Event of Default specified in Section 5(a)(vii)(4) or, to the extent analogous thereto, (8).

(b)   *Right to Terminate Following Termination Event.*

(i)   *Notice.* If a Termination Event occurs, an Affected Party will, promptly upon becoming aware of it, notify the other party, specifying the nature of that Termination Event and each Affected Transaction and will also give such other information about that Termination Event as the other party may reasonably require.

(ii)   *Transfer to Avoid Termination Event.* If either an Illegality under Section 5(b)(i)(1) or a Tax Event occurs and there is only one Affected Party, or if a Tax Event Upon Merger occurs and the Burdened Party is the Affected Party, the Affected Party will, as a condition to its right to designate an Early Termination Date under Section 6(b)(iv), use all reasonable efforts (which will not require such party to incur a loss, excluding immaterial, incidental expenses) to transfer within 20 days after it gives notice under Section 6(b)(i) all its rights and obligations under this Agreement in respect of the Affected Transactions to another of its Offices or Affiliates so that such Termination Event ceases to exist.

If the Affected Party is not able to make such a transfer it will give notice to the other party to that effect within such 20 day period, whereupon the other party may effect such a transfer within 30 days after the notice is given under Section 6(b)(i).

Any such transfer by a party under this Section 6(b)(ii) will be subject to and conditional upon the prior written consent of the other party, which consent will not be withheld if such other party's policies in effect at such time would permit it to enter into transactions with the transferee on the terms proposed.

(iii) *Two Affected Parties.* If an Illegality under Section 5(b)(i)(1) or a Tax Event occurs and there are two Affected Parties, each party will use all reasonable efforts to reach agreement within 30 days after notice thereof is given under Section 6(b)(i) on action to avoid that Termination Event.

(iv) *Right to Terminate.* If: —

(1) a transfer under Section 6(b)(ii) or an agreement under Section 6(b)(iii), as the case may be, has not been effected with respect to all Affected Transactions within 30 days after an Affected Party gives notice under Section 6(b)(i); or

(2) an Illegality under Section 5(b)(i)(2), a Credit Event Upon Merger or an Additional Termination Event occurs, or a Tax Event Upon Merger occurs and the Burdened Party is not the Affected Party,

either party in the case of an Illegality, the Burdened Party in the case of a Tax Event Upon Merger, any Affected Party in the case of a Tax Event or an Additional Termination Event if there is more than one Affected Party, or the party which is not the Affected Party in the case of a Credit Event Upon Merger or an Additional Termination Event if there is only one Affected Party may, by not more than 20 days notice to the other party and provided that the relevant Termination Event is then continuing, designate a day not earlier than the day such notice is effective as an Early Termination Date in respect of all Affected Transactions.

(c)    **Effect of Designation.**

(i)    If notice designating an Early Termination Date is given under Section 6(a) or (b), the Early Termination Date will occur on the date so designated, whether or not the relevant Event of Default or Termination Event is then continuing.

(ii)    Upon the occurrence or effective designation of an Early Termination Date, no further payments or deliveries under Section 2(a)(i) or 2(e) in respect of the Terminated Transactions will be required to be made, but without prejudice to the other provisions of this Agreement. The amount, if any, payable in respect of an Early Termination Date shall be determined pursuant to Section 6(e).

(d)    **Calculations.**

(i)    **Statement.** On or as soon as reasonably practicable following the occurrence of an Early Termination Date, each party will make the calculations on its part, if any, contemplated by Section 6(e) and will provide to the other party a statement (1) showing, in reasonable detail, such calculations (including all relevant quotations and specifying any amount payable under Section 6(e)) and (2) giving details of the relevant account to which any amount payable to it is to be paid. In the absence of written confirmation from the source of a quotation obtained in determining a Market Quotation, the records of the party obtaining such quotation will be conclusive evidence of the existence and accuracy of such quotation.

(ii)    **Payment Date.** An amount calculated as being due in respect of any Early Termination Date under Section 6(e) will be payable on the day that notice of the amount payable is effective (in the case of an Early Termination Date which is designated or occurs as a result of an Event of Default) and on the day which is two Local Business Days after the day on which notice of the amount payable is effective (in the case of an Early Termination Date which is designated as a result of a Termination Event). Such amount will be paid together with (to the extent permitted under applicable law) interest thereon (before as well as after judgment) in the Termination Currency, from (and including) the relevant Early Termination Date to (but excluding) the date such amount is paid, at the Applicable Rate. Such interest will be calculated on the basis of daily compounding and the actual number of days elapsed.

(e) **Payments on Early Termination.** If an Early Termination Date occurs, the following provisions shall apply based on the parties' election in the Schedule of a payment measure, either "Market Quotation" or "Loss", and a payment method, either the "First Method" or the "Second Method". If the parties fail to designate a payment measure or payment method in the Schedule, it will be deemed that "Market Quotation" or the "Second Method", as the case may be, shall apply. The amount, if any, payable in respect of an Early Termination Date and determined pursuant to this Section will be subject to any Set-off.

(i) **Events of Default.** If the Early Termination Date results from an Event of Default: —

(1) *First Method and Market Quotation.* If the First Method and Market Quotation apply, the Defaulting Party will pay to the Non-defaulting Party the excess, if a positive number, of (A) the sum of the Settlement Amount (determined by the Non-defaulting Party) in respect of the Terminated Transactions and the Termination Currency Equivalent of the Unpaid Amounts owing to the Non-defaulting Party over (B) the Termination Currency Equivalent of the Unpaid Amounts owing to the Defaulting Party.

(2) *First Method and Loss.* If the First Method and Loss apply, the Defaulting Party will pay to the Non-defaulting Party, if a positive number, the Non-defaulting Party's Loss in respect of this Agreement.

(3)  *Second Method and Market Quotation.* If the Second Method and Market Quotation apply, an amount will be payable equal to (A) the sum of the Settlement Amount (determined by the Non-defaulting Party) in respect of the Terminated Transactions and the Termination Currency Equivalent of the Unpaid Amounts owing to the Non-defaulting Party less (B) the Termination Currency Equivalent of the Unpaid Amounts owing to the Defaulting Party. If that amount is a positive number, the Defaulting Party will pay it to the Non-defaulting Party; if it is a negative number, the Non-defaulting Party will pay the absolute value of that amount to the Defaulting Party.

(4)  *Second Method and Loss.* If the Second Method and Loss apply, an amount will be payable equal to the Non-defaulting Party's Loss in respect of this Agreement. If that amount is a positive number, the Defaulting Party will pay it to the Non-defaulting Party; if it is a negative number, the Non-defaulting Party will pay the absolute value of that amount to the Defaulting Party.

(ii)   *Termination Events.* If the Early Termination Date results from a Termination Event: —

(1)  *One Affected Party.* If there is one Affected Party, the amount payable will be determined in accordance with Section 6(e)(i)(3), if Market Quotation applies, or Section 6(e)(i)(4), if Loss applies, except that, in either case, references to the Defaulting Party and to the Non-defaulting Party will be deemed to be references to the Affected Party and the party which is not the Affected Party, respectively, and, if Loss applies and fewer than all the Transactions are being terminated, Loss shall be calculated in respect of all Terminated Transactions.

(2)  Two Affected Parties. If there are two Affected Parties: —

(A)  if Market Quotation applies, each party will determine a Settlement Amount in respect of the Terminated Transactions, and an amount will be payable equal to (I) the sum of (a) one-half of the difference between the Settlement Amount of the party with the higher Settlement Amount ("X") and the Settlement Amount of the party with the lower Settlement Amount ("Y") and (b) the Termination Currency Equivalent of the Unpaid Amounts owing to X less (II) the Termination Currency Equivalent of the Unpaid Amounts owing to Y; and

(B) if Loss applies, each party will determine its Loss in respect of this Agreement (or, if fewer than all the Transactions are being terminated, in respect of all Terminated Transactions) and an amount will be payable equal to one-half of the difference between the Loss of the party with the higher Loss ("X") and the Loss of the party with the lower Loss ("Y").

If the amount payable is a positive number, Y will pay it to X; if it is a negative number, X will pay the absolute value of that amount to Y.

(iii)  *Adjustment for Bankruptcy.* In circumstances where an Early Termination Date occurs because "Automatic Early Termination" applies in respect of a party, the amount determined under this Section 6(e) will be subject to such adjustments as are appropriate and permitted by law to reflect any payments or deliveries made by one party to the other under this Agreement (and retained by such other party) during the period from the relevant Early Termination Date to the date for payment determined under Section 6(d)(ii).

(iv)  *Pre-Estimate.* The parties agree that if Market Quotation applies an amount recoverable under this Section 6(e) is a reasonable pre-estimate of loss and not a penalty. Such amount is payable for the loss of bargain and the loss of protection against future risks and except as otherwise provided in this Agreement neither party will be entitled to recover any additional damages as a consequence of such losses.

## 7.  Transfer

Subject to Section 6(b)(ii), neither this Agreement nor any interest or obligation in or under this Agreement may be transferred (whether by way of security or otherwise) by either party without the prior written consent of the other party, except that: —

(a)   a party may make such a transfer of this Agreement pursuant to a consolidation or amalgamation with, or merger with or into, or transfer of all or substantially all its assets to, another entity (but without prejudice to any other right or remedy under this Agreement); and

(b)   a party may make such a transfer of all or any part of its interest in any amount payable to it from a Defaulting Party under Section 6(e).

Any purported transfer that is not in compliance with this Section will be void.

## 8.   Contractual Currency

(a)   *Payment in the Contractual Currency.* Each payment under this Agreement will be made in the relevant currency specified in this Agreement for that payment (the "Contractual Currency"). To the extent permitted by applicable law, any obligation to make payments under this Agreement in the Contractual Currency will not be discharged or satisfied by any tender in any currency other than the Contractual Currency, except to the extent such tender results in the actual receipt by the party to which payment is owed, acting in a reasonable manner and in good faith in converting the currency so tendered into the Contractual Currency, of the full amount in the Contractual Currency of all amounts payable in respect of this Agreement. If for any reason the amount in the Contractual Currency so received falls short of the amount in the Contractual Currency payable in respect of this Agreement, the party required to make the payment will, to the extent permitted by applicable law, immediately pay such additional amount in the Contractual Currency as may be necessary to compensate for the shortfall. If for any reason the amount in the Contractual Currency so received exceeds the amount in the Contractual Currency payable in respect of this Agreement, the party receiving the payment will refund promptly the amount of such excess.

(b)   *Judgments.* To the extent permitted by applicable law, if any judgment or order expressed in a currency other than the Contractual Currency is rendered (i) for the payment of any amount owing in respect of this Agreement, (ii) for the payment of any amount relating to any early termination in respect of this Agreement or (iii) in respect of a judgment or order of another court for the payment of any amount described in (i) or (ii) above, the party seeking recovery, after recovery in full of the aggregate amount to which such party is entitled pursuant to the judgment or order, will be entitled to receive immediately from the other party the amount of any shortfall of the Contractual Currency received by such party as a consequence of sums paid in such other currency and will refund promptly to the other party any excess of the Contractual Currency received by such party as a consequence of sums paid in such other currency if such shortfall or such excess arises or results from any variation between the rate of exchange at which the Contractual Currency is converted into the currency of the judgment or order for the purposes of such judgment or order and the rate of exchange at which such party is able, acting in a reasonable manner and in good faith in converting the currency received into the Contractual Currency, to purchase the Contractual Currency with the amount of the currency of the judgment or order actually received by such party. The term "rate of exchange" includes, without limitation, any premiums and costs of exchange payable in connection with the purchase of or conversion into the Contractual Currency.

(c)    *Separate Indemnities.* To the extent permitted by applicable law, these indemnities constitute separate and independent obligations from the other obligations in this Agreement, will be enforceable as separate and independent causes of action, will apply notwithstanding any indulgence granted by the party to which any payment is owed and will not be affected by judgment being obtained or claim or proof being made for any other sums payable in respect of this Agreement.

(d)    *Evidence of Loss.* For the purpose of this Section 8, it will be sufficient for a party to demonstrate that it would have suffered a loss had an actual exchange or purchase been made.

### 9.    Miscellaneous

(a)    *Entire Agreement.* This Agreement constitutes the entire agreement and understanding of the parties with respect to its subject matter and supersedes all oral communication and prior writings with respect thereto.

(b)    *Amendments.* No amendment, modification or waiver in respect of this Agreement will be effective unless in writing (including a writing evidenced by a facsimile transmission) and executed by each of the parties or confirmed by an exchange of telexes or electronic messages on an electronic messaging system.

(c)   *Survival of Obligations.* Without prejudice to Sections 2(a)(iii) and 6(c)(ii), the obligations of the parties under this Agreement will survive the termination of any Transaction.

(d)   *Remedies Cumulative.* Except as provided in this Agreement, the rights, powers, remedies and privileges provided in this Agreement are cumulative and not exclusive of any rights, powers, remedies and privileges provided by law.

(e)   *Counterparts and Confirmations.*

(i)   This Agreement (and each amendment, modification and waiver in respect of it) may be executed and delivered in counterparts (including by facsimile transmission), each of which will be deemed an original.

(ii)   The parties intend that they are legally bound by the terms of each Transaction from the moment they agree to those terms (whether orally or otherwise). A Confirmation shall be entered into as soon as practicable and may be executed and delivered in counterparts (including by facsimile transmission) or be created by an exchange of telexes or by an exchange of electronic messages on an electronic messaging system, which in each case will be sufficient for all purposes to evidence a binding supplement to this Agreement. The parties will specify therein or through another effective means that any such counterpart, telex or electronic message constitutes a Confirmation.

(f)   *No Waiver of Rights.* A failure or delay in exercising any right, power or privilege in respect of this Agreement will not be presumed to operate as a waiver, and a single or partial exercise of any right, power or privilege will not be presumed to preclude any subsequent or further exercise, of that right, power or privilege or the exercise of any other right, power or privilege.

(g)   *Headings.* The headings used in this Agreement are for convenience of reference only and are not to affect the construction of or to be taken into consideration in interpreting this Agreement.

## 10.   Offices; Multibranch Parties

(a)   If Section 10(a) is specified in the Schedule as applying, each party that enters into a Transaction through an Office other than its head or home office represents to the other party that, notwithstanding the place of booking office or jurisdiction of incorporation or organisation of such party, the obligations of such party are the same as if it had entered into the Transaction through its head or home office. This representation will be deemed to be repeated by such party on each date on which a Transaction is entered into.

(b)   Neither party may change the Office through which it makes and receives payments or deliveries for the purpose of a Transaction without the prior written consent of the other party.

(c)   If a party is specified as a Multibranch Party in the Schedule, such Multibranch Party may make and receive payments or deliveries under any Transaction through any Office listed in the Schedule, and the Office through which it makes and receives payments or deliveries with respect to a Transaction will be specified in the relevant Confirmation.

## 11.   Expenses

A Defaulting Party will, on demand, indemnify and hold harmless the other party for and against all reasonable out-of-pocket expenses, including legal fees and Stamp Tax, incurred by such other party by reason of the enforcement and protection of its rights under this Agreement or any Credit Support Document to which the Defaulting Party is a party or by reason of the early termination of any Transaction, including, but not limited to, costs of collection.

## 12.   Notices

(a)   *Effectiveness.* Any notice or other communication in respect of this Agreement may be given in any manner set forth below (except that a notice or other communication under Section 5 or 6 may not be given by facsimile transmission or electronic messaging system) to the address or number or in accordance with the electronic messaging system details provided (see the Schedule) and will be deemed effective as indicated: —

> (i)   if in writing and delivered in person or by courier, on the date it is delivered;

(ii)    if sent by telex, on the date the recipient's answerback is received;

(iii)    if sent by facsimile transmission, on the date that transmission is received by a responsible employee of the recipient in legible form (it being agreed that the burden of proving receipt will be on the sender and will not be met by a transmission report generated by the sender's facsimile machine);

(iv)    if sent by certified or registered mail (airmail, if overseas) or the equivalent (return receipt requested), on the date that mail is delivered or its delivery is attempted; or

(v)    if sent by electronic messaging system, on the date that electronic message is received,

unless the date of that delivery (or attempted delivery) or that receipt, as applicable, is not a Local Business Day or that communication is delivered (or attempted) or received, as applicable, after the close of business on a Local Business Day, in which case that communication shall be deemed given and effective on the first following day that is a Local Business Day.

(b)    *Change of Addresses.* Either party may by notice to the other change the address, telex or facsimile number or electronic messaging system details at which notices or other communications are to be given to it.

## 13.    Governing Law and Jurisdiction

(a)    *Governing Law.* This Agreement will be governed by and construed in accordance with the law specified in the Schedule.

(b)    *Jurisdiction.* With respect to any suit, action or proceedings relating to this Agreement ("Proceedings"), each party irrevocably:—

(i)    submits to the jurisdiction of the English courts, if this Agreement is expressed to be governed by English law, or to the non-exclusive jurisdiction of the courts of the State of New York and the United States District Court located in the Borough of Manhattan in New York City, if this Agreement is expressed to be governed by the laws of the State of New York; and

(ii)    waives any objection which it may have at any time to the laying of venue of any Proceedings brought in any such court, waives any claim that such Proceedings have been brought in an inconvenient forum and further waives the right to object, with respect to such Proceedings, that such court does not have any jurisdiction over such party.

Nothing in this Agreement precludes either party from bringing Proceedings in any other jurisdiction (outside, if this Agreement is expressed to be governed by English law, the Contracting States, as defined in Section 1(3) of the Civil Jurisdiction and Judgments Act 1982 or any modification, extension or re-enactment thereof for the time being in force) nor will the bringing of Proceedings in any one or more jurisdictions preclude the bringing of Proceedings in any other jurisdiction.

(c)    *Service of Process.* Each party irrevocably appoints the Process Agent (if any) specified opposite its name in the Schedule to receive, for it and on its behalf, service of process in any Proceedings. If for any reason any party's Process Agent is unable to act as such, such party will promptly notify the other party and within 30 days appoint a substitute process agent acceptable to the other party. The parties irrevocably consent to service of process given in the manner provided for notices in Section 12. Nothing in this Agreement will affect the right of either party to serve process in any other manner permitted by law.

(d)    *Waiver of Immunities.* Each party irrevocably waives, to the fullest extent permitted by applicable law, with respect to itself and its revenues and assets (irrespective of their use or intended use), all immunity on the grounds of sovereignty or other similar grounds from (i) suit, (ii) jurisdiction of any court, (iii) relief by way of injunction, order for specific performance or for recovery of property, (iv) attachment of its assets (whether before or after judgment) and (v) execution or enforcement of any judgment to which it or its revenues or assets might otherwise be entitled in any Proceedings in the courts of any jurisdiction and irrevocably agrees, to the extent permitted by applicable law, that it will not claim any such immunity in any Proceedings.

## 14.   Definitions

As used in this Agreement: —

*"Additional Termination Event"* has the meaning specified in Section 5(b).

*"Affected Party"* has the meaning specified in Section 5(b).

*"Affected Transactions"* means (a) with respect to any Termination Event consisting of an Illegality, Tax Event or Tax Event Upon Merger, all Transactions affected by the occurrence of such Termination Event and (b) with respect to any other Termination Event, all Transactions.

*"Affiliate"* means, subject to the Schedule, in relation to any person, any entity controlled, directly or indirectly, by the person, any entity that controls, directly or indirectly, the person or any entity directly or indirectly under common control with the person. For this purpose, "control" of any entity or person means ownership of a majority of the voting power of the entity or person.

*"Applicable Rate"* means: —

(a)   in respect of obligations payable or deliverable (or which would have been but for Section 2(a)(iii)) by a Defaulting Party, the Default Rate;

(b)   in respect of an obligation to pay an amount under Section 6(e) of either party from and after the date (determined in accordance with Section 6(d)(ii)) on which that amount is payable, the Default Rate;

(c)   in respect of all other obligations payable or deliverable (or which would have been but for Section 2(a)(iii)) by a Non-defaulting Party, the Non-default Rate; and

(d)   in all other cases, the Termination Rate.

*"Burdened Party"* has the meaning specified in Section 5(b).

*"Change in Tax Law"* means the enactment, promulgation, execution or ratification of, or any change in or amendment to, any law (or in the application or official interpretation of any law) that occurs on or after the date on which the relevant Transaction is entered into.

*"consent"* includes a consent, approval, action, authorisation, exemption, notice, filing, registration orexchange control consent.

*"Credit Event Upon Merger"* has the meaning specified in Section 5(b).

*"Credit Support Document"* means any agreement or instrument that is specified as such in this Agreement.

*"Credit Support Provider"* has the meaning specified in the Schedule.

*"Default Rate"* means a rate per annum equal to the cost (without proof or evidence of any actual cost) to the relevant payee (as certified by it) if it were to fund or of funding the relevant amount plus 1% per annum.

*"Defaulting Party"* has the meaning specified in Section 6(a).

*"Early Termination Date"* means the date determined in accordance with Section 6(a) or 6(b)(iv).

*"Event of Default"* has the meaning specified in Section 5(a) and, if applicable, in the Schedule.

*"Illegality"* has the meaning specified in Section 5(b).

*"Indemnifiable Tax"* means any Tax other than a Tax that would not be imposed in respect of a payment under this Agreement but for a present or former connection between the jurisdiction of the government or taxation authority imposing such Tax and the recipient of such payment or a person related to such recipient (including, without limitation, a connection arising from such recipient or related person being or having been a citizen or resident of such jurisdiction, or being or having been organised, present or engaged in a trade or business in such jurisdiction, or having or having had a permanent establishment or fixed place of business in such jurisdiction, but excluding a connection arising solely from such recipient or related person having executed, delivered, performed its obligations or received a payment under, or enforced, this Agreement or a Credit Support Document).

*"law"* includes any treaty, law, rule or regulation (as modified, in the case of tax matters, by the practice of any relevant governmental revenue authority) and *"lawful"* and *"unlawful"* will be construed accordingly.

*"Local Business Day"* means, subject to the Schedule, a day on which commercial banks are open for business (including dealings in foreign exchange and foreign currency deposits) (a) in relation to any obligation under Section 2(a)(i), in the place(s) specified in the relevant Confirmation or, if not so specified, as otherwise agreed by the parties in writing or determined pursuant to provisions contained, or incorporated by reference, in this Agreement, (b) in relation to any other payment, in the place where the relevant account is located and, if different, in the principal financial centre, if any, of the currency of such payment, (c) in relation to any notice or other communication, including notice contemplated under Section 5(a)(i), in the city specified in the address for notice provided by the recipient and, in the case of a notice contemplated by Section 2(b), in the place where the relevant new account is to be located and (d) in relation to Section 5(a)(v)(2), in the relevant locations for performance with respect to such Specified Transaction.

*"Loss"* means, with respect to this Agreement or one or more Terminated Transactions, as the case may be, and a party, the Termination Currency Equivalent of an amount that party reasonably determines in good faith to be its total losses and costs (or gain, in which case expressed as a negative number) in connection with this Agreement or that Terminated Transaction or group of Terminated Transactions, as the case may be, including any loss of bargain, cost of funding or, at the election of such party but without duplication, loss or cost incurred as a result of its terminating, liquidating, obtaining or reestablishing any hedge or related trading position (or any gain resulting from any of them). Loss includes losses and costs (or gains) in respect of any payment or delivery required to have been made (assuming satisfaction of each applicable condition precedent) on or before the relevant Early Termination Date and not made, except, so as to avoid duplication, if Section 6(e)(i)(1) or (3) or 6(e)(ii)(2)(A) applies. Loss does not include a party's legal fees and out-of-pocket expenses referred to under Section 11. A party will determine its Loss as of the relevant Early Termination Date, or, if that is not reasonably practicable, as of the earliest date thereafter as is reasonably practicable. A party may (but need not) determine its Loss by reference to quotations of relevant rates or prices from one or more leading dealers in the relevant markets.

*"Market Quotation"* means, with respect to one or more Terminated Transactions and a party making the determination, an amount

determined on the basis of quotations from Reference Market-makers. Each quotation will be for an amount, if any, that would be paid to such party (expressed as a negative number) or by such party (expressed as a positive number) in consideration of an agreement between such party (taking into account any existing Credit Support Document with respect to the obligations of such party) and the quoting Reference Market-maker to enter into a transaction (the "Replacement Transaction") that would have the effect of preserving for such party the economic equivalent of any payment or delivery (whether the underlying obligation was absolute or contingent and assuming the satisfaction of each applicable condition precedent) by the parties under Section 2(a)(i) in respect of such Terminated Transaction or group of Terminated Transactions that would, but for the occurrence of the relevant Early Termination Date, have been required after that date. For this purpose, Unpaid Amounts in respect of the Terminated Transaction orgroup of Terminated Transactions are to be excluded but, without limitation, any payment or delivery thatwould, but for the relevant Early Termination Date, have been required (assuming satisfaction of eachapplicable condition precedent) after that Early Termination Date is to be included. The ReplacementTransaction would be subject to such documentation as such party and the Reference Market-maker may, ingood faith, agree. The party making the determination (or its agent) will request each ReferenceMarket-maker to provide its quotation to the extent reasonably practicable as of the same day and time(without regard to different time zones) on or as soon as reasonably practicable after the relevant EarlyTermination Date. The day and time as of which those quotations are to be obtained will be selected in goodfaith by the party obliged to make a determination under Section 6(e), and, if each party is so obliged, afterconsultation with the other. If more than three quotations are provided, the Market Quotation will be thearithmetic mean of the quotations, without regard to the quotations having the highest and lowest values. Ifexactly three such quotations are provided, the Market Quotation will be the quotation remaining afterdisregarding the highest and lowest quotations. For this purpose, if more than one quotation has the samehighest value or lowest value, then one of such quotations shall be disregarded. If fewer than three quotationsare provided, it will be deemed that the Market Quotation in respect of such Terminated Transaction or groupof Terminated Transactions cannot be determined.

*"Non-default Rate"* means a rate per annum equal to the cost (without proof or evidence of any actual cost)to the Non-defaulting Party (as certified by it) if it were to fund the relevant amount.

*"Non-defaulting Party"* has the meaning specified in Section 6(a).

*"Office"* means a branch or office of a party, which may be such party's head or home office.

*"Potential Event of Default"* means any event which, with the giving of notice or the lapse of time or both,would constitute an Event of Default.

*"Reference Market-makers"* means four leading dealers in the relevant market selected by the partydetermining a Market Quotation in good faith (a) from among dealers of the highest credit standing whichsatisfy all the criteria that such party applies generally at the time in deciding whether to offer or to makean extension of credit and (b) to the extent practicable, from among such dealers having an office in the samecity.

*"Relevant Jurisdiction"* means, with respect to a party, the jurisdictions (a) in which the party isincorporated, organised, managed and controlled or considered to have its seat, (b) where an Office throughwhich the party is acting for purposes of this Agreement is located, (c) in which the party executes thisAgreement and (d) in relation to any payment, from or through which such payment is made.

*"Scheduled Payment Date"* means a date on which a payment or delivery is to be made under Section 2(a)(i) with respect to a Transaction.

*"Set-off"* means set-off, offset, combination of accounts, right of retention or withholding or similar rightor requirement to which the payer of an amount under Section 6 is entitled or subject (whether arising underthis Agreement, another contract, applicable law or otherwise) that is exercised by, or imposed on, suchpayer.

*"Settlement Amount"* means, with respect to a party and any Early Termination Date, the sum of: —

(a)   the Termination Currency Equivalent of the Market Quotations (whether positive or negative) for each Terminated Transaction or group of Terminated Transactions for which a Market Quotation is determined; and

(b)    such party's Loss (whether positive or negative and without reference to any Unpaid Amounts) for each Terminated Transaction or group of Terminated Transactions for which a Market Quotation cannot be determined or would not (in the reasonable belief of the party making the determination) produce a commercially reasonable result.

*"Specified Entity"* has the meanings specified in the Schedule.

*"Specified Indebtedness"* means, subject to the Schedule, any obligation (whether present or future, contingent or otherwise, as principal or surety or otherwise) in respect of borrowed money.

*"Specified Transaction"* means, subject to the Schedule, (a) any transaction (including an agreement with respect thereto) now existing or hereafter entered into between one party to this Agreement (or any Credit Support Provider of such party or any applicable Specified Entity of such party) and the other party to this Agreement (or any Credit Support Provider of such other party or any applicable Specified Entity of such other party) which is a rate swap transaction, basis swap, forward rate transaction, commodity swap, commodity option, equity or equity index swap, equity or equity index option, bond option, interest rate option, foreign exchange transaction, cap transaction, floor transaction, collar transaction, currency swap transaction, cross-currency rate swap transaction, currency option or any other similar transaction (including any option with respect to any of these transactions), (b) any combination of these transactions and (c) any other transaction identified as a Specified Transaction in this Agreement or the relevant confirmation.

*"Stamp Tax"* means any stamp, registration, documentation or similar tax.

*"Tax"* means any present or future tax, levy, impost, duty, charge, assessment or fee of any nature (including interest, penalties and additions thereto) that is imposed by any government or other taxing authority in respect of any payment under this Agreement other than a stamp, registration, documentation or similar tax.

*"Tax Event"* has the meaning specified in Section 5(b).

*"Tax Event Upon Merger"* has the meaning specified in Section 5(b).

*"Terminated Transactions"* means with respect to any Early Termination Date (a) if resulting from a Termination Event, all Affected Transactions and (b) if resulting from an Event of Default, all Transactions (in either case) in effect immediately before the effectiveness of the notice designating that Early Termination Date (or, if "Automatic Early Termination" applies, immediately before that Early Termination Date).

*"Termination Currency"* has the meaning specified in the Schedule.

*"Termination Currency Equivalent"* means, in respect of any amount denominated in the Termination Currency, such Termination Currency amount and, in respect of any amount denominated in a currency other than the Termination Currency (the "Other Currency"), the amount in the Termination Currency determined by the party making the relevant determination as being required to purchase such amount of such Other Currency as at the relevant Early Termination Date, or, if the relevant Market Quotation or Loss (as the case may be), is determined as of a later date, that later date, with the Termination Currency at the rate equal to the spot exchange rate of the foreign exchange agent (selected as provided below) for the purchase of such Other Currency with the Termination Currency at or about 11:00 a.m. (in the city in which such foreign exchange agent is located) on such date as would be customary for the determination of such a rate for the purchase of such Other Currency for value on the relevant Early Termination Date or that later date. The foreign exchange agent will, if only one party is obliged to make a determination under Section 6(e), be selected in good faith by that party and otherwise will be agreed by the parties.

*"Termination Event"* means an Illegality, a Tax Event or a Tax Event Upon Merger or, if specified to be applicable, a Credit Event Upon Merger or an Additional Termination Event.

*"Termination Rate"* means a rate per annum equal to the arithmetic mean of the cost (without proof or evidence of any actual cost) to each party (as certified by such party) if it were to fund or of funding such amounts.

*"Unpaid Amounts"* owing to any party means, with respect to an Early Termination Date, the aggregate of (a) in respect of all

Terminated Transactions, the amounts that became payable (or that would have become payable but for Section 2(a)(iii)) to such party under Section 2(a)(i) on or prior to such Early Termination Date and which remain unpaid as at such Early Termination Date and (b) in respect of each Terminated Transaction, for each obligation under Section 2(a)(i) which was (or would have been but for Section 2(a)(iii)) required to be settled by delivery to such party on or prior to such Early Termination Date and which has not been so settled as at such Early Termination Date, an amount equal to the fair market value of that which was (or would have been) required to be delivered as of the originally scheduled date for delivery, in each case together with (to the extent permitted under applicable law) interest, in the currency of such amounts, from (and including) the date such amounts or obligations were or would have been required to have been paid or performed to (but excluding) such Early Termination Date, at the Applicable Rate. Such amounts of interest will be calculated on the basis of daily compounding and the actual number of days elapsed. The fair market value of any obligation referred to in clause (b) above shall be reasonably determined by the party obliged to make the determination under Section 6(e) or, if each party is so obliged, it shall be the average of the Termination Currency Equivalents of the fair market values reasonably determined by both parties.

IN WITNESS WHEREOF the parties have executed this document on the respective dates specified below with effect from the date specified on the first page of this document.

.......................................................    .......................................................

|                        |                        |
|:----------------------:|:----------------------:|
| (Name of Party)        | (Name of Party)        |

By: ............................................    By: ............................................

   Name:                                          Name:

   Title:                                          Title:

   Date:                                          Date:

**(Multicurrency — Cross Border)**

# ISDA®

International Swap Dealers Association, Inc.

# SCHEDULE
# to the
# Master Agreement

dated as of .....................................

between ............................................. and .............................................
    ("Party A")                    ("Party B")

Part 1. **Termination Provisions.**

(a)    *"Specified Entity"* means in relation to Party A for the purpose of: —

Section 5(a)(v),   .........................................................................

Section 5(a)(vi),   .........................................................................

Section 5(a)(vii),   .........................................................................

Section 5(b)(iv),   .........................................................................

and in relation to Party B for the purpose of: —

Section 5(a)(v),   .........................................................................

Section 5(a)(vi),   .........................................................................

Section 5(a)(vii),   .........................................................................

Section 5(b)(iv),   .........................................................................

(b)  *"Specified Transaction"* will have the meaning specified in Section 14 of this Agreement unless another meaning is specified here ...................................................................................................................
...................................................................................................................

(c)  The *"Cross Default"* provisions of Section 5(a)(vi)
will/will not * apply to Party A
will/will not * apply to Party B

If such provisions apply: —

*"Specified Indebtedness"* will have the meaning specified in Section 14 of this Agreement unlessanother meaning is specified here ...................................................................................................................
...................................................................................................................

*"Threshold Amount"* means ...................................................................................................................
...................................................................................................................

(d)  The *"Credit Event Upon Merger"* provisions of Section 5(b)(iv)
will/will not * apply to Party A
will/will not * apply to Party B

(e)  The *"Automatic Early Termination"* provision of Section 6(a)
will/will not * apply to Party A
will/will not * apply to Party B

(f)  *Payments on Early Termination.* For the purpose of Section 6(e) of this Agreement: —

   (i)   Market Quotation/Loss * will apply.

   (ii)  The First Method/The Second Method * will apply.

(g)  *"Termination Currency"* means ...................................., if such currency is specified and freely available, and otherwise United States Dollars.

(h)  *Additional Termination Event* will/will not apply*. The following shall constitute an Additional Termination Event: — ...................................................................................................................
...................................................................................................................

---

* Delete as applicable.

..................................................................................................

..................................................................................................

..................................................................................................

..................................................................................................

For the purpose of the foregoing Termination Event, the Affected Party or Affected Parties shall be: — .....................

..................................................................................................

## Part 2. **Tax Representations.**

(a)   ***Payer Representations.*** For the purpose of Section 3(e) of this Agreement, Party A will/will not* make the following representation and Party B will/will not* make the following representation: —

It is not required by any applicable law, as modified by the practice of any relevant governmental revenue authority, of any Relevant Jurisdiction to make any deduction or withholding for or on account of any Tax from any payment (other than interest under Section 2(e), 6(d)(ii) or 6(e) of this Agreement) to be made by it to the other party under this Agreement. In making this representation, it may rely on (i) the accuracy of any representations made by the other party pursuant to Section 3(f) of this Agreement, (ii) the satisfaction of the agreement contained in Section 4(a)(i) or 4(a)(iii) of this Agreement and the accuracy and effectiveness of any document provided by the other party pursuant to Section 4(a)(i) or 4(a)(iii) of this Agreement and (iii) the satisfaction of the agreement of the other party contained in Section 4(d) of this Agreement, provided that it shall not be a breach of this representation where reliance is placed on clause (ii) and the other party does not deliver a form or document under Section 4(a)(iii) by reason of material prejudice to its legal or commercial position.

(b)   ***Payee Representations.*** For the purpose of Section 3(f) of this Agreement, Party A and Party B make the representations specified below, if any:

---

* Delete as applicable.

(i)  The following representation will/will not\* apply to Party A and will/will not apply to Party B: —

It is fully eligible for the benefits of the "Business Profits" or "Industrial and Commercial Profits" provision, as the case may be, the "Interest" provision or the "Other Income" provision (if any) of the Specified Treaty with respect to any payment described in such provisions and received or to be received by it in connection with this Agreement and no such payment is attributable to a trade or business carried on by it through a permanent establishment in the Specified Jurisdiction.

If such representation applies, then: —

*"Specified Treaty"* means with respect to Party A ..............................

*"Specified Jurisdiction"* means with respect to Party A ....................

*"Specified Treaty"* means with respect to Party B ..............................

*"Specified Jurisdiction"* means with respect to Party B ....................

(ii)  The following representation will/will not\* apply to Party A and will/will not\* apply to Party B: —

Each payment received or to be received by it in connection with this Agreement will be effectively connected with its conduct of a trade or business in the Specified Jurisdiction.

If such representation applies, then: —

*"Specified Jurisdiction"* means with respect to Party A ....................

*"Specified Jurisdiction"* means with respect to Party B ....................

(iii)  The following representation will/will not\* apply to Party A and will/will not\* apply to Party B: —

(A) It is entering into each Transaction in the ordinary course of its trade as, and is, either (1) a recognised U.K. bank or (2) a recognised U.K. swaps dealer (in either case (1) or (2), for

---

\* Delete as applicable.

purposes of the United Kingdom Inland Revenue extra statutory concession C17 on interest and currency swaps dated March 14, 1989), and (B) it will bring into account payments made and received in respect of each Transaction in computing its income for United Kingdom tax purposes.

(iv)   Other Payee Representations: — ...................................

................................................................................................

................................................................................................

................................................................................................

N.B. The above representations may need modification if either party is a Multibranch Party.

## Part 3.  **Agreement to Deliver Documents.**

For the purpose of Sections 4(a)(i) and (ii) of this Agreement, each party agrees to deliver the following documents, as applicable: —

(a)   Tax forms, documents or certificates to be delivered are: —

| Party required to deliver document | Form/Document/ Certificate | Date by which to be delivered |
|---|---|---|
| ....................................... | ....................................... | ....................................... |
| ....................................... | ....................................... | ....................................... |
| ....................................... | ....................................... | ....................................... |
| ....................................... | ....................................... | ....................................... |
| ....................................... | ....................................... | ....................................... |

(b)    Other documents to be delivered are: —

| Party required to deliver document | Form/ Document/ Certificate | Date by which to be delivered | Covered by Section 3(d) Representation |
|---|---|---|---|
| ............................ | ........................ | ........................ | Yes/No* |
| ............................ | ........................ | ........................ | Yes/No* |
| ............................ | ........................ | ........................ | Yes/No* |
| ............................ | ........................ | ........................ | Yes/No* |
| ............................ | ........................ | ........................ | Yes/No* |

Part 4. **Miscellaneous.**

(a)    *Addresses for Notices.* For the purpose of Section 12(a) of this Agreement: —

Address for notices or communications to Party A: —

Address: ...................................................................................

Attention: .................................................................................

Telex No.:................................    Answerback: ......................

Facsimile No.: ...........................    Telephone No: ...................

Electronic Messaging System Details:

Address for notices or communications to Party B: —

Address: ...................................................................................

Attention: .................................................................................

Telex No.:................................    Answerback: ......................

Facsimile No.: ...........................    Telephone No.: .................

Electronic Messaging System Details: ......................................

---

* Delete as applicable.

(b)    ***Process Agent.*** For the purpose of Section 13(c) of this Agreement: —

Party A appoints as its Process Agent ....................................

Party B appoints as its Process Agent ....................................

(c)    ***Offices.*** The provisions of Section 10(a) will/will not* apply to this Agreement.

(d)    ***Multibranch Party.*** For the purpose of Section 10(c) of this Agreement: —

Party A is/is not* a Multibranch Party and, if so, may act through the following Offices: —

..............................    ..............................    ..............................

..............................    ..............................    ..............................

Party B is/is not* a Multibranch Party and, if so, may act through the following Offices: —

..............................    ..............................    ..............................

..............................    ..............................    ..............................

(e)    ***Calculation Agent.*** The Calculation Agent is ...................., unless otherwise specified in a Confirmation in relation to the relevant Transaction.

(f)    ***Credit Support Document.*** Details of any Credit Support Document: — ........................................................................

........................................................................

........................................................................

........................................................................

(g)    ***Credit Support Provider.*** Credit Support Provider means in relation to Party A, ....................................................................

........................................................................

........................................................................

---

* Delete as applicable.

Credit Support Provider means in relation to Party B,

.............................................................................................................

.............................................................................................................

(h)   *Governing Law.* This Agreement will be governed by and construed in accordance with English law / the laws of the State of New York (without reference to choice of law doctrine) *.

(i)   *Netting of Payments.* Subparagraph (ii) of Section 2(c) of this Agreement will not apply to the following Transactions or groups of Transactions (in each case starting from the date of this Agreement / in each case starting from ........................ *)

.............................................................................................................

.............................................................................................................

.............................................................................................................

(j)   *"Affiliate"* will have the meaning specified in Section 14 of this Agreement unless another meaning is specified here

.............................................................................................................

.............................................................................................................

**Part 5. Other Provisions.**

---

* Delete as applicable.

# Appendix E

## ISDA Master Agreement Schedule Explained

In the following section, we give a step-by-step explanation of a typical ISDA master agreement schedule between a trader and a bank.

*Agreement dated as of June 26, 2004* between

Corex Trading Limited (Party A)

and XYZ Bank Limited (Party B).

[First of all, the Schedule names the two counterparties to the agreement that want to trade with one another.]

### Part 1: Termination

In this Agreement:

1.  "Specified Entity" means in relation to Party A for the purpose of:

    Section 5(a)(v):   [Default under specified transactions]
    Section 5(a)(vi):  [Cross Default]
    Section 5(a)(vii): [Bankruptcy]
    Section 5(b)(iv):  [Termination event — credit event upon merger]

    "Specified Entity" means in relation to Party B for the purpose of:

    Section 5(a)(v):   Not applicable
    Section 5(a)(vi):  Not applicable

Section 5(a)(vii):  Not applicable

Section 5(b)(iv):  Not applicable

[This is about Party B getting as much credit cover as possible against Party A in the event of defaults. In this example, under Section 5, XYZ Bank Ltd does not have to give these assurances back to Corex Trading Ltd. Corex, though, is basically agreeing that if it defaults on any OTC contract with XYZ, XYZ has the right to close out all transactions under this agreement. Note that Credit Support providers of Corex Trading Ltd (e.g., its parent company) are automatically joined to this provision in the 1992 ISDA Master Agreement.

The aim of the Specified Entity provision is to draw in those organizations whose capital is closely correlated to that of Corex Trading. Banks rarely offer this provision because most of the assets of its group will be in the bank itself and they see little point in opening themselves to the risk of Corex, for example, closing out trades under this agreement through the default of a small bank subsidiary in another agreement with Corex Trading Ltd or one of its specified entities.]

2.    "Specified Transaction" will have the meaning specified in Section 14 of this Agreement.

[Section 14 is in the Master Agreement and unless it states otherwise, which in this example it does not, it refers to any OTC derivatives transaction existing in another agreement between the parties to this Schedule or their affiliates or specified entities. The bottom line is that if Corex Trading has lots of swaps and OTC options positions with XYZ Bank, and a subsidiary of Corex Trading — EFG Trader — decides under another agreement with XYZ Bank to enter into a swap with XYZ, and EFG Trader then goes bust and defaults then, under this agreement, XYZ Bank could go back and close out Corex's positions. Changes in Specified Transaction provisions are being proposed which could widen the scope beyond OTC transactions being in default to allow the party not in default to close out all transactions with the defaulting party.]

3.    "Cross Default" means that the provisions of Section 5(a)(vi) will apply to Party A and Party B.

[This provision catches contractual terms and payment defaults in relation to borrowed money in agreements between the two parties to this agreement and their specified entities or credit support providers with any third party. Such a default has to exceed a defined limit, termed the "threshold amount". This means that if Corex Trading Ltd or any companies in its group, or any company that is providing credit support in this agreement to permit trading between Corex and XYZ, defaults on any agreement under which it has borrowed money, then XYZ Bank Ltd can close out the transactions under this agreement.]

"Specified Indebtedness" will have the meaning specified in Section 14 of this Agreement except that (i) such term shall not include obligations in respect of deposits received in the ordinary course of a party's banking business and (ii) there shall be added at the end thereof "or any money otherwise raised whether by means of issue of notes, bonds, commercial paper, certificates of deposit or other debt instruments, under financial leases, deferred purchase schemes or under any currency or interest rate swap or exchange agreement of any kind whatsoever or otherwise."

[In this schedule, XYZ Bank Ltd is extending what the borrowing of money is related to — for example, notes, bonds, commercial paper … or financial leases. The bank wants to protect itself against the higher risk of Corex Trading Ltd, working on the notion that a default somewhere else in some loan or lease etc. may be the early-warning sign of possible bankruptcy occurring. XYZ then has the ability to close out its OTC positions and control its losses. In this section, XYZ has excluded the banking deposits it may receive from its bank customers, which is quite common. Technically, these deposits are money borrowed by the bank from its customers, so some may argue over this. The usual problem faced by a bank is that its customer account deposits are very large and would easily breach any threshold amount level.]

"Threshold Amount" means with respect to Party A an amount of US$10,000,000 or the US dollar equivalent of any obligations stated in any other currency, currency unit, or combination thereof, with respect to Party B, an amount equal to 5% of stockholders equity as of the end of its most recently completed fiscal year (or its equivalent in any currency).

[The threshold amount is the amount of money or limit of specified indebtedness, below which XYZ Bank cannot trigger its close-out rights under this agreement's cross-default clause. In this case, for Corex Trading Ltd, the limit is US$10 million. XYZ Bank is a huge entity and its capital base can be very variable. So, instead of a fixed monetary amount, a formula based on a percentage of stockholders' equity is used. This is quite common for Wall Street refiners; that is, financial institutions trading in the energy derivatives markets.]

4.   "Credit event upon merger": The provisions of Section 5(b)(iv) will apply to Party A and Party B as amended in the following paragraph:

Whether, for the purposes of Section 5(b)(iv) of this Agreement, the resulting, surviving or transferee entity (hereinafter "Y") is "materially weaker" shall be a matter to be determined in the reasonable discretion of the other party. Notwithstanding the foregoing, the creditworthiness of Y shall not be determined to be materially weaker if Y agrees to and does within two local business days of demand provide eligible credit support (as defined in the Credit Support Annex) in an amount equal to or in excess of the delivery amount (as defined in the Credit Support Annex) on the basis that the threshold for Y shall be zero notwithstanding anything to the contrary in the Credit Support Annex and thereafter maintains such eligible credit support in accordance with the Credit Support Annex as amended by this provision.

[Sometimes, to avoid dispute, parties to an ISDA Schedule will be specific as to what "materially weaker" actually means for the purposes of their agreement. For example, in this case it might define this as: "If either Corex Trading Ltd or XYZ Bank Ltd fails to maintain a long term, unsecured, and unsubordinated debt rating of at least BBB as determined by Standard & Poor's Ratings Group, or Baa3 as determined by Moody's investors Service Inc." These ratings are used because anything below these is generally considered to be non-investment grade or perhaps even junk-bond status. Terminology like this may be used in a Schedule between two large entities, perhaps two large banks. Enron almost certainly suffered as a result of OTC transactions being closed out when its rating was lowered, because others who had only put cover against default on a trade or borrowing of money in their schedule had to wait whilst they saw Enron going down fast but not defaulting on loans as banks tried to bail them out. Needless to say, what defines a "default" has been under great scrutiny in the world of OTC derivatives since Enron.]

A credit event shall also occur if
   (a)   any person or entity acquires directly or indirectly the beneficial ownership of equity securities having the power

to elect a majority of the board of directors of X, any credit support provider of X or any applicable specified entity of X or otherwise acquires directly or indirectly the power to control their policy making decisions; or (b) X, any credit support provider of X or any applicable specified entity of X enters into any agreement providing for any of the credit events specified in Section 5(b)(iv) of the Agreement or in clause (a) above.

5.   The "Automatic early termination" provision of Section 6(a) will apply to Party A and Party B.

[Automatic early termination has an impact on events of default on bankruptcy. The effect of this provision is that all transactions under the agreement are deemed terminated as of a date immediately before a winding-up order is presented against the defaulting party and immediately at the time bankruptcy proceedings are instituted against the defaulting party in all other cases. This means that the non-defaulting party can exercise its rights outside the insolvency proceedings. Parties generally choose to include this section in a Schedule some 80% of the time. There are some countries, though, in which it is always advisable to use this section 6(a) — a fully updated list of such countries is available from ISDA (www.isda.org)]

6.   Payments on early termination. For the purpose of Section 6(e) of this Agreement:
    (i)   The market quotation method will apply;
    (ii)  The loss method will apply; and
    (iii) The second method will apply.

[In the energy markets there are three choices on how to calculate the amount owed between the counterparties in the event that contracts are terminated early and payment is required. The market quotation is very popular, as it is simple to use for plain-vanilla instruments such as fixed for floating swaps, where there is typically good liquidity. It involves obtaining a series of usually three or four quotations from market makers (not brokers) for the replacement value of the derivatives to be terminated. If the derivatives to be terminated are more complex than plain-vanilla swaps, there could be problems obtaining reasonable quotes from the market makers. In such circumstances, loss could be used as a fallback and put in the Schedule as a fallback provision. Loss is the non-defaulting party's "good faith" determination of its losses and costs (minus its gains) in respect of replacing terminated transactions. Last but not least, the loss method basically means the defaulting party has to pay anything it owes to the non-defaulting party, but if the non-defaulting party owes the defaulting party money it has no obligation to pay any amount to the defaulting party until it has received confirmation that all transactions have been terminated under this schedule, and that all obligations (matured or unmatured) of the defaulting party or any of its affiliates to the non-defaulting party or any affiliate of the non-defaulting party have been made.]

7.    "Termination Currency" means the currency selected by the party which is not the defaulting party or the affected party, as the case may be, or where there is more than one affected party the currency agreed by Party A and Party B. However, the termination currency shall be one of the currencies in which payments are required to be made in respect of transactions. If the currency selected is not freely available, or where there are two affected parties and they cannot agree on a termination currency, the termination currency shall be United States Dollars.

[Simply, this is the currency into which all derivatives transactions are converted on close-out and settlement. The above section 7 illustrates very common wording in ISDA Schedules. It allows the non-defaulting party to choose the currency. If the currency chosen for any reason is not freely available, the Schedule defaults to U.S. dollars.]

8.    "Additional termination event" shall apply as given in paragraphs following the interpretation.

[Additional termination events include change of control, ratings downgrade (as in the case of Enron), even the death or resignation of key men (where the counterparty is a small entity or one controlled perhaps by key management), breach of agreements, and sovereign event (maybe the company is based in a politically unstable region). The following example shows wording for change of ownership and ratings downgrade.]

Change of ownership: Mega Corporation either directly or indirectly ceases to own directly or indirectly 51% of the issued share capital of Corex Small Traders Ltd carrying voting rights in ordinary circumstances in a general meeting of shareholders, or a comparable meeting of Corex Trading Ltd or otherwise directly or indirectly ceases to control the board of directors of Corex Trading

Ltd and/or Corex Trading Ltd ceases to be a fully consolidated subsidiary of Mega Corporation.

Downgrade: (i) S&P, or Moody's, or both rate the long-term, unsecured, unsubordinated debt obligations of Corex Trading Ltd or XYZ Bank Ltd at least three modifiers (a modifier being 1, 2, or 3 for Moody's, or plus, neutral, minus for S&P) lower than the highest rating which had previously applied (from the date of this agreement) to the long term unsecured, un-subordinated debt obligations of Corex Trading Ltd, or XYZ Bank Ltd.

(ii) Corex Trading Ltd or XYZ Bank Ltd cease to be rated by both S&P and Moody's.

For the purposes of the foregoing termination event, the affected party shall be the party that was downgraded or ceased to be rated.

[This is self explanatory: if the rating gets too badly affected then OTC derivatives contracts under this agreement can be terminated by the "affected" party.]

## Part 2: Tax Representations

[Tax representations are left over from the early years of OTC derivatives when there was uncertainty even in the United States as to whether a payer's tax authority would levy a withholding tax on settlement payments made on OTC swaps transactions. The ISDA agreement covers both counterparties against any withholding tax ever being required to be paid on any derivative settlements via Section 2(d)(i)(4) of the Master Agreement, which makes it the responsibility of the payer (the company sending the payment) to ensure that the payee (the company receiving the payment) gets full payment. The payer must gross up the payment to the payee so that the payee receives, after deduction of the payer's jurisdictional withholding tax, the full settlement required on the derivatives trade. We have only come across one such jurisdiction — Thailand — in which there was a clear withholding-tax issue for energy derivatives. Any organization entering into an ISDA agreement with a new counterparty should get a legal opinion on the country with which they are going to be dealing.]

### Payer tax representations

1.   For the purpose of Section 3(e) of this Agreement, both parties make the following representation:

It is not required by any applicable law, as modified by the practice of any relevant governmental revenue authority, of any Relevant Jurisdiction to make any deduction or withholding for or on account of any Tax from any payment (other than interest under Section 2(e), 6(d)(ii), or 6(e) of this Agreement) to be made by it to the other party under this Agreement.

[Relevant jurisdiction in the ISDA Schedule refers to the payer's home jurisdiction, where the office actually executing the trades is based, the jurisdiction where it executed the Agreement and also the jurisdiction from which it makes payments, including settlement payments, for any transactions under this agreement.]

In making this representation, it may rely on

(i)    the accuracy of any representation made by the other party pursuant to Section 3(f) of this Agreement;

(ii)   the satisfaction of the agreement of the other party contained in Section 4(a)(i) or 4(a)(iii) and the accuracy and effectiveness of any document provided by the other party pursuant to Section 4(a)(i), or 4(a)(iii) of this Agreement; and

(iii)  the satisfaction of the agreement of the other party contained in Section 4(d).

Provided that it shall not be a breach of this representation where reliance is placed on Clause (ii) and the other party does not deliver a form or document under Section 4(a)(iii) by reason of material prejudice to its legal or commercial position.

[The payer tax representation actually does not include default interest payments or any interest that could be charged due to an early termination payment. This section is standard, and there are a few jurisdictions where ISDA may not have been tested and some where overseas payment and or tax regulations have been outpaced by the local adoption of derivatives instruments usage. Where it does not appear in an ISDA Schedule, it is always advisable to query it.]

## Payee tax representations

2.    For the purpose of Section 3(f), both parties make the following representation:

Each payment received or to be received by it in connection with this Agreement relates to the regular business operations of the party (and not to an investment of the party).

[The section above is not always included because of the existence of many double tax treaties around the world which have income and interest provisions giving protection against withholding taxes.]

## Other representations

1.    Each party represents and warrants to the other (which shall be deemed to be repeated by each party on each date on which a transaction is entered into) that (a) there has been no material adverse change in its financial condition since the last day of the period covered by its most recently prepared audited financial statement and that "Accuracy of specified information" as provided for in Section 3(d) will apply to the financial information which a party is required to deliver to the other party under this Schedule, and (b) It is entering into this Agreement and each transaction as principal (and not as agent or in any other capacity, fiduciary or otherwise).

2.    Each party will be deemed to represent to the other party on the date on which it enters into a transaction that (absent a written agreement between the parties that expressly imposes affirmative obligations to the contrary for that transaction) (a) It is acting for its own account, and it has made its own independent decisions to enter into that Transaction and as to whether that Transaction is appropriate or proper for it based upon its own judgment and upon advice from such advisers as it has deemed necessary. It is not relying on any communication (written or oral) of the other party as investment advice or as a recommendation to enter into that transaction; it being understood that the information and explanations related to the terms and conditions of the transaction shall not be considered investment advice or a recommendation to enter into that Transaction. No communication (written or oral) received from the other party shall be deemed to be an assurance or guarantee as to the expected results of that transaction; that (b) it is capable of assessing the merits of and understanding (on its own behalf or through independent professional advice), and understands and accepts, the terms, conditions, and risks of that transaction. It is also capable of assuming, and assumes, the risks of that transaction; and that (c) the other party is not acting as a fiduciary for or an adviser to it in respect of that transaction.

3.    Absence of litigation. Section 3(c) of the Agreement is hereby amended by limiting the definition of "affiliate" for the purposes of this representation to such affiliates, if any, as may be a specified entity for purposes of Section 5(a)(v).

[Below is a standard list of documents often required by banks entering into an ISDA Agreement with a corporate entity before trading begins. Here it will also note what documents are exchanged after each derivatives trade/transaction. Obtaining a certified copy of a board resolution authorizing execution of the agreement is very important, otherwise trade conducted may not be enforceable on one or both parties to the agreement. In practical terms, counterparties may say that it will take three months or more to get such a resolution, but it is worth waiting for.]

## PART 3: Documents to be delivered

For the purpose of Section 4(a)(i) and (ii) of this Agreement each party agrees to delivery of the following documents, as applicable:

| Party required to deliver document | Form/document/ certificate | Date by which to be delivered | Covered by Section 3(d) representation |
|---|---|---|---|
| Party A | A certified copy of a board resolution authorizing the execution, delivery, and performance of this Agreement and each Confirmation executed hereunder together with the names, titles, and specimen signatures of the persons entitled to execute this Agreement and each Confirmation executed hereunder. | On or before execution hereof and if any change in authority has occurred prior thereto, on or before the execution of each Confirmation. | Yes |

| Party A | In respect of each transaction an accepted Confirmation signed by an authorized signatory. | Within 24 hours of receipt of the relevant Confirmation from Party B. | Yes |

| Party A | A capacity certificate in the form attached to this Agreement as Appendix A. | On or before execution hereof. | Yes |

## Part 4: Miscellaneous provisions

[Don't be fooled by the term "Miscellaneous"; it is still important. In Part 4, parties set out their contact details for notices, mainly for administrative purposes.]

1. Address for Notices. For the purpose of Section 12(a):

   Address for notices or communications to Party A: Corex Trading Ltd

   Address: 27 Old Gloucester Street, London, WC1N 3XX, United Kingdom

   Attention:

   Telex No: 12345          Answerback: ABCSTrader

   Facsimile No: +44 207 681 2076          Telephone No:

   Address for notices or communications to Party B: XYZ Bank Limited,

   Address: Bank of England Road, London, United Kingdom.

   Attention: Swaps Back Office (Confirmations only)
   Mr Paul French (All other notices or communications)

   Telex No: 98238 XYZ

   Facsimile No: +44 123456 7890

   Telephone No: +44 207 12345678

2.    Process Agent. For the purpose of Section 13(c):

[A process agent will usually need to be appointed if a party is not incorporated in England, if the ISDA is under English Law (which is the preferred industry norm for the majority of OTC energy contracts outside the United States) or not incorporated in New York for a New York law-based agreement. So if an organization does not have an office or is not incorporated in these jurisdictions, it will need to nominate an organization or lawyer in London or New York to act on its behalf. A process agent receives writs, termination notices, or other legal documentation associated with the ISDA agreement.]

Party A appoints as its Process Agent:

Party B appoints as its Process Agent:    Not applicable

["Not applicable" for Party B indicates that XYZ Bank Ltd is incorporated in England (as this example is under English law), or it would indicate that it was incorporated under New York law if this contract was under New York law. XYZ Bank can accept legal notices directly; it does need a process agent.]

3.    Offices. The provision of Section 10(a) will not apply.

[Section 10(a) provides that if one of the companies signing this Schedule enters into a derivatives trade through one of its branches, its obligations will be the same as if it had executed the trade through its head office.]

4.    Multibranch party. For the purpose of Section 10(c):

Party A is not a multibranch party.

Party B is not a multibranch party.

[If Section 10(c) did apply, it would mean that both companies signing this Schedule were effectively providing an implied payment guarantee for any derivatives trades entered into by their branch offices. The benefit of being multibranch is that an organization, via one ISDA agreement with its head office, can permit all its branches to trade with the other counterparty.

It might read like this:-

"(d) Multibranch party. For the purposes of Section 10(c) of this agreement: Party A is a multibranch and may act through the following Offices: (-) Tokyo, Singapore, Frankfurt, London, New York, Houston."

Party B can also put down whether it wants to use the multibranch clause.]

5.   Calculation agent. The calculation agent is Party B, unless otherwise specified in a Confirmation in relation to the relevant transaction.

[This is the counterparty in the agreement that has to determine the floating-rate values and calculate payments. It is usual for a financial institutional trader such as a bank to insist that it is the calculation agent where the agreement is with a corporate hedger or a trader that is not a financial institution. Whoever is not the calculation agent will always have to double-check the calculation agent's figures and can dispute any big differences. Most of the time, with Platts price-related energy derivatives, any difference in calculations often arises from the calculation agent simply not picking up on a change of the Platts price for a particular day, as the correction of the price may have been published much later in the contract month. If the counterparties cannot agree on who will be the calculation agent, they can agree to be co-calculation agents. The calculation agent also has to establish whether a "market disruption event" has occurred and remedy it (see point 12 under part 5 in this example Schedule).]

6.   Credit support document. Details of any credit support document

In respect of Party A: Parental Guarantee Dated December 10, 2002

In respect of Party B: Not applicable

[This is where any form of unconditional and irrevocable credit support against derivatives transactions under this ISDA Schedule is specified. For example, in OTC energy swaps, the majority of companies utilize "irrevocable standby letters of credit (LCs)" from a bank, "bank guarantee" or, less often, parental guarantees from their parent holding company, if a subsidiary. In our example, Party A, Corex Trading Ltd, is offering a parental guarantee from its parent, Mega Corporation.]

7.   Credit support provider

Credit support provider means in relation to Party A: Mega Corporation

[Mega Corporation is the parent company offering the Parental Guarantee noted in paragraph 6 above, so it is named here.]

Credit support provider means in relation to Party B: Not applicable

8.    Governing Law. This Agreement will be governed by and construed in accordance with the laws of England.

[This example is showing English law. As mentioned earlier, the two key laws and jurisdictions used are English and New York State. Any other jurisdiction should be avoided unless an organization is prepared to get legal advice on the fact that the new jurisdiction's law will not have an adverse impact on ISDA provisions and the Master Agreement. ISDA contracts are already well tested under English and New York State law. For reference, if this example ISDA Schedule were under New York law, paragraph 8 would read "This Agreement will be governed by and construed in accordance with the laws of the State of New York (without reference to choice of law doctrine)".]

9.    Netting of payments. Subparagraph (ii) of Section 2(c) of the Agreement will not apply to all transactions under this Agreement starting from the date of this Agreement.

[This provision is where the counterparties choose the scope of payment netting to be applied to the agreement. The wording that is chosen is often limited by how advanced their risk-management systems are. An organization should not feel pressured into any complex netting-of-payment wordings. Organizations should liaise with their back office to ensure systems can automate the netting required or, if not, that they are prepared to allocate human resources to process it.

The wording in this example is the standard chosen by default by the majority of banks and traders in the energy derivatives arena. When "Subparagraph (ii) of Section (c) applies (as above) it means that "Single Transaction Netting" (same product, same currency, and same value date) applies. This means that the two parties to this Schedule do not have to make payments to each other, but the one who owes the most money has to pay the difference between the two amounts to the counterparty.

The other choices organizations can make on payment/ settlement netting are
  •    Cross-product netting: For more than one derivatives trade, for different products, in the same currency and due for payment on the same date.
  •    Multiple transaction netting: For more than one derivatives trade of the same type, in the same currency and due for payment on the same date.

If an organization wants to leave its options open, starting with the simplest form of netting and then, if it can handle it operationally later on, move on to more complex netting, it could agree with its counterparty on the following wording

"Netting of Payments. (i) Subparagraph (ii) of Section 2 (c) will apply to all transactions under this agreement unless otherwise specified in a Confirmation in relation to the relevant transaction."]

## Part 5: Other provisions

The following changes are made to this Agreement:

1.   Definitions. This Agreement incorporates, and is subject to and governed by, unless otherwise specified in a Confirmation, the 2000 ISDA Definitions published by the International Swaps and Derivatives Association, Inc. (the "2000 Definitions") and the 1993 ISDA Commodity Derivatives Definitions ("1993 Definitions"). In the event of any inconsistency between the provisions of this Agreement and the 2000 Definitions and/or the 1993 Definitions, this Agreement will prevail. In the event of any inconsistency between the provisions of the 2000 Definitions and the 1993 Definitions, the 1993 Definitions will prevail. In the event of any inconsistency between the provisions of any Confirmation and this Agreement or the 2000 Definitions or the 1993 Definitions, such Confirmation will prevail for the purpose of the relevant transaction. In the event of any inconsistency between the provisions of this Schedule and the Agreement this Schedule shall prevail.

[This example Schedule operates under the ISDA 2000 definitions, and the 1993 ISDA Commodity Derivatives provisions, which cover energy OTC derivatives transactions/trades.]

2.   Change of account. At the end of Section 2(b) add the following words:

"provided that, if any new account of the notifying party is not in the same jurisdiction as the original account, the other party shall not be obliged to pay any greater amount and shall not receive any lesser amount as a result of such change than would have been the case if such change had not taken place."

[Under a ISDA Master Agreement, the parties can give each other five local business days' notice of a change of their banking account details for payments. The reason this paragraph has been included in this example is to protect both parties from potential withholding-tax charges and foreign-exchange controls that might arise from the other counterparty moving its bank account to another jurisdiction.]

3.    Pari Passu. Party A hereby agrees that it will ensure that its payment and delivery obligations under this Agreement rank at all times at least pari passu in all respects with all of its other unsecured and unsubordinated obligations (except for those which are mandatorily preferred by operation of law).

[In this example, XYZ Bank is getting Corex Trading Ltd to ensure that any unsecured debt it owes to XYZ Bank through settlement payments due on trades under this ISDA contract will rank equally with other unsecured and unsubordinated obligations in any winding up (liquidation) of Corex Trading Ltd. It is very important for corporates to understand this clause as it can only be given if it is true. Advice should be taken on this clause if it turns up in a schedule being proposed by another counterparty.]

4.    Confirmations. Each confirmation shall be in the standard form used by Party B from time to time or in such other form as the parties may agree. With respect to each transaction, Party B shall on, or promptly after, the trade date send Party A a Confirmation. Party A shall promptly sign and return a copy of the Confirmation or advise any discrepancy between the Confirmation and Party A's own records where upon the parties will promptly agree on the text of a replacement Confirmation for signature by Party A.

[This is self-explanatory. However, it is worth noting that, increasingly, wording for the acceptance of electronic confirmations in the energy-trading industry is being placed into ISDA Schedules. Several organizations have electronic-confirmations systems for energy-swaps deals. These include Intercontinental Exchange (www.intcx.com), which has also launched such a system for trades executed via its ICE platform. NYMEX also has electronic confirmation of OTC deals registered via its online system, ClearPort.

Following is an example of wording used to allow acceptance of electronic confirmations:

"Electronic Confirmations. Where a transaction is confirmed by means of an electronic messaging system that the parties have elected to use to confirm such transaction, such confirmation will constitute a "Confirmation" as referred to in this agreement."]

5.   Automatic early termination. If automatic early termination is specified as applying to a party in Part 1 point 5 above, that Party shall upon the occurrence of an event of default notify it immediately to the other Party and provided further that automatic early termination shall not apply to either party if the event of default concerned is the presentation of a winding-up petition which is withdrawn without advertisement. In the event of absence of such notice on the day of the occurrence of the event of default, the defaulting Party shall fully indemnify the non-defaulting Party on demand against all expense, loss, damage, or liability that the non-defaulting Party may incur in respect of this Agreement and each transaction as a consequence of movements in interest, currency, exchange, or other relevant rates or prices between the early termination date and the local business day on which the non-defaulting Party first becomes aware that the early termination date has occurred under Section 6(a). The non-defaulting Party may for this purpose convert any expense, loss, damage, or liability to the termination currency.

6.   Early Termination. At the end of Section 6 add the following Sections 6(f) and (g):

"(f) *Conditions of Certain Payments.* Notwithstanding the provisions of Section 6(e), the non-defaulting Party shall have no obligation to make any payment on early termination to the defaulting Party unless and until the non-defaulting Party shall have received confirmation satisfactory to it in its sole discretion (which may include an unqualified opinion of its counsel) that (i) in accordance with Section 6(c)(ii) of the Agreement, no further payments or deliveries under Section 2(a)(i) or 2(e) in respect of terminated transactions will be required to be made and (ii) each specified transaction shall have terminated pursuant to its specified termination date or through the exercise by a party of a right to terminate and all obligations owing under each such specified transaction shall have been fully and finally performed; and

(g) (i)   Without affecting the provisions of this Agreement requiring the calculation of certain net payment amounts, all payments under this Agreement will be made without set-off or counterclaim; provided, however that any amount (the "early termination amount") payable to one party (the Payee) by the other party (the Payer) under Section 6(e) in circumstances where there is a defaulting Party or one affected Party in the case where a termination event under Section 5(b) (i) to (v) inclusive has occurred, will, at the option of the party ("X") other than the defaulting Party or the affected Party (and without prior notice to the defaulting Party or affected Party), be reduced by its set-off against any amount(s) (the "other agreement amount") payable (whether at such time or in the future or upon occurrence of a contingency) by the Payee to the Payer (irrespective of the currency, place of payment, or booking office of the obligation) under any other agreement(s) between the Payee and the Payer or instrument(s) or undertaking(s) issued or extended by one party to, or in favor of, the other party (and the other agreement amount will be discharged promptly and in all respects to the extent it is so set-off). X will give notice to the other party of any set-off effected under this Section.

(ii)   For this purpose, either the early termination amount or the other agreement amount (or the relevant portion of such amounts) may be converted by X into the currency in which the other is denominated at the rate of exchange at which X would be able, acting in a reasonable manner and in good faith, to purchase the relevant amount of such currency.

(iii)   If an obligation is unascertained, X may in good faith estimate that obligation and set-off in respect of the estimate, subject to the relevant party accounting to the other when the obligation is ascertained.

(iv)   Nothing in this Section 6(g) shall be effective to create a charge or other security interest. This Section 6(g) shall be without prejudice and in addition to any right of set-off, combination of accounts, lien, or other right to which any party is at any time otherwise entitled (whether by operation of law, contract, or otherwise)."

7.   Transfer. Rights and obligations under this Agreement or any Transaction may not be transferred, in whole or in part, except upon the prior written consent of both parties and any such transfer made without such consent shall be void.

[Often counterparties, for reassurance that the other party will accept a reasonable transfer of rights and obligations under the ISDA Agreement, will insert the following phrase: "which consent shall not be unreasonably withheld".]

8.   Default rate. The default rate shall mean 1% over LIBOR compounded on a daily basis where "LIBOR" on any day shall mean the one-month London Interbank Offered Rate as reported in *The Financial Times* or if *The Financial Times* ceases publication temporarily or permanently, such other newspaper published in London as Party B may determine.

[If one of the counterparties defaults on a payment then the other counterparty is entitled to charge interest on monies owed.]

9.   Physical Delivery. Unless specifically stated to the contrary in a signed Confirmation, no physical delivery by either party shall take place under the terms of this Agreement and transactions entered into hereunder shall be settled in cash only.

[ISDA OTC derivatives trades in energy are all cash-settled.]

10.   Telephone recording. Each party to this Agreement acknowledges and agrees to the electronic recording of telephone conversations between the parties (including any director, officer, employee, agent, or representative thereof) and whether by one or other or both of the parties and that any such recording may be submitted in evidence to any court or in any proceedings for the purpose of establishing any matters pertinent to any transaction.

[Electronic trading platforms are making progress in penetrating the OTC energy market, but outside the United States the market practice is still generally to trade over the telephone. Consent has to be given for the recording of telephone conversations if such are to be used for any legal purposes in the future.]

11.   Designated account details for US dollar payments.
   (a)   In the case of Party A: As specified by Party A when returning the Confirmation from Party B.

[or the counterparty can state its banking details under this Agreement and it can change them in the future by giving five local business days' notice.]
(b)   In the case of Party B:
     Name of bank:    XYZ Bank Ltd
     Account number:  08231-89178236-73624-02
     Account name:    XYZ Bank derivatives receipts

12.   "Market Disruption Event" means the occurrence of any of the following events in the reasonable determination of the calculation agent:
   (a)   Price source disruption;
     [where, a settlement price is not available for some reason; for example, it has not been published by the reference agency (say, Platts) on a day it would normally be available]
   (b)   Trading suspension;
     [A look-a-like swap would settle, for example, against a futures-market settlement price each day during the pricing period, if the futures market was suspended.]
   (c)   Disappearance of commodity reference price;
     [where a publisher stops publishing the price reference counterparties are using as the floating price reference on a derivatives trade]
   (d)   Material change in formula;
   (e)   Material change in content; and
   (f)   Trading limitation.

15.   Disruption fallbacks relating to commodity transactions:
   The following disruption fallbacks (as defined in the 1993 Commodity Definitions) shall be applicable in each case in the order in which they appear:
   (i)   in respect of any transaction having a calculation period or calculation periods which are greater than or equal to one calendar month:
     (a)   Average daily price disruption, with maximum days of disruption equal to five;
     (b)   Fallback reference price;
     (c)   Negotiated fallback;
     (d)   The Parties shall appoint a single independent expert to determine an alternative pricing method. If the parties fail to agree on the appointment of an expert,

the Chairman for the time being of the Institute of Petroleum in the United Kingdom shall be requested by either party to make such appointment within two days of request. An expert, if appointed, shall be deemed not to be an arbitrator but shall render his decision as an expert and his determination shall be final and binding upon both parties save in the event of manifest error or fraud; and

[In this example, where everything else fails, both Parties will in the end approach the Chairman of the Institute of Petroleum as an expert to establish the price.]

(e)  No fault termination.

(ii)  in respect of any transaction having a calculation period or calculation periods which are less than one calendar month:

(a)  Average daily price disruption, provided that the maximum days of disruption shall be zero where the calculation period is less than or equal to two commodity business days; one, where the calculation period is between three and five commodity business days inclusive; two, where the calculation period is between six and ten commodity business days inclusive; three, where the calculation period is between 11 and 15 commodity business days inclusive; and four, where the calculation period is greater than 16 commodity business days inclusive;

(b)  Fallback reference price;

(c)  Negotiated fallback;

(d)  The Parties shall appoint a single independent expert to determine an alternative pricing method. If the parties fail to agree on the appointment of an expert, the Chairman for the time being of the Institute of Petroleum in the United Kingdom shall be requested by either party to make such appointment within two days of request. An expert, if appointed, shall be deemed not to be an arbitrator but shall render his decision as an expert and his determination shall be final and binding upon both parties save in the event of manifest error or fraud; and

(e)  No fault termination.

All determinations and calculations hereunder by the calculation agent shall be made in good faith, in the exercise of its commercially reasonable judgment and only after consultation with the other party.

16.   Commencement date. This Agreement is deemed to have come into effect on December 15, 2005

| Corex Trading Ltd | XYZ Bank Limited |
|---|---|
| By: | By: |
| Name: | Name: |
| Title: | Title: |
| By: | By: |
| Name: | Name: |
| Title: | Title: |

## Additional notes

- ### Withholding tax and ISDA

Counterparties should undertake detailed legal and tax analysis at the start of their business relationship to ensure that no withholding tax is likely to be charged in any of the jurisdictions through which the counterparty proposes to trade OTC derivatives. ISDA's legal infrastructure makes provisions against being caught out by withholding tax by making the counterparty pay the net amount (net of any taxes payable in their home country).

- ### Netting and ISDA agreements

The ISDA Master Agreement has established international contractual standards governing privately negotiated derivatives transactions to reduce legal uncertainty and allow for the reduction of credit risk through netting of contractual obligations. Ensuring the enforceability of the netting provisions of the ISDA Master Agreement remains a key initiative for ISDA, because of its importance in reducing the credit risk arising from the OTC derivatives business. ISDA's work in this area has resulted in a series of laws being passed in various countries to ensure legal certainty surrounding the process of netting in those nations.

Around 36 countries have already confirmed acceptance of netting procedures in OTC transactions via the ISDA Master Agreement and this number continues to grow. ISDA's website (www.isda.org) has regular updates on legal opinions by country and results of the operational surveys and swaps-trading volumes reported annually by ISDA members.

# Index